Religion and Modernity in India

Religion and Modernity in India

edited by
Sekhar Bandyopadhyay
Aloka Parasher Sen

OXFORD
UNIVERSITY PRESS

OXFORD
UNIVERSITY PRESS

Oxford University Press is a department of the University of Oxford.
It furthers the University's objective of excellence in research, scholarship,
and education by publishing worldwide. Oxford is a registered trademark of
Oxford University Press in the UK and in certain other countries.

Published in India by
Oxford University Press
YMCA Library Building, 1 Jai Singh Road, New Delhi 110 001, India

ISBN-13: 978-0-19-946778-5
ISBN-10: 0-19-946778-1

Typeset in ScalaPro 10/13
by The Graphics Solution, New Delhi 110 092
Printed in India by Replika Press Pvt. Ltd

Contents

SEKHAR BANDYOPADHYAY

ALOKA PARASHER SEN

Introduction*

Theory

'**M**odernity is easy to inhabit but difficult to define,' wrote Dipesh Chakrabarty in his *Habitations of Modernity* (2002: xix). In his view, modernity is always defined against its 'other', that is, the premodern or the non-modern. Yet, the advent of modernity has never meant a complete break with the past and hence scholars of modernity have always talked about incomplete or imperfect modernization. In India it is widely recognized that modernity came through the conduit of colonial rule, as Britain's imperial mission was to make India modern. In other words, as Peter van der Veer has recently put it, here 'modernity has been mediated by imperialism' (2014: 214). The Indian elite embraced the shibboleth of modernity and began to imagine their society in the light of post-Enlightenment rationalism, science, democracy, secularism, and progress—the attributes of European modernity. Yet, her premodern, or what is often described as the 'traditional', has refused to disappear. During the colonial period, India was constantly compared with what Chakrabarty in

---

* We are indebted to Benjamin Kingsbury for providing valuable research assistance for writing this Introduction.

his *Provincializing Europe* has called a 'hyperreal "Europe"', and was condemned for being insufficiently modern (2000: 40–1). Coming to the more recent times, A. Raghuramaraju has argued that the story of Indian modernity needs to be narrated in the 'present continuous' tense. It 'is a good example of a society that is neither pre-modern nor distinctly modern. It is a society where modernity has to [continually] reckon with the pre-modern' (2011: 2–3). It has been variously described as alternative modernity or plural modernities or modernities at large. Indeed, among the many certitudes of modernity that have been questioned, the expected demise of religion and the disenchantment of the world are arguably the most significant ones. As Prasenjit Duara has recently pointed out, even Max Weber, who argued about the emergence of modern Western civilization through a process of rationalization and disenchantment, had to trace its origins in religious ideas, namely Protestant ethics (Duara 2015: 1). Yet, there are intellectual constraints as well, as we rarely have been able to think of religion except within the context of Enlightenment values—or what Derrida once said, 'within the limits of reason alone' (quoted in Needham and Rajan 2007: 22).

In India the very conceptualization of 'religion' and its interaction with the colonial modernity constitute a problematic area of historical interpretation. It was initially through the imagination of Indology, presented to us by nineteenth-century European scholarship, that the study of Indian religions—their genesis and historical journey— began. This entry, however, impeded the understanding of the vast religious diversities and cultural patterns that were preserved in and produced through local and folk traditions embedded more often in memory rather than texts, which the Orientalists were focusing on. Moreover, writing the past is deeply entwined with the way we perceive and live our present. It has been well established by scholars that studies on religion in the context of classical India had become a contesting ground for some of the earliest endeavours by the imperialist and Orientalist writings seeking to mould and perpetuate certain types of interpretations. For instance, there was a comfort with which 'India', as a total object of study, was seen as a monolithic whole. More commonly, a great emphasis on unearthing only the textual traditions led to the image of a highly 'spiritual' and 'exotic' land bereft of any political or economic agency. The nationalist writings on classical

India seemed whole-heartedly indebted to the Orientalists in terms of providing fodder for their major thrust to depict India in glorious terms through the prism of its religious thought. In fact, with them, as well as with other schools of historical interpretations, the making of the historical narratives about religion in India went hand in hand with the creation of the 'source' and 'fact' of its past. For the nationalist school in particular, this kind of history only solidified their attempts at writing about the past from the perspective of the dominant modern 'self'. For example, our attention is drawn to the examples of men such as Bankim Chandra Chatterjee who sought 'to graft the discourse of history on a structure of feeling indigenous in character' (Kumar 1991: 11). However, by relying only on the high culture of Hinduism to retrieve this essence, the other diverse traditions of the Indian subcontinent were lost sight of. Thus, an abstracted idea of Indian spirituality became Indian nationalism's most potent ideological weapon to be deployed against Western imperialism and materialism (van der Veer 2014: 32). In postcolonial India, we therefore cannot talk about our past without the essential and immediate history of the last 200 years. This has resulted in a set of complex conjunctures wherein Indians have now lost the sensibility of identifying the difference between 'India's essential past' and 'its historical connection to the empire' (Dirks 1990: 28). It can thus be argued that history needs to be repositioned as an enabler to retrieve and recover horizontally an expansive, vertically a deeper, and socially—and in terms of religious identities—a more inclusive past. Thus, the post-Independence dilemmas for the Indian historians have not been only about generating the 'source' for writing about the past of its religious groups, but how the 'discourse' of history, a handmaiden to understand the coming of the modern, could be made more inclusive. However, as pointed out by Dipesh Chakrabarty, the muse of 'Indian History' was caught in the impossible situation of being able to only mimic 'a certain "modern" subject of "European" history' and was thus 'bound to represent a sad figure of lack and failure' (Chakrabarty 1992: 18–19).

Therefore, moving beyond the Orientalist and nationalist concerns and searching for alternative modernities, there is now renewed interest across disciplines in the ways in which different groups have negotiated the interface between religion and modernity in India.

This is particularly significant in contemporary India since 'Religious Studies' as a discipline has not been part of the Indian curriculum for study in the Social Sciences. In an impressive survey of the study of religion and its historiographies, it has been pointed out recently that 'within the methodological scope of the Study of Religion the importance of history seems to have receded in past decades, with sociological, political, ethnographic and cognitive approaches coming to the fore' (Otto, Rau, and Rüpke 2015: 3). Out of these circumstances arose lively debates on whether the scientific study of religions was particularly 'Western' and how one should produce non-Eurocentric, comparative, and multi-perspective studies based also on the practice of religion and not merely on its beliefs. The present volume reflects this diversity of disciplines and perspectives, while being inclusive of the historical study of religion as well.

The extant narratives reveal two aspects of this renewed interest that has impacted subsequent studies. First of all, the works of sociologists and anthropologists have revealed that religions may be a crucial source of ethical values and not just a source of 'false consciousness' as Marxist historians had been suggesting a few decades ago. Historians now recognize the enormous diversity and complexity across space and time in the ways in which religious symbols and myths have evolved, and emphasize the need to deconstruct monolithic ideas of religion and society. As Ashis Nandy has argued, there is always 'that other India which is neither pre-modern nor anti-modern but only non-modern' (Nandy 1998: 74). They are in 'constant dialogue with their pasts, not defensively, but as a way of accessing their own tacit knowledge'. For them religion is an integral part of that past, and they believe that their path to progress might be through this knowledge of their uncolonized self, embedded in the past (Nandy 2002: 2). In other words, the traditional past remains, in real ways, a part of their modern social present. And when one looks at this perspective through the prism of a place or locality, one is confronted with a community's flexible notions of space and time, as for them the past is not an alien land (de Certeau 1988: viii–ix), but a living present. It is here that the tenacity of thoughts, emotions, and social relations emanating out of a deep study of religious sensibilities permits us to capture a space between the past and the present, between the modern and the premodern—a space that allows us to move beyond binaries for narrating religious and cultural practices. In this context, elaborating on the ways early Indian religious traditions interacted with each other, Kapila Vatsyayan wrote: 'There was a notion of space in terms of place, locale, region and country and the universe. There were different spatial orders (*loka*) as there were different temporal (*kala*). The two together provided the basis of multiple identities and local distinctiveness' (Vatsyayan 2005: 42). The notions of both tradition (*paramparā*) and time and space were thus in constant negotiation with each other to provide enough of a dynamic flow of ideas around religious belief, faith, and ritual, which had a very different historical structure and role when compared to those emanating from the Semitic traditions. Hence, the introduction of secularism and religion as static and given social categories during the course of India's modernization during the twentieth century has only obscured the understanding of religion both on the academic plane and in the political arena in contemporary times.

This leads us to the second issue about religion and modernity, which is about the idea of secularism, believed to be an important component of political modernity, based on the premise of the democratic principles of equality and egalitarianism (Chandoke 1999: 4). There is a growing discontent with secularism both in theory and in practice, as it is not just considered as the religion's other; in a postcolonial world the concept is expected to perform complex functions of nation-building (Needham and Rajan 2007). The ideological uses of religion in generating nationalist exclusivism and fundamentalism in India have attracted considerable scholarly attention. While construction of national identities is in itself a modern activity (Kaviraj 2004: 108), Peter van der Veer has argued that 'religion has been crucial in the formation of national identity not only in India but also in supposedly secular and modern Britain' (van der Veer 2001: 3). According to another recent study, 'the religion/state nexus in India was ever (and remains) a work in progress', as every Indian state had established some kind of relationship with religion and that 'no government in South Asia has ever observed the Enlightenment principle of Church–State separation' (Copland et al. 2012: 253). Gurharpal Singh, on the other hand, has argued recently that the Indian Constitution, though did not establish a 'wall of separation' between the state and the church (or religion), at least established a 'no preference doctrine', showing no special privileges to any religion. In his opinion, this Indian secularist compromise broke down only recently—in the 1990s, since when he dates the 'return of religion' in public life and the 'decline of the secular state' in India (Singh 2013: 140–1). However, to what extent this secular compromise was actually practised in real politics by the successive governments before the 1990s is of course a matter of debate (see Chapter 2 in this book).

Peter van der Veer in his most recent book—a comparative study of China and India—has traced the historical evolution of this 'no preference doctrine' or what he calls the idea of 'neutrality'. He starts with a bold assertion of the obvious, stating: 'There is no opposition between being modern and being religious' (2014: 9). In his view, 'religion-magic-secularity-spirituality is an integral part of modernity' (10), and the connections between these concepts were established through the mediation of imperialism, which identified the Oriental societies as traditional and superstitious. It was through encounter with such characterization that secularism was historically constructed as 'atheism' in communist China and 'neutrality' in nationalist India (226–7).

Ashis Nandy, however, looks at the idea of neutrality not as a historical construct, but rather as a historically given tradition of the non-modern in India. In his view, there have always been two ways of looking at secularism. In the 'Western' model, secularism meant a complete separation between the church and the state, relegating religion to a private sphere. But there was also a 'non-Western' model in which religion might be allowed a public role, but the state was expected to maintain equidistance from and show equal respect to all religions. The principles of toleration and accommodation were naturally built into this model. In India, he argues, while the Western-educated middle classes embraced the rationalist Western model of secularism, the general people—the 'non-modern Indians'—have remained attached to the more 'accommodative and pluralist meaning' of the term (Nandy 2002: 68–9).

So, for Nandy, it is not a question of India being imperfectly modern, as Copland and others would argue, but it is India having to choose between two parallel and competing models of modernity—one Western and the other indigenous. And here Nandy makes another interesting observation. As the process of modernization progresses, he argues, the Western model becomes hegemonic and the accommodative model recedes to the background. This Western modernity has another pathology: it makes the political use of religion more aggressive and violent: '[A]s India gets modernized, religious violence is increasing', while in the premodern past, religious riots were 'rare and localised' (Nandy 2002: 78–9). This critique of modernity and secularism by Nandy and other postcolonial thinkers has raised the complaint of indigenism, but in fairness to Nandy, his engagement with the premodern past is not of uncritical valourization. It is more in the nature of critical traditionalism, where the past is not neglected or ignored, but lessons are learnt from it.

Very recently, Prasenjit Duara, in his *The Crisis of Global Modernity* (2015), has come up with a powerful new intervention in this debate. Drawing his empirical evidence from Chinese and Indian religious traditions, he argues that the 'idea of transcendence'—which he defines as 'a source of non-worldly *moral authority* that can speak back to power' or 'a critique of existing conditions that draws on a non-worldly moral authority [italics original]'—has survived in a secular age. There are divergent trends in these religious traditions, some which are abhorrent to circulatory trends of capitalist modernity, while others have adapted to these new trends. The two spheres of the 'secular' and the 'religious' survive together through a dialogic process ('dialogical transcendence'), which is not dialectical in a Hegelian sense where one paradigm negates or supersedes the other. It is rather a process of 'traffic' where both spheres can survive through 'coexistence' and 'unacknowledged "borrowings"' of ideas from one another. It is through this process of 'dialogical transcendence', he argues, that self-formation in Asian societies has taken place over the last two centuries (Duara 2015: 1–17).

In a similar vein, Leela Gandhi's work on 'affective communities' makes a poignant connection between ideas shared across different intellectual traditions drawn from both secular and religious domains that could still find resonance with each other. Her examples of transnational friendships are from the colonial context (1878–1914) with a focus on understanding spirituality through, among other things, vegetarianism, animal rights, marginalized lifestyles, subcultures, and religious traditions that cohabited with each other. This, she argues, produced very complex and contesting networks of collaborations when Indians were in fact involved in a deep anti-colonial struggle.

She retrieves this historical juncture and outlays how, what she calls, 'anti-colonial cosmopolitan activists' created 'affective communities' (Gandhi 2006: 1) calling for social justice and political action. Most importantly, she emphasizes that they drew on ideas that emanated from both the modern and premodern realms to create empathy for a struggle that had to have ethical underpinnings. Their ethics of friendship transcended the immediacy of their particular locations and provided an improvisatory and inclusive means of 'co-belonging', clearly emphasizing on the condition of the 'other' in this cohabitation.

This burgeoning and complex theoretical literature establishes one important central point, that religion and modernity are not necessarily in opposition to each other—the two cohabit in a complex, plural, transient, and historically evolving relationship. This literature therefore raises several important questions about the place of religion in Indian modernity: Are the modern uses of religion so radically different from medieval or premodern uses? Has modernity transformed religion into homogenized and exclusive entities by purging its plural and accommodative characteristics? How has religion been used and adapted to construct modern collective or bounded identities? In what ways do religious ideas and practices interrupt and modify modern secular politics? How have different regimes deployed religious symbols and ideas? How have different religious communities and networks combined and also separated religion and politics? How do hitherto marginalized communities draw upon religions even as they definitively reject some aspects of it, such as hierarchy? How do different agents, say diasporic communities, especially women, sustain and revise religious ideas of purity or auspiciousness in non-Indian contexts? To address some of these questions, the New Zealand India Research Institute and the School of Social Sciences at the University of Hyderabad convened a conference, and papers presented there have been compiled into this book.

Method

The distinctiveness of this book lies partly in its methods. The essays here seek to address some of those questions mentioned earlier through specific empirical case studies. These cases have been taken from everyday experiences of people following a variety of religions, such as Hinduism, Islam, Christianity, or tribal religions. This is where the present collection stands apart from other collections, which focus either on a particular religious group, in most cases the Hindu nationalists, or only on ethical and moral crises of religions under modernity. To cite a few examples, *Making India Hindu* (2005), edited by David Ludden, explores the genealogies, politics, and consequences of Hindu majoritarianism following the demolition of the Babri Masjid at Ayodhya. Majoritarian Hindu nationalism, it argues, is a modern effort to organize collective identities and cannot be understood except in the context of Indian and global modernity: the vicissitudes of national politics, the pressures of the world economy, and even, in the private sphere, the changing patterns of family life. Its focus remains exclusively on the Hindus. On the other hand, *Ethical Life in South Asia* (2010), edited by Anand Pandian and Daud Ali, addresses a renewed scholarly interest in ethics and morality, which it sees as a response to the proliferating moral conundrums of modernity. It is interested in how modern institutions—states, markets, and schools—encourage or discourage ethical traditions: for example, how fragments of the pre-colonial past have been reinvented as part of nationalist and religious revivalism, or how the economics and culture of neoliberal globalization have put pressure on South Asian ethical traditions. Its primary concerns remain ethics, morality, and institutions. The other comparable collection, *Secularism and Religion-Making* (2011), edited by Markus Dressler and Arvind-Pal S. Mandair, seeks to demonstrate the interdependence, rather than the opposition, of the religious and the secular within modernity. It also explores how the strict opposition between religious-nationalist and state-secularist discourses has been sustained by the Enlightenment notion that religion must remain outside the public realm. It suggests that undermining this opposition might help to open up alternative models of secular society.

The present collection, by contrast, does not confine itself to any particular religion or part of the country, or to abstract ethical issues, but treats religion as a sociological category and examines its relationship with modernity in its quotidian social experiences, practices, and political representations in a variety of physical and temporal locales. It uses what John Walliss (2002) has described as the concept of 'reflexive traditions', which can bring out the ways in which the behaviour and knowledge that make up religious traditions are constantly revised under the impact of modernity. The essays in this collection seek to show that the relationship between religion and modernity is dialogic and not dualistic—it is indeed akin to what Duara (2015: 3) has described as 'dialogical transcendence'. While some of the essays consciously bring in the oral tradition and cultural practices of communities, there are others that, by focusing on major textual traditions, have permitted us to present dynamically interacting textures of society—historically and in our contemporary times—engaging with modernity in divergent ways.

It is also important to emphasize that this collection of empirical studies has consciously brought in the idea of inclusivity by factoring in the small and local contexts that clearly bring in the perspectives of marginalized 'other' groups. They create an intellectual space for discussion on pastoral and tribal communities, the gay community, women, and other excluded groups, while not ignoring discussions on the more mainstream political and socially privileged sections in our midst. Writing on the past and the present has to be seen as deeply entwined with the way we perceive our social milieu as horizontally more expansive and vertically deeper and more inclusive. This endeavour suggests that we can no longer compartmentalize the various seminal traditions of the Indian subcontinent, and that each needs to be looked at in terms of networks, each dynamically interacting with the other. This book therefore seeks to retrieve from everyday religious practices, material traditions, and cognitive texts the textures of social change that involve women and marginal social and regional groups who represent difference, but at the same time are linked to a larger whole. The emergence of these networks—their sustenance, mutation, and transformation—we argue, should become the central focus of India Studies in our times.

The Book

The book consists of twelve chapters grouped into four distinct thematic sections. In the first section on 'Modernity, Religion, and Secularism', T.K. Oommen, in Chapter 1, sets out the broad theoretical framework for interrogating the supposed epistemological dualism between religion and modernity, which is the central theme of this book. He suggests that we should begin by looking at the provisions of secularism in the Indian constitution and their imperfect implementation by the post-Independence Indian state. In the interface between tradition and modernity, he asserts that four interrelated processes can be found to have happened, and these are homogenization, pluralization, traditionalization, and hybridization. These processes led to the reinvention of tradition both as religious reform and as religious fundamentalism. Therefore, he argues, to assume that religion will disappear as modernity advances is not just simplistic but utterly false.

In the next densely theoretical chapter (Chapter 2), Aditya Malik looks at the ritual of possession as practised in the Central Himalayas to interrogate the assumptions of modernity as a liberating force that ensures freedom from religion. Survival of such rituals, he states, is a reminder of the past, which modernity is supposed to have displaced. The fact that it is continually thriving even in recent times shocks and challenges the foundations of the modern nation-state based on the notions of science, technology, and rationality and compels us to rethink the modern ideas of agency and subjectivity.

The essays in the section on 'Modernity, Religion, and the Communities' look at four specific empirical situations to illustrate the complex dialogic relationship between religion and modernity in colonial as well as postcolonial India. Will Sweetman (Chapter 3) looks at how an existing religious tradition got reinvented as a result of the project of colonial modernity. He critically looks at the construction of Dravidian culture in south India through the discursive intervention of Christian missionaries, who were credited with developing such hallmarks of modernity as print culture and the wide extension of literacy. It is arguable, according to Sweetman, that the single most consequential missionary contribution to modern south Indian culture was the dissemination of the Dravidian idea. The essay examines its missionary formulation through a critical reading of missionary Robert Caldwell's two texts, and a much older, early eighteenth-century missionary account of the Tamil religion, which was revised in the mid-nineteenth century to take account of Caldwell's work on both the Shanars and the Dravidian languages. It demonstrates that the idea of a distinctive south Indian religious tradition was much older than the Dravidian idea. It owed less to missionary dislike for

Brahmanism, and more to concerns, especially on the part of Lutheran missionaries, to establish a 'folk-church' (Volkskirche) which would be at once Christian and deeply rooted in south Indian culture.

The second essay in this section by Ranjeeta Dutta (Chapter 4) focuses on the Śrīvaiṣṇavas in the Tamil region and discusses their reinvention of religious identity through the modernization process in colonial south India. She argues that there was the development of multiple indigenous modernities through which the educated middle class recast their traditions through the frame of religious identities. The Śrīvaiṣṇava modernity generated a specific consciousness of belonging to a religious community and, within that consciousness, the brahmanical status was reiterated and related to the larger subcontinental brahmanical identity. This modern community consciousness was further linked to the larger discourse of Tamil tradition, Hinduism, and the nation. Consequently, a modern public sphere was created in which the Brahman Śrīvaiṣṇava self influenced the modern discipline of history. A series of history writings evolved which, while discussing the Śrīvaiṣṇava past, projected a consolidated and seamless history. This narrative diluted the multiple traditions of caste and regions existing historically within the Śrīvaiṣṇava community, thus creating a new homogenized modern self.

In the next essay, we move to the north and to the interventions of the postcolonial state in society with special focus on a marginalized community. Alok Pandey and R. Siva Prasad (Chapter 5) examine the impacts of recent modernization projects of the Indian state on a pastoral forest-dwelling community—the nomadic Van Gujjar of the Himalayas. The essay looks at two interrelated aspects of this process: first, the strong connection between the Van Gujjars' nomadic pastoral lifestyle and their religion; and second, the government Forest Department's attempt at their sedentarization, forcing them to abandon their nomadic pastoral way of life. The state sees the nomadic pastoral culture as an antithesis to its projected model of modernity and also destructive of its biodiversity conservation efforts. So, it encourages them to take up agriculture. But their removal from their natural resource base not only affects their livelihood, it also displaces their religion and identity. The essay shows how this physical and spiritual displacement effected by the process of modernization results in an increase in religious fundamentalism and conflict within the community—a point that in a way buttresses Ashis Nandy's argument mentioned earlier.

In the last essay in this section, Pushpesh Kumar (Chapter 6) looks at another minority group—the Muslim gay community in India—which gets marginalized under the process of homogenization of religious norms in the age of global modernity. While medieval Islamic society, literature, and culture, he asserts, left space for diversity of sexual orientation and practices, the influence of modernity has led to universalization of heteronormativity in Indian Muslim society. The daily lived experiences of the urban gay Muslims in contemporary India show that at least in the urban–metropolitan areas, they inhabit a hybrid terrain comprising the internet and cyberspace, with mobile intimacy, civil society, and NGO (non-governmental organization) connections exposing them to ideas of sexual citizenship. Yet, they do not wish to renounce their religious identity and therefore cannot avoid the heteronormativity and homonegativity of their family, community, and the religious world. The universalizing and homogenizing tendencies of modernity, the essay argues, thus ultimately shrink the space for pluralism and further marginalize a minority group.

The essays in the next section on 'Secularism, Religion, and Politics' discuss the contentious relationship between colonial legacies and the postcolonial state and between religion and politics in modern India, and interrogate the problematic notion of the communal–secular binary. Contesting the familiar nationalist narrative, Aparna Devare (Chapter 7) presents a different reading of the Muslim League leader M.A. Jinnah's politics. By drawing on his writings, speeches, and events from his life, she demonstrates that Jinnah never envisaged a theocratic state in imagining Pakistan, but was fundamentally secular. Jinnah believed in secularization of religion, first by confining it to the private sphere during the first half of his life (if at all) and then bringing it into public life purely in political terms (that is the call for Muslim representation and political mobilization). Generalizing from this, she claims that the formation of Pakistan and the ongoing attempts by the Hindu right to search for religious purity created homogeneous nation-states, and that religion-based identities were fundamentally secularist or modern projects.

In the second essay in this section, Sekhar Bandyopadhyay (Chapter 8) also questions the secular–communal binary in analysing the ideological dilemmas of the Hindu Mahasabha immediately after Independence and Partition. The Working Committee of the Mahasabha decided to initiate an internal debate to 'reorient' its ideological position within the new demographic realities of post-Partition India. Did a Hindu-majority India need an exclusively Hindu political party, asked some of its leaders. But in the end, the debate did not result in any major reorientation of the Mahasabha's policies, as the conservative section staunchly held its ground against the reformists, and the debate was somewhat derailed by the political fallout of the assassination of Mahatma Gandhi. But the debate raised serious questions about modernity, citizenship, and the role of religion in postcolonial Indian politics. It also brought out the pluralism within a major Hindu nationalist group and showed that the Hindu right was not a political monolith that could easily be pigeonholed into the communal/secular categories of the familiar nationalist narrative.

In the third essay in this section, B.L. Biju (Chapter 9) looks at the modern political-party system in Kerala, organized into a bipolar coalition system—one group led by the Communist Party of India (Marxists) (CPI [M]) and the other by the Congress (the Indian National Congress party). But in a society where the communities are highly politically mobilized, Biju argues, there is always pressure from them on political parties. The essay shows how this community-based pressure politics works in Kerala's bipolar coalition system. The central argument of this essay is that both the coalitions, despite their modern secularist ideologies, actually perform the function of gatekeepers and carriers of religious as well as communal forces in politics.

In the last essay in this section, N. Sudhakar Rao and M. Ravikumar (Chapter 10) look at the interface between religion and politics in the present Telangana state (formerly a part of Andhra Pradesh) through the ritual of honouring a female deity whose power was acknowledged even by the Nizam. Although this ritual is organized at different places in Hyderabad city around the same time as *bonalu* (a Hindu goddess festival celebrated in Telangana, particularly Hyderabad and Secunderabad, during July–August), the temple and the ritual in the old city became particularly prominent due to the location of the temple surrounded by the majority Muslim population. Here, tempers often run high when processions are organized; several times in the past Hindu–Muslim communal conflicts, riots, and assaults have flared up when the bonalu was organized, disturbing the peace and tranquility of the entire city. The essay argues that in the modern-day context, a religious ritual needs to be understood in its political context, thus compelling a rethinking of religious–secular binary.

The two essays in the last section deal with the 'Religious Practices of the Diaspora', showing how religion works in the lives of expatriate Indians in the most modern living conditions in the Western world. Aparna Rayaprol's essay (Chapter 11) looks at the process of cultural reproduction through a Hindu temple in the American city of Pittsburgh, Pennsylvania. In these temples, rituals are often transformed to suit the needs of the host communities, and change and sometimes even secular values are promoted. But the emphasis remains firmly on the preservation of 'tradition', religion being its most important defining principle. It impacts women particularly adversely, as it reinforces patriarchal authority and emphasizes the 'Eastern' notions of women being the custodians of tradition as a counterpoint to the career-oriented feminist ideology and the 'Western' notions of sexism related to the politics of body. However, equally important is the way, she argues, how a temple provides a cultural space where Hindu religious activities and teachings become constitutive of a collective diasporic identity that remains connected to the home country, its current religious movements, and also their overt—and of course modern—political agendas.

In the last essay in this collection, Brent Otto and Robyn Andrews (Chapter 12) focus on the Anglo-Indian community, which identifies as Christians both in their metropolitan habitats in India as well as in the diaspora. Yet, the story of their religiosity, particularly in the diasporic situations, is far from monolithic and defies some of the presumed categories and patterns one might find with other immigrant groups. The stability of the religious practices of the Anglo-Indians moving into the diaspora demonstrates how essential Christian faith is to Anglo-Indian identity, and that through religion Anglo-Indians find (or actively claim) a place of belonging where their lives can become 'settled' in a new country. The ways in which some Anglo-Indian migrants have adapted their religious practice to Western secularism, individualism, and other attributes of modernity are consistent with the acute need of this minority to adapt to changing circumstances outside of its control. In other words, religion anchors Anglo-Indian identity in a believing community of belonging—a notion that is in itself a product of modernity. Yet here lies their ambiguity as well because, unlike the recent secularist trend in Western modernity, they are reluctant to push their religion to a private space.

Since the last two decades of the twentieth century, there have been a number of studies and debates around the understanding of religion in India. Some of these have provided wholesome critiques of the way these studies originated, entwined as they were in the search for a modern identity of the nation-state. This quest has dominated the academic scene. For the last three decades, the various disciplines of the social sciences in India have also tended to encompass the study of religion within their ambit. However, they have moved away from its traditional definition as part of the literature based on Indological Studies. In this book, against the background of these debates, we provide the challenges posed in the teaching and researching of India's religious diversity from the perspective of specific religious and social contexts—the region and the locality. This is clearly witnessed in the inclusion in this volume of emphasis on bringing in gender issues, the importance of the everyday and folklore, politics, and religion and the practices of marginal groups, as well as the diaspora.

We conclude that for purposes of teaching in classrooms in India and in South Asian Studies departments abroad, the social science disciplines should become more inclusive in their subject content. Increasingly, the seekers of this knowledge in class/caste/ethnic terms have become more varied, demanding a change in the way social sciences are taught in contemporary times. In the various regions of the subcontinent, new histories of their respective distant pasts have come to be written from a regional perspective and, outside India, the so-called 'Indian' diaspora now seeks to grapple with its roots—sometimes at tandem with how Indians in India see as theirs. Hopefully, this book will cater to the intellectual demands of all these varied groups who want to understand India's religion as well as her modernity.

Bibliography

Chakrabarty, Dipesh. 1992. 'Postcoloniality and the Artifice of History: Who Speaks of "Indian" Pasts?'. *Representations* 37(Winter): 1–26.

————. 2000. *Provincializing Europe: Postcolonial Thought and Historical Difference.* Princeton and Oxford: Princeton University Press.

————. 2002. *Habitations of Modernity: Essays in the Wake of Subaltern Studies.* Delhi: Permanent Black.

Chandoke, Neera. 1999. *Beyond Secularism: The Rights of Religious Minorities.* New Delhi: Oxford University Press.

Copland, Ian Mabbett, Asim Roy, Kate Brittlebank, and Adam Bowles. 2012. *A History of State and Religion in India.* London and New York: Routledge.

De Certeau, Michel. 1988. *The Writing of History*, translated by Tom Conley. New York: Columbia University Press.

Dirks, Nicholas. 1990. 'History as a Sign of the Modern'. *Public Culture* 2(2): 25–33.

Dressler, Markus, and Arvind-Pal S. Mandair, eds. 2011. *Secularism and Religion-Making.* Oxford: Oxford University Press.

Duara, Prasenjit. 2015. *The Crisis of Global Modernity: Asian Traditions and a Sustainable Future.* Cambridge: Cambridge University Press.

Gandhi, Leela. 2006. *Affective Communities: Anticolonial Thought, Fin-de-Siecle Radicalism, and the Politics of Friendship.* Durham: Duke University Press.

Kaviraj, Sudipta. 2004. 'Tragedy, Irony and Modernity'. In *Postcolonial Passages: Contemporary History-Writing on India*, edited by Saurabh Dube. New Delhi: Oxford University Press.

Kumar, Ravinder. 1991. 'Exploring the Historical Conjuncture'. *Social Scientist* 19(9–10): 5–18.

Ludden, David, ed. 2005. *Making India Hindu: Religion, Community, and the Politics of Democracy in India*, 2nd edition. New Delhi: Oxford University Press.

Nandy, Ashis. 1998. *The Intimate Enemy: Loss and Recovery of Self under Colonialism.* New Delhi: Oxford University Press.

————. 2002. *Time Warps: Silent and Evasive Pasts in Indian Politics and Religion.* London: Hurst & Co.

Needham, Anuradha D., and Rajeswari S. Rajan. 2007. 'Introduction'. In *The Crisis of Secularism in India*, edited by Anuradha D. Needham and Rajeswari S. Rajan, 1–44. Durham and London: Duke University Press.

Otto, Bernd-Christian, Sussane Rau, and Jörg Rüpke. 2015. 'History and Religion'. In *History and Religion, Narrating a Religious Past*, edited by Bernd-Christian Otto, Sussane Rau, and Jörg Rüpke (with the support of Andrés Quero-Sánchez). Berlin and Boston: De Gruyter GmBH.

Pandian, Anand, and Daud Ali, eds. 2010. *Ethical Life in South Asia.* Bloomington: Indiana University Press.

Raghuramaraju, A. 2011. *Modernity in Indian Social Theory*. New Delhi: Oxford University Press.

Singh, Gurharpal. 2013. 'Religion, Politics and Governance in India, Pakistan, Nigeria and Tanzania: A Comparative Framework'. In *Interrogating India's Modernity: Democracy, Identity and Citizenship*, edited by Surinder S. Jodhka, 135–65. New Delhi: Oxford University Press.

van der Veer, Peter. 2001. *Imperial Encounters: Religion and Modernity in India and Britain*. Princeton and Oxford: Princeton University Press.

————. 2014. *The Modern Spirit of Asia: The Spiritual and the Secular in China and India*. Princeton and Oxford: Princeton University Press.

Vatsyayan, Kapila. 2005. 'From Interior Landscapes into Cyberspace: Fluidity and Dynamics of Tradition'. In *Culture and the Making of Identity in Contemporary India*, edited by Kamala Ganesh and Usha Thakkar, 39–50 (The Asiatic Society of Mumbai Bicentenary Volume). New Delhi: Sage Publications.

Walliss, John. 2002. *The Brahma Kumaris as a 'Reflexive Tradition': Responding to Late Modernity*. Aldershot: Ashgate.

PART ONE

MODERNITY, RELIGION, AND SECULARISM

1

T.K. OOMMEN

Society, Religion, and Modernity in Postcolonial India*

Terms such as 'society', 'religion', and 'modernity' are in wide currency; yet it cannot be said that there exists consensus among social scientists with regard to their conceptualizations. For example, society was conceptualized in myriad ways and these were conditioned by the kind of social transformations taking place at different points in time. Dichotomous constructions were in vogue when the transition from agrarian to industrial or from feudal to capitalist societies was taking place. With the advent of colonialism, a trichotomy—First, Second, and Third Worlds—assumed saliency. The postcolonial world is believed to have given birth to a global society. Yet, when we refer to a society, we have in mind an entity which has specific territorial, cultural, political, and economic referents.

* This constitutes the text of the first keynote address at the International Conference on Society, Religion and Modernity in India organized at the School of Social Sciences, University of Hyderabad, in collaboration with the New Zealand India Research Institute, on 28–29 November 2013.

I

Today there are sociologists who abandoned the very term 'society'—once believed to be the fulcrum of their discipline—and now prefer the terms 'mobility' (Urry 2000), 'global network' (Castells 1998), or 'multidimensional social spaces' (Bourdieu 1977), to mention just three substitutes for society. Yet, we are still stuck with the term 'society' as explicated by Bauman:

> ... the term 'society' as used by well-nigh all sociologists regardless of their school loyalties is, for all practical purposes, a name for an entity identical in size and composition with the nation-state.... Further, ... with hardly any exception, all the concepts and analytical tools currently employed by social scientists are geared to a view of the human world in which the most voluminous totality is a 'society', a notion equivalent for all practical purposes, to the concept of the nation state. (1973: 43, 78)

Most social scientists unhesitatingly refer to India as a nation-state and pursuantly as a 'society' in the sense in which Bauman equated the two entities. But I suggest that this is utterly simplistic and indeed confusing for several reasons: First, a nation-state relentlessly pursues the ideal of cultural homogenization, but the Indian state not only accommodates but also celebrates cultural heterogeneity. India has 22 officially recognized languages and no official or national religion, although 82 per cent of its population is categorized as Hindu as of now. Second, most nations, that is, territorially anchored linguistic communities, in the Indian polity did not seek their own sovereign states, but renounced them and settled for provincial states—they are state-renouncing nations (Oommen 2004: 121–43). Third, the hyphenated term 'nation-state' conflates state and nation, which violates the empirical reality of polities such as India (Oommen 1997). Therefore, India should be designated as a national state which is a conglomeration of several societies that coexist in one sovereign state (Oommen 2006). This means 'society' in postcolonial India is an aggregation of several societies, each one of which has its own specificities. The binding factor in India is common citizenship of a complex polity in which a multiplicity of cultures coexist: single citizenship common to several 'nations'. This understanding of the nature of Indian society drastically alters the terms of discourse of the theme of this conference, particularly because the Indian republic hosts a wide variety of religions.

The first settlers of India (Adivasis) were subjected to internal colonialism[1] by both Aryan and Muslim invaders. The Adivasis did not share the religions of Hindus (Aryans or Dravidians) and Muslims. Through the processes of political and economic domination and cultural assimilation, the Adivasis, except those in northeast India, were absorbed into the Indian polity. It is also necessary to distinguish between retreatist and replicative colonialisms (Oommen 1999: 67–84) because postcolonial societies differ based on the type of colonialism to which they are subjected. When British colonizers retreated from India after two centuries, they left indelible marks on the territorial, political, and economic features of India but not so much on the cultural, particularly religious, characteristics of India.

Religions in India may be grouped into three broad categories based on the sources of their origin. First are those religions that are perceived to be native to India, including: (*a*) the primal vision of the indigenous people of India (Adivasis); (*b*) Hinduism (Aryan and Dravidian); and (*c*) Indian protestant religions such as Buddhism, Jainism, and Sikhism. The second category comprises those religious communities that migrated to India to escape persecution in their ancestral home lands—Jews, Zoroastrians, and Baha'is—and adopted India as their homeland. The third refers to religions perceived to be the products of conquest and colonialism—Islam and Christianity respectively—although an overwhelming majority of them are converts from local religions and castes.

Armed with this understanding of Indian society, let us dissect the interface between religion and modernity in postcolonial India. In replicative colonialism, the colonizers transform the colony into their settlement and transplant their religion and language[2] in addition to moulding its polity and economy. In contrast, under retreatist colonialism, the cultural dimensions are retained and their specificity is maintained. When the British left, after two centuries of colonialism, barely 1.5 per cent of the people of the Indian subcontinent were Christians, although pre-colonial and pre-British Christianity did exist in India.[3] And, contrary to common perception, the Christian population in northeast India expanded fivefold in India counting from 1951, the year of the first census in independent India (Downs

2003: 381–400). Thus, it is not only that Christianity in India existed in pre-colonial times, but also that its postcolonial expansion in India has been substantial. This nullifies two popular stereotypes: (*a*) that Christianity in India is a colonial transplant and (*b*) that Indian religions are eroded due to colonialism.

Both the British colonial policy and the nature of religions which existed in pre-British India caused this slow growth of Christianity in India. First, there was hardly any formal cooperation between the British colonial state and the European missionaries. Queen Victoria's proclamation of 1858 stated: 'Firmly relying ourselves on the truth of Christianity, and acknowledging with gratitude the solace of religion, We disclaim alike the Right and the Desire to impose our convictions on any of our subjects' (quoted in Firth 1976: 189). That is, the British colonial administration professed official neutrality towards the different religions of India.[4] Second, the two major religions present in colonial India, Hinduism (70 per cent) and Islam (25 per cent), were well developed and serious competitors to the colonizer's religion, namely Christianity, which spread mainly either among the tribal population (Scheduled Tribes [STs]) whose religion was not well formed or among those who were placed lowest in the caste hierarchy (Scheduled Castes [SCs]) and treated as 'untouchables' by caste Hindus.

It is also pertinent to recall two aspects of Christian conversion movements here. Throughout the middle years of the nineteenth century, educated upper-caste men and women converted to Christianity, although in small numbers, on the basis of personal convictions. By the third decade of the nineteenth century, mass conversion movements among STs, SCs, and Other Backward Classes (OBCs; who were above the ritual pollution line but were socio-economically backward) reached their peak (Firth 1976). If the first type of conversion prompted Westernization/modernization of the converts, the second usually facilitated the retention of much of the traditional lifestyle of converts as these were group conversions. The second aspect refers to the approach followed by the missionaries which in turn were of two types. The first of these was represented by Alexander Duff (1806–78), the Scottish missionary based in Calcutta, who wanted to transform Calcutta's Bengalis into Scottish Presbyterians. He was convinced that the route to India's progress lay in Western religion and culture. In contrast, the English missionary

William Carey aimed at introducing the basic influence of Christianity into the existing structures of Indian society and culture. Carey wanted Indian Christians to be rooted in Indian culture (Kopf 1969). The point of this brief excursus into history is to reveal that colonialism did not fundamentally alter the religious landscape in India, and even those who did embrace the religion of the colonizer mainly followed the line pursued by Carey. B.P. Sircar echoed this sentiment in 1910 thus: '... before India can be Christianized, Christianity must be nationalized' (quoted in Abraham 1947: 26).

II

Given this historical backdrop, how do we situate religion in postcolonial India? Under replicative colonialism, the religion of the colonizer becomes the dominant religion of the postcolonial society either because the majority of the population comprises migrants and their descendants from the colonizer country or because the indigenous people do not have a sophisticated religion to resist the imposition of the colonizer's religion. Thus, in the New World consisting of the Americas, Australia, and New Zealand, Christianity became the dominant religion.[5] This meant that the political 'problem' in colonial India, which was subjected to retreatist colonialism, was between the two dominant religions—Hinduism and Islam—eventuating in partition based on religious grounds, although attempts were made to evolve a synthetic culture that would fuse the two (see, for example, Prasad 1941 and Kabir 1955). The way forward was to establish a 'secular' polity, even though the Indian population was predominantly Hindu (82 per cent). It was in the constitutional notion of secularism that one had to locate the interface between religion and modernity in postcolonial India.

In the West, secularism is juxtaposed with religiosity and there are at least three connotations of secularization. These Western connotations are (*a*) separating humans and society from the transcendental and the divine; (*b*) relegating religion to the private realm of human activity;[6] and (*c*) institutionalizing rationality through a process of displacing religiosity. Incidentally these conceptualizations of secularization go hand in hand with the Western notions of modernization. The first and second are proximate to the conceptualization of modernity as structural differentiation mainly attributed to Émile Durkheim, the French sociologist. The third notion of secularization is isomorphic with the conceptualization of modernity as an onward march of rationality attributed to Max Weber, the German sociologist.[7]

Although there are several Indian social scientists who fall in line with one or the other notion of Western secularism (and modernity), the Indian constitution conceptualizes secularism as (*a*) the dignified coexistence of all religions and (*b*) the state keeping equal distance from all religions, notions which are in consonance with the empirical reality of India. To facilitate this, the Republic of India abandoned the idea of an official or national religion. However, this does not mean that the phenomenon of religiosity has declined in independent India and, even if it did, its measurement is problematic. While most religions have their organizational structures in the form of churches or their equivalents, Hinduism does not have any such structure; it is famously described as a way of life by the philosopher-statesman Radhakrishnan. Therefore, it is extremely tortuous to measure the decline of religiosity in Hinduism or understand the increase in secularity or modernity in Indian society.[8] Viewed from the opposite side, through India's constitutional lens of secularism, one can discern the increase in inter-religious harmony through the decrease in inter-religious conflicts popularly known as 'communal riots' in South Asia.

As per the National Crime Records Bureau (NCRB), Ministry of Home Affairs, Government of India, there were 797,576 riots during 1971–80, which works out to be 13.07 riots per one lakh (100,000) population per year. The situation during 1989–98, a decade later, was more or less the same, with the total number of communal riots being 792,392—an annual average of 11 riots per one lakh population. But what is appalling is that independent India does not have a legal instrument to deal with the recurring communal riots, to prevent and punish those who cause and rehabilitate those who are victims of these riots. And the Communal Violence (Prevention, Control, and Rehabilitation of Victims) Bill of 2006 is not yet an Act.

A National Commission for Minorities (NCM) was established in 1992 by the Government of India. Its mandate includes violations of the rights of religious minorities and looking into specific complaints regarding such violations. The complaints are entertained from both individuals and minority religious organizations. During 1993–5, that is, for a period of three years, NCM received 350 complaints per year, almost one complaint per day. For the years 2001–3, that is, for a period of another three years, NCM received 2,625 complaints per year, registering an annual increase of 7.5 times.[9]

It is not possible to propose causal explanations for the variations in complaints received by NCM during the two time chunks. And yet it is pertinent to recall here that during 1987–95 the party in power and which led the union government was one that endorsed the principle of secularism as conceptualized in the Indian constitution. In contrast, during the latter period (1999–2003), the government was led by a party which believed in establishing a Hindu *rashtra* (nation) in India. It can be stated without any fear of contradiction that the religious value-orientation upheld by the party in power necessarily influences the quantum of violence against religious minority communities. The contents of complaints received by NCM are indicative of the causes of prevailing inter-religious tension: non-recognition by the governments (provincial and central) of minority-managed institutions of education and health, unlawful interference by the governments in the management of these institutions, and refusal of governments to locate such institutions in areas inhabited mainly by minorities.[10]

Having referred to the positive orientation of the Indian constitution to conceptualize secularism in a way that would accommodate religious diversity and promote communal harmony, it is necessary to refer to some of the grave praxiological aberrations by the Indian state. I will refer only to three instances to make my point.

From 1871 onwards, a religious category designated as 'primitive' was listed in the Indian census. In 1901, those who belonged to this category comprised 2.92 per cent of the population, which increased to 3.28 per cent by 1911. After 1911, the term used was 'tribal religion', which accounted for 3.09 per cent in 1921 and 2.36 per cent in 1931 (there was no census in 1941 due to World War II). In 1951, tribal religion as a category disappeared from free India's census and was absorbed into the category of Hinduism, excluding those individuals who embraced one of the world religions such as Buddhism, Christianity, or Islam. The Scheduled Tribes of India number 451 and their population is 8.6 per cent, that is, about 100 million, most of who practise their traditional religion in part or in full. Admittedly, to deny religious identity to this vast population is wrong in letter and spirit as per the constitutional understanding of secularism, namely according equal respect to all religions.[11]

The second instance of the Indian state denying religious identity to minorities occurs in the expansive definition of Hinduism. Thus, the Hindu Code Bill includes Buddhists, Jains, and Sikhs along with Hindus in its scope. One may argue that these religions are offshoots of Hinduism, but they maintain that they have distinct identities which should be reflected in their separate civil codes. Therefore, to encapsulate them under the rubric of Hinduism through the Hindu Code Bill is patently against the spirit of Indian secularism as enunciated in the Indian constitution.[12] While Jains accept this expansionist definition, Buddhists protest meekly and Sikhs vociferously against it.

The third instance of the Indian state flouting the spirit of secularism is flagrant in that it denies not only identity but also equity and justice to a segment of Indian citizenry. Given the fact that India's traditional caste hierarchy not only denied equality but also sanctioned and institutionalized inequality based on Hindu theological doctrines, it was but appropriate that the Indian constitution introduced the policy of protective discrimination, popularly referred to as 'reservation', a set of special entitlements to those who were stigmatized as 'untouchables' but referred to as Scheduled Castes in legal parlance. In 1950, through the Constitution (Scheduled Castes) Order, usually referred to as the Presidential Order, the SCs who professed Hinduism were provided certain special entitlements. Faced with protests from the SCs of Sikh background, these entitlements were extended to them in 1954. After a prolonged struggle, the SCs of Buddhist background were also brought under this Order in 1990. But those members of the Scheduled Castes who embraced Christianity and Islam are denied these entitlements even today. That is, it was not only the principle of treating citizens belonging to different religions with equal respect that was violated, but also that of providing them equality of opportunity, flouting the letter and spirit of secularism.[13]

The point I am making by citing these three instances (and several others could be added) is that there is a yawning gap between the promises of secularism in India's constitution and its practice by the Indian state. More distressing is the fact that these praxiological aberrations are in tune with the vision of the Hindu rashtra upheld by Hindutva ideologues (see Golwalkar 1939 and Savarkar 1949).

III

Let me conclude this chapter by referring to an unstated but implicit assumption in formulating the theme of the conference, namely Western epistemological dualism and the displacement syndrome it implies. This means that as a society modernizes, several of its traditional aspects are displaced, religion being one of the guaranteed casualties. I have argued for long that this is not always true even in the West, but certainly not in India. The process that is taking place in India is partial retention and partial displacement (see Oommen 1975: 163–80), which defies the tenets of epistemological dualism. Which is to say that in the interface between tradition and modernity, four interrelated processes can and often occur; they are homogenization, pluralization, traditionalization, and hybridization (Oommen 2005: 149–69). This is applicable in the case of an interface between religion and modernity too.

Homogenization of cultural patterns and institutional arrangements is widely believed to be a necessary accompaniment to modernization, and religion is not exempt from this. I have earlier alluded to the absence of 'church' in Hinduism, but functional equivalents of church, such as the Rashtriya Swayamsevak Sangh (RSS), did emerge to regulate behaviour and reinforce belief and succeeded in the case of a section of Hindus. The idea of institutionally trained clergy was absent and perhaps unnecessary in Hinduism because Brahmans could inherit this role. But the possibility of a trained clergy cutting across caste divisions is gradually emerging and some of the provincial states have established institutions to train Hindu clergy. Indeed, the expression 'semitization of Hinduism'[14] frequently heard in India today is an indication of homogenization across Hindu religious sects and even caste categories in certain aspects. On the other hand, religions such as Christianity and Islam often attempt to indigenize their religions to adapt to the local situations without changing their basic belief systems and canonical rituals.[15] Thus 'glocalization', combining the global and the local elements, often occurs in the case of most religions, indicating the limits of homogenization implicated in and attributed to modernity.

Homogenization is not possible because of selective displacement of certain traditional aspects and glocalization. On the other hand, selective retention of certain traditional aspects and accretion of new ones also take place. These processes in combination give birth to pluralization. Hinduism, as practised in different parts of India, differs not only because of the multiplicity of gods and texts but also because of differing emphases bestowed on them by different sects, each of which is prominent in different regions and areas within them. While it is true that plurality is an inherent feature of Hinduism, it is not impervious to the demonstration effect of the praxis of other religions. For example, in the villages of Kerala, the introduction of Ravi Pathasalas (Sunday schools) to teach scriptures in Hindu temples, imitating Sunday schools conventionally conducted by Christian churches, is gaining popularity. This is widely believed to be an example of RSS influence.

The homogenizing tendency of modernization often gives birth to loss of meaning, an erosion of identity, particularly to the dominant or majority religions. This leads to the revivalist syndrome, the resurrection of roots manifesting in a process of traditionalization. Even as societies modernize, they are often keen to retain their national heritages and give expression only to specific forms of modernity, as articulated in the notion of 'Indian modernity'. This may prompt reinvention of tradition both as religious reform and as religious fundamentalism. If religious reform is an effort to re-read the texts taking into account the changes in socio-cultural contexts, religious fundamentalism is the proclivity to read the texts ignoring changes in the context. When traditionalization relapses into the search for cultural purity, it engenders cultural relativism, the belief that one's culture is superior to other cultures, and hence needs to be maintained in its pristine purity. Religion is frequently in the forefront of cleansing societies of alien accretions, that often being a function of modernization. The tendency to identify religions of Indian origin as 'national' (an instance of Hindu expansionism) and religions of non-Indian origin as alien (an instance of Hindu exclusivism) is rampant among a section of Hindus, although the presence of these 'alien' religions is several centuries old—twenty centuries in the case of Christianity and thirteen in the case of Islam. That is, homogenization based on religions demoralizes and alienates these 'alien' religious communities, which is against the professed accommodative spirit of both Hinduism and modernity.

I have referred to the plurality of traditions in religions, and this is particularly true of Hinduism. This fact gives birth to conflicts between different traditions in addition to the conflict between tradition and modernity. Generally speaking, the conflict between tradition and modernity is a conflict between the hegemony of tradition and the homogenizing tendency of modernity. But when multiple traditions emerge and exist in a society, the struggle is to establish the hegemony of one of these traditions, be they sectarian groups within a religion or proximate religions such as Hinduism, Buddhism, and Jainism. Apart from the horizontality of religious traditions, their verticality too is important. This is true in India because of the multiplicity of little traditions and a few great traditions. While modernity, particularly postmodernity, erodes great traditions, it is not averse to bestowing dignity to little traditions because of its egalitarian orientations. Understandably, this is often a breeding ground for tensions and conflicts between the homogenizing and diversifying tendencies of modernity. Above all, conflicting value orientations of different religious traditions—polytheism and monotheism, cosmocentrism and homocentrism, gradual assimilation and sudden proselytization—all have the potentiality to unleash violence and tension in the context of modernization, which find frequent expression in India. This is particularly prominent in the tensions between Hinduism, the majority religion, and Islam, the most numerous minority religion.

Finally, the cross-breeding of the traditional and the modern, the local and the global, the little and the great, and the Indic and non-Indic religious traditions gives birth to religious hybridity. Hybridization is different from pluralization in that it is neither coexistence nor elaboration. It is an effort to innovate and mutate in the religious context, often manifesting in syncretism. The tendency on the part of believers, when faced with stresses and strains in life, to seek solace in godheads and places of worship other than their own original faiths is common in India. Thus, hybridity in the religious context is simultaneous engagement with both the local and the global as well as the Indic and the alien. This is why people are often surprised and even upset that when religious communities are in conflict, as people belonging to opposite camps help, cooperate, and protect each other. Once again the problem arises from the tendency to theorize and ignore empirical reality. Some theorists think that hybridity is the product of simultaneous engagement with both tradition and modernity and the local and the global (cf. Pieterse 1994: 161–84). What I am alluding to is that there is no set pattern here. Depending on the context, it could be simultaneous or successive, mutually contradictory or reinforcing.

The four processes identified—homogenization, pluralization, traditionalization, and hybridization—while impacting on both religion and modernity, produces a society whose complexity increases exponentially. Therefore, to assume that as modernity advances religion will disappear is not just simplistic but utterly false. True, new permutations and combinations will emerge that will give birth to diversity. That is why I suggested at the very outset that instead of opting for the engineered homogeneity of the nation-state of western Europe, India should consciously endorse the idea of national state that not only tolerates or accommodates cultural diversity but also celebrates it. The logical derivation of this proposition is enunciating and celebrating religious pluralism instead of envisioning modernity as a cauldron in which religion will melt away.

Notes

1. A few decades ago Hechter (1975) referred to internal colonialism with regard to Britain. Both the colonialisms that I am referring to here are external, but internal colonialism too existed in India prior to the advent of European colonialism (Oommen 2013: 1–16), although this is not recognized by Indian social scientists.

2. It is rewarding to hypothesize the varying focus of Protestant and Catholic colonizers. It seems that while the latter focused on religion, the former concentrated on language. Thus, in Asia, in both Philippines (colonized by Catholic Spain) and Goa (colonized by Catholic Portugal), substantial attention was given to Christianization. In contrast, in the Indian subcontinent mainly colonized by Britain, the focus was on spreading the English language.

3. Pre-colonial Christianity came to Kerala in India in the first century AD through St Thomas, an apostle of Jesus Christ. There were only two other sites where pre-colonial Christianity existed, namely Egypt (Coptic Christians) and Ethiopia (Orthodox Christians). Pre-British Portuguese Christianity was transplanted in the sixteenth century mainly in Goa.

4. This is in contrast to the policy pursued with regard to the promotion of English language rendered notorious through Thomas Macaulay's Minute on Education (1835).

5. In fact decolonization itself implies two different trajectories. Replicative colonialism only calls for the cutting off of the umbilical cord or 'slaying of the European father' (see Lerner 1957). In contrast, retreatist colonialism calls for a vigorous and often prolonged anti-colonial struggle against the colonizer for liberating the colony.

6. I have argued elsewhere that these conceptualizations are not tenable (Oommen 1990: 112–23) but that should not deflect our attention here.

7. There are two other notions of Western modernity: the history-making project which eventuates in revolution, the progenitor of which is Karl Marx; and the compression of time and space usually attributed to Georg Simmel (Oommen 2001: 1–16). As these are not pertinent to the present analysis, I will not explore them further here.

8. The typical 'method' invoked to understand the decline of religiosity in countries populated by Christians is to count the decline of church attendance and, in the case of Islamic countries, it is to understand the decrease in the number of times one prays, the prescribed periodicity being five times a day.

9. The data for the years left out are either not available or not kept systematically.

10. An elaborate report that focuses on the social, economic, and educational status of Muslims in India (Government of India 2006), who account for nearly 13 per cent of the Indian population and number 140 million, paints a graphic picture of discrimination against them.

11. The Indian state is not the sole culprit in this context. Indian sociologists and social anthropologists too endorsed the view that the tribes of India are 'backward Hindus'. The pioneer in this effort was G.S. Ghurye (1943).

12. This encapsulation of Jains, Buddhists, and Sikhs under the rubric of Hinduism is precariously proximate to the notion of Hindutva propounded by Savarkar (1949).

13. The big divide one witnesses here is that between those who profess religions of Indian origin and those who pursue religions of alien origin, an idea so dear to Hindu militants and initially propounded by Golwalkar (1939).

14. The three Semitic religions being Judaism, Christianity, and Islam.

15. Members of all religious communities tend to participate in the social rituals prevalent in linguistic regions associated with local festivals, while the political rituals associated with Independence Day and Republic Day are designated as 'national' in which all religious communities participate.

Bibliography

Abraham, C.E. 1947. *The Founders of the National Mission Society of India*. Madras: National Missionary Society of India.

Bauman, Z. 1973. *Culture as Praxis*. London: Routledge and Kegan Paul.

Bourdieu P. 1977. *Outline of a Theory of Practice*. Cambridge: Cambridge University Press.

Castells, M. 1998. *The Information Age*, vol. 3. Oxford: Blackwell.

Downs, Frederick S. 2003. 'Christian Conversion Movements in Northeast India'. In *Religious Conversion in India: Modes, Motivations and Meanings*, edited by Rowena Robinson and Sathianathan Clarke, 381–400. New Delhi: Oxford University Press.

Firth, C.B. 1976. *An Introduction to Indian Church History*. Madras: Christian Literature Society.

Ghurye, G.S. 1943. *The Aborigines—So Called—and Their Future*. Poona: Gokhale Institute of Politics and Economics.

Golwalkar, M.S. 1939. *We or Our Nationhood Defined*. Nagpur: Bharat Prakashan.

Government of India. 2006. *Social, Economic and Educational Status of the Muslim Community in India*. New Delhi: Government of India (Cabinet Secretariat).

Hechter, Michael. 1975. *Internal Colonialism: The Celtic Fringe in British National Development 1536–1966*. London: Routledge and Kegan Paul.

Kabir, Humayan. 1955. *The Indian Heritage*. Bombay: Asia Publishing House.

Kopf, D. 1969. *British Orientalism and Bengal Renaissance: The Dynamics of Modernization: 1713–1865*. Calcutta: Firma K.L. Mukhopadhyay.

Lerner, Max. 1957. *America as a Civilisation*. New Delhi: Allied Publishers.

Oommen, T.K. 1975. 'Possibilities for the Realisation of a Consensus between India's Past and Her Modern Society'. *Delo* (special issue on India and the West) XXI(2): 163–80.

———. 1990. *State and Society in India*. New Delhi: Sage Publications.

———. 1991. 'Internationalization of Sociology: A View from Developing Countries'. *Current Sociology* 39(1): 67–84.

———. 1997. *Citizenship, Nationality and Ethnicity: Reconciling Competing Identities*. Cambridge: Polity Press.

———. 2001. 'Multiple Modernities and the Rise of New Social Movements: The Case of India'. *Indian Social Science Review* 3(1): 1–16.

———. 2004. 'New Nationalisms and Collective Rights: The Case of South Asia'. In *Ethnicity, Nationalism and Minority Rights*, edited by Stephen May, Tariq Modood, and Judith Squires, pp. 121–43. Cambridge: Cambridge University Press.

————. 2005. 'Challenges of Modernity in an Age of Globalization'. In *Comparing Modernities: Pluralism versus Homogeneity (Essays in Homage to Shmuel N. Eisemstatt)*, edited by Eliezer Ben Rafel and Yitzhak Stanberg, 149–69. Leiden: Brill.

————. 2006. *Understanding Security: A New Perspective*. Delhi: MacMillan.

————. 2013. 'Adivasis of Bharat: Victims of Erroneous Conceptualization and Inappropriate Policies'. Occasional Paper Series I, 1–16. Bhopal: Indira Gandhi Rashtriya Manav Sangrahalaya.

Prasad, Beni.1941. *The Hindu–Muslim Question*. Allahabad: Indian Press.

Pieterse, J.N. 1994. 'Globalization as Hybridization'. *International Sociology* 9(2): 161–84.

Savarkar, V.D. 1949. *Hindutva—Who Is a Hindu?* New Delhi: Bharat Sahitya Sadan.

Urry, J. 2000. *Sociology beyond Societies: Mobilities for the Twenty-First Century*. London: Routledge.

2

ADITYA MALIK

Possession, Alterity, Modernity*

Whereas possessed bodies were likely to be approached as anachronistic bodies influenced by beliefs that the scholar did not hold, I have argued for an approach that both acknowledges that the possessed body is powerful and that scholarly studies of possession are produced by a desire to be in proximity to alterity, which is often masked as an intellectual desire to explain possession.

—Mary Keller, *The Hammer and the Flute* (2002)

A boundary is not that at which something stops, but as the Greeks recognized, the boundary is that from which something begins its presencing.
—Martin Heidegger, *Building, Dwelling, Thinking* (1971)

This chapter is based on ethnographic materials collected during several field trips to the Central Himalayan region of Kumaon.[1] While the text I present here does not itself contain ethnographic materials, it is a prelude to a more detailed analysis of an ethnography of so-called possession rituals that I have documented in the field along with temple narratives, devotees' stories, and quasi-legal petitions associated with Goludev, the Kumaoni 'god of justice' and other

---

* This constitutes the text of the second keynote address at the International Conference on Society, Religion and Modernity in India organized at the School of Social Sciences, University of Hyderabad, in collaboration with the New Zealand India Research Institute, on 28–29 November 2013.

*nyāy-kārī devtā*s or deities linked to granting justice in the Central Himalayas.[2] In broad terms, this chapter asks questions about the meanings of religious phenomena such as 'possession' vis-à-vis notions of the individual and modernity in India in contexts where social existence is explained in terms of forces that are not only human, but also non-human and divine.

Goludev is the principal deity or *iṣṭadevtā* of almost all 'high' and 'low' caste communities including Thakur or Rajput, Dalit, and Brahman living in the northern province of Kumaon. Goludev's devotees are able to solicit his mediation or intervention in matters of justice (a category used in this context to cover a wide range of life concerns) in two predominant ways. The first way of requesting his mediation is through the submission of written petitions (*manauti*)[3] in his main temples at Chittai (near Almora, Almora district), Ghoda Khal (near Bhavali, Nainital district), and Champavat (Champavat district). The first two temples are administered by Brahman priests of the Panth and Joshi lineages respectively,[4] and the third one by members of the Nath Gosain community. The temples are described as 'courts of justice' (*kaccheri* or *darbār*).[5] The second manner of soliciting his advice and intervention is through an oracular ritual called *jāgar* (see Krengel 1999; Leavitt 1997; and Malik 2009, 2010, 2011, 2014, 2015, and 2016).

Manautis or petitions vary in size, from a few lines to a page or several pages. The majority of the petitions I have been able to document are in Hindi, but many are written in a mixture of Hindi and English, and sometimes Kumaoni. The tone of the petitions is often intimate and personal, as though the writers have no other avenue to express their feelings and concerns. Petitions may also refer directly to legal matters being dealt with in secular courts such as an impending prison sentence or a property dispute. The composition of the petitions, besides often being a hybrid of Hindi and English, can be a combination of legal and devotional language.

The jāgars are rituals that involve the possession or rather embodiment of the deity through designated individuals. The deity's presence is invoked through the ritual narration of the deity's story. There is a powerful element of suffering, pain, injustice, and even death that is innermost to their stories.[6] When these incidents are retold during the telling of the narrative, they produce feelings of anger and passion in the deities, accelerating their embodiment. Once the deities are embodied, they 'dance' and speak to family members. It is through this dialogue that the diagnosis of 'injustice' construed in different ways, both legal and non-legal, and its resolution in forms of 'justice' (*nyay*) can begin to occur.

The focus of this chapter is primarily on the implications of scholarly, theoretical, and, to a degree, popular understandings of 'possession' not only with regard to the jāgars of Goludev but, more broadly, in respect of a bounded, impermeable subjectivity grounded in the idea of the individual that in turn occupies a central place in the ideological and philosophical underpinnings of modernity both in India and elsewhere.

Framing Possession

There has been a steady fascination—perhaps even an obsession—with the spectacle of 'possession' in South Asia and beyond not only in the field of religious studies, but also within anthropology, psychology, sociology, literary history, linguistics, and medical disciplines (Smith 2011: 3).[7] Early European missionaries in India, for example, described rituals of possession as wild, demonic acts of frenzy far removed from the kind of 'religion' they were familiar with. The first Danish protestant missionary in India, Bartholomeus Ziegenbalg, mentions 'devil dancers' in his *Genealogie der malabarischen Götter* (Genealogy of Malabar gods) in 1713. In subsequent missionary writings on India, and on 'Hindoos' in particular, 'devil dancers' become like a requisite trope along with 'devil worship' (Schoembucher 1993: 239).[8] This negatively laden meaning of possession has, in a sense, continued to the present day, even while the scholarly disciplines of religious studies and anthropology grow in self-reflexivity. Although missionaries such as Ziegenbalg condemned possession as degenerate and *pagan*, they had 'no difficulty in seeing possession as an ecstatic religious experience ... Western social scientists have had a much more ambiguous attitude ... most anthropologists think that a person cannot really become possessed by divine or demonic beings, and that phenomena such as possession have to be regarded as an expression of other events or conditions, for which more rational explanations have to be found' (Schoembucher 1993: 240). Possession, by and large, is still considered something abnormal or pathological, something that the scholar, psychiatrist, or medical doctor needs to explain in terms of symbolic behaviour, psychological trauma, social oppression, psycho-pathological disease, resistance to colonialism, neo-liberalism, or patriarchy, as the case may be, or simply as a function of powerful embodied belief—at best a kind of *body hexis* to borrow a term from the French sociologist Pierre Bourdieu.[9]

While we encounter an enormous variety of possession rituals from the vast majority of cultures, including South Asian,[10] possession as a state of 'being another' or of 'not being oneself' is still treated as something of an anomaly. Why is it so? Why is such consistent academic attention given to it? And why is it rarely taken for what it is: a multi-sensory bodily practice, which, like asceticism, yoga, meditation, or other forms of personal cultivation (and an assortment of ritual practices involving the invocation of *presence* other than that which is known to belong to one's own immediate self), is central to the diagnosis, healing, and resolution of concerns that people deal with?[11]

Any conversation about possession—from the most casual to the most scholarly—is therefore usually accompanied by the question 'Is this real?'[12] 'Can something like this really happen—especially in this day and age?' or 'Do you believe in this?' The implication is that 'today', that is, at this present moment of history, we have somehow overcome and transcended superstitious, irrational modes of existence that plagued the past. We have, in fact, overcome tradition. But as the anthropologist Bruno Latour discerningly notes: 'The past comes back with a vengeance in modernity.'[13] The amazement and scepticism that people have towards 'possession' is, in fact, located wherever modernity—in whatever form, 'Eastern' or 'Western'—flourishes.[14] Modernity seems to promise us a clear, uncluttered present and purposeful future of which we are in control. It promises us freedom from unreflexive aspects of tradition and, more pertinently, from *religion* and its various expressions. Possession, on the other hand, suggests a relinquishment of control accompanied by a loss of self, memory, and identity rooted in uncertainty with regard to agency and authorship.

Is it at all possible to *understand* rather than reduce or explain possession within the ideological and discursive framework of modernity? Can possession, with its implicitly different comprehension of subjectivity and agency, contribute to a *breakthrough*, so to speak, from the global forms of impasse that seem to be the legacy of modernity?

While both terms—possession and modernity—admittedly resist simple and easy definitions, it is worthwhile to begin by attempting to provide working delineations.

Possession and Modernity: A Binary Tale

A definition of modernity—even a working one—is possibly more elusive than that of possession, perhaps because modernity ascribes to itself a mode of self-reflexivity and is therefore constantly revising its own meaning.[15] But modernity, above all, also distinguishes itself from that which is antiquated, traditional, or 'old'. In this sense modernity is always an oppositional term that marks itself off from that which is considered to be *not modern*, which, in straightforward temporal terms, is the *past*, or more accurately from a past that can be considered unreflexive. To be modern is to be in the 'now' or present time, but also to be new. In eleventh-century Europe, for example, 'in order to count oneself among the *moderni* one had to distinguish oneself from the *antiqui*' (Benavides 1998: 186; italics original). Already present during the medieval period in Europe, but also today, '[the] condition of modernity presupposes an act of self-conscious distancing from a past or a situation regarded as naïve. This self-extrication, however, is in principle an endless task ...' (Benavides 1998: 187–8). Modernity has been identified with a series of rejections and acts of distancing. In fundamental terms, it rejects the notion of religion, that is, 'of a sacramental view of reality and of anthropomorphic conceptions of the divinity, as well as even more radically ... any notion of transcendence' (Benavides 1998: 190). Along with this oppositional shift, modernity has also moved 'from the organic to the mechanic; from the corporate to the individual; from hierarchy to equality; from an understanding of reality in which everything resonates with everything else ... to one built around precision and the increasing differentiation of domains' (Benavides 1998: 190). One could add to this list the universally taken-for-granted binary oppositions between mind and body, subject and object, subject and 'other-subject', nature and culture, analytic and synthetic, rational and non-rational, Occident and Orient, and so on. These radical acts of distancing but also of the fixity of being and identity, are furthermore enshrined in the political and cultural institutions of law and social justice, education and rationality, secularism and democracy, technological advancement and research, the separation and preservation of public and private spheres, and so on, even in the idea of 'multiculturalism'.

A definition of 'possession' may appear easier to approach than a definition of modernity, although the answer to the question: 'What is possession?' can be equally daunting and complex. As Fredrick Smith (2011: 3) points out, the response '... could be one or two sentences in length, or it could stretch to ten volumes'. Janice Boddy, in her wide-ranging review of the scholarly literature on possession, begins with a succinct description:

> Spirit possession commonly refers to the hold exerted over a human being by external forces or entities more powerful than she. These forces may be ancestors or divinities, ghost of foreign origin, or entities both ontologically and ethnically alien.... *Possession*, then is a broad term referring to an integration of spirit and matter, force or power and corporeal reality, in a cosmos where the boundaries between an individual and her environment are acknowledged to be permeable, flexibly drawn, or at least negotiable. (1994: 407; emphasis original)[16]

But what exactly does it mean to say that 'the boundaries between an individual and her environment are acknowledged to be permeable'? Is it even possible as 'modern subjects' to know what this means not just in a theoretical sense but in real, experiential terms? Does this suggest a different understanding of Self or indeed of Being that needs to be stated? What are the implications of this statement for our understanding of the 'I' that seemingly constitutes the core of a person?[17] The 'I' that simultaneously occupies as well as produces the category of the individual is constituted by *thought* or thinking. This shift in the notion of self occurs through the epistemic radicalism of Descartes whose thought is founded on the idea of 'radical doubt' through which '[he] can affirm that he is not nothing because he is conscious of being something in and through the very act of consciousness itself' (Winquist 1998: 227). It is thinking that therefore causes the notion of 'I' to arise, which then in turn views itself as a separate, bounded entity consisting of a body and mind with singular and unique thoughts and experiences. Within this framework, the thinking or conscious 'I' begins to occupy a place of primacy over Being as 'the point of reference for the determination of meaning ...' (Winquist 1998: 227).

These questions become fundamental to our understanding of 'possession' as outlined earlier, and as will be discussed in this study from the Central Himalayas. Again, as Boddy (1994: 410) incisively observes:

> Spirit possession research has been characterized by a fundamental tension between reductive, naturalizing or rationalizing approaches on the one hand and contextualizing, more phenomenological approaches on the other. Studies constructed along lines of the former are more readily amenable to comparison, but insofar as they render phenomena in Western commonsense or scientific terms, they suspend epistemological inquiry of those terms and are at best incomplete, at worst culturally solipsistic.

Clearly, in instances of possession, the 'I' and its corollaries of the person, of the individual, of singularity, and of agency cease to have primacy as points of reference. They seem to be on 'hold' or in suspension as other forces 'take over' or operate, as boundaries seem to dissipate allowing for ever widening circles of divine or malevolent agency 'in which persons suddenly and inexplicably lose their normal set of memories, mental dispositions, and skills, and exhibit entirely new and different sets of memories, dispositions, and skills' (Becker [1993: 11] cited in F. Smith 2011: 3). But does the 'I' we are assuming here have an existence that is primarily grounded in the kind of 'thinking I' that Descartes and our modern notions of the individual suggest? Moreover, what does 'environment' mean in the definition of possession provided by Boddy? What is 'environment' constituted by? Humans? Deities? Animals? Animate entities? Non-animate entities? The acknowledgement of permeability between the individual and her or his environment has fundamental implications for Self and its other. Clearly, an acknowledgement of permeability of 'flexibly drawn' boundaries implies that the Self and the other are neither oppositional, nor complementary, nor even relational. The relationship may involve all of these possibilities, and yet go beyond them to be identified through equivalence, enmeshing, and continuity. It may involve a Moebius-like quality in which the inner and outer merge seamlessly, creating only a mirage-like impression of separate surfaces (Handelman and Shulman 2004: 44). On one level, the difference between the Self and the other appears real, but on another level, it may become illusory. Thus, we require some other, radical way of imagining the conundrum of the Self and the other that seems to lie at the very nucleus of the phenomenological enquiry into Being. It is not sufficient to put this difference in the formulation of the relationship of the Self and the other to a cultural context, since this relativizes the theoretical force of these formulations. The reversal of the 'anthropological gaze' towards the 'demystification', for example, 'of "universalist," "objectified" categories of Western sociology [or anthropology, philosophy, and so forth]', raises several deeply problematic yet critical issues if we are ever to move beyond being 'culturally solipsistic' while legitimately formulating alternative theoretical frameworks derived from the philosophical speculations of 'other' cultures. As Veena Das (1995: 33) astutely notes:

> ... the possibility of transcending his own ideology through an intellectual appropriation of other values is open to the Western anthropologist, but the Indian anthropologist has no legitimate way of applying the same method to the ideology of his own culture. The knowledge categories of non-Western cultures are simply unanchored beliefs, while Western categories have the status of scientific and objective truths.... Other cultures acquire legitimacy only as objects of thought, never as instruments of thought.

Being Another[18]

The foregoing questions bring us to an exploration of another—for the purposes of this chapter, critical—term, which is *alterity*, perhaps the very cornerstone upon which religion and religious experience are grounded. As Csordas (2004: 164) argues: 'Alterity is the phenomenological kernel of religion. Insofar as alterity is part of the structure of being in the world—an elementary structure of existence—religion is inevitable, perhaps even necessary.' But what does alterity mean, and how am I using the word? Alterity has most recently been employed in postcolonial studies to indicate the existence and condition of the colonized, and the cultural 'other'. 'Otherness' therefore pertains to the linguistic, political, epistemological, and imperial mechanisms through which the cultural and colonized 'other' is constructed. From an anthropological perspective, alterity is often understood 'as referring to political, racial, ethnic, gender, class, religious otherness—the otherness that is the occasion for identity politics, war, conflict, violence' (Csordas 2004: 173). Amongst these many divisive and colonizing aspects of otherness, there is also the important sense in which it is used to describe the condition of women in both First- and Third-World situations as being the 'other' of men. Hannah Arendt, for example, states that '*alteritas* or otherness belongs to everything not just to the marginalized. Because all our definitions and concepts are distinctions—we say what something is by distinguishing it from other things—difference is our human condition' (Arendt [1958: 176], cited in Cutting-Gray 1993: 41). Moreover, '"alterity" reconceived in terms of multiplicity opens the possibility for the community of plurality...' (Arendt [1958: 176], cited in Cutting-Gray 1993: 41). This re-conceptualization of alterity as multiplicity brings us to a further philosophical and religious differentiation of the term.

But what is the sense in which I intend to use the term 'alterity'? I wish to use the term in a layered or stratified sense that carries traces of the meanings I have outlined previously, but also applies a different sense. Since I will be talking about an aspect of South Asian culture which, speaking from a colonial context, can be regarded as the 'other', my use of alterity must also include the meaning it has as describing the 'culturally other'. I also use it in the sense of women being 'other', as the stories and the event I will be recounting from the Central Himalayas reveal. The fact that women can and are viewed as the 'other' is particularly relevant to the discussion of possession when we take into account the seemingly overwhelming preponderance of the participation of women in the vast majority of scholarly materials collected from different cultures the world over. Erika Bourguignon (2004: 557) notes:

> As has been reported again and again, it is primarily women who evidence possession by spirits, enacting their presence. This is the case in which spirits are invited to participate in rituals, whether for worship or for accommodation and healing. In such situations, women are often participants and leaders, patients and healers. In situations in which illness and disorders of various kinds are ascribed to malevolent entities that take control of human bodies and must be exorcised, it is mostly women who are their victims.

However, it is not the simple statistical fact of the predominance of women in such rituals that is sufficient to label them 'other' in the context of male participation and perhaps even regulation of possession rituals. It is, as Bourguignon and others attempt to explain, the fact that women—because of their lesser status to men and the concomitant condition of emotional, financial, social, and domestic oppression—utilize the complex ritual, narrative as well as somatic and psychological mechanisms of possession to regain and reinstate their voice through socially and religiously legitimate means. The embodied state of alterity expressed through the ritual processes of possession then becomes, in this explanatory model, a channel for *symbolic action*. The religious or spiritual views expounded by the women (or men) in such ritual contexts are in reality not what they are being stated as (the presence of divine or malevolent beings); rather these are mostly 'unconscious' strategies adopted by socially deprived actors. This symbolic explanation, however, is problematic inasmuch as it endorses a particular view of the 'other' (in the sense of both culture and gender) while propping up a set of values and possibilities germane to modernity.

And, finally, perhaps in the most critical sense, I use the word alterity to describe the possibility of multiplicity and permeability in the phenomenal world *and* the possibility of divine presence in human life. But there is a radical departure here, I think, from our usual philosophical understanding of the 'other', whether human, non-human, or divine. In fact, I would like to bring in the notion of 'another', rather than 'other'. But what does or can 'another' mean here? Two perspectives are presented: one stems from the intellectual tradition of anthropology; the other is rooted in Indian philosophical thought. While the first seems to contain a plea for a new formulation of social relationships and identity, the latter is primarily ontological in its direction. I would like to suggest that both routes of responding to the question of the Self and the other, though seemingly divergent in their temporal, cultural, and intellectual heritage, merge and fuse. In their fullest expression, each exchanges substance with the other: the social in its deepest application invokes the ontological; the ontological in its sharpest form is grounded in the social. Ghassan Hage (2009), for example, talks about the anthropological gaze as being about the possibility of *being another*. This idea, he suggests, implies the idea of *excess* that is grounded in potentiality rather than actuality. In other words, any given social situation or identity has the promise of being more than what it appears to be, is represented as, or is perceived to be. Actuality, on the other hand, is grounded on a notion of 'what is' or of *stasis* and 'predictability' rather than in a dialectic that can result in an unpredictable (re)configuration of 'what is'. Hage calls the ability to *be another* 'radical alterity'. Radical alterity thus moves beyond the chasm between the Self and the other upon which much of anthropological, historical, and philosophical thought is based. But one might ask what is this capacity to be another based upon? What, in fact, allows human beings to participate in, gain from, and even relish the world of possibility that is implicit in the capacity to be 'more than oneself'? First, the world of actuality or fixity needs to be pierced, broken down, and critiqued. How is this done? It is done, to begin with, by an acknowledgement of the existence and power of 'actuality' as a pervasive perception of what is considered to be *real*.[19] The real as in that which is limited, defined, immovable, and bounded. The 'real' as a commitment to fixity and petrifaction under the paradoxical guise of progress, change, and modernity—as the justification for cynically continuing to operate in the way 'things have always been', and so forth. But how does the real come to be constituted in such a way as to be devoid of possibility? There is a 'collapsing together', so to speak, between the real and the true in the world of actuality. Hage points out that the markers of this world are both fatalism and naturalness. In other words, the actual world is presented as though it is a given and naturally existing world in which events take place in a predetermined and therefore fatalistic manner.

In Upanishadic and Vedantic thought, neither divinity nor other sentient or non-sentient entities are *fundamentally* 'other' (*anya*). The perception of difference or 'otherness' rests on entities possessing name (*nama*) and form (*rupa*), but not on ontological distance or difference. On the ontic level of Being or Self (Atman/Brahman),[20] there is, in fact, no 'other'. All there is, is 'Self, 'Consciousness', or 'Being'. Brahman, Being, or Self cannot, however, be directly apprehended through words or language. It is 'not this, not this'. The philosopher Śaṃkara, however, states that Brahman or 'It' 'can be indirectly designated, for example, by the word "I". The word "I" directly denotes my ego (*ahaṃkāra*), but since the ego is a reflection of the true Self, as the mirror image is a reflection of the fact reflected in it, one can use the word "I" nonmetaphorically to indicate the Self. But all such usage presupposes ... the operation of ignorance, a failure on our part to discriminate the true Self from the *jīva*, ego, or whatever'(Potter 1981: 60; italics original).

Therefore, while on a purely phenomenological and linguistic level there is an 'I' and a 'You' and a 'World', and so forth, on an ontological and experiential level, these distinctions dissolve, leaving no separation between me, you, and the world.[21] While this perspective may seem historically and culturally antiquated, being ascribed to ancient India, it is a perspective that is found, at least on a discursive level, amongst many members of India's contemporary population, both rural and urban. As a philosophical position and as a 'popular' discourse, it needs to be taken as seriously as the philosophical traditions discussed previously. Alterity here, as Arendt suggests, is reconceived as multiplicity, but this multiplicity encompasses more than the immediate arena of human relationships, more than the multiplicity of cultures and individual perspectives. In theory, it covers all possible entities and all past, present, and future possibilities. It approaches the question of a 'community of plurality' through the simultaneous acknowledgement of the reality of multiplicity on the one hand and its dissipation, dissolution, and illusory nature through 'non-duality' on the other.

As Boddy then puts it, the study of possession is about 'how the parameters of selfhood might shift or be constituted differently in societies other than the anthropologist's own' (1994: 422). Pertinent for our understanding of these differently constituted parameters of selfhood are also Piatigorsky's (1985: 217) observations on a phenomenology of Indian religion in which he discusses, among other categories, 'the structure of religious consciousness', which 'can be defined as a complex whole, the related elements of which produce in their totality a complete model of religious behaviour, i.e. of the religion'. Piatigorsky applies the idea of 'the structure of religious consciousness' to various aspects of Hindu religion, including that of the concept of god (*deva*) that 'implies a specific kind of differentiation fundamentally different from the concept of God (and from pagan gods) in Mosaic religion' (Piatigorsky 1985: 217). The concept of 'a god' is particularly relevant for our conceptualization of possession in the Indian context, since

... taken at a given time and in a given place ... a god is present as an *iṣṭadevtā* (chosen deity), that is, a phenomenon in which the idea of the god momentarily present coincides in time and space with that of his devotee and is merged with him in the context of a particular subjective religious situation. As in the case of *ātman-brahmān*, the subject and object of worship are not opposed to one another but seen as two instances of manifestations of the same entity. (Piatigorsky 1985: 219; italics original)

This notion of identity or equivalence between subject and object, particularly in the instance of worship and ritual, is crucial to how we view 'possessed bodies' in the Indian context. The body is the middle ground, so to speak, in which both the dual and the non-dual manifest, in which human and divine interchange, swap around, merge, become one, but also become two. Thus, in the southern Indian Śaiva Siddhanta tradition that describes Śiva's sojourn into the 'Forest of Pines',

> There is no room ... for severe dualisms of any kind. The non-dual god is the world, and he never changes—which is to say all changes are included within him. The middle precludes the dual. By the same token, middle space is the only locus for interaction—again, the forest as we know it, where Siva meets others.... From the middle, only from the middle, one can move in any direction. But none of this is given— certainly not presence, not 'being,' not movement toward or into being. It has to be made where potential exists—interactively at that, in that space between. (Handelman and Shulman 2004: 44)

The interactive 'between space' is the *space of ritual* in which presence is urged and drawn out into existence but is never taken for granted.

Following on from this, we can state that non-duality is a framework within which to place our understanding of possession in the Indian cultural and religious situation. Non-duality is a context in which the question of the Self and the other, of alterity, is addressed in a fundamentally distinct manner to which 'Western'-situated philosophical ideas address and resolve this question. It may be counter-argued that the philosophical position of non-duality briefly outlined earlier is merely indicative of a single standpoint within several other divergent philosophical systems in India, and that the former represents an elite if not exclusive view that has little bearing on the so-called level of folk or popular religion and culture to which possession rituals belong. However, it can be asserted with good reason that the manner in which the question of multiplicity in the phenomenal world and diversity within the social universe is 'explained' on a popular, non-elite level is through precisely the same philosophical discourse: the 'many' is the 'one'.[22] Difference, while 'real' on the level of everyday transaction, is 'illusory' on a transcendental level. This transcendental level becomes immanent if the misrecognition of the reality of the ephemeral person/individual is acknowledged.

What this suggests is the possibility, as various scholars describe it, of a multidimensional, porous, permeable, fluid identity or Self, or even 'no-Self' or Self as 'no-thing', that not only reinforces but also elicits a full engagement with the world.[23] Again, this notion of a 'decentred' or even non-existent Self approaches the phenomenological and existentialist view of Self and of Being that is carved out against the background of *no-thing*. Thus, we have somewhat overlapping conclusions regarding the nature of Self or Being. The responses and scope of these conclusions, however, diverge and vary.[24] The existential view overlays *no-thing* with a particular pessimistic meaning: that life has no purpose as such (Sartre [1943] 1966), but it also reinstates nothing as the background or source for the creation of all possibility, and of *some-thing* (Heidegger [1927] 1962). Here again, the focus is primarily on the Being of human being, and of the possibility of intersubjectivity as framed by social and political relationships between human individuals. In contrast, in the Indian context outlined previously, the constructed, social, or phenomenal Self is the source of an existential condition of bondage which gives rise to feelings of fear, anxiety, anger, greed, power, violence, and so on, because of a fundamental misrecognition involving the illusory and ephemeral nature of the bounded and therefore limited, individualized, egocentric Self that is concerned with its own immediate personal survival (this can be extended to include community, religion, tradition, territory, nation, and so forth). Freedom from these forms of emotional and physical constraints lies in the acknowledgement of the primordial misrecognition.

The possibilities of 'Self' explored earlier are intertwined in any discourse of possession, particularly in the South Asian context. Thus, for example, to return to Boddy's brief definition, there is the use of the term 'individual' which, as we have seen, is grounded in Western notions of person and Self. This is accompanied by the idea of 'permeability' and 'flexibility' when it comes to boundaries between an individual and their environment. The latter possibility is grounded as we have seen in non-Western notions of Self and person that, at least in the Indian context, have no fixed or lasting reality. The language of the hermeneutic framework for interpreting possession is therefore itself a hybrid one, crisscrossing—perhaps unconsciously—between the notions of individuality and fixity that researchers themselves carry and 'blurred', fluid boundaries and identities encountered in the field. These entangled, hybrid, perhaps fused, and yet oftentimes divergent views of Self are a crucial component in arriving at a critical, and perhaps radical new understanding of what we have been calling 'possession' and how we talk about it.

The reader may find this discussion of 'premodern' and 'modern' notions of subjectivity and agency incongruous to materials I am exploring from the Central Himalayas involving a Hindu deity. Let me briefly state here why I think this discussion is relevant. As much as I would like simply to describe what happens in the narratives and rituals I have encountered, I cannot do so without using categories and conceptual frameworks that are inextricably tied up with the colonial and postcolonial enterprise of scholarship, particularly the scholarship dealing with South Asia and India, which has, of course, along with the nebulous category of the 'Orient', had the dubious status of being Europe's quintessential 'other'. As Veena Das (1995: 25) succinctly states '... there is a peculiar double bind which traps the non-Western anthropologist who wishes to relate experience and representation, gained through membership of her society, when constructing the anthropological text. I should not be understood as saying there is some kind of "given" or "neat" experience of their own societies available to non-Western anthropologists.' In a sense, much of what I am exploring is my own attempt to unravel the taken-for-granted conceptual underpinnings and biases of the way I perceive the powerful experiences I have encountered during my fieldwork with regard to Goludev.[25]

The Play of Conversation

I refer here to Heidelberg philosopher Hans-Georg Gadamer's explication of 'Dialogue and Conversation'.[26] Gadamer (1979: 347) uses the metaphor of conversation to describe how we can enter into a dialogue that leads to understanding (*Verstehen*).

> [It] is a process of two people understanding each other. Thus it is a characteristic of every true conversation that each opens himself to the other person, truly accepts his point of view as worthy of consideration

and gets inside the other to such an extent that he understands not a particular individual, but what he says. The thing that has to be grasped is the objective rightness or otherwise of his opinion, so that they can agree with each other on a subject. (Cited in M.K. Smith 2001)

Gadamer argues that knowledge is not fixed or static, but that it arises out of a dialogic process of interaction. This dialogic process involves each 'speaker' or 'participant' to both acknowledge and 'unconceal', so to speak, their inherent prejudices or 'horizons'.[27] Without engaging in this process of revealing or 'unconcealment' of prejudices, there can be no fruitful dialogue or understanding. While Gadamer stresses the importance of texts and their interaction within a history of interpretation, his idea of conversation is particularly crucial because it suggests the oral and spoken nature of dialogue and therefore 'emergent' nature of knowledge:

> What emerges in its truth is the logos, which is neither mine nor yours and hence so far transcends the interlocutors' subjective opinions that even the person leading the conversation knows that he does not know.... What characterizes a dialogue, in contrast with the rigid form of statements that demand to be set down in writing, is precisely this: that in dialogue spoken language—in the process of question and answer, giving and taking, talking at cross purposes and seeing each other's point—performs the communication of meaning that, with respect to the written tradition, is the task of hermeneutics. (2004: 361).

Gadamer's idea of conversation—like his notion of play—can be likened to a medial plane in which the subjectivity of the speakers (or players as the case may be) is not in the foreground. It is the conversation (or game) that is in the foreground, having an existence that is almost independent of the speakers. The speakers, in fact, enter and explore the emerging terrain of the conversation that unfolds as they speak.[28] This is quite distinct, for example, to a discussion or debate that involves one speaker convincing the other speaker through argument or persuasion of the validity of their point of view. A dialogue, on the other hand, involves a willingness to be open such that a third possibility emerges from the conversation that may or may not have the quality of a conclusion. In fact, the 'end' of a conversation may be 'inconclusive'; the point being one of revealing or 'unconcealing' a series of insights or questions that the theme of the conversation calls upon or draws out from itself.

Individual human beings or communities represent 'points of view' or horizons (to put it in Gadamer's language) that are constituted by inherent and often unexamined biases or prejudices that determine the constraints or limitations of any given horizon. Each horizon, I am suggesting, also represents a world that is constituted by ideas (language) and actions (practices). In discussing or encountering a phenomenon like 'possession' what we run into, as I mentioned earlier, is a convergence or mixing of points of view or horizons, each carrying its own set of (pre-)judgments or prejudices. Assuming that the body in possession is played upon by 'social and biological forces,' that are themselves constituted by a chorus of voices, the 'reality' of possession is made up of a set of hybrid discourses and practices consisting of academic ('Western') and non-academic ('non-Western')[29] ideologies concerning Self, body, power, agency, and so forth, together with academic practices (fieldwork) and non-academic practices (ritual). I am describing this as a swirl because of the shifting, indeterminate, and fluid nature of the interactions between these horizons, which, like spoken conversation, is constantly moving or changing, is sometimes fragmented like utterances, and is both ephemeral and unpredictable. Moreover, the notion of a swirl also suggests an interplay of voices that coalesces into an unconscious eddy that is not always self-reflexive in the sense Gadamer suggests of 'unconcealing' hidden prejudices and given 'always-already' ways of perceiving.

Possession as Radical Alterity

> I am most surprised by those moments when I have felt as if the sentences, dreams, and pages that have made me so ecstatically happy have not come from my own imagination—that another power has found them and generously presented them to me.[30]

I began this chapter by saying that I would explore the possibility of alterity in the context of what is commonly called 'possession'. I have suggested that possession can be imagined as a bodily practice, like asceticism, yoga, breathing exercises, meditation, or other forms of personal cultivation that educe divine presence or power. Moreover, I have indicated that 'alterity' as the possibility of the participation and intervention of the 'divine other' in human life exists because of and through a social *conversation* involving several voices and perspectives belonging to both the scholar and devotees. I would like to conclude this chapter with some further remarks about 'possession', and 'alterity' in the context of 'possession'. First, I would like to point out again that there is an ongoing preoccupation, indeed fixation, with possession within scholarly disciplines. Why is so much attention paid to the study of possession rituals in different cultures? And, furthermore, why is there such an effort to explain possession within the different theoretical frameworks that, for the most part, reduce the phenomenon to a set of symbolic behaviours, unconscious beliefs, psychopathology, and so on? I am suggesting that the desire to both study possession and explain it within frameworks that objectify it and are, in fact, experientially disengaged from it stems from the challenge that possession poses to the dominant view that religion itself is separate from the public domain permeated by the secular, being rooted in the private domain of individual belief. But more than that, possession, I think, occupies one of the significant interstices of the modern age by transgressing and transcending binary categories with which modernity so dearly identifies itself. Modernity, as I pointed out earlier, crystallizes through a series of acts involving critical distancing: the individual from community, community from cosmos, culture from nature, equality from hierarchy, mind from body, and so on. These acts of distancing, furthermore, necessarily result in sets of binary, oppositional categories, since modernity itself is predicated and defined on the fundamental distancing between the modern/innovative/new and the ancient/traditional/old. As I mentioned previously, we cannot know whether we are the 'moderni' unless we can contrast ourselves with that which we define as 'antiqui'. The discursive category of modernity therefore must continuously create, and in its political manifestations also *intentionally* perpetuate the existence of antagonistic dualities without which it loses legitimacy and force as an intellectual and political ideology. To continue along the lines mentioned previously, to be modern then is to both live and fervently believe in a society that values and, indeed, sustains divisions between the public and private, human and divine, human and non-human or animal, secular and religious, individual and community, mind and body, and, last but not least, bounded or 'buffered self' and porous or 'permeable self'. While these dichotomous categories may seem neutral on paper, in practice they are far from not.[31]

Thus, these oppositional categories involve a suppression in many instances of one of the pairings: the secular is clearly valourized over the religious which may continue to exist, but only in the private sphere; humans are valourized over non-humans, specially animals, such that their survival can take place at the cost of the extinction of several thousand other species; the mental (mind) is valued over the biological (body) that it can presumably control, understand, and analyse; the individual is given value over the community in his or her quest for personal success, and so forth. It is to live in a political state that administers fixed categories of social identity in which *excess*, in the sense of Hage's definition, is undermined or even denied. Moreover, the individual is understood to be driven by an inner capacity to shape and manage his or her life. There is little recourse in the context of modernity to invoke forces or powers that lie beyond or even hidden within the individual's capabilities when it comes to the explanation of his or her actions.[32]

Possession, however, challenges these precise yet value-laden categorizations that lie at the source of modernity and its expression in the modern, secular nation-state, and therefore there is a necessity to explain possession through reductionist categories. The fact is, we do not know how to deal with it. Possession is somehow that very 'vestige' of that past—like its larger, problematic counterpart, religion—that shocks, amazes, and perhaps even embarrasses us in its continued and even thriving survival within the realms of the scientific, technological, and rational. To allow possession to represent what it is, that is, the possibility of a multidimensional, 'porous' Self that is both created and operates in a public rather than private ritual domain, and the possibility of alterity in the sense of divine 'intervention' as such (whether in the public or private domain), is to question the foundations of a modern secular state built on the notion of the bounded, separate individual who is in complete control of his or her life and destiny. Possession, therefore, in a fundamental manner, forces us to rethink modern notions of agency and subjectivity. As the possibility of quite literally being another, possession, then, represents the tangible prospect of a *radical alterity*, which goes beyond even the social, secular meaning that Hage seems to be thinking of. In view of the somewhat uncertain status of the ideological arrow of modernity in terms of the ecological and political disasters we are encountering today, divine embodiment itself represents one possibility of an alternative understanding of the 'Self' and of other ways of being for human beings that we can take seriously if we are to authentically explore new possibilities for the future of being human.[33]

Notes

1. Over the past four–five years, I have made a number of field trips to Kumaon and collected a large and extremely fascinating body of materials including (*a*) approximately forty-five hours of film documenting intense, complex, and often long, ritual performances (*jāgar*) involving the embodiment of human mediums through Goludev and other local deities such as Kalbisht and Gangnath; (*b*) four or five hundred 'legal' petitions (*manauti*) offered to Goludev in his temples that are treated as courts of law (*darbār/ kaccheri*) by his devotees; and (*c*) sixty to eighty hours of additional interviews with priests, ritual specialists, and devotees. I have also visited his three main temples that are located in different districts of Kumaon, each representing an important incident in the deity's life.

2. See my (2016) work, *Tales of Justice and Rituals of Divine Embodiment*. Broadly speaking, my book addresses questions concerning the multiple meanings of justice, agency, religion, and modernity in India.

3. Although written petitions are the most tangible and visible forms of manautis, petitions or requests for the fulfilment of wishes and desires can also be made in an interior, 'mental' manner.

4. Priests of the Panth lineage claim to have migrated together with their deity from the western Indian region of Maharashtra some generations ago. See below for an alternative explanation.

5. The temple at Ghoda Khal has also become the location for marriage ceremonies, particularly for couples who do not have the endorsement of their families by virtue of, for example, belonging to different social backgrounds (that is, castes) or religious communities (for example, Hindu and Sikh). On such occasions, the priest is able to administer a marriage certificate for the bride and bridegroom for which Goludev acts as witness. The certificate issued by the priest is legally binding, and once it is handed in to a civil court, a state-endorsed marriage certificate must be issued by court authorities.

6. For example, both Kalbisht and Gangnath are murdered treacherously, and appear subsequently in dreams of devotees demanding proper worship. Goludev, whose father is a king, is abandoned at birth by jealous step-mothers who blindfold and truss-up his mother while claiming that she has given birth to a stone-grinder as well as a grinding stone!

7. As Boddy (1994: 407) notes: 'In contrast to anthropological accounts of the body or of time, spirit possession has long been an explicit topic of inquiry; it has rarely missed a theoretical beat. Discourse on the subject is thematic for the discipline as a whole in its confrontation with the Other, continuously affirming our identity as anthropologists.'

8. See also Sweetman (2004) for an account of Ziegenbalg's writings.

9. F. Smith (2011: 10) points out that Bourdieu draws on Aristotle's *Nichomachean Ethics* in his utilization of the term *hexis*, which 'is a form of body memory in which local enculturation is achieved ... [it is] the way the body is used to express itself in ritual that communicates to the observer changes in consciousness'. Furthermore, as Sax and Weinhold (2010) show, hexis 'subverts the mind-body dichotomy that ... forces us to misunderstand the nature of possession' (quoted in F. Smith 2011).

10. See, for example, Janice Boddy's extensive review of the literature on possession (1994). It is interesting to note, however, that Boddy seems to largely gloss over South Asia (with the exception of Kapferer's (1991 [1983]) and Obeyesekere's (1981) work in Sri Lanka) in her list of geographical and cultural regions covered by scholars working on possession, even though possession would appear to be, in both historical/textual and contemporary terms, an ubiquitous phenomenon in that part of the world. See, for example, Assayag and Tarabout (1999), Berreman (1963), Brubaker (1978), Brueckner (1995), Claus (1984), Daniel (1984), Erndl (1993), Ferrari (2011), Freed and Freed (1964), Freeman (1993), Fuller (1992), Gaenszle (2002), Gellner (1994), Gold (1988), Kakar (1983), Knipe (1989), Leavitt (1997), Malik (2009, 2011, 2015, 2016), Mayaram (1999), Sax (2002, 2009), Sax and Weinhold (2010), Schoembucher (1993, 2006), F. Smith (2006, 2011), and Sontheimer (1976).

11. It should be noted of course that the term 'possession' covers a variety of states, conditions some of which are afflictive and disease-causing (malevolent) and others diagnostic and healing (benevolent).

12. As F. Smith (2011: 3) states: 'A number of questions must be asked of possession at the outset, especially with regard to ... disease and healing. First, is possession "real"? This is another way of accessing the complementary question: What is possession?' While Frederick Smith and other scholars devote considerable effort towards answering the second question, the first is never fully addressed, excepting to say that possession is 'real' but only as a belief or as symbolic action or performance, and so forth.

13. In a public lecture at Delhi University, entitled 'The Politics of Nature: East–West Perspectives' (6 January 2011). See also Latour (1993).

14. See, for example, Eisenstadt (2000) and Kaviraj (2005) for the idea of 'multiple' modernities.

15. There is of course an enormous body of work on modernity. Only a small fraction of this complex scholarship is represented here.

16. See also F. Smith (2011: 3).

17. See F. Smith's lucid discussion on the problematic use of terms such as experience, person, self, and consciousness, especially when translating these categories into Indic cultural contexts to explain occurrences such as possession (2006: 115ff).

18. See, for example, Shail Mayaram's (1999) article in *La Possession en Asie du Sud*.

19. I am using 'real' in contradistinction to Lacan's use of 'the real' to denote the unnamable, authentic, infinite Being or Self that is prior to language and independent of our sensory experience. 'Real', as it is being used here, means exactly the opposite: it is the anchoring of authenticity (erroneously) in the experience of our senses, and in a descriptive or frozen use of language in which words are expected to map the world, and names and labels become essences.

20. Piatigorsky (1985: 218) points out that 'in the various early Hindu movements and schools *ātman–brahman* figures side by side with other structures, such as *mārga* (path), *bhakti* (devotion), *bhagavān* (lord), and so forth. Some of these were reinterpreted in the context of other structures, although persisting as a self-sufficient source of identification and interpretation [italics original]'.

21. This eliding of the individuated, singular, separate Self, as Kapila Vatsyayan notes, is also the concern and goal of Indian artistic and performative principles, especially those espoused in Bharata's *Natyasastra*, which the author himself describes as a 'theory of practice' (*prayogashastra*) regarding dance. The goal of artistic creation is to induce 'aesthetic relish' (*rasa*). The inducement of this aesthetic experience rests, however, on 'the eschewing of the particular "I" ... only to evoke a single "unified" luminosity. This is the singular *rasa* of the beginning and the end: all else is play (*līlā*, *kridā*) of forms of specific configurations serving a very important and indispensable, but nevertheless ephemeral function [italics original]' (Vatsyayan 1996: 103–4).

22. The matter of what constitutes folk or popular religion within Hinduism on both a conceptual and ethnographic level is one that has received considerable attention through the work of Sontheimer (2005) and Fuller (1992). Stereotypically, folk Hinduism has been considered as being devoid of the kind of metaphysical and philosophical reflection that signifies Brahmanical Hinduism. However, this is indeed questionable, as this view mirrors the prejudices 'elite' forms of religion might harbour towards 'non-elite/folk' forms of religion. It is important, though, to note the sheer corporality and immediate presence of a god or goddess in folk religious ritual and

practice, unlike in the brahmanical situation in which deities may exist in a separate extraterrestrial location (*svarga*) (Sontheimer 2005: 315).

23. The notions of multiplicity and multidimensionality, while having an ontological meaning here, are to be found in other areas of creativity as well, such as in the perception and formulation of textual traditions, art, dance, and music. For example, Vatsyayan, in her incisive study of the *Natyasastra*, points out that '[t]he composer of the text [Bharata] consciously creates a fluid text ... the statements made by its author sound familiar as distantly related to the post-modern discussion on a text ... the author himself allows for varied interpretations and readings, even modifications of his own injunctions' (Vatsyayan 1996: 38–9).

24. Again as Sax (2002: 9) points out:

> Hindu theories of self, both learned and popular, are remarkably similar to the ruminations of postmodernists and social constructionists, and it is nothing short of scandalous that this similarity has been so little noticed in the West. The irony has been captured nicely by Bharati, who points out that whereas conventional Indian social scientists have consistently attempted to assimilate Western ideas, Western social scientists have equally failed to take Indian ideas seriously ...

25. This is the name of the deity whose narratives and rituals I am examining in this book.

26. See also the Sanskrit notion of *samvād* or dialogue.

27. Prejudice and (pre-)judgments are strong words. I prefer to use the word 'concern' to indicate the issues or questions speakers are dealing with in their lives, which they then bring to a conversation.

28. 'As in play, it rests on a common willingness of the participants in conversation to lend themselves to the emergence of something else, the *Sache* or subject matter which comes to presence and presentation in conversation'' (Gadamer 2004: xvii).

29. This binary division between academic as Western and non-academic as non-Western is of course a simplification of a much more complex and intricate matter.

30. From the Turkish author Orhan Pamuk's Nobel Lecture: 'My Father's Suitcase', Stockholm, 7 Decemeber 2006.

31. See Latour (1993) on the 'post-human' condition.

32. The idea of a subjectivity that is not solely rooted in 'conscious', personal volition, is, of course, close to the experience of many artists, writers, musicians, and creative individuals including scholars and scientists. Although creative insight may be often experienced as spontaneous, 'unexplained', or even 'channelled', this fact rarely enters scholarly discourse as the latter has to do with the very opposite of 'insight' and spontaneity, namely reason, logic, argument, rational thought, and so on.

33. In saying this I am not in anyway suggesting that 'possession' or ritual embodiment should be taken up as a practice that will address or solve the problems that face us today, but that views on how being human is both conceptualized and practised in the world are in urgent need of alternate imaginings.

Bibliography

Agrawal, C.M. 1992. *Golu Devata: The God of Justice of Kumaon Himalayas*. Almora: Shree Almora Book Depot.

Arendt, Hannah. 1958. *The Human Condition*. Chicago: The University of Chicago Press.

———. 1974 [1958]. *Rahel Vernhagen: The Life of a Jewess*, translated by Richard Winston and Clara Winston. New York: Harcourt Brace Jovanovich.

Asad, Talal. 1993. *Genealogies of Religion*. Baltimore: Johns Hopkins University Press.

Assayag, J. and G. Tarabout, eds. 1999. *La Possession en Asie du sud: Parole, Corps, Territoire*. Paris: Editions de L'École des Hautes Études en Sciences Sociales (Collection, Purusartha, 21).

Bailey, Greg. 1983. *The Mythology of Brahmā*. New York: Oxford University Press.

Bauemer, Bettina. 1995. 'The Play of the Three Worlds: The Trika Concept of Lila'. In *The Gods at Play*, edited by W. Sax, 35–49. New York: Oxford University Press.

Becker, C.B. 1993. *Paranormal Experience and Survival of Death*. Albany: SUNY Press.

Benavides, Gustavo. 1998. 'Modernity'. In *Critical Terms for Religious Studies*, edited by Mark C. Taylor, 186–204. Chicago: The University of Chicago Press.

Berreman, Gerald D. 1963. *Hindus of the Himalayas*. Berkeley: University of California Press.

Brubaker, Richard. 1978. *The Ambivalent Mistress: A Study of South Indian Village Goddesses and Their Religious Meanings*. Chicago: The University of Chicago Press.

Brückner, Heidrun. 1995. *Fürstliche Feste: Texte und Rituale der Tulu-Volksreligion an der Westküste Südindiens*. Wiesbaden: Harrassowitz.

Boddy, Janice. 1994. 'Spirit Possession Revisited: Beyond Instrumentality'. *Annual Review of Anthropology* 23: 407–34.

Bourguignon, Erika. 2004. 'Suffering and Healing, Subordination and Power: Women and Possession Trance'. *Ethos* 32(4): 557–74.

Claus, Peter J. 1984. 'Medical Anthropology and the Ethnography of Spirit Possession'. *Contributions to Asian Studies* 18: 60–72.

Coburn, Thomas B. 1991. *Encountering the Goddess: A Translation of the Devi-Māhātmaya and a Study of Its Interpretation*. New York: SUNY Press.

Csordas, Thomas J. 2004. 'Asymptote of the Ineffable: Embodiment, Alterity, and the Theory of Religion'. *Current Anthropology* 45(2): 163–85.

Cutting-Gray, Joanne. 1993. 'Hannah Arendt, Feminism, and the Politics of Alterity: "What Will We Lose If We Win?"' *Hypatia* 8(1): 35–54.

Daniel, Valentine E. 1984. *Fluid Signs: Being a Person the Tamil Way*. Berkeley: University of California Press.

Das, Veena. 1995. *Critical Events: An Anthropological Perspective on Contemporary India*. New Delhi: Oxford University Press.

Eisenstadt, S.N. 2000. 'Multiple Modernities'. *Daedalus* 129(1): 1–29.

Erndl, Kathleen. 1993. *Victory to the Mother: The Hindu Goddess of Northwest India in Myth, Ritual and Symbol*. New York: Oxford University Press.

Ferrari, Fabrizio, ed. 2011. *Health and Religious Rituals in South Asia: Disease, Possession and Healing*. London: Routledge.

Falk, Harry. 1986. *Brüderschaft und Würfelspiel—Untersuchungenzur Entwicklungsgeschichte des vedischen Opfers*. Freiburg: Hedwig Falk.

Freed, S.A. and R.S. Freed. 1964. 'Spirit Possession as Illness in a North Indian Village'. *Ethnology* 3: 152–71.

Freeman, Richard. 1993. 'Performing Possession: Ritual and Consciousness in the Teyyam Complex of Northern Kerala'. In *Flags of Fame: Studies in South Asian Folk Culture*, edited by H. Brückner, L. Lutze, and A. Malik, 109–38. Delhi: Manohar.

Fuller, Christopher J. 1992. *The Camphor Flame: Popular Hinduism and Society in India*. Princeton: Princeton University Press.

Gadamer, Hans-Georg. 1979. *Truth and Method*. London: Sheed and Ward. (Originally published in German in 1960 as *Wahrheit und Methode: Grundzügeeinerphilosophischen Hermeneutik* [Tübingen: Mohr Siebeck].)

———. 2004. *Truth and Method*, 2nd revised edition, translated and revised by Joel Weinsheimer and Donald G. Marshall. London: Continuum.

Gaenszle, Martin. 2002. *Ancestral Voices: Oral Ritual Texts and Their Social Contexts among the Mewahang Rai of East Nepal*. Berlin: Lit Verlag.

Gellner, David N. 1994. 'Priests, Healers, Mediums and Witches: The Context of Possession in the Kathmandu Valley'. *Man* (n.s.) 29(1): 27–48.

Gold, Ann Grodzins. 1988. 'Spirit Possession Perceived and Performed in Rural Rajasthan'. *Contributions to Indian Sociology* (n.s.) 22: 35–63.

Handelman, Don, and D. Shulman. 2004. *Siva in the Forest of Pines: An Essay on Sorcery and Self-Knowledge*. New Delhi: Oxford University Press.

Hage, Ghassan. 2009. 'Anthropology and the Passion for the Political'. Inaugural Distinguished Lecture for the Australian Anthropological Society. State Library of New South Wales, Sydney, 8 December. Available at https://www.youtube.com/watch?v=wgWpXqZl0sE (last accessed 10 May 2016).

Heesterman, Jan C. 1985. *The Inner Conflict of Tradition*. Chicago: The University of Chicago Press.

Heidegger, Martin. [1927] 1962. *Being and Time*. London: SCM Press. (Originally published in German in 1927 as *Sein und Zeit* [Tübingen: Max Niemayer Verlag].)

———. [1951] 1971. 'The Origin of the Work of Art' and 'Building, Dwelling, Thinking'. In *Poetry, Language, Thought*, translated by Albert Hofstadter, 15–86 and 141–60. New York: Harper and Row.

Hesse, Hermann. 1998. *Siddhartha*. Boston: Shambhala Publications. (Originally published in German in 1922 as *Siddhartha: Eine indische Dichtung*.)

Kakar, Sudhir. 1983. *Shamans, Mystics and Healers: A Psychological Enquiry into India and Its Healing Traditions*. Oxford: Oxford University Press.

Kapferer, Bruce. 1991 [1983]. *A Celebration of Demons: Exorcism and the Aesthetics of Healing in Sri Lanka*. Bloomington: Indiana University Press.

Kaviraj, Sudipto. 2005. 'An Outline of a Revisionist Theory of Modernity'. *European Journal of Sociology* 46(3): 497–526.

Keller, Mary. 2002. *The Hammer and the Flute: Women, Power and Spirit Possession*. Baltimore: Johns Hopkins University.

Knipe, David. 1989. 'Night of the Growing Dead: A Cult of Virabhadra in Coastal Andhra'. In *Criminal Gods and Demon Devotees: Essays on the Guardians of Popular Hinduism*, edited by Alf Hiltebeitel, 123–56. New York: SUNY Press.

Krengel, Monika. 1999. 'Spirit Possession in the Central Himalayas'. In *La Possession en Asie du sud: Parole, Corps, Territoire*, edited by J. Assayag and G. Tarabout, 265–88. Paris: Editions de L'École des Hautes Études en Sciences Sociales (Collection, Purusartha, 21).

Kumar, Nita. 1995. 'Class and Gender Politics in the Ramlila'. In *The Gods at Play: Lila in South Asia*, edited by W. Sax, 156–76. New York: Oxford University Press.

Latour, Bruno. 1993. *We Have Never Been Modern*. Cambridge, MA: Harvard University Press.

Leavitt, John, ed. 1997. *Poetry and Prophecy: The Anthropology of Inspiration*. Ann Arbor: University of Michigan Press.

Macann, Christopher. 2007. *Being and Becoming: A Genetic Interpretation of the Being of Human Being*, part I: *General Metaphysics*. London and Bordeaux: Online Originals.

Malik, Aditya. 2009. 'Dancing the Body of God: Rituals of Embodiment from the Central Himalayas'. *SITES: A Journal of Social Anthropology and Cultural Studies* 6(1): 80–96.

————. 2011. 'Is Possession Really Possible? Towards a Hermeneutics of Transformative Embodiment in South Asia'. In *Health and Religious Rituals in South Asia: Disease, Possession and Healing*, edited by F. Ferrari, 17–32. London: Routledge.

————. 2014. 'Temples, Travels and Territories'. In *Wege zum Heil(igen)? Sakralität und Sakralisierung in hinduistischen Traditionen*, edited by K. Steiner and H. Brueckner, 195–202. Wiesbaden: Otto Harrasowitz Verlag.

————. 2015. 'The *Darbar* of Goludev: Possession, Petitions and Modernity'. In *The Law of Possession*, edited by W. Sax and H. Basu, 193–225. New York: Oxford University Press.

————. 2016. *Tales of Justice and Rituals of Divine Embodiment: Oral Narratives from the Central Himalayas*. New York: Oxford University Press.

Mayaram, Shail. 1999. 'Sprit Possession: Reframing Discourses of the Self and Other'. In *La Possession en Asie du sud: Parole, Corps, Territoire*, edited by J. Assayag and G. Tarabout, 101–31. Paris: Editions de L'École des Hautes Études en Sciences Sociales (Collection, Purusartha, 21).

Nabhan-Warren, Kristy. 2011. 'Embodied Research in Writing: A Case for Phenomenologically Oriented Religious Studies Ethnographies'. *Journal of the American Academy of Religion* 79(2): 378–407.

Obeysekere, Gananath. 1981. *Medusa's Hair: An Essay on Personal Symbols and Religious Experience*. Chicago: University of Chicago Press.

O'Leary, Joseph. 2006. 'Where all the Ladders Start: Apophasis as Awareness'. Available at josephsoleary.typepad.com.

————. 2008. 'Theological Resonances of "Der Satz vom Grund"'. Available at josephsoleary.typepad.com.

Piatigorsky, A. 1985. 'Some Phenomenological Observations on the Study of Indian Religion'. In *Indian Religion*, edited by R. Burghart and A. Cantlie, 208–58. London: School of Oriental and African Studies.

Potter, Karl H., ed. 1981. *Advaita Vedanta up to Samkara and His Pupils*. Delhi: Motilal Banarsidas.

Sartre, Jean-Paul. [1943] 1966. *Being and Nothingness: A Phenomenological Study on Ontology*, translated by Hazel Barnes. New York: Washington Square Press.

Sax, William. 2002. *Dancing the Self: Personhood and Performance in the Pandav Lila of Garhwal*. New York: Oxford University Press.

————. 2009. *God of Justice. Ritual Healing and Social Justice in the Central Himalayas*. New York: Oxford University Press.

Sax, W. and J. Weinhold. 2010. 'Rituals of Possession'. In *Ritual Matters: Dynamic Dimensions in Practice*, edited by C. Brosius and U. Hüsken, 236–52. Delhi: Routledge.

Schoembucher, Elisabeth. 1993. 'Gods, Ghosts and Demons: Possession in South Asia'. In *Flags of Fame: Studies in South Asian Folk Culture*, edited by H. Brückner, L. Lutze, and A. Malik, 239–67. Delhi: Manohar.

———. 2006. *Wo Götter durch Menschen Sprechen: Bessessenheit in Indien*. Berlin: Dietrich Reimer Verlag.

Silburn, Lilian 1955. *Instant et cause: Le discontinudans la pensée philosophique de l'Inde*. Paris: J. Vrin.

Smith, Frederick. 2006. *The Self Possessed: Deity and Spirit Possession in South Asian Literature and Civilization*. New York: Columbia University Press.

———. 2011. 'Possession in Theory and Practice'. In *Health and Religious Rituals in South Asia: Disease, Possession and Healing*, edited by F. Ferrari, 3–16. London: Routledge.

Smith, M.K. 2001. 'Dialogue and Conversation'. In *The Encyclopaedia of Informal Education*, available at www.infed.org/bibio/b-dialog.htm.

Sontheimer, Günther-Dietz. 1976. *Biroba, Mhaskoba und Khandoba: Ursprung, Geschichte und Umwelt von pastoralen Gottheiten in Maharashtra*. Wiesbaden: Franz Steiner Verlag.

———. 2005. 'Hinduism: The Five Components and Their Interaction'. In *Hinduism Reconsidered*, edited by H. Kulke and G.D. Sontheimer, 305–24. New Delhi: Manohar.

Sweetman, Will. 2004. 'The Prehistory of Orientalism: Colonialism and the Textual Basis for Bartholomaus Ziegenbalg's Account of Hinduism'. *New Zealand Journal of Asian Studies* 6(2): 12–38.

Thieme, Paul. 1952. 'Brahman'. *Zeitschrift der Deutschen Morgenlaendischen Gesellschaft* 27: 100–37.

Van Kooij, K.R. 1972. *Worship of the Goddess according to the Kalikapurana*. Leiden: Brill.

Vatsyayan, Kapila. 1996. *Bharata: The Natyasastra*. New Delhi: Sahitya Akademi.

Winquist, Charles E. 1998. 'Person'. In *Critical Terms for Religious Studies*, edited by Mark C. Taylor, 225–38. Chicago: University of Chicago Press.

PART TWO

MODERNITY, RELIGION, AND THE COMMUNITIES

3

WILL SWEETMAN

The Dravidian Idea in Missionary Accounts of South Indian Religion

Christian missionaries were pioneers in a number of fields that were integral to the development of modernity in South Asia, especially in south India. The first printing presses were run by missions, from tentative beginnings in the sixteenth century and then with greater continuity and impact from the early eighteenth century onwards (H. Liebau 2014). Mission schools were also central to the wide extension of literacy, and their efforts to establish schools for girls are particularly notable (Kent 2004: 141). Nevertheless, it is arguable that the single most consequential missionary contribution to modern south Indian culture is to be found elsewhere, in the dissemination of the Dravidian idea. It was a Company official, Francis Whyte Ellis, who—building on the work of Indian grammarians—first demonstrated as early as 1816 that the Dravidian languages are interrelated and are not derived from Sanskrit (Trautmann 2006). But it was the missionary Robert Caldwell who, forty years later, brought the Dravidian idea to wide public attention in his *Comparative Grammar of the Dravidian or South-Indian Family of Languages* (1856). Ravi Vaitheespara, building to some extent on the work of K. Sivathamby, has argued that Caldwell and another missionary, George Pope, contributed significantly to the early formation of the Dravidian ideology, the political and cultural ramifications of which remain with us today.

Vaitheespara argues that 'the ideological origins of Dravidian nationalism can be traced not only to the historical tensions that existed between Sanskritic and local vernacular cultures in south India but more importantly to the modern reconfigured articulation of these tensions inspired by Missionary Orientalism' (Vaitheespara 2002: 28). He identifies two 'key moments' in the development of Dravidian nationalism. The first was the demonstration of the distinct genealogy of south Indian languages and Caldwell's coining of the term 'Dravidian' to refer to them. This moment Vaitheespara also characterizes more broadly as 'the separation of Brahmans and Non-Brahmans' (1999: 54). The second moment follows as a consequence of the first:

> Caldwell's work had a phenomenal impact, for aside from laying the ideological foundation for Dravidian nationalism it opened up a whole field of scholarly inquiry into things 'Dravidian'. After Caldwell's achievement, others launched a search for a distinctly 'Dravidian' religion and culture. This was the beginning of the second key moment in the evolution of Dravidian ideology. (Vaitheespara 1999: 53)

The key missionary figure in this second moment is Pope, and his most important contribution was identifying Śaiva Siddhanta as 'a peculiarly Tamil religion' (Vaitheespara 1999: 66). For Vaitheespara, missionary interest in identifying a distinct Dravidian culture, including Śaiva Siddhanta as a distinctive Dravidian religion—as *the* Dravidian religion—was driven by antipathy towards Brahmanism, which missionaries saw as the primary obstacle to the conversion of India.[1] There is little doubt that missionaries regarded Brahmans and brahmanical thought, including the *varna* ideology, as significant obstacles to conversion (Oddie 2006: 342–3), and that this contributed to their enthusiasm for currents in Indian religion which ran counter to Brahmanism.[2] However, the idea of a distinctive south Indian religious tradition (the second moment), in fact, long predates the Dravidian idea (the first) in missionary writing. Moreover, missionary interest in such a religious tradition was primarily driven not by antipathy towards Brahmanism, although that was present, but rather by a concern, especially on the part of German Lutheran missionaries and those whom they influenced (including Caldwell), to establish a *Volkskirche*, a 'national church', which would be at once Christian and deeply rooted in south Indian culture.

Lutheran Mission in South India and the Caste Question

It was precisely the concern for a Volkskirche which was cited by German Lutherans in defence of their stance on caste that ran counter to a developing Protestant consensus on the incompatibility of Christian conversion and caste consciousness in the mid-nineteenth century.[3] Protestant missions in India had been established in Tranquebar in Tanjore by German Lutherans commissioned by the Danish king in 1706 (Hudson 2000). In many respects, they pioneered what became integral parts of Protestant missionary strategy, including translation of the Bible into Indian languages, dissemination of printed tracts, and running schools. Even their tolerance of caste distinctions among former Hindus who converted to Christianity was shared to a greater or lesser degree by many other Protestant missions until the 1820s. The first Protestant missions in the north of India had been established towards the end of the eighteenth century, and at first missionaries there were 'willing to tolerate a degree of caste distinction both in their schools and among their converts' (Forrester 1980: 25). From about the third decade of the nineteenth century, however, a much stricter line was taken against caste in the north. In south India, declining support from Germany and Denmark resulted in the Lutheran missions coming under the effective control of the Anglican Society for the Propagation of the Gospel (SPG) from 1825. The Lutheran clergy, whose orders were not recognized by the Church of England, suffered the indignity of having to be reordained. Despite the developing Anglo-Saxon Protestant intolerance of caste in the north, the SPG permitted the formerly Lutheran missions to continue their practice of tolerating caste on the basis that the spiritual equality of believers in Christ was 'in no way incompatible with the various distinctions of rank and degrees in society which are recognised in the Gospel itself' (Forrester 1980: 34).

In the 1840s, the newly established, and passionately Lutheran, Leipzig Missionary Society began to reclaim the territory and the tradition of the old Tranquebar mission. Like the founders of the

Tranquebar mission, the new Leipzig missionaries, and especially Heinrich Cordes, the first of them, and Karl Graul, *Missiondirektor* from 1844, took a flexible approach to the issue of caste.[4] According to Graul, the Leipzig missionaries saw 'caste among the Native Christians in the light of a national institution, devoid of its superadded heathenish basis' (quoted in Sharpe 1998: 132). He argued that while the practices of Indian Christians and Hindus had the same outward form, they were not in fact understood in the same way: 'Two do the same, which is yet not the same' (*'Zwei thun dasselbe, was doch nicht dasselbe ist'*; quoted in Sharpe 1998: 133.) Sharpe notes the influence on Graul of German Romanticism. This not only emphasized the distinctive identity of different peoples [*Völker*]—each with its own culture [*Kultur*] based on, among other things, a shared language, religion, and form of social organization—but was also profoundly Indophilic: 'In the Romantic scale of values, no non-Western culture stood higher than that of India in respect of natural virtue' (1998: 135). Already thus predisposed to a sympathetic view of caste, the Leipzig missionaries were also the inheritors of what Sharpe characterizes as a 'hierarchical and bitterly anti-democratic' social theory. Their 'vision of society was ... least of all egalitarian; rather it presupposed something not altogether different from a caste system of *Amt* and *Stand*' (Sharpe 1998: 128).[5] The Leipzig society's position on caste led to a long-running and bitter dispute[6] with other missionary societies who saw their own efforts to eradicate caste consciousness among their congregations undermined by the ease with which converts and even whole congregations were able to change their affiliation and align themselves with churches of the Leipzig society. When Graul visited the Leipzig mission stations—he was in India from December 1849 to August 1852—the caste debate was never far from his mind, and his *Reise* [Travels] record many conversations on the question with missionaries of all societies.[7] He found that there were 'many Anglican missionaries whose private convictions with respect to the caste issue [stood] in secret contradiction to the official practice, prescribed from above' (Graul 1855: II, 69).

Lutheran Missionary Accounts of South Indian Religions

The founder of the Tranquebar mission was also a pioneering scholar of Indian religions. Bartholomäus Ziegenbalg assembled a library of well over a hundred Tamil religious texts, on the basis of which he wrote two substantial volumes on south Indian Hinduism—*Malabarian Heathenism* (1711) and *The Genealogy of the Malabarian Gods* (1713)—and a series of smaller works, translations, and letters dealing with the same material. Although Ziegenbalg was aware of Sanskrit and its importance for brahmanical religion, he seems never to have regarded it as important to learn Sanskrit and wrote that while 'the Brahmins make much of' the Vedas, they do not allow others even to see, much less to read, them. Instead the 'idolatrous worship' of Tamil Hindus is established on the Puranas, together with the Agamas and Shastras, which are found 'in all sorts of languages' among the common, non-Brahman people (K. Liebau 1998: 94). I have argued elsewhere that in part this is because the primary sources of Ziegenbalg's textual collection were the libraries of the non-Brahman Śaiva *mathams* (religious institutions housing ascetic lineages), which in turn was the result of the extended familial networks on which Ziegenbalg relied for acquiring books (Sweetman and Ilakkuvan 2012: 29–38). For Ziegenbalg, it was the Tamil Puranas, especially the *Tiruvilaiyadal puranam*, and other Tamil works which were the primary sources of his own writings on Hinduism. While these works—like all Tamil literature—are far from untouched by the Sanskrit tradition, they do represent a form of Hindu religion which is distinctively Tamil. Ziegenbalg does note the difficulties that converts experienced when they were disowned by their family and caste, but it cannot be said that any special antipathy towards Brahmans or the caste system animates his presentation of South Indian Hinduism as a distinctively Tamil religion. It was simply all he knew, and while he notes Sanskrit's association with the north, he has no knowledge of the north beyond what he read in the Tamil versions of the myths of Krishna's exploits in Vrindavan or Rama's birth in Ayodhya.

Ziegenbalg's works were not immediately published, but they were circulated among both missionaries and friends of the mission in Europe. In the century and a half following his premature death (at the age of 37) in 1719, the *Genealogy* appeared in four heavily redacted versions.[8] The most interesting of these for our purposes are a German edition in 1867 and an English translation in 1869 (Germann 1867; Metzger 1869). A German edition of Ziegenbalg's *Genealogy* had been planned by Graul, but following his death, also premature, in 1864, the task fell to his pupil Wilhelm Germann. Germann had already established himself as a mission historian with his biography of another of the Tranquebar missionaries, J.P. Fabricius, who had revised Ziegenbalg's translation of the Bible into Tamil (Germann 1865). In 1867, Germann also dispatched for publication an account of the founding of the mission and a collection of primary sources relating to the mission (Germann 1868). His edition of Ziegenbalg's *Genealogy* is, however, not merely the publication of another primary source, but was conceived as a necessary contribution to the development of a Tamil church.

For Graul and Germann, as for other German Protestant missionaries of the nineteenth century, the conversion of individuals to Christianity was only an 'initial step in missionary work. The ultimate aim was the establishment of a ... *Volkskirche*' (Fiedler 1996: 13; italics original). Although Christian, such a church would have to be deeply rooted in the *Volkstum*,[9] in this case, the Kultur of the Tamil country. In his plan for a series of Tamil translations, also cut short by his death, Graul had spoken of the necessity for missionaries to study the literature of the people among whom they worked. Knowledge of Christian literature alone was insufficient and would yield only a 'poor and wooden' preaching. It was in the literature of a people that the missionary would find crystallized the spirit of the people (*der Geist des Volkes*). There, he writes:

> The folk-errors [*Volksirrthümer*] lie open to the sun but there too is most clearly to be seen the 'red threads' of the truth, which run through even the most mendacious heathenism, offering a welcome foundation for the Gospel message.[10]

For Germann, the publication of Ziegenbalg's *Genealogy* was in part an attempt to sway the colonial authorities in India to take up the work left unfinished by Graul and to publish a series of Tamil works and commentaries that would shed light on the religious and intellectual history of south India, just as the works of the British Sanskritists in Calcutta had done for the north. This would not only be in the spirit of Ziegenbalg, but would, says Germann, 'discharge a duty to a people who must degenerate through the influx of western, albeit Christian, education if not given access at the same time to their own classical heritage through an education appropriate to their nationality' (Germann 1867: xii). Such a loss of their national character [*Entnationalisirung*] would corrupt the divine ordering of the world. At the very least, Germann hoped the British authorities would allow classical Tamil works to be prescribed for University examinations instead of 'relatively worthless translations from Sanskrit' (1867: xii). In his edition of the *Genealogy*, Germann set out to meet what he took to be the 'urgent practical need' for a mythological handbook for south India as a counterpart to the many mythological works in English which were oriented only to the north (1867: viii). Germann had other axes to grind in his edition of the *Genealogy*, notably about the choice of the word *deva* for God in the revised Tamil translation of the Bible, but this was secondary to his primary purpose of helping to establish the basis for a Tamil church, by ensuring that missionaries 'became members of the *Volk*, familiar with their manner of thought and their literature, with all their weaknesses and benefits' (Germann 1867: xii).

In editing—or, rather, thoroughly bowdlerizing—Ziegenbalg's work, Germann drew heavily on more recent European accounts of India. He used a wide range of works by both missionaries and others, including missionaries such as the Abbé Dubois and William Ward and secular scholars including H.H. Wilson, Christian Lassen, and Friedrich Max Müller. It was, however, from Graul's works—notably his account of his own travels, the *Reise in Ostindien*—that he took the primary narrative which he uses to unify the disparate elements in Hinduism as they are presented in Ziegenbalg's work.

> As the Brahmins pressed toward the south they found there as the original religion [*Urreligion*] the devil-worship in which still today the lower classes are entrapped. As their gods proved not powerful enough to overcome the devil-worship, they entered into a sort of union. (Germann 1867: 153)

The degree to which the two had mixed varied, and the south Indian 'devil worshippers' had been unwilling to accept the Brahmins' attempts to dress their practices in Brahmanical garb. Germann continues by noting that, among the Shanars, resistance to Brahmanism amounted to outright struggle. The Shanars are therefore identified as the true representatives of original devil worship (*Dämonendienst*) of the south (Germann 1867: 181, 164).

This picture resonates deeply with the presentation of the Shanars in Caldwell's *Tinnevelly Shanars*, first published in 1849.[11] The Shanars, writes Caldwell, 'are Hindus not of the Brahmanical, but of the Tamil or aboriginal race' (1849: 5), and while they 'nominally acknowledge as deities some of the most renowned of the gods of the Brahmanical mythologies … generally speaking they know only their names, and a few popular myths in which they figure as heroes.'[12] Their 'only real faith', Caldwell concludes 'is demonolatry' (1849: 9). Caldwell's *Tinnevelly Shanars* was enormously influential, and it is therefore no surprise that Germann's presentation of the Shanar religion was shaped by it. However, while Germann does cite *Tinnevelly Shanars*,[13] he cites 'my dear teacher, Dr Graul' (Germann 1867: viii) twice as often, and, on occasion, opposes Graul's interpretation to Caldwell's.[14] And it was Graul's conception of the Shanars as the representatives of 'non-Brahmin-dom' (*Nichtbrahmanenthum*) that shaped Germann's understanding of Shanar tradition as the true Volkstum of the Tamils. For Graul, as we have seen, the spirit of a people is crystallized in their literature, and it is therefore not surprising to find that he emphasizes the distinctive character of what he—anticipating Caldwell—refers to already in April 1850 as the 'the so-called Dravida language family'. The context is his description of Mangalore, which he characterized as 'a little Bombay' in its mix of peoples, languages, and religions. The most widely spoken languages were Kannada and 'the true language of the people [*Volkssprache*]', Tulu. Both belonged to 'the so-called Dravida language family', the crown of which, however, is Tamil. The 'dominant religions yield nothing to the colourful mixture of languages' but as with language, so with religion, Graul identifies 'the original religion of the people' (*die ursprüngliche Volksreligion*), which is 'demon-worship'" (*Dämonen-Dienst*) (Graul 1850: 111).[15]

The origins of the Dravidian idea—and even the term 'Dravida' for the languages of the south—long predate Graul (Trautmann 2006: 175–6), but it is nevertheless worth exploring the proximate sources of his use of the idea. Despite his wide travels to mission stations throughout the south Indian region, including Tirunelveli and Idaiyangudi, and his constant reports of meeting missionaries of all societies, Graul never reports meeting Caldwell,[16] and Caldwell—so far as I have been able to determine—did not use the term 'Dravidian' in print prior to Graul. Graul does cite Caldwell's *Tinnevelly Shanars*, but Andreas Nehring notes that there is no trace in his papers of any dependence on Caldwell in respect to the Dravidian idea (2003: 143). Graul had, however, met other missionaries among whom the idea— if not the name—of a Dravidian language family was current.

Graul met, briefly, John Stevenson in his house on Malabar Hill in Bombay in January 1850 (Graul 1854–6: I, 33). Stevenson, at first a missionary but by then a chaplain to the East India Company, had just published the first part of an article entitled 'Observations on the Grammatical Structure of the Vernacular Languages of India' in the *Journal of the Bombay Branch of the Royal Asiatic Society* (Stevenson 1849). Thomas Trautmann (1997: 158) summarizes Stevenson's argument as 'saying that there is one and only one pre-Sanskritic ancestral language of India, and that it is Dravidian'. However, the account of Mangalore in which Graul first introduces 'the so-called Dravida language family' was written from Ketti in the Nilgiris in April 1850 where, just a week earlier, he had met the missionaries Bernhard Schmid and Peter Schaffter in Udhagamandalam (Graul 1854–6: I, 279). According to the account of his colleague Schaffter, Schmid had joined the German Carl Rhenius with the Church Missionary Society in Tinnevelly (Palayamkottai) in 1820, but by 1830, his health had forced him to retire first to the Nilgiris and subsequently, from late 1836 to December 1845, to Europe (Schaffter 1844: 44, 74).[17] In the mid-1830s, Schmid had followed Rhenius out of the Church Missionary Society and appealed to Halle for financial support (Nehring 2003: 142). Schmid was typical of the missionary scholar, studying both languages and, after his return from Europe, the natural history of the Nilgiris. He published a series of articles on both subjects in periodicals such as *The Madras Journal of Literature and Science*, *The Journal of the Bombay Branch of the Royal Asiatic Society*, and the *Oriental Christian Spectator*, edited by Stevenson's missionary and scholarly colleague John Wilson in Bombay. In 1829, Schmid had written that 'the Tamils, the Malabarians or Maleialians, the Telingians, and the Kannadians form the tribe of original inhabit- ants and share a fundamental language (*Grundsprache*) which is more or less mixed with Sanskrit words' (Nehring 2003: 145).[18] In 1836, he published 'Observations on Original and Derived Languages', in which he wrote: 'The construction of the Tamul, Maleialam, Karnataka and Telugu (I think also that of the Konkanese and Orissa), is most strictly conformed to the rules of a genuine *original* language [emphasis original]'—an original language being one 'formed by a nation through their own mental exertion' rather than 'the violent interference and intermixture of one or more other languages' (Schmid 1836: 121, 123). Neither Stevenson nor Schmid uses the term 'Dravidian', instead referring to 'the southern family' of Indian languages and 'the four principal languages of the Madras Presidency', respectively.

As Trautmann has shown, the idea of a Dravidian family of languages was current among many scholars in India from the early nineteenth century, and indeed implicit earlier still in Indian grammatical traditions. Both Graul and Caldwell were heir to these discussions, although, as Trautmann notes, Caldwell 'was not excessively generous in giving credit to his predecessors' (Trautmann 2006: 74). While there is, therefore, no reason to suppose that Graul was dependent upon Caldwell in relation to the Dravidian idea, there is some evidence to suggest that Caldwell's understanding of a Dravidian linguistic and religious cultural complex distinct from the Sanskritic and Brahmanical tradition owed something to the Lutheran understanding of the Tamil Volkstum, as well as to the discussions mapped by Trautmann.

Early in his missionary career, Caldwell had spent an extended period in Madras with Heinrich Cordes, the first of the new Lutheran missionaries, and it is possible, although difficult to substantiate, that Caldwell had imbibed something of the character of Lutheran understanding of mission from his contacts with him and other Leipzig missionaries, and from his careful study of their predecessors in the older Lutheran missions. In March 1841, at a time when he was contemplating leaving the London Missionary Society, Caldwell wrote to his sister contrasting the work of the German missionaries in villages with the work of English societies in towns and European settlements, noting that 'all the German missionaries whose names are so celebrated and who produced such results in India, lived nearly on a level with the natives and among the natives' (Wyatt 1894: 66). He learnt German so 'that I might be able to make use of the vast stores of Indian learning accumulated by German scholars' (Wyatt 1894: 111). Caldwell wrote an early and enthusiastic review of Germann's 1867 edition of Ziegenbalg's *Genealogy*, noting Germann's use of Graul's

Reise, which he called 'the work of a careful enquirer and accurate observer' (Caldwell 1867: 2). He lamented that works such as Graul's *Reise* and Lassen's *Indische Alterthumskunde* had not been translated into English, and welcomed the plan to translate Ziegenbalg's *Genealogy*. Caldwell also knew Schaffter[19] and, through him, may well have met Schmid after his return from Europe in 1845.

We should not overstate the degree of this possible influence. Caldwell differed sharply from the Lutherans on the caste question, arguing that 'the retention of caste distinctions' was the reason that 'Christian life and missionary zeal had sunk to a low point' in the old Lutheran missions and adding that the Leipzig missionaries who had revived the old Lutheran stations were a 'lamentable exception' to the general Protestant effort to discourage caste (Caldwell 1857: 11, 17). Graul gave as good as he got, arguing that it had been Lutherans— Christian Friedrich Schwartz and Christian Wilhelm Gericke—who had sown the seeds for the harvest which the Anglicans were now reaping (Graul 1854–6: III, 42). Referring directly to Caldwell's work at Idaiyangudi, he argued that the number of converts and communicants demonstrated that 'the so-called general awakening in Tinnevelly cannot truly be called a pentecostal outpouring of the Holy Spirit', and suggested that most of those who had converted had been influenced by 'external grounds' (Graul 1854–6: III, 224). Nevertheless, Caldwell's account of the Shanar religion is strikingly congruent with Lutheran thought regarding a Volkstum. Of the Shanars' lack of distinct conception of an afterlife, he writes:

> They have, it is true, a primitive Tamil word denoting 'a spirit' or ghost; but the word which denotes the soul, according to the Christian or philosophical meaning of the term, is a Sanscrit one, belonging consequently *to the terminology of a different religion*. (Caldwell 1849: 10; emphasis added)

Thus, Caldwell, like Graul and Germann, finds in language the key to understanding the religious character of a people.

Vaitheespara does acknowledge that Caldwell was, and was conscious of being, heir to a longer missionary tradition of writing on India. He mentions Caldwell's admiration of the German Protestant missions, and even notes that Schmid 'is reputed to have noted the independence of South Indian languages as early as 1836'

(Vaitheespara 2002: 39–40). The missionary he singles out for influence on Caldwell is, however, the Catholic Abbé Jean-Antoine Dubois. Vaitheespara notes in particular the anti-Brahmanical element in Dubois's work, and his controversial claim that the conversion of India was rendered impracticable by 'the spiritual and intellectual power that the Brahmans exercised over the rest of the castes' (Vaitheespara 2002: 42). There is an irony here in that Dubois was not the primary author of the text that made him famous, the *Description of the Character, Manners, and Customs of the People of India, and of Their Institutions, Religious and Civil*, first published in 1817. This was in fact based on an earlier text by the eighteenth-century French Jesuit Gaston-Laurent Cœurdoux (Murr 1987). Cœurdoux's text is very much the culmination of a long Jesuit tradition which regarded caste distinctions as a matter of social rank, tolerable in the church if purged of their religious associations.[20] The more profound influence on Caldwell in his formulation of the Dravidian idea is, however, to be attributed to other Protestant missionaries. The Dravidian idea was widely canvassed among these missionary scholars in the first half of the nineteenth century, and it was rooted in a still older tradition of reflection about the nature of Tamil culture and religion which begins with Ziegenbalg's intensive study of Tamil literature. While missionary antipathy to Brahmans is undoubtedly also a factor, it is to the concern with Tamil Kultur or Volkstum that we owe the missionary elaboration of the Dravidian idea and all the consequences that flowed therefrom.

Notes

1. 'The missionaries were impelled in this project by their belief that Brahmanism and the caste system posed the greatest obstacle in the way of Christian conversion in South India.... The major impulse in much of the missionary support for a distinctly Dravidian religion, again, was their antipathy towards Brahminism and what was considered to be its latest manifestation, neo-Vedantism' (Vaitheespara 2002: 28, 31). See also Vaitheespara (1999: 52–3).

2. Vaitheespara's more tentatively phrased suggestion that Caldwell's demonstration of the distinct origins of the Dravidian languages 'might have been intended by him to weaken the power and influence of Brahmans and

Brahmanism in South India, in order to facilitate the progress of Christianity there' (Ravindiran 1996: 85) is, as he notes (1996: 102), harder to demonstrate.

3. This was expressed in the so-called Minute on Caste agreed on at the Madras Missionary Conference, a meeting of all Protestant mission agencies in India, in 1850. The Minute proclaimed, 'Caste ... is one of the greatest obstacles to the progress of the Gospel in India ... whatever it may have been in its origin, it is now adopted as an essential part of the Hindu religion.' On the responses of Lutherans—both missionaries and their Tamil congregations—see Sweetman (2007).

4. On the history of the Danish-Halle/Leipzig mission in the nineteenth century, and its position on caste, see Sharpe (1998) (from where much of the information given here is derived) and Bergunder (2000). Stephen Neill (1985: 407) prefers to emphasize Graul's acceptance that caste should eventually, if only slowly, be eliminated from the church.

5. Sharpe describes this as the 'first, and perhaps the most important of the Leipzig missionaries' convictions' (1998: 127). See also Bergunder (2000: 33).

6. See, for example, Graul (1851) and Pope (1853).

7. See Graul (1854–56). Some sections—including one which make early reference to 'the so-called Dravida language family' (discussed later)—had earlier appeared in German missionary periodicals.

8. A study of these editions as indices of changing European attitudes towards Hinduism during the period in which colonial rule was established is in preparation.

9. *Volkstum*, often regarded as untranslatable, was first used in Friedrich Ludwig Jahn's *Deutsches Volkstum* (1813) to refer to the unique character or cultural identity of a people, in opposition to that of other peoples: 'It designates the strength given a people by its organic unity' (Crépon, Cassin, and Moatti 2014: 756).

10. 'Dort findet sich der Geist des Volkes krystallisirt; dort lassen sich die herrschenden Gedanken und Neigungen belauschen; dort liegen die Volksirrthümer klar gesponnen an der Sonnen,—und dort ziegen sich auch am deutlichsten die 'rothen Fäden' der Wahrheit, die selbst das lügenhafteste Heidenthum durchziehen—und dem Boten des Evangeliums willkommne Anknüpfspukte gewähren' (Graul 1854: 23).

11. I am grateful to Ulrike Schröder for making available to me a copy of Caldwell's *Tinnevelly Shanars*. The work was withdrawn from circulation by Caldwell following protests from Shanars at the representation of their traditions, and has become scarce. See Hardgrave (1969: Chapter 3), and Schröder (2009: 172–6).

12. 'Again, some of the wealthier and more educated Shanars may appear to hold the Brahmanical doctrine of the transmigration of souls; but their

belief in it is merely nominal, and only exhibited in half-earnest' (Caldwell 1849: 11).

13. He also cites other works on Tinnevelly, including Pettitt (1851).

14. See, for example, Germann (1867: 190–1). Graul's account of the religion of the Shanars was published in the second volume of the Indian section of his *Reise* (Graul 1854–6: II, 125–9). Graul does cite *Tinnevelly Shanars* in this volume, but not when discussing Shanar *religion*.

15. The phrase 'so-called Dravida language family', is repeated in the first volume of Graul's *Reise in Ostindien* (Graul 1854–6: I, 350). In an article published in *Das Ausland* in 1855, Graul refers to Tamil as the foremost among the Indian aboriginal languages (*Ursprachen*) referred to by the name 'Dravida' (cited in Nehring 2003: 144).

16. Nor is Graul among the 'Distinguished Visitors to Tinnevelly' or 'Men I Met in Tinnevelly' recorded by Caldwell (Wyatt 1894). Caldwell travelled through Tinnevelly in early 1851. Caldwell reports going to the Nilgiris for health reasons in 1851 and spending almost a year there, which is perhaps why they did not meet.

17. An essay in the *Madras Journal of Literature and Science*, published in July 1836, says Schmid 'is still at Ootacamund' (Schaffter 1844: 156). Schmid's obituary in the *Madras Journal of Literature and Science*, to which he was a regular contributor, records his return from Europe at the end of 1845.

18. I have not been able to consult the source, which was published in 1837. Although Nehring says this was written in 1829, it was published in 1837, and may be the free translation' of his 1836 essay (see next note) which Schmid describes in his journal. The latter, he says, 'embodied the results of my philological inquiries and observations during the last 28 or 30 years' ('Obituary Notice' 1857: 144).

19. Schaffter and Caldwell accompanied George Spencer, the bishop of Madras, on his tour of the Tinnevelly mission in 1845 (Spencer 1846: 42).

20. For an analysis of the differences between Dubois and Cœurdoux on caste, see Sweetman (2007).

Bibliography

Bergunder, Michael. 2000. 'Geschichte der Leipziger Mission'. In *Quellenbestände der Indienmission 1700–1918 in Archiven des deutschsprachigen Raums*, edited by Erika Pabst and Thomas Müller-Bahlke, 32–4. Halle: Verlag der Franckeschen Stiftungen zu Halle.

Caldwell, Robert. 1849. *The Tinnevelly Shanars: A Sketch of Their Religion, and Their Moral Condition and Characteristics, as a Caste*. Madras: Printed by

Reuben Twigg, at the Christian Knowledge Society's Press, Church Street, Vepery.

———. 1856. *A Comparative Grammar of the Dravidian or South-Indian Family of Languages*. London: Harrison.

———. 1857. *Lectures on the Tinnevelly Missions*. London: Bell & Daldy.

———. 1867. 'Genealogy of the Malabar Gods'. *Madras Times*, 5 December, 2.

Crépon, Marc, Barbara Cassin, and Claudia Moatti. 2014. 'People/Race/ Nation'. In *Dictionary of Untranslatables: A Philosophical Lexicon*, edited by Barbara Cassin, Emily Apter, Jacques Lezra, and Michael Wood, translated by Steven Rendall, Christian Hubert, Jeffrey Mehlman, Nathanael Stein, and Michael Syrotinski, 751–63. Princeton: Princeton University Press.

Fiedler, Klaus. 1996. *Christianity and African Culture: Conservative German Protestant Missionaries in Tanzania, 1900–1940*. Leiden: Brill.

Forrester, Duncan B. 1980. *Caste and Christianity: Attitudes and Policies on Caste of Anglo-Saxon Protestant Missions in India*. London: Curzon.

Germann, Wilhelm. 1865. *Johann Philipp Fabricius: Seine Funfzigjahrige Wirksamkeit im Tamulenlande*. Erlangen: Verlag von Andreas Deichert.

———. 1867. *Genealogie der Malabarishen* [sic] *Götter. Aus eigenen Schriften und Briefen der Heiden zusammengetragen und verfasst von Bartholomaeus Ziegenbalg, weil. Propst an der Jerusalems-Kirche in Trankebar*. Madras: Printed for the Editor at the Christian Knowledge Society's Press.

———. 1868. *Ziegenbalg und Plütschau: Die Gründungsjahre der Trankebarschen Mission. Ein Beitrag zur Geschichte des Pietismus nach handschriftlichen Quellen und ältesten Drucken*. Erlangen: Verlag von Andreas Deichert.

Graul, Karl. 1850. 'Des Herrn Missions-Directors Karl Graul vierteljährliche Mittheilungen aus einer Missionsreise nach Ostindien'. *Missionsnachrichten der Ostindischen Missionsanstalt zu Halle*, 2(1): 101–27.

———. 1851. *Explanations Concerning the Principles of the Leipzig Missionary Society, with regard to the Caste Question*. Madras.

———. 1854. 'Zweck und Plan einer Tamulischen Bibliothek in Uebersetzung mit Erklärungen'. *Missionsnachrichten der Ostindischen Missionsanstalt zu Halle*, 6: 22–30.

———. 1854–6. *Reise in Ostindien von December 1849 bis October 1852*. 3 vols. Leipzig: Dörffling & Franke.

Hardgrave, Robert L. 1969. *The Nadars of Tamilnad: The Political Culture of a Community in Change*. Berkeley: University of California Press.

Hudson, D. Dennis. 2000. *Protestant Origins in India: Tamil Evangelical Christians, 1706–1835*. Richmond: Curzon.

Kent, Eliza F. 2004. *Converting Women: Gender and Protestant Christianity in Colonial South India*. Oxford: Oxford University Press.

Liebau, Heike. 2014. 'Translocal Networks: Tranquebar Mission Press in Eighteenth-Century South Asia'. In *Beyond Tranquebar: Grappling across Cultural Borders in South India*, edited by Esther Fihl and A.R. Venkatachalapathy, 496–518. Hyderabad: Orient BlackSwan.

Liebau, Kurt. 1998. *Die Malabarische Korrespondenz: Tamilische Briefe an deutsche Missionare; eine Auswahl*. Sigmaringen: Thorbecke.

Metzger, G.J. 1869. *Genealogy of the South-Indian Gods: A Manual of the Mythology and Religion of the People of Southern India*. Madras: Higginbotham & Co.

Murr, Sylvia. 1987. *L'Inde philosophique entre Bousset et Voltaire*, vol. I: *Mœurs et coutumes des Indiens (1777)*; vol. II: *L'indologie du Père Cœurdoux*. Paris: École française d'Extrême Orient.

Nehring, Andreas. 2003. *Orientalismus und Mission. Die Repräsentation der tamilischen Gesellschaft und Religion durch Leipziger Missionare 1840–1940*. Wiesbaden: Harrassowitz.

Neill, Stephen. 1985. *A History of Christianity in India*, vol. II: *1707–1858*. Cambridge: Cambridge University Press.

Oddie, Geoffrey A. 2006. *Imagined Hinduism: British Protestant Missionary Constructions of Hinduism, 1793–1900*. New Delhi: Sage.

Pettitt, George. 1851. *The Tinnevelly Mission of the Church Missionary Society*. London: Seeleys.

Pope, George Uglow. 1853. *The Lutheran Aggression: A Letter to the Tranquebar Missionaries, regarding 'Their Position, Their Proceedings and Their Doctrine'*. Madras: American Mission Press.

Ravindiran, V. 1996. 'The Unanticipated Legacy of Robert Caldwell and the Dravidian Movement'. *South Indian Studies*, 1(1): 83–110.

———. 1999. 'Discourses of Empowerment: Missionary Orientalism in the Development of Dravidian Nationalism'. In *Nation Work: Asian Elites and National Identities*, edited by Timothy Brook and Andre Schmid. Ann Arbor: University of Michigan Press.

Schaffter, Peter Paul. 1844. *Histoire de la mission du Tinnévelly*. Bâle: J.J. Schweighauser.

Schmid, Bernhard. 1836. 'Observations on Original and Derived Languages'. *Madras Journal of Literature and Science*, IV(12): 121–7.

Schröder, Ulrike. 2009. *Religion, Kaste und Ritual. Christliche Mission und tamilischer Hinduismus in Südindien im 19. Jahrhundert*. Halle: Verlag der Franckeschen Stiftungen zu Halle.

Sharpe, Eric. 1998. '"Patience with the Weak": Leipzig Lutherans and the Caste Question in Nineteenth-Century South India'. In *Religious Traditions in South Asia: Interaction and Change*, edited by Geoffrey A. Oddie, 125–37. Richmond: Curzon.

Spencer, George Trevor. 1946. *Journal of a Visitation-Tour through the Provinces of Madura and Tinnevelly: In the Diocese of Madras, in August and September 1845.* London: Francis and John Rivington.

Stevenson, John. 1849–51. 'Observations on the Grammatical Structure of the Vernacular Languages of India'. *Journal of the Bombay Branch of the Royal Asiatic Society*, 3: part 1: 71–76; part 2: 1–7, 196–202.

Sweetman, Will. 2007. 'Colonialism All the Way Down? Religion and the Secular in Early Modern Writing on South India'. In *Religion and the Secular: Historical and Colonial Formations*, edited by Timothy Fitzgerald, 117–34. London: Equinox.

Sweetman, Will, and R. Ilakkuvan. 2012. *Bibliotheca Malabarica: Bartholomäus Ziegenbalg's Tamil Library.* Pondicherry and Paris: Institut français de Pondichéry / École française d'Extrême Orient.

'Obituary Notice [Doctor Bernhard Schmid]'. *Madras Journal of Literature and Science*, 19(44): 143–6.

Trautmann, Thomas R. 1997. *Aryans and British India.* Berkeley and Los Angeles: University of California Press.

————. 2006. *Languages and Nations: The Dravidian Proof in Colonial Madras.* New Delhi: Yoda Press.

Vaitheespara, Ravi. 2015. *Religion and Nation in South India: Maraimalai Adigal, the Neo-Saivite Movement and Tamil Nationalism, 1876–1950.* Oxford: Oxford University Press.

Vaitheespara, Ravindran. 2002. 'Caste, Hybridity and the Construction of Cultural Identity in Colonial India: Maraimalai Adigal and the Intellectual Genealogy of Dravidian Nationalism, 1800–1950'. PhD dissertation, University of Toronto.

Wyatt, J.L., ed. 1894. *Reminiscences of Bishop Caldwell.* Madras: Addison & Co.

4

RANJEETA DUTTA

Locating the Self, Community, and the Nation

Writing the History of the Śrīvaiṣṇavas of South India

In a monograph written exclusively on the Śrīvaiṣṇava *brāhmaṇas* sometime in 1930, the author, D.B.K. Rangachari, in the introductory section (1986 [1930]: 1) stated:

> The Sri Vaishnava Brahmanas form now an exclusive group adopting certain customs based on beliefs in which they have implicit faith. But in most of their general ritualistic observances they do not differ from the other groups of Brahmans. As a matter of fact all Brahmanas, to whatever section they belong, follow one of the Vedas and in the ceremonies they have to perform they adopt the rituals as laid down in the sûtras pertaining to their Vedas.... Further, there is a belief current amongst several of the Sri Vaishnava community that the Sri Vaishnava Brahmanas existed as a separate class from very early times, almost suggesting that they constitute a very distinct class quite different from the other sections of the Brahmans. A careful scrutiny of the Vaishnava traditional account at once disproves of this claim.

A Śrīvaiṣṇava brāhmaṇa himself, Rangachari, while asserting such an identity, was also eager to relate to the pan-Indian brāhmaṇa identity. Feeling apprehensive that the association with the larger brāhmaṇa community could be severed, Rangachari soon after painstakingly went into details of similarities in ritual practices between a Śrīvaiṣṇava brāhmaṇa and a brāhmaṇa. Such an anxiety of maintaining a dual identity based on the traditional frame of religion in a regional context (in this case the Śrīvaiṣṇava tradition in the Tamil region) as well as a caste (the brāhmaṇa *varṇa*) that had a pan-Indian presence and hierarchical superiority was evident in the early twentieth century and defined the brahmanical self vis-à-vis the religion and the community. Simultaneously, the self had to articulate its identity with reference to the idea of modernity and the nation generated by the establishment of the colonial state (Pandian 2007: 17–101). This essay therefore aims to analyse the ways in which a small community of the Tamil Śrīvaiṣṇava brāhmaṇas with a long historicity reconfigured themselves in the late nineteenth and early twentieth centuries in the context of colonial modernity and the cultural and political processes such a modernity generated. Consequently, this interaction led to the development of a specific indigenous modernity of the Tamil Śrīvaiṣṇava brāhmaṇas in which secularization and religion presupposed each other.

In its literal sense, modernity, and the notion of the modern, emphasizes upon creating a sanitized secular sphere in which religion has no public role, its practice and ideas relegated to an individual's private life. It has been well argued that such an ideal of modernity was problematic for any culture, and the Indian case was no exception (for details, see Bilgrami 1998: 380–417; van der Veer 2001: 3–54; Asad 2003: 1–20). Though on the one hand, the colonial state in India in its later stages strove to maintain a secularity that aimed at non-interference in native religions and ceded the space of religious control to the missionary activities, on the other hand, it 'also provided the grounds for articulating and bringing into new identities as much as it sought to freeze identities' (Pandian 2007: 11). One such identity that was recast in response to colonial modernity was the brahmanical identity. The modern colonial state produced a new 'framework for education, jobs, and social interactions'; reduced the social position of the brāhmaṇas due to the superior authority of the British; and in many ways, facilitated the development of a homogeneous institutionalized Hinduism in the nineteenth and twentieth centuries (van der Veer 2001: 20–3; Frykenberg 1997: 90). These colonial dynamics posed a challenge to the brāhmaṇa identity in general and the regional brahmanical identity in particular (Frykenberg 1997: 31–3). Thus, the brāhmaṇas worked out a strategy that attempted to validate their status by simultaneously claiming to be the legitimate inheritors of the tradition that would 'authenticate' their brahmanical existence and at the same time declare them to be modern (Frykenberg 1997: 37). This balancing of tradition and modernity was particularly challenging for the Tamil-speaking brāhmaṇas. They had to identify not only with the pan-Indian brahmanical practices, but also with the modern institutionalized religion of Hinduism, thus 'authenticating' their traditional moorings. Simultaneously they were also under stress to establish their modern identity by associating with the colonial state and the new concept of the Indian nation. Conversely, this reinvention in many ways also influenced the colonial modernity.

Therefore, the Śrīvaiṣṇava modernity, as a part of the brahmanical modernity, generated a specific consciousness of belonging to a religious community, and within that consciousness, the brahmanical status and the pan-Indian association were reiterated. Consequently, such a modernity created a public sphere in which histories of the Śrīvaiṣṇava community and history writings in the late nineteenth- and early twentieth-century south India were worked upon as predominantly the history of the Śrīvaiṣṇava brāhmaṇas that set the template for the subsequent histories. Thus, religion and religious identity coalesced with the modern discipline of history and generated a specific kind of regional Tamil brāhmaṇa modernity.

The essay is divided into two sections. The first section will provide the historical frame of community identities. The purpose of the discussion on the historical context is to provide an understanding of the points for departure and convergence between the modern and historical identity of being a Śrīvaiṣṇava. The next section will seek to understand the self-perception of the Śrīvaiṣṇava community as reflected in its history writing, primarily authored by the brāhmaṇas within the context of religious consciousness in nineteenth- and twentieth-century south India. Since it will not be possible to discuss the various themes in the history writing, the biographical depiction of Rāmānuja, one of the important Śrīvaiṣṇava *ācāryas* (spiritual teachers or leaders) in the eleventh century, will be critically analysed to show that this kind of representation of the past for a community located within the frame of modernity was never a homogeneous exercise and had points of variations and conflicts, highlighting and generating complex identities that went beyond the brahmanical Śrīvaiṣṇava self.

I

The Śrīvaiṣṇavas are a Vaiṣṇava community of south India. The community considers Viṣṇu and his consort Lakṣmī as their supreme godhead, and regards the Sanskrit Vedas and the *Nālāyira Divya Prabandham* (*NDP*; the 4,000 Tamil hymns of the Ālvārs, the early Vaiṣṇava saints) as its main scriptures. The community has two distinct groups, the Vaṭakalais and Teṅkalais. The Vaṭakalais regard the Varadarājaswamī temple at Kāñcīpuram (Kāñcīpuram district, Tamil Nadu) as their institutional centre and give precedence to the Sanskrit Vedas over the Tamil ones and therefore are considered to be conservative in outlook. The Teṅkalais represent the Tamil tradition with Śrīraṅgam (Tiruchchirapalli district, Tamil Nadu) as their institutional centre and regard the *Draviḍa Vedas* or the Tamil hymns of the early Vaiṣṇava saints, the Ālvārs (fifth to eighth centuries) as their scripture and are considered to be more broad based with a large non-brāhmaṇa following. There are three religious figures or ācāryas whom the Śrīvaiṣṇavas regard as most reverent: Rāmānuja (traditional dates: c. 1017–1137 CE), who belonged to eleventh and twelfth centuries and, credited with bringing together the social basis and the intellectual philosophy together into one organization and one community, is considered the most important ācārya; Vedāntadeśika (traditional dates: c. 1268–1369 CE), located in the thirteenth century, who is considered to have established the ideas and practices of the Vaṭakalai sub-tradition; and, finally, Maṇavāḷamāmuṇi (traditionally c. 1370–1442 CE), located in the fourteenth century, who is considered as the founding ācārya of the Teṅkalai sub-tradition. Both the Vaṭakalais and Teṅkalais believe that the lineages of their respective ācāryas were derived from the direct 'legitimate' descendants of Rāmānuja.

The Śrīvaiṣṇavas as a community existed before the thirteenth century CE, as is evident in the hymns of the Ālvārs, whose time period was approximately between the fifth and eighth centuries

CE (Hardy 1983: 241–480; Champakalakshmi 1996: 135–63). The hymns, individually as well as collectively, reflected the consciousness of being a Śrīvaiṣṇava. Based upon complete devotion or *bhakti* to Viṣṇu, the hymns advocated that being a devoted Śrīvaiṣṇava was superior to being a brāhmaṇa (Champakalakshmi 1996: 151–2). The priority of the community over a caste status was accompanied by the emphasis on Tamil as a scriptural language at par with Sanskrit (Champakalakshmi 1996: 150–1). The temple became the focus of this devotion, as it was considered the place where a transcendental God made himself accessible. The Āḷvārs delineated a sacred geography comprising one and eight centres or *divyadesams*, thereby demarcating a spatial identity for the community (Champakalakshmi 1996: 151–2; Hardy 1983: 256– 61). In the temple inscriptions, too, the presence of the Śrīvaiṣṇava community can be discerned from the phrase 'Śrīvaiṣṇava rakśasaī' (for the protection of the Śrīvaiṣṇavas).[1]

From the ninth and tenth centuries onwards, the community was dominated by ideologues with Sanskritic and brahmanical orientations. Known as the ācāryas, they wrote theological treatises, mostly in Sanskrit, and attempted to create a tradition that linked the hymnal phase to the tradition they were consolidating. The collection and compilation of the Tamil hymns of the Āḷvārs into a corpus of 4,000 songs, that is the *NDP*, sometime in the ninth and tenth centuries by the ācāryas was a crucial step in this direction.[2] Some attempts were also consciously made to evolve an institutional structure for the Vaiṣṇava community when a part of the *NDP*, that is, the *Tiruvāymoḷi* of Nammāḷvār (one of the Āḷvārs in the seventh century CE), was collected and put to music in the Raṅganāthasvāmī Temple at Śrīraṅgam and Uttaramērūr in the eleventh century (Sastri 1975: 479–80).

It was in the second quarter of the twelfth century CE that the Viśiṣṭādvaita philosophy of Rāmānuja imparted the much-needed theological orientation to the community. It was the first school of thought to challenge Śaṅkara's monistic (that is, non-dualism) philosophy of Advaita (eighth century CE) and the concept of *nirguṇa brahmaṇa* and presented an alternative model for the perception of divinity. Rāmānuja's philosophy was based on 'qualified monism' (that is, Viśiṣṭādvaita) where the divine had attributes that became the focus of worship.

However, a systematic philosophy projecting a normative tradition with the institutionalization in the temples and the *maṭhas* (monastic establishments) began to develop only from the thirteenth century CE. A written textual tradition evolved that comprised various genres of texts, namely the commentaries (*vyākhyānas*) and hagiographies (*guruparamparās*). These texts acquired a scriptural status. The development of Śrīvaiṣṇavism into a well-demarcated community with a cohesive identity can be traced in these texts. The *Prabandham* and the works of Rāmānuja became the subject of several commentaries. This led to the development of several interpretations, which gradually crystallized into distinct philosophies themselves. However, it was the hagiographies or the guruparamparās that delineated the history of the community.[3] The life stories of the Āḻvārs and ācāryas were the subjects of the hagiographical narratives. These narratives exemplified the Śrīvaiṣṇava ideals of devotion, sacrifice, and community identity. Particularly significant was the life story of Rāmānuja in which the concept of the 'guru' was emphasized upon, whereby the latter was delineated as superior to god. This concept of guru exemplified in Rāmānuja's biography set the tone for the delineation of the life stories of the subsequent ācāryas, including Vedāntadeśika and Maṇavāḷamāmuṉi. The language of the texts comprising the textual tradition was mostly a mixture of Tamil and Sanskrit and was representative of the philosophy of *ubhaya–vedānta*, that is, dual Vedas comprising the *NDP* as the Tamil Veda and the Vedas as the Sanskrit Vedas. This was significant; for the first time, a notion of a scripture in Tamil was introduced.[4] A certain duality in the construction of religious traditions, due to constant interaction between the mainstream Sanskritic tradition and regional/local or vernacular forms with shifting emphases between the Sanskritic and the vernacular at different points of historical time, was represented as well as accelerated by this philosophy of ubhaya–vedānta. The hagiographies as well the commentaries reflected often a proclivity or even an assertion of the Sanskritic tradition or the Tamil one. This duality became the ideological basis for the Śrīvaiṣṇava community's schism into the Vaṭakalai (northern) and Teṉkalai (southern) sects in the latter period. Such a schism assumed significant ramifications for the temple disputes and interactions with the colonial state and influenced the Śrīvaiṣṇava modernity in the late nineteenth and twentieth centuries.

Providing an integrative paradigm and a cohesive community structure, the normative tradition as articulated in the texts and ritual practices was documented in the temple inscriptions. The fusion of the Tamil with the Sanskrit was institutionally represented in the increasing non-brāhmaṇa participation in the temple activities. One such non-brāhmaṇa group was the weaver community of the *kaikkōḷas* who had significant links with the temples and became an important social group that the religious tradition attempted to incorporate in order to project a liberal outlook (Ramasvamy 1985: 35–62; Mines 1984: 11–51).[5] Rāmānuja is supposed to have introduced temple reforms to include the non-brāhmaṇa participation in the ritual and temple activities.[6] The relevance of the varṇa status became a part of the theological discourses in the commentarial texts and other philosophical treatises (Hardy 2007: 29–49). The projection of a low-caste background of the Āḻvārs, and equating the Tamil *NDP* with the Vedas, the development of a scriptural traditions, and popularization of the temples through the Agamic forms of worship, all contributed towards the construction of a popular social base. Hence, by the end of the thirteenth century CE, Śrīvaiṣṇavism emerged as an organized religious community, which provided the context for interaction within and outside the community. Such a reorientation of the community tradition took place against the background of social change, migrations, and urbanization that led to the rise of the non-brāhmaṇa groups both politically and economically (Appadurai 1978: 11–46; Stein 1989: 14–38; Karashima 1994: 43–145).

A consolidated analysis of the Śrīvaiṣṇava textual tradition shows that the complex community identity can be encapsulated within three concepts, namely uniformity, multiplicity, and duality (Dutta 2005: 248–53). *Uniformity* implied belonging to a single Śrīvaiṣṇava community. The textual tradition whose component texts developed as scriptures of the community reiterated the normative notion of a single homogeneous uniform community. A cohesive and distinct identity was constructed around Visnu with his spouse Lakṣmī as the universal divine couple. The scriptures further developed this uniform identity in the charismatic portrayal of Rāmānuja. Therefore, the idea of a uniform identity meant belonging to a single Śrīvaiṣṇava community with Rāmānuja as its head. Uniformity became the dominant theme in all the sectarian hagiographies that provided the respective sects with a lineage. The origin of the lineage in most of cases was traced to Rāmānuja. In this manner, each sect with its lineage claimed to represent the uniform Śrīvaiṣṇava community. Projection of a uniform community became important for establishing claims in the competitive spheres of resource control in the temples. It represented an integrative framework, whereby devotees could be from any section of the society. Therefore, the concept of uniformity made the caste ascription secondary to that of a community.

Multiplicity implied that within the overarching Śrīvaiṣṇava community there were sub-communities with their respective traditions. Multiple identities were based on caste, region, matha, and individual ācāryas, that is, the *svayamācāryas*. Plural identities were evident at two levels—one, at the level of a Śrīvaiṣṇava believer; two, at the level of a Śrīvaiṣṇava ācārya. For a Śrīvaiṣṇava brāhmaṇa believer, the basic affiliation was related to his family deity, followed by his ācārya and ācārya's matha or temple, and finally a brahmanical temple. For a non-brāhmaṇa believer, affiliatory pattern included his occupational or caste status, followed by the village deity, the region, then the ācārya who may be the *maṭhadhipati* (the head of a matha) or an *ācāryapurusa* or svayamācārya, and finally a brahmanical temple. In the multiple identities, the ācārya emerged as the focal point in which the pre-existing affiliations converged. The concept of a guru was epitomized in the ācārya who was the spiritual guide as well as the initiator of the community. Hence, of all the levels of identities, the one at the level of the ācārya became important as it linked the disparate groups into the mainstream Śrīvaiṣṇava community, through the ācāryic institutional organization. The ācāryas then became the disseminator of Śrīvaiṣṇavism by re-articulating the tradition according to the changing context and need of the community. These religious leaders projected an independent identity that became the basis for establishing power and authority and a large following. In this context, the composition of a genealogy to create an antiquated lineage became an important textual exercise for the Śrīvaiṣṇavas in the post-Rāmānuja period, particularly when the religious leaders tried to establish a strong institutional organization with a large following. Hence, within the community, multiplicity created a hierarchy of identities, with the ācāryic one at the top, followed by the identities of the brāhmaṇas and the non-brāhmaṇa elites. At the bottom of the hierarchy were those groups of non-brāhmaṇas who occupied a marginalized varṇa status within the caste system.

Today, the division into the Vaṭakalai and Teṅkalai sects represents the *duality* within the Śrīvaiṣṇava community. Vaṭakalai, meaning north—that is, the northern part of the Tamil region with Kāñcīpuram as the religious centre—is supposed to be Sanskritic, therefore brahmanical in orientation. Teṅkalai, that is, the southern part of the Tamil region with Śrīraṅgam as the centre is projected as adhering to the Prabandhic or the Tamil tradition. The identity of a Vaṭakalai and Teṅkalai has become an enduring one so much so that even the historical past of the Śrīvaiṣṇava community is identified along these sectarian lines. Similarly, the institutional set-ups of the temples and maṭhas have acquired the sectarian affiliations, as is evident from the religious centres of the sects, Kāñcīpuram (Vaṭakalai) and Śrīraṅgam (Teṅkalai) respectively.

Thus, the Śrīvaiṣṇava community identity can be understood through the analysis of the textual tradition, as characterized by *uniformity*, *multiplicity*, and *duality*. It is also stated that the community emerged as a coherent structure when the normative tradition, as represented in the texts, evolved a religious philosophy that became the ideological basis of the institutions and the pilgrimage process in post-twelfth century CE. However, none of these categories through which the community identity has been understood were stabilized until the end of the sixteenth century CE. They were constantly evolving and modified upon, and contributed to the fluidity in the community consciousness and its sectarian affiliations. The socio-political context against which the identity construction took place and crystallized thereafter also contributed to the fluidity within the Śrīvaiṣṇava community.

II

Certain shifts in the policies of the colonial administration and the idea of secularity that underlined the colonial modernity influenced the identities of the Śrīvaiṣṇavas. First, the community was gradually ossified into Vaṭakalais and Teṅkalais, which emerged as clear sectarian categories, vested with specific temple rights and authorities from the eighteenth century onwards when the British rule was established in south India. Second, a process of creating the brahmanical self and a homogeneous community manifested simultaneously in the new enterprise of history writing. Such a project was perhaps a response to the institutional reconfiguration in the colonial state that eroded the older system of community control and identity. Thus, the history writing probably had the purpose of providing a sense of past that the Śrīvaiṣṇavas could identify with, and hence prevent their deracination.

In the pre-British period, the king acted as the arbitrator of disputes by virtue of being the 'protector' of the temple. This required him to interact with the temple. The orders of the king were not 'legislative' but 'administrative', whereby there was neither cogent legal frame nor a coherent bureaucracy that dealt with the temple matters (Appadurai 1981: 214). However, the ruler intervened according to the need of the hour and did not have any permanent hold over the temple whose affairs were managed by different Śrīvaiṣṇava groups. At the same time, the ruler interacted with the sectarian leaders through the temple for a share in the temple honours that gave him political and economic control over resources (Appadurai 1981: 63–104).

This was the politico-cultural universe with which the British had to negotiate when they took over as rulers in south India (Appadurai 1981: 17). From the eighteenth century onwards, a series of interactions between the colonial government and the temple authorities began. The colonial state's takeover of the temple managements, opposed strongly by the British missionaries, was an attempt to secularize and push religious control to the margins of the political and public spheres. It should be noted that the colonial state did not require the sanction of the temple for legitimizing their authority. However, they had to negotiate 'with the structural and cultural needs of the temple community' during various conflicts between different Śrīvaiṣṇava groups in the temple (Appadurai 1981: 17). As a solution, the colonial state provided the Śrīvaiṣṇavas 'with a fresh set of categories within which to frame their interests in the redistributive process of the temple' (Appadurai 1981: 17). Arjun Appadurai points out that the principles that determined the management of the temple, its control, and the authority within it underwent a process of transformation with the British expanding their involvement in the temple on one hand, but refusing to mediate in the disputes on the other, preferring the help of the native people as intermediaries and arbitrators (Appadurai 1981: 215–17). Such an ambivalent attitude on the part of the colonial state created complexities leading to situations of disputes over the temple rights.

However, from nineteenth century onwards, the colonial administration began to withdraw from the temple conflicts as arbitrators and shifted litigation cases to the court. The language of the judiciary required clear-cut bureaucratic categories for defining the rights of control and, therefore, the need arose to establish distinct sectarian identities cutting across the regional frontiers based on common interests. Subsequently, the Śrīvaiṣṇavas, one of the groups affected by these measures, found themselves administratively marginalized in their very own institutions. The maṭhas, ācāryapurusas, the Vaṭakalais, and Teṇkalais had to reorient their interactions and privileges vis-à-vis the colonial state. The classic universal modernity separating the sacred and the secular was at work here, although it needs to be stated that colonial modernity was a dynamic process that negotiated with and was influenced by its interaction with the Indian context. It is this shift from the state to the Anglo-Indian court with a codified legal system as the conciliator of temple disputes that characterized one of the dimensions of colonial modernity. Now, the temple authorities had to deal with the judiciary and not the state. This was an unfamiliar situation for the Śrīvaiṣṇavas who were, until now, used to interacting with the state and the rulers at the time of disputes. As a reaction, the fluidity of the religious boundaries began to be somewhat hardened. The pre-existing alignments across the Sanskrit and Tamil traditions gradually crystallized into distinct sects of the Vaṭakalais and Teṇkalais respectively.

Thus, the traditional religious consciousness articulated mainly through the institutional frame of the temple was now being reconfigured and reformulated. In his research on the Śrī Pārthasārathīsvāmī temple at Triplicane in Chennai, Arjun Appadurai remarks:

> In the pre-British period, the term *Teṇkalai* appears to have indicated a pan-regional schism in the Śrī Vaisnava community in South India, which had temple control as one of its competitive expressions. In the early British period, at least in the Śrī Pārtasārati Svāmi Temple, it appears to have become a primary and *contrastive* category, whereby certain Sri Vaisnavas in Triplicane resisted the attempts of other Vaisnavas

called the Vaṭakalai to share in the control of the temple. In the first half of the nineteenth century, through the actions of the British revenue officials, this de facto eighteenth century *Teṇkalai* victory was made the basis of a potentially far-reaching piece of bureaucratic codification, whereby the election of the trustees for the temple was henceforth to be 'left to the suffrage of the community of the Tengala sect as has heretofore been customary.' By this time, the term *Teṇkalai* had lost its pan-regional, theological, and ritual connotations and become a potential sociopolitical category, denoting the local constituency that was to control the temple. (Appadurai 1981: 215–16; italics original)

While on one hand colonial modernity's distance from religion had ramifications for the Śrīvaiṣṇava identity as Vaṭakalai and Teṇkalai, on the other hand it led to a rise of identity consciousness which made the Śrīvaiṣṇava brāhmaṇas embark on a project of writing the history of the community. As stated in the previous section, the awareness of belonging to a distinct Śrīvaiṣṇava community can be traced back to the historical past in textual traditions and to the institutional structures of the temples and the maṭhas. The modern writings on the community that started emerging around the late nineteenth and especially early twentieth centuries presented a consolidated and seamless history that, in many ways, diluted the multiple traditions of caste and regions existing within the Śrīvaiṣṇava community and created a new exclusive homogeneous modern self. The varied documentations were either hardly registered or completely ignored. The works of several important thinkers and nationalists such as Ālkondaville Gōvindāchārya, C.R. Srinivasa Aiyengar, S. Krishnaswami Aiyangar, V. Rangachari, and so on, focused on the Ālvārs and ācāryas till Rāmānuja and a few extended it to Vedāntadeśika and Maṇavāḷamāmuni.[7] However, while independent documentations of the temples and the maṭhas existed, they were not a part of the histories that were being written.

It needs to be stated that while using the textual sources, especially the guruparamparās and the *stotras* (praise poems), these modern writings often overlooked the variations in the narratives and the complexities arising from them. Hence, the identity of a Śrīvaiṣṇava in the late nineteenth and twentieth centuries in the public domain essentially meant being a brāhmaṇa adhering to the reverential lineage of the Ālvārs and ācāryas till Rāmānuja. Consequently, such an interaction led to the thematic accent on the homogeneous delineation of the past, in which the Ālvār phase and the life of the ācāryas till Rāmānuja received prominence. The avowed dissent of the Ālvārs in general and Rāmānuja in particular against the caste hierarchy highlighted the notion of social reform. As a result, the subsequent phase in which the split into Vaṭakalai and Teṅkalai took place was virtually ignored. Finally, the non-brāhmaṇas such as the Śāttada Śrīvaiṣṇavas, who had a significant share in the temple authorities in the sixteenth century, were almost left out from this delineation of the past.[8]

Why was such a unilinear homogeneous identity delineated? To look for answers to this question, it is crucial that one examines the audience such writings addressed and the contexts in which they were articulated. It needs to be stated here that while the project of history writing had become an integral part of the nationalistic agenda, there were parallel history writings that on one hand reformulated definite religious identities and on the other repositioned them within the larger, universalistic historical narratives of Hinduism and the nation (see Oberoi 1994: 1–17). Therefore, the authors of such particular histories were products of a historical process that attributed to them their lineage, in this case the Śrīvaiṣṇavas. But this was now being refashioned and written in a manner so that they could become a part of the larger nationalist discourse and discursive dialogues related to the ideas of Hinduism. Hence, the focus was on composing uniform seamless histories that obliterated multiple voices and in this case, these voices were often at variance with each other.

How was the process of relating the particular to the universal achieved by the Śrīvaiṣṇavas? The writings of Ālkondaville Gōvindāchārya, S. Krishnaswami Aiyangar, and C.R. Srinivasa Iyengar articulated for the first time a modern community consciousness that linked the larger discourse of the Tamil tradition to Hinduism and the nation with the modern agenda of social reforms.[9] It should be noted that three of them lived between the late nineteenth and mid-twentieth centuries and belonged to the Madras Presidency, were nationalistic in their outlook, and also were Śrīvaiṣṇava brāhmaṇas. In addition, they were a part of the modern colonial state and followed modern secular professions. Ālkondaville Gōvindāchārya was a thinker–scholar, though an engineer by profession; S. Krishnaswami Aiyangar was a historian trained in the discipline of history and employed at Madras University; and C.R. Srinivasa Iyengar was a nationalist leader.

The attempt to be an integral part of Hinduism affected the history in two ways: one, secularizing the history writings; and two, focusing on the themes of social reform and protest against the caste hierarchy. With regard to the secularization of history writing, especially of the Śrīvaiṣṇava community, an alternate sphere of articulation of the religious consciousness emerged in the non-religious domain of history writing in which history was the modern discipline. Significantly, the histories were now not being written by the religious specialists—the ācāryas and the *jīyars* (heads of the maṭhas) who had composed the hagiographies. Now they were being composed by individuals well versed in English language, trained in the modern educational institutions, and acquiring degrees that certified them as specialists in modern disciplines, one of them being history. As mentioned earlier, Ālkondaville Gōvindāchārya was an engineer by training; C.R. Srinivasa Aiyengar was a law graduate who practised at Madras High Court and went on to become the Advocate-General of the Madras Presidency in 1916; and S. Krishnaswami Aiyangar acquired a degree from the University of Madras, worked as a lecturer in Bangalore, was elected a member of the Royal Asiatic Society in 1908, and finally, in 1914, was appointed as the head of the Department of Indian History and Archaeology at the University of Madras (editor's note in Gōvindāchārya 1982; Clooney 2004: 103–24). Thus, religion and community history were not marginalized. Rather they were taken from the limited confines of the tradition and imported to a secular, non-religious sphere of history writing using the modern tools of the discipline. Interestingly, the traditional Śrīvaiṣṇava texts continued to inform this writing and remained the main sources. Thus, now the Śrīvaiṣṇava was linked to the modernity that gave him a secular space to re-articulate his religious identity. Further, secularization was observed when the history of the Śrīvaiṣṇavas became a part of the modern discipline of history in the universities, its theology and religious personalities discussed in the classroom and not just in the sacred precincts of the maṭhas and the temples. Seminars began to be organized and their history became the subject of memorial lectures. For instance, in 1916, T.A. Gopinath Rao, a scholar in religious iconography, delivered a lecture on the history of the Śrīvaiṣṇavas in the Sir Subrahamanyya Ayyar Lecture series at University of Madras (Rao 1923).

With regard to the theme of social reform and dissent, this Śrīvaiṣṇava modernity articulated itself against certain intellectual trends that predisposed its history writing. The Orientalist discourse of the nineteenth century, attributing a unitary character to 'bhakti marg' (path of devotion), held that this 'bhakti religion'—primarily a Vaiṣṇava religion—possessed strong reformist tendencies to purge the polytheistic and monistic trends. This also posited Vaiṣṇavism against the Advaita of Śaṅkara that gave precedence to knowledge over devotion (Grierson 1907: 539, 544). Concomitant with the Orientalist discourse, there was a vibrant discussion amongst Indian scholars during this period on the notion of bhakti, religion, and religious philosophies. These scholars argued over the provenance of the term 'bhakti movement' and the influence of Vaiṣṇavism on medieval bhakti (Sharma 1987: 291–332; Hawley 2007: 209–25; Dalmia 1997: 338–429). Since Śrīvaiṣṇavism was associated with Vaiṣṇavism, it could have been assumed that reformatory capabilities were naturally an intrinsic part of it.

The terms of debates and discussions in the Tamil intellectual environment were informed not only by Orientalism, but also by the ideas of reforms, the Dravidian movement, and the national movement. Such an orientation can be traced back to the discursive domain of nineteenth-century India in which the discussions on social reforms influenced by the nationalist perspective were a response to the perceptions of religion: in this case, what came to be regarded as Hinduism. There was a debate amongst the middle-class Indian intelligentsia on the question of Hindu self-identity and Indian self-identity against the background of colonialism. The reformist agenda was linked with the stirring of the social consciousness and consolidation of Hinduism. However, although it is important to consider the consequences of the encounter with the West and the new equations that the colonial state and colonialism posed, the role of the Theosophical Society in the redefinition of Hinduism and its influence upon a specific delineation of the past was crucial (Sen 2007: 107–37). The ideas of the non-brāhmaṇa movement focusing on the language issue impacted the cultural and intellectual sphere, which had consequences for the Tamil literature (Venkatachalapathy 2006: 89–113). The Tamil literary canon, comprising religious and didactic texts including the commentaries, hymnal corpus, and hagiographies, was contested with the influence of the Dravidian movement and restructured. A modern literary canon comprising the old Cankam texts emerged based on the notion of 'antiquity in secular, historical terms' spanning more than a millennium (Venkatachalapathy 2006: 97). The older canon was now reduced to the category of bhakti literature with mere religious significance and was secondary to the secular Cankam literary tradition, with love, war, and heroism as important literary tropes. The development of print technology and the concomitant print culture made several of these old Cankam texts readily available. The underlying principle of the new canon, now purged of religious texts, was the assertion of Tamil as an ancient language and castigation of Sanskrit and the caste structure, both now considered as alien to the southern context and therefore irrelevant (Venkatachalapathy 2006: 104–10).

Amidst the background of the Orientalist discourse, ideas of social and religious reform, and Dravidian movements, it became crucial for the upper-caste Tamil intelligentsia to attribute the epithet of 'the great reformer and religionist of the twelfth century' to Rāmānuja and emphasize the Śrīvaiṣṇava tradition with an illustrious history of inclusivism and protest. Therefore, one of the important themes of the Śrīvaiṣṇava history, which these scholars focused upon, was the biography of Rāmānuja. The perspectives in these biographies influenced the development of some of the enduring images of Rāmānuja that not only circulated within the south Indian context but also became the basis of understanding and perceiving him at the pan-Indian level—an image of a benign saint who was not only a great exegete, but also a champion of the oppressed and the poor, stridently arguing against the caste hierarchy. His philosophy of the Viśiṣṭādvaita was perceived to have had a seminal impact on the medieval bhakti, for it made the act of *prapatti* or spiritual salvation through surrender to God accessible to everybody, irrespective of the individual's caste status. The biographies of Rāmānuja considered this idea revolutionary and radical. The larger frame of reference that resonated in these writings was that Rāmānuja was a 'social reformer'.

The nationalistic agenda becomes evident when the Śrīvaiṣṇava thoughts were juxtaposed against the Christian ones and declared superior. Their writings, especially on Rāmānuja, were informed by a comparative analysis with Christianity and Western categories of philosophical thought. Though seen in the writings of the Orientalists, even the Indian scholars were not disengaged from such a methodology. Ālkondaville Gōvindāchārya was one of the few Indians who, at the beginning of the twentieth century, used such an analytical tool to highlight the superiority of an Indian and associated the Śrīvaiṣṇava religious traditions with it. His work, *Life of Rāmānujacharya*, carries long footnotes explaining and countering the 'Christians' and their perception of Indian religion. A comparative analysis between Rāmānuja's ideas and personality with Christian saints such as St Augustine continued and was an important part of the discursive scholarly tradition (Clooney 2004: 103–24). One can also see similar ideas in the works of S. Krishnaswami Aiyangar, who vehemently denied that Christianity and the church at Mylapore influenced Śrīvaiṣṇavism and Rāmānuja, as the original Vaiṣṇava ideas came from the Ālvārs who in turn influenced Rāmānuja.

There was also a significant parallel consciousness of the religious self—in this case, a distinct brahmanical self—which also related to the modernity in its own ways. Assigning the agency of change to the 'Western-educated, upper-caste males', the reformist discourse in the nineteenth century focused on the brāhmaṇa religious figures, especially Śaṅkara and Rāmānuja, along with Caitanya and Maharashtrian saint-poets (Sen 2007: 108–9). The reformers realized that without the stirring of mass consciousness, the reforms of customs and traditions had no relevance. It is in this context that the image of Rāmānuja as a compassionate social reformer was juxtaposed with that of Śaṅkara. Within the topical discourse of social reforms, analysts of this period ignored the fact that the same set of narratives that reinforced Rāmānuja's status as a 'social reformer' were either absent from all the hagiographies or at variance with each other. It needs to be highlighted that by drawing from the religious reserves and projecting the idea of Rāmānuja as a reformer, the scholars, mostly brāhmaṇas, were using a conservative medium whose perception of egalitarianism was confined merely to the experiential aspects of devotion and maintaining the traditional social balance. This upper-caste initiative of projecting religious leaders as reformers was countered by the non-brāhmaṇa movement during the same period. It has been pointed out that the leader of the non-brāhmaṇa

Dravidian movement, E.V. Ramaswamy, popularly known as Periyar, rejected the reforms.

Thus, it was clearly not the Orientalist influence so much as the influence of the ideas of reform that seemed to have highlighted the notion of a progressive liberal personified in Rāmānuja. In addition, the attack on religion for perpetuating caste and inequality also could have led to a reassertion of the past to counter the accusation of inequity. Interestingly, while on the one hand the biographies on Rāmānuja projected him as a great social revolutionary, on the other they upheld caste values as essential for the moral order of the universe. In this connection, Ālkondaville Gōvindāchārya's *The Life of Rāmānujāchārya: The Exponent of Viṣishṭādvāita Philosophy*, written in 1906, becomes important. While calling Rāmānuja a great revolutionary, Gōvindāchārya's comment on the hagiographical narratives on contestation of the *varṇāśramadharma* (the four-fold caste system) did not condemn it; rather it justified its existence for the preservation of the universe. On the episode of Rāmānuja beseeching Tirukacci Nambi, a non-brāhmaṇa, to be his teacher, Gōvindāchārya commented: 'Rāmānuja admitted the legality and expediency of the caste system, and yet he felt it ought to be disregarded in special case', which was the case of him having non-brāhmaṇa teachers (Gōvindāchārya 1906: 60).

Gōvindāchārya then went to provide a long footnote, quoting from the speech of N.N. Ghosh at the Hare Anniversary Meeting in 1904 on the 'vexed question of caste in India, which the Christian will not understand.... For the purposes of spiritual evolution, a segregation of classes and occupations was considered necessary ...' (1906: 59fn2). Further, Gōvindāchārya's own comments (1906: 59fn2) to this quote were as follows:

> The warning voice against promiscuous intercourse and admixture of castes is found in the *Bhagavad-Gita*, I, 40 to 44; which may be read by all the devotees of this Holy Bible, and laid to heart before venturing to anathematize the caste-institution of India ...

Why was Gōvindāchārya so defensive about the validity of caste system? Was it because he was a brāhmaṇa? Was he also reacting to the Christian missionaries who critiqued this social order? To answer these questions, a detailed analysis of his works is required, which could be the theme of another research endeavour.

This essay thus discussed the complex interaction between secularization, modernity, and religion in late nineteenth- and twentieth-century south India, focusing on the case of the Śrīvaiṣṇavas in the Tamil region. It argued that the colonial state in India created a modern space in which they strove to maintain a secularity that aimed at non-interference in native religions and ceded the space of religious control to missionary activities. Simultaneous to this project of colonial modernity was the development of multiple indigenous modernities through which the educated middle-class Indians recast the traditions—mainly religious traditions—they had inherited, and reinvented themselves in this new modern context through the frame of religious identities. The Śrīvaiṣṇava modernity too was one such modernity that generated a specific consciousness of belonging to a religious community and, within that consciousness, the brahmanical status was reiterated and related to the larger brahmanical identity. This modern community consciousness further linked the larger discourse of the Tamil tradition to Hinduism and the nation with the modern agenda of social reforms. Consequently, such modernity created a public sphere in which the brāhmaṇa Śrīvaiṣṇava self influenced the modern discipline of history. A series of history writings evolved which, while discussing the Śrīvaiṣṇava past, projected a consolidated and seamless history that diluted the multiple traditions of caste and regions existing historically within the Śrīvaiṣṇava community, thus creating a new, exclusive, and homogeneous modern self.

Notes

1. See, for instance, Srinivasan (1982).

2. Tradition credits Nāthamuni with the collection, compilation, and edition of the hymns, which were scattered and lost. Nāthamuni is considered as the first ācārya of the Śrīvaiṣṇava community and lived in Viranārāyaṇacaturvedimangalam, a brāhmaṇa village (*brahmadeya*). The hagiographical narratives tell us that after listening to ten hymns sung by a group of devotees who visited his village at some point of time, Nāthamauni undertook a journey to various temples in south India where the Tamil hymns of the Āḻvārs were sung. He is said to have got in touch with Nammāḻvār spiritually through the latter's disciple, Madurakavi, who was also an Āḻvār. Thereafter, with the help of his disciples, Nāthamauni set the hymns to divine music in the temple at Viranārāyaṇacaturvedimangalam at the behest of God.

The narrative of the recovery of the lost tradition has historical basis, though overstated by theology. For details, see Hardy (1983: 248); Hardy (2001: 42–5); Dutta (2014: 67–72).

3. Some of the well-known Śrīvaiṣṇava hagiographical texts or *guruparamparās* are: Paṇḍita (1978); Perumāḷjīyaruḷiya (1979); and Mudaliyar (1952).

4. The mixture of Tamil and Sanskrit is called the Maṇipravāḷa. For details, see Venkatachari (1978: 1–46).

5. The Kaikkoḷa Mudalis are prominently mentioned in the inscriptions at the Śrī Venkaṭeśvara Temple at Tirumalā Tirupati. For details, see Sastri (1930: 241–308).

6. For instance, see Oḷugu (1961).

7. The following works have been used in this section: Gōvindāchārya (1906); Gōvindāchārya 1982; Aiyengar (1908); Aiyangar, Chariar, and Rangacharya (1911); Rao (1923); V. Rangachari (1914–15a), (1914–15b), and (1917).

8. For details on the Śāttada Śrīvaiṣṇavas, see Stein (2004: 81–101) and Lester (1994: 39–53).

9. For a study of social reforms in relation to Hinduism and the nation, see Dalmia (1997) and (2007); Sen (2007) and (2008 [2005, 2003]).

Bibliography

Aiyangar, S. Krishnaswami, Rajagopala Chariar, and M. Rangacharya. 1911. *Sri Ramanujacharya: A Sketch of His Life and Times*. Madras: G.A. Natesan & Co. Publishers.

Aiyengar, C.R. Srinivasa. 1908. *The Life and Teachings of Sri Ramanujacharya*. Madras: R. Venkateshwar & Co.

Appadurai, Arjun. 1978. 'Kings, Sects and Temples in South India, AD 1350 to 1700'. In *South Indian Temples: An Analytical Reconsideration*, edited by Burton Stein, 11–46. Delhi: Vikas Publishing House.

———. 1981. *Worship and Conflict under Colonial Rule*. Cambridge: Cambridge University Press Reprinted in 1983 (New Delhi: Orient Longman.)

Asad, Talal. 2003. *Formations of the Secular: Christianity, Islam and Modernity*. Stanford: Stanford University Press.

Bilgrami, Akeel. 1998. 'Secularism, Nationalism and Modernity'. In *Secularism and Its Critics*, edited by Rajeev Bhargava, 380–417. New Delhi: Oxford University Press.

Champakalakshmi, R. 1996. From Devotion and Dissent to Dominance: The *Bhakti* of the Tamil Alvars and Nayanars'. In *Tradition, Dissent and Ideology: Essays in Honour of Romila Thapar*, edited by R. Champakalakshmi and S. Gopal, 135–63. New Delhi: Oxford University Press.

Clooney, Francis X. 2004. 'Śrīvaiṣṇavism in Dialogue, c. 1900: Alkondavilli Govindacharya as a Comparative Theologian'. *Journal of Vaisnava Studies*, 13(1): 103–24.

Dalmia, Vasudha. 1997. *The Nationalization of Hindu Traditions: Bhāratendu Hariśchandra and Nineteenth-Century Banaras*. New Delhi: Oxford University Press.

———. 2007. 'The Only Real Religion of the Hindus'. In *The Oxford India Hinduism Reader*, edited by Vasudha Dalmia and Heinrich von Stietencron, 90–128. New Delhi: Oxford University Press.

Dutta, Ranjeeta. 2005. 'Community Identity and Sectarian Affiliations: The Srivaisnavas of South India (From Tenth to the Seventeenth Century)'. Unpublished PhD Dissertation, Centre for Historical Studies, Jawaharlal Nehru University, New Delhi.

———. 2014. *From Hagiographies to Biographies: Rāmānuja in Tradition and History*. New Delhi: Oxford University Press.

Frykenberg, Robert E. 1997. 'The Emergence of "Modern Hinduism"'. In *Hinduism Reconsidered*, edited by Gunther Sontheimer and Herman Kulke, 82–107. Delhi: Manohar.

Gōvindāchārya, Ālkondaville. 1906. *The Life of Rāmānujāchārya: The Exponent of Viṣishṭādvaita Philosophy*. Madras: S. Murthy & Co.

———. 1982. *The Holy Lives of the Azhvars or the Dravida Saints*. Reprint, Bombay: Anantacharya Indological Research Institute.

Grierson, George A. 1907. 'Bhakti Marga'. In *Encyclopedia of Religion and Ethics*, vol. 2, edited by James Hastings, 539–51. Edinburgh: T. & T. Clark.

Hardy, Friedhelm. 1983. *Viraha-Bhakti: The Early History of Kṛṣṇa Devotion in South India*. New Delhi: Oxford University Press.

———. 2001. 'The Formation of Śrīvaiṣṇavism'. In *Charisma and Canon: Essays on the Religious History of the Indian Subcontinent*, edited by Vasudha Dalmia, Angelika Malinar, and Martin Christof, 42–5. New Delhi: Oxford University Press.

———. 2007. 'A Radical Assessment of the Vedic Heritage: The *Ācāryahrdayam* and Its Wider Implications'. In *The Oxford India Hindu Reader*, edited by Vasudha Dalmia and Heinrich von Stietencron, 29–49. New Delhi: Oxford University Press.

Hawley, John Stratton. 2007. 'Introduction'. *International Journal of Hindu Studies*, 11(3): 209–25.

Karashima, Noboru. 1994. *Towards a New Formation: South Indian Society under Vijayanagar Rule*. New Delhi: Oxford University Press.

Lester, Robert C. 1994. 'The *Śāttada* Śrīvaiṣṇavas'. *Journal of American Oriental Society*, 114(1): 39–53.

Mines, Mattison. 1984. *The Warrior Merchants: Textiles, Trade and Territory in South India*. Cambridge: Cambridge University Press.

Mudaliyar, Arangasvami, ed. 1952. *Panniāyirappaḍi Guruparamparāprabhā-vam*. Madras: Lifco.

Oberoi, Harjot. 1994. *The Construction of Religious Boundaries: Culture, Identity and Diversity in the Sikh Tradition*. New Delhi: Oxford University Press.

———. 2007. 'The Only Real Religion of the Hindus'. In *The Oxford India Hinduism Reader*, edited by Vasudha Dalmia and Heinrich von Stietencron, 90–128. New Delhi: Oxford University Press.

Oḷugu, Kōil. 1961. *The Chronicle of the Srirangam Temple with Historical Notes*, edited by V.N. Hari Rao, 49–155. Madras: Rochouse and Sons.

Pandian, M.S.S. 2007. *Brahmin and Non Brahmin: Genealogies of the Tamil Political Present*. New Delhi and Ranikhet: Permanent Black.

Paṇḍita, Garuḍa Vāhana. 1978. *Divyasūricaritam*, with Hindi rendering by Pandita Madhvacharya, edited by T.A. Sampathakumaracharya and K.K.A. Venkatachari. Bombay: Ananthacharya Research Institute.

Perumāḷjīyaruḷiya, Piṇbaḷagiya. 1979. *Āṟayirappaḍi Guruparamparāprabhāvam*, edited by Shri Tirukrishnaswami Ayyangar. Tirucci: Puttur Agraharam.

Ramasvamy, Vijaya. 1985. *Textiles and Weavers in Medieval South India*. New Delhi: Oxford University Press.

Rangachari, D.B.K. 1986 [1930]. *The Sri Vaishnava Brahmans*. Delhi: Gian Publishing House.

Rangachari, V. 1914–15a. 'The Life and Times of Sri Vedanta Desika'. *Journal of the Bombay Branch of the Royal Asiatic Society*, 24: 277–312.

———. 1914–15b. 'The Successors of Ramanuja and the Growth of Sectarianism among the Sri-Vaishnavas'. *Journal of the Bombay Branch of the Royal Asiatic Society*, 24: 102–36.

———. 1917. 'The History of Sri Vaishnavism: From the Death of Sri Vedanta Desika to the Present Day'. *Quarterly Journal of the Mythic Society*, 7(2 [January]): 106–18; and 7(2 [April]): 197–209.

Rao, T.A. Gopinatha. 1923. *The History of Śrīvaiṣṇavas*. Sir Subrahmanya Ayyar Lectures, Madras.

Sastri, K.A. Nilkantha. 1975. *The Colas*, vol. 2. Madras: Madras University.

Sastri, S. Subrahmanya. 1930. *Report on the Devasthanam Collections with Illustrations*. Tirupati: Tirumala Tirupati Devasthanam Epigraphical Series.

Sen, A.P. 2007. 'The Idea of Social Reform and Its Critique among Hindus of Nineteenth-Century India'. In *Development of Modern Indian Thought and the Social Sciences, History of Science, Philosophy and Culture in Indian Civilization*, edited by Sabyasachi Bhattacharya, vol. 10, part 5, 107–37. New Delhi: Oxford University Press.

———. 2008 [2005, 2003]. *Social and Religious Reform: The Hindus of British India*. New Delhi: Oxford University Press.

Sharma, Krishna. 1987. *Bhakti and the Bhakti Movement: A New Perspective: A Study in the History of Ideas*. New Delhi: Munshiram Manoharlal.

Srinivasan, P.R., gen. ed. 1982. *South Indian Inscriptions, vol. 24: Inscriptions of the Ranganathasvami Temple.* Srirangam: Archaeological Survey of India.

Stein, Burton. 1989. *Vijayanagara: The New Cambridge History of India.* Cambridge: Cambridge University Press.

———. 2004. 'Social Mobility and Medieval South Indian Hindu Sects'. In *Religious Movements in South Asia,* edited by David Lorenzen, 81–101. New Delhi: Oxford University Press. Originally published in 1968 in *Social Mobility and the Caste System in India: An Interdisciplinary Symposium,* edited by James Silverberg, 78–94 (Paris: Mouton).

van der Veer, Peter. 2001. *Imperial Encounters: Religion and Modernity in India and Britain.* Delhi: Permanent Black.

Venkatachalapathy, A.R. 2006. *In Those Days There Was No Coffee: Writings in Cultural History.* New Delhi: Yoda Press.

Venkatachari, K.K.A. 1978. *The Maṇipravāḷa Literature of the Śrīvaiṣṇava Ācāryas.* Bombay: Anantacarya Indological Institute.

5

ALOK KUMAR PANDEY

R. SIVA PRASAD

Sedentarization and Changing Contours of Religious Identities

The Case of the Pastoral Van Gujjars of the Himalayas

It is important to note that a considerable number of marginalized communities in India, for instance, the Van Gujjars, depend on natural resources such as forests, common grazing lands, lakes, and so forth, for eking out a living. Their relationship with natural resources is a symbiotic one and usually reflected in socio-religious expressions. This is largely revealed in their daily and seasonal activities linked not only to natural resources but even to other living and non-living beings, such as wild and domesticated animals, plants, and other species. In light of this, any changes due to development and modernity have to be analysed using the cultural logic of the members of the 'Societies of Nature', as they are referred to by Philip Descola (1992), who operate them. They consider natural resources as the creation of the supernatural and, in some cases, the residence of the divine. Hence, natural resources are not merely physical spaces or materials but also sacred spaces. It is in relationship with the sacred that the continuity of life may be comprehended for these communities. People's perception of nature is thus formulated by religion and religious practices. Hence, it is through religion that these communities conceptualize their everyday lives and their relationship with nature. Therefore, we need to acknowledge the role of religion in linking people with natural resources.

Contrary to this, the state views the dependence of the communities on natural resources as a threat. The communities are blamed for indiscriminate use and ruthless destruction of forests and natural resources. Further, communities' presence in forest areas is seen as a threat to wildlife. The state declares forests as protected areas or national parks and denies the traditional rights of communities to stay and access their resources. Modernity in the form of scientific management of protected areas results in ousting of communities from their traditional environs. This conception of state with regard to the relationship between people and natural resources alters the relationship between nature and culture when communities are removed in the name of development from their dwellings in the forest and denied access to natural resources.

Altering the Nature–People Relationship

A nation-state uses the notion of modernity to design development policies and programmes as a part of 'nation-building'. Multipurpose projects such as dams, mining projects, industrial corridors, special economic zones (SEZs), and declaration of protected areas are aspects of such modernizing projects.

For the conservation of biodiversity, the state adopts a 'scientific' approach as part of its scientific experiment to restore nature to an assumed pristine beauty by removing communities from their natural-resource base. The scientific view is that people's presence in the forests is detrimental to its rejuvenation, as they indiscriminately exploit forest resources. Reason and logic are invoked to support the argument that 'nature' free of people will rejuvenate by itself and return to a 'Garden of Eden' untouched by human beings, which is contrary to the facts of history (Savory 1991; Rangarajan 2008; Thapar 2008).

The removal of people from their resource base alters the religious ideas, practices, and identity of these communities. In a new context (outside the forest or natural-resource base), relations of people with the natural resources alter both within and outside the community. Since these communities are dependent on natural resources for their livelihood, in an altered resource context their traditional livelihood is difficult to be pursued. On the other hand, development initiatives by the state to improve the lives of nomadic communities results in sedentarizing them. Further, agriculture is imposed as an appropriate livelihood that is alien to these communities. The sedentarization results in a complete break between people, livelihoods, and natural resources. Hence, it leads to altering livelihoods and social relations in the context of new livelihoods and resources. The new livelihood—in most cases, agriculture—is difficult to adopt as it requires a specialized knowledge, given that these communities have never practised agriculture in the past. The communities, hence, are susceptible to vulnerability as they become dependent on the knowledge and resources of the dominant others. This changing context of livelihoods, resources, and social relations forces the communities to redefine their identity and relationship with nature. In this context of modernity, the indigenous communities are drawn into the 'mainstream' world, particularly through the processes of the state's initiatives. Modernity is inherent in this process of state-making, while the costs are paid by indigenous communities as they are at the receiving and sacrificing end of development.

Conceptualization of Modernity and Tradition

Modernity is a relational term. The origin of the concept suggests a differentiation in religious beliefs and practices. It is viewed to differentiate the Christian era from the pagan (Wade 2007). According to Turner, modernity 'arises with the spread of Western imperialism in the sixteenth century' (1990: 6) and continues with the dominance of capitalism, the acceptance of scientific procedures, and the separation of the household from the economy. In a broad sense, the anthropology of modernity is 'what results from the diversified impact of capitalism on social formations across the world', and the 'impact of western scientific rationality and other formalized, calculative rationalities (in the Weberian sense)' (Wade 2007: 50). Anthropology engages with what Wade identifies as 'resignification and hybridization', that is, an analysis to explain and understand how local cultures accept, reject, modify, reconcile, or syncretize objects and ideas entering from the global context, hence generating not a single modernity but 'multiple modernities', a term introduced by Shmuel Eisenstadt and emphasized by other scholars (Eisenstadt 2000; Ben-Rafael and Sternberg 2005; Kumar and Welz 2003; Oommen 2005). 'The variability of modernities was accomplished above all through military and economic imperialism and colonialism, effected through superior economic, military, and communication technologies' (Eisenstadt 2000: 14). The process that by the end of twentieth century covered the entire world it was identified by Eisenstatd as the first true wave of globalization. This change brought in the idea that some societies are ahead of the others. In Latour's understanding, everyone is modern, which implies that the modernity is not of the Western kind; 'rather it is a way of contesting the Eurocentric assumption that some are "ahead" of others on a scale of progress' (Wade 2007: 51–2). Modernity is associated with a spatial origin and spread. Wade points out that Englund and Leach (2000) view modernity having a scaling connotation wherein it is seen as large scale and global, while its opposite tradition is small scale and confined to the local space. Inherent in this view is that Western modernity came first and moulded the rest of the world. It is, then, the bigger context for other processes, and transforms traditional societies towards modernization.

Modernity and tradition are usually analysed as a dichotomy. Tradition and modernity cannot be completely comprehended as concepts merely opposite to each other. 'The misunderstanding of modern society that excludes its traditional features is parallel by a misdiagnosis of traditional society that underestimates its modern potentials' (Rudolph and Rudolph 1987: 5). We need to understand the complex processes that are involved in the ways tradition and modernity interact as they are didactically related rather than dichotomously. Kahn calls for an understanding of the anthropological realities of modernity in a way that does not place the West in opposition to the rest of the world. '[M]odernization and traditionalization are very often *simultaneous processes*' (Kahn 2001: 663; emphasis original). Wade's way out of this teleology and scaling is to see '... all social forms as coeval and at the same scale or rather [see] all forms of periodization or historicization and all attempts as scaling (creating figure/ground devices) as constructions, whether analytic or "popular," with political effects' (Wade 2007: 53).

Harri Englund and James Leach suggest that 'modernity' has become 'a buzzword to such an extent that we must distinguish a meta-narrative from the word and make it clear from the outset that our focus is on the former' (2000: 226). The word 'modernity' may or may not carry a meta-narrative. 'The situations faced by modernizing societies are universal, even though the solutions will more often than not be unique for each society' (Black 1966: 164, cited in Englund and Leach 2000: 228). This observation calls for analyses of particular societies, as modernization assumes multiple forms (Englund and Leach 2000).

As modernity gains hold, it is believed that religion would weaken, or even vanish. Secularization theory suggests that modernity necessarily brings about a decline in religion, differentiation between religious and other institutions, and privatization of religion. This happens as 'rationality and science' begin to replace superstition, magic, and religion, what Max Weber calls the 'disenchantment of the world' (Oommen, cited in Kumar and Welz 2003). However, this proposition of replacement is empirically falsified (Hervieu-Léger 2005; Berger 2012). For Berger, secularization is replaced by the theory of pluralization and a religious revival around the world (Casanova 2010). Casanova proposes that

> ... we think of processes of secularization, of religious transformations and revivals, and of processes of sacralisation as ongoing mutually constituted global processes, rather than as mutually exclusive developments. Much of the difficulty in analyzing processes of secularization, religious transformation and sacralisation in our global age as simultaneous rather than as mutually exclusive processes derives from the tendency to use the dichotomous analytical categories sacred/profane, transcendent/immanent, and religious/secular, as if they were synonymous and interchangeable, when in fact they correspond to historically distinctive, somewhat overlapping but not synonymous or equivalent social systems of classification. The sacred tends to be immanent in pre-axial societies, transcendence is not necessarily religious in some axial civilizations, and obviously much contemporary immanent secular reality (the nation, citizenship, the individual, inalienable rights

to life and freedom) tends to be sacred in our modern secular age.
(2010: 3)

According to Berger, '[M]odernity does not so much change the
what of religious faith, but the *how*' (2012: 316; italics original). He
further contends that '... modernity does not necessarily produce a
decline of religion; it does necessarily produce a deepening process of
pluralization—a historically unprecedented situation in which more
and more people live amid competing beliefs, values and lifestyles'
(2012: 313). Secularization also leads to religion reorganizing itself to
meet the challenges that modernity leaves (Hervieu-Leger 1990: S15).
As Oommen (2005) suggests, the rise of a global culture is not possible as there are four interrelated processes in the creation of a global
culture in the era of multiple modernities. These are homogenization,
pluralization, traditionalization, and hybridization. For him, homogenization and hegemonization imply that the minority and weaker
sections are assimilated into the mainstream dominant culture. This
hegemonizing feature is countered by the marginalized groups in
search of their roots, hence resulting in revivalism and traditionalization (Oommen 2005; Kumar and Welz 2003). Oommen rightly argues
that '[i]t is not that that traditionalization is an autonomous process in
itself. It is a reactive process of homogenization and hegemonisation
that it implies' (Oommen, cited in Kumar and Welz 2003: 103).

In light of the aforementioned arguments, we can conceptualize
that in the current globalized world, with its emphasis on exploiting
natural and human resources for profit, it would lead to dispossession
and dismemberment of the marginalized (which includes pastoralists, nomadic and tribal communites, and the rural poor). Further, this
would result in depletion of resources; denial of access to resources;
loss of identity, livelihoods, and knowledge; disruption of culture; and
so on, leading to disharmony and unrest. In this entire process, the
state acts as the dominant player on the side of those who try to usurp
the resources of the indigenes. This one-sided version of 'development' that engulfs the so-called modernity leaves no choice for the
deprived who are forced to accept what is thrust on them. In such an
event, marginal communities reconfigure their cultural practices and
their negotiations with nature and the dominant others.

It is pertinent to note that the mainstreaming agenda of the state
has resulted in religious conflict and the hardening of identities

within the community. Further, once a community is dislodged from its traditional environment and livelihood, it redefines its social and cultural conditions, and thereby its identity, in the new setting. In this changing context, they experience a complete break from their traditional livelihood, practices, and environment. The changes brought in by the shift in economic activities result in altered religious and cultural practices. They redefine social relationships and identities from within and without. In the relocated context, dormant identities surface resulting in competing identities as there is a stronger interference of external orthodox ideologies in the life of the communities. The competing identities manifest in religious conflicts that were absent in their earlier context of forest-based pastoralism.

Pastoral Van Gujjars and Transhumance

Many of the traditional communities had access to natural resources through which they eked out their livelihood. These communities included the pastoralists, peripatetics, forest-dwelling tribals, and the rural depressed castes, including artisans and service castes. The process of marginalization has something to do with resources and access to them. It is important to note that the resources in the past were communally owned, controlled, and managed. People had access to and use-rights over them. The process of the state taking over community resources is one of the major factors for increasing the pace of marginalization of a large majority of these communities. The state always thought of sedentarizing the nomadic communities to settle them as a part of its modernizing and mainstreaming agenda. Thus, the process of sedentarization also coincided with the process of 'modernization'. It is in this context that the present chapter deals with the process of sedentarization of Van Gujjars of the Himalayas and its consequences.

Traditionally, the nomadic Muslim Van Gujjar (*van* in Hindi means forest, and Gujjar is the name of the community) are transhumant grazers. Nomadic pastoralism[1] for the Gujjars is a cultural way of life enmeshed with ecology. The Van Gujjars (Gujjars from now on) live in the forest of Uttarakhand and depend on it for their survival. They seasonally move to the high-altitude grasslands in the Himalayas[2] during the summer and return to the Siwalik plains in the winter. In the plains, they live in huts (*chan*) constructed in the forests of Uttarakhand. They depend on their water-buffalo (*mais*) herds to eke out their livelihood. The forest and grasslands are central to their lives, as their buffaloes eat the leaves of tree branches that are lopped (*path badhno*) by them. In high-altitude mountains, grasslands are the source of food for the buffaloes. The milk from the buffaloes is sold to diary owners known as Banias in Dehradun, the capital of Uttarakhand, and the Hindu pilgrim town of Haridwar.

On 12 August 1983, parts of the forests of Uttarakhand (erstwhile Uttar Pradesh) were declared as Rajaji National Park (RNP). This culminated in the termination of the traditional rights of the Gujjars in the forests. The process of removal of the Gujjars from the forest continues: with several families still to be identified as beneficiaries of the relocation package of the state, not all Gujjars have left the forest. Technically, for a forest area to be denoted as a national park, there should be no human presence in it. Thus, the removal of the Gujjars from their traditional dwelling has led to an alteration in their access to resources, livelihood, and identity.

Short-term nomadic movements occur in the plains (known as *des*) of Uttarakhand. The Gujjars during the winter season migrate to the hills in the lesser Himalayas (*kandi*) for lopping of trees and return to their homesteads (known as *dera*) in the plains at the end of the lopping season. Long-term migration is when the Gujjars migrate to the high-altitude mountain (locally called *paad*) grasslands (*panjal*) and return to the des in the winter months. Local migration spans anywhere between 20 and 35 kilometres. Long-term migration covers approximately 200 kilometres or sometimes even more. During the summer months, the relocated Gujjars migrate to new grazing areas in the district of Bijnor, Uttar Pradesh. This migration is relatively new.

State Forest Policy and the Van Gujjar

Historically, up to the Mughal period, there was minimum interference of the ruling regimes in the management and use of common property resources (CPR) of the people (Singh 1986). The colonial state began interfering by regulating the relationship between people and the CPR through some enactments. It resulted in the denial of use by declaring forests as 'reserved' or 'protected' territories. Colonial laws permitted the declaration of forests as state property. Such enforcement of laws altered the relationship between people and their livelihood-earning resource. Such exclusionary laws not only altered people and resource relations, but also changed people's view of the state. People began witnessing interference through stronger state regulation in their resource use. The colonial Forest Department introduced a permit system for the access to and use of forest resources. These were reflected in the Forest Working Plans prepared once in every ten years that guided the department's strategies.

The forest policy of the state of Uttarakhand[3] can be categorized into three phases: the colonial phase from 1815 to 1947, the postcolonial phase from 1947 to 1972, and the post-1972 phase when the Wildlife Protection Act was passed. The colonial forest policy concentrated on commercial forestry for generating revenue by the sale of wood and forest resources. Hence, people's use of the forest was seen as destructive to the forest, as it reduced the resources that the British administration wanted to usurp. The postcolonial phase was only a continuation of the colonial legacy which perceived the people's presence in the forest and its use for their livelihood as harmful to the forest. Hence, a complete removal of these communities from the forests was the only solution to 'save' them from destruction. The colonial administration protected forests for their commercial interests, while in the postcolonial phase, this was done for the 'conservation' of forests.

The Wildlife Protection Act enacted in 1972 was the watershed for an increase in the scale of formation of wildlife parks and protected areas. It seems fitting to highlight the introduction of the Wildlife Protection Act that impacted communities which depended directly on forests and other natural resources for living. Communities dependent on large tracts of forest areas, waterscapes, and landscapes for their livelihood were ousted from these areas. Currently, the model preferred by the state to conserve nature is the one that removes communities away from the resources they depend on.

The state declared its claim over forests and land by introducing the permit system. The system aimed at regulating people's access to natural resources and acted as a means of generating revenue. The permit allows a large number of buffaloes to graze but allows only a small number of buffaloes to feed on the leaves lopped by the Gujjars.

There is a fundamental difference between the notion of property between the state of Uttarakhand and the Gujjars living in its forests. For these Gujjars, natural resources are a common property, and buffalo herds and forests for lopping are privately owned by them.

The colonial and postcolonial phases, through the working plans, devised rules for the Gujjars' access to forests. Thus, Gujjar pastoral life was dictated by the policy of the Forest Department. The number of buffaloes allotted for grazing and lopping varied. Resource access by the rotational lopping method deprived fodder to Gujjar livestock, thereby impacting their livelihood. Further, the reduction in grasslands due to a shift to the commercial forestry programme and the planting of eucalyptus trees had serious bearing on the Gujjars. Ali, a Gujjar, remarked that the Forest Department began planting eucalyptus trees in the Tarai region during 1965–7. This prevented the undergrowth of grass for their buffaloes to graze. The indigenous tree species were replaced by commercial trees that deprived the Gujjar buffaloes of tree fodder, leading to a decline in milk yield.

The foresters viewed the traditional grazing and lopping practices of the Gujjars as destructive to the forest. Hence, they felt that their practices had to be regulated or stopped. This had implication for the livelihood of Gujjars and their relationships with the other communities. It also affected their relationship with the natural-resource endowments. Gadgil and Guha observe that 'the colonial state radically defined property rights, imposing on the forest a system of management whose priorities sharply conflicted with earlier systems of local use and control' (Gadgil and Guha 1992: 264).

The colonial notion that grazing cattle and people's use of the forest led to its destruction and was absolutely incompatible with forest conservancy took precedence in determining people's relationship with nature. The perception that the traditional management practice of setting grass on fire for its rejuvenation is detrimental to forests gained primacy. The local people's presence in the forest was discouraged. There was a growing insensitivity towards traditional forest-management practices of the people. Their customary rights to access resources were obstructed, as colonial administrators were of the view that the 'native ... imagined that he had a prescriptive right to hack and hew when and where he desired' (Atkinson 1973: 870). The areas where the locals felled trees and grazed cattle were demarcated and declared as restricted areas, and their access was declared unauthorized. One can perceive how resource bases used for survival by communities were suddenly declared as restricted areas, thereby depriving people of their livelihood. The British dictated the terms and conditions that determined the relationship between people and their commons. They exercised authority by declaring people's rights in them as unlawful as against that of the government. Atkinson wrote that the '[g]overnment could at any time step in and appropriate any portion required for its own use or for settlement with others, so long as sufficient land were left for grazing purposes to each village' (1973: 871). In 1873, 'waste lands', more than a thousand acres in local subdivisions, were marked off as 'government waste', making community commons the property of the colonial administration. The process of appropriating community commons was done by denying people's access to resources. Wherever resource use was a customary right, it was declared illegal, and privileges, under the head of concessions, were granted as a favour from the colonizers to the local people.

Without a scientific study, the British declared forests where cattle grazed to be of poor quality. The quality of soil was poor as these were grazing grounds for livestock. 'In other places where the soil is poor, but more especially where the numerous cattle stations formerly existed, and where in consequence the young trees suffered continually from being lopped, barked, and otherwise injured, and where they were more exposed to repeated fires, the trees are knotted, crooked, and with poor heads' (Atkinson 1973: 855).

Gujjars were under the constant vigil of the colonial administration. Their numbers and movements were often restricted. They were not allowed to move freely to access resources as these movements were against the principles and practices of 'scientific' forestry, and they had to obtain permission from the governments of the territories in which they moved. For those Gujjars who migrated to Sirmour and other areas in Himachal Pradesh (erstwhile Punjab state), cattle-grazing numbers were restricted to 500 in the British territory of Bushahr. Gujjars who migrated to Sirmour could not enter the British territory, but had to go along the Giri River (Dangwal 1997). These regulations were meant to restrict the number of cattle, their place of movement, and further restrict their traditional migratory routes. The effort of the British administration was to make the Gujjars' life difficult. Tough measures were suggested by a few officers. For instance, W.R. Fisher wrote:

> If my plan of excluding Gujars from Jaunsar and Bawar be adopted to the limited extent I have already explained, it will be necessary to establish police guards at Songota bridge on the Tons river, and at Lakha Mandal on the Jamuna river, during the months of March and April, when the Gujars go up into the hills; and to prevent them from passing through Jaunsar on their return, a police guard should be stationed at the Tenni bridge, over the Tons river, during the month of October. Passes for the number of buffaloes which will be admitted will be issued in October when Gujars leave the hills, by the forest officers of the Tons and Jaunsar Division. (cited in Dangwal 1997: 424)

The issue of passes after the 'Gujars leave the hills' was a shrewd strategy to reprimand Gujjars for violating the restricted number of cattle permitted to migrate.

The issue of passes by the forest officers was a method of keeping a constant check on the Gujjars and their livestock. Gujjars had to follow the same migratory routes that were fixed for moving up and down the hills. Here, they were not allowed to stray off the route; if they did, they would be immediately taken into custody and prosecuted for trespassing. The constant gathering of Gujjars for permits to migrate to the hills became a menace for the officers. Fisher suggested that a fee of one rupee should be charged per animal at Kalsi, before they departed for the higher ranges. It was hoped that this would discourage the Gujjars from going to the hills:

> Apart from grazing tax, Gujars were also to pay security money. This was first proposed by the Conservator of Forest, Central Circle, in 1902. He argued that Gujars were careless and violated regulations. To ensure their proper behavior he suggested a security rate. This security was to be returned if Gujars behaved properly, otherwise it was to be retained by the Forest Department. (cited in Dangwal 1997: 426)

Finally, eight annas per animal was levied. By 1921, the Gujjars were charged two rupees per buffalo, one rupee per cow, and eight annas per pony and donkey (Dangwal 1997). Gujjars were thus victims of the harsh forest policy. It is obvious that the officer decided what was to be 'appropriate Gujjar behaviour'. They had to face harassment at the hands of the officers for their survival. This provided a scope for creating a wedge among the Gujjars—some found themselves in the good books of the authorities and, hence, benefitted from this relationship. One of the key Gujjar informants narrated how his father had taken care of a British forest officer during an overnight stay at his dera. In return for this hospitality, the officer granted him the licence to possess a rifle.

It seems clear that the British devised the fee system based on the number of buffaloes reared by the Gujjars. The non-Gujjar villagers, in comparison, were charged lower rates. While on the one hand, the Gujjars were restricted from accessing forest resources, they were permitted to pursue their customary practices in fragments on the other. In addition, the British policy of permitting the nomadic Gujjars access to grazing areas while denying the same right to others created hostility between the Gujjars and the dominant Hindu communities and other sheep- and goat-grazers. The Gujjars who supplied milk to the cantonment and lumbermen working in the forests were permitted access to forest resources in the Garhwal region of Uttarakhand (Gadgil and Guha 1992).

Rajaji National Park and the Sedentarization of the Van Gujjars

After the intention to form the national park by the Forest Department, many Gujjar families have been removed from the forest and many more are still being displaced from their traditional habitats. This is not a mere separation of people from their natural setting, but a separation of a people from their traditional livelihood. However, the community is divided over the issue of vacating the park. The park is now 'protected' from the Gujjars and their pastoral way of life. The number of families or even the population of the Van Gujjars living in Uttarakhand is not available. Given that the Gujjars are nomadic or living within the forest, the state fails to register their numbers. The existing statistics regarding their population seem inaccurate. The Rural Litigation and Entitlement Kendra (RLEK), an NGO in Dehradun, estimates 5,532 Gujjars residing in the Rajaji National Park, with 12,278 heads of buffaloes (RLEK 1996, cited in Vania 1997). According to a study conducted by the Wildlife Institute of India (WII), the population of Gujjars in eight ranges of the park was 5,477 who belonged to

494 deras (households) and owned 13,150 buffaloes (Rajvanshi and Dasgupta 2005). The US Fish and Wildlife Service observed that there were 5,477 Gujjars inside the park (1998–9). According to the documents from the Relocation Officer, Uttarakhand Forest Department, the livestock population was 12,161. According to another study, the WII identifies 1,390 families living in RNP (Mishra et al. 2007).

A total of 1,390 families are declared eligible by the State Forest Department for relocation from RNP to two colonies which we will call Basti I and Basti II. They are identified as beneficiaries of the relocation package. Out of this, 512 families have been relocated in Basti I and another 613 in Basti II. In Basti II, 265 families are yet to occupy the land allotted to them. The total number of beneficiaries identified by the Forest Department for Basti II is 878 families. Although, on record, 613 families have accepted the land allotted to them, not all of them stay in Basti II. Many Gujjar families from Basti II, who stay with their kin in the forest (both in Rajaji National Park and in reserve forests surrounding the park), have been refusing to vacate the park as their names are absent from the relocation list. According to the Gujjar leaders and other Gujjars, 1,608 families are yet to be considered part of the relocation package.

There is a contestation between the Forest Department and Gujjars over the number of beneficiaries. Although the state identified 1,390 families as beneficiaries for relocation from RNP and allotted them agricultural land outside the forest, many Gujjar families have been left out. The Gujjars have taken the issue to the Forest Department, claiming that 1,608 families are omitted from the beneficiary list. In other words, 1,608 families (excluding 1,390 beneficiary families) are to be included in the list of beneficiaries of relocation from RNP. The 1,608 families are 'left-out' families (also identified as 'chutae hua parivar') and have not been allotted land. They are protesting their removal from the forest without compensation. Simultaneously, their traditional right of access to forests has been terminated, as it is a national park.

After the declaration of RNP, beneficiaries were identified based on a permit system that was issued during the colonial and postcolonial period. After the notification of the park, no new permits were issued. The permit system allotted forest areas and grasslands to Gujjars for grazing their buffaloes. It regulated the number of livestock in a particular area of the forest. It also determined how many Gujjar families could stay in the forest. If the Gujjars were short of buffaloes, their kin would graze their livestock along with the holders of the permit.

In 1987, through a government order, the Forest Department identified 512 families to be relocated. Although this was only a small fraction of the total number of Gujjar families in the park, the community realized that only a few would benefit while most Gujjar families would be losers in this relocation process. Representations were made to consider other families as beneficiaries too. In 1994, the Gujjars met Saifuddin Soz, the then minister of Environment and Forests. Gujjars made their case to the minister for the management of the forest to be handed over to the Gujjars, as they had been traditionally living in the forest and had better knowledge about it. Their nomadic pastoral way of life was harmonious, as it allowed resources to rejuvenate during their absence while they were away. The minister asked the Gujjars to give up their hope of becoming owners of the forest (JPAM 1998). The meeting led to a new definition of identifying a beneficiary: only an adult Gujjar who was married and had children qualified. Based on this new definition of a beneficiary, 878 Gujjar families were identified to be given land as a compensation for being removed from RNP.

From the community's perspective, cultural factors, such as the definition of age, adulthood, and marriage, were overlooked, and this created further confusion in identifying beneficiaries. The Gujjars did not traditionally maintain or record their date of birth. One was simply born. The estimation of the age of a teenage Gujjar or adult (eighteen years or above) became an issue in the relocation process for the state. The Gujjars would claim a boy to be an 'adult', but the Forest Department would reject the claim and not allot land to the 'adult' Gujjar. Even when the Gujjars claimed that a boy was married and pointed to the fact that he sported a moustache (a sign of physical maturity), the claim to a family and land was denied by the Forest Department. This further created conflict between the people and the Forest Department. This issue of allotting land under the relocation scheme has been a persisting problem between the state and the Gujjars. After various disputes and court cases between the two, a decision was arrived at to allot land to every family identified as an adult married male, his wife, and children. This cultural aspect of age, if taken into consideration for the purpose of allotting land, could have been dealt with dextrously. Now more families are demanding land based on the new definition of age that considers a married Gujjar eligible to receive a piece of land. The outcome of such lapse has resulted in another 1,608 Gujjar families not identified as beneficiaries of the relocation package of the Forest Department.

Competing Religious Identities

After the relocation from Rajaji National Park, Gujjar identity has altered. In the context of the forest, the Gujjars would identify themselves as forest–dwellers—'Van Gujjar'. After relocation, they would refer to themselves with pride as Gujjars who once lived in the forest. Since relocation, they are claiming more of an Islamic identity, visible in their practices in the village to which they have been relocated.

Gujjars are Sunni Muslims who are divided into two groups (*firka*): Deobandi and Barelwi. This division was not prominent in the forest context and Gujjars were not particular about the subdivision. They maintained that, in the forest context, while they were either Deobandi or Barelwi, they were all Muslim. After their relocation, the divide among the Gujjars has grown wider.

There has been a mixed opinion on the origins of the religious division between the Gujjars in the forest. Mir Gujjar, a sexagenarian, stated that since his youth in the forest he has been a Barelwi. Mam Gujjar mentioned that he was a Deobandi and he had converted to the Barelwi sect thirty-five years previously. Khanu felt that the division became apparent in 1985. Prior to the split in the community, all Gujjars offered holy food, known as *fathyah*, though today it is only offered by the Barelwis. Isa Gujjar, an octogenarian, commented that the split was Allah's wish: because the Gujjars were living immoral lives, the end of the world (*tabahi*) was near. The Bareilly *peer* (seminary head of the Barelwi sect) has been visiting the Gujjars in the Chilla Range forest, now part of the Rajaji National Park. There is a general agreement that the Deobandis are more in number in Basti I. There are a few households where the husband and wife belong to different sects. Marriage between individuals of different sects takes place in the relocated villages despite discouragement from the Bareilly peer.

The Gujjars' identity does not merely rest with being Islamic but the division is significant. The Barelwi Gujjars offer holy food known as fathyah, which the Deobandis do not. Fathyah is offered to their ancestors, Rasool Peer (Prophet Mohammed), and Allah. The Deobandi Gujjars accuse the Barelwis of being grave-worshippers, as they visit various Sufi Muslim tomb-shrines (*mazhar* or *dargah*) asking for their prayers to be fulfilled, which the Deobandis do not consider holy. Some even refer to the Barelwis as nonbelievers (*kafir*). The Deobandis do not offer *niyaz* (a religious gathering where fathyah is offered) after their relatives die. The Barelwis read the Sunnat[4] in the name of Mohammed, while the Deobandis do it in Allah's name. The Deobandis, when attending the fathyah ritual of the Barelwis, do not raise their open palms up to the level of their chest, which is a necessary gesture. They keep their palms on their thighs while squatting, which the Barelwis see as a sign of disrespect.

The conflict between the divisions is apparent on the day of Eid when both offer namaz at the Eidgah (place of offering namaz) in the relocated village. The Deobandis and Barelwis refuse to offer namaz together. The two sects often get into an argument over who would offer namaz first. In the past, fights have also erupted between the two over this. The Barelwis claim a superior status and want to offer namaz first. The Deobandis refuse to offer namaz at the Eidgah after the Barelwis. After many discussions, a resolution was arrived at, and the Gujjars agreed to offer namaz on Eid separately: first the Barelwis, then the Deobandis. Loudspeakers are attached to tractors and brought to the Eidgah, an open field next to a mosque where the Gujjars gather. It is used to amplify the 'Eid ki namaz' and the message by the cleric belonging to the seminary. They teach the Gujjars the Islamic way of life. The religious leaders of the two divisions are non-Gujjars. They come from outside to try and influence the Gujjars to adhere to their way of Islamic life. The seminary headquarters of both the divisions sponsor the construction of mosques in the relocated colony. As the ideology of both the divisions is different, the clerics socialize with the Gujjars of their form of Islam. The presence of non-Gujjar Muslim clerics belonging to the different sects is promoting a form of religious practice that is creating a divide amongst the Gujjar community.

The construction of the Barelwi mosque began in 2008 with funds received from Peer Miyan of Bareilly. The Barelwi and Deobandi Gujjars do not offer namaz in each other's mosques. The Barelwi believe in Rasool Peer, while the Deobandis believe that Rasool is another human who is one amongst the Deobandis. The Barelwis argue that it is Rasool Peer who has shown the path to Allah, and thus cannot be ignored in their prayers. As the myth goes, when Rasool Peer died, Allah sent a beautiful chest (*sandook*) to take him to heaven, but he refused and stayed back on Earth. This is the reason why people offer namaz in Mecca as it is the tomb of Rasool Peer. Deobandis believe that praying to Rasool is like praying to a human, while the Barelwis believe that if one does not believe in Rasool one is against the tenets of the Quran and Islam and that one has abandoned his faith (*iman se lautna*). Hence, they are not Muslim. While offering namaz, the Barelwis chant 'La Iillah Rasool Allah'; the Deobandis also recite this, but do not believe in Rasool Peer. The peer of the Barelwi sect asked the Barelwis not to give their girls in marriage to the Deobandis, and not to eat with them. The peers ask: 'When one is not forging relations then why eat with them' (*jab ristha nahin karna tou khana kyo khana?*).

Gujjars did not construct mosques while in the forest as they were not permitted to do so by the Forest Department. In the forest, one of the homesteads was used on a regular basis for offering namaz. As they lopped and grazed their buffaloes, Gujjars used to spread their shawls (*pattis*) on the floor, facing west towards Kabah (a building at the centre of Islam's most sacred mosque, Al-Masjid Al-Haram, in Mecca, Saudi Arabia), and offer namaz. On Fridays, Gujjars would come to the nearby towns and offer namaz in a mosque along with other Muslims. The Gujjars of Mudhal Soth, Chilla Range, used to offer namaz in the mosque at the Chilla power-house. In the forest, Gujjars appointed a *hafiz* (Muslim cleric) to teach their children to read and write in Arabic and Urdu, and also the Quran (*Kalam Pak*). The hafiz used to stay in one of the Gujjar deras. A salary was paid by collecting a fee of 50 rupees per month from each student who learnt at the temporary school. One of the deras was used as a school. Teachers were not employed to teach other subjects or languages. In some cases, children were sent to madrasas. Depending on the sect, a few Gujjar children were sent to Deoband and Bareilly to Muslim seminaries to receive training to become a hafiz.

In the relocated village, Gujjars offer namaz in the mosque being constructed through funds they themselves contributed. Officially, the government sanctioned the construction of two mosques. Currently, there are eleven mosques in Basti II. Each harvest season Gujjars contribute 50 kilograms of wheat towards the construction and functioning of the mosque. Gujjars who do not have grains make a monetary donation of 500 rupees. The members of the Barelwi sect consulted the peer at Bareilly, who recommended the construction of the mosque and contributed funds for its construction. A maulvi is employed to teach the Gujjars Islamic practices. Children learn to read and write Urdu and Arabic in the mosque. Each child pays the hafiz 50 rupees for his or her education. The hafiz guides the Gujjars during different namaz timings. He also conveys the message of the Quran and guides the Gujjars through various Islamic rituals during the holy month of Ramzan.

On the approach of the Ramzan month after relocation, the men of the Lodha clan (one of twenty-one clans that the Gujjars are organized into) in one of the sectors in Basti II felt that walking to the main mosque to offer Trabi[5] was tedious, especially during the monsoons as the rains made the place wet. In the dark, people, especially the older Gujjars, found it difficult to walk to the mosque. A Chouhan-clan Gujjar volunteered to contribute his land for the construction of a mosque so that the people living close by could offer namaz and read Salat and Trabi. He felt that he would receive *sabab* (good fortune) and the *salamat* (well-being) of Allah Tala (the almighty Allah) if he granted land for a mosque. It is considered a good deed by the Gujjars. The Lodhas and Chouhans in these sectors belong to the Barelwi sect. On the decided date, the Gujjars gathered on the Chouhan's land earmarked for the construction of the mosque. The plot of land for the mosque measured 20 feet by 20 feet based on their traditional measure.[6] The Gujjar members, on a 10-rupee stamp paper, wrote that the contribution was being made in the name of Allah. The document stated that the Chouhan was giving the land in the name of Allah to the community out of his own will and had not been forced to do so by anyone. The witnesses under whose supervision the land was given for the mosque put their thumb impressions along with that of the contributor of the land. After their relocation, Gujjars have been careful about legal processes. They documented the contribution of land to avoid any dispute. In the forest, they did not set much store to legal documents as proof of ownership or user rights as they were ignorant about its importance. During the process of relocation, the Gujjars were asked to furnish proof in the form of paper documents issued by the Forest Department to establish that they traditionally resided in the forests of RNP and it was only then that they realized the significance of legal documents. After this, Gujjars were careful not to misplace any official papers. At times, anticipating its use in the future, *any* piece of paper given by the government office is preserved.

The next day, a political council (*penchi*) was summoned to discuss the details of the contributions and the selection of the mosque-management committee. A consensus was arrived at regarding the contribution to be made for the construction of the mosque. It was also decided to employ a hafiz to teach the Gujjars the customary way of offering namaz and reading the Trabi. It is believed by the Gujjars that if one does not offer namaz during the year, but does so during the whole month of Ramzan and reads the Trabi, one receives good fortune (sabab). At the penchi, member names were proposed for each activity, that is, for collection of money, purchase of plastic sheets, mugs, and so forth. A president, vice-president, and a secretary were nominated for the mosque committee as office bearers. Each member's merits and demerits regarding their responsibilities associated with the mosque were discussed. Signatures were taken from each office-bearer and a few witnesses to finalize the proposal to construct the mosque. A fathyah was offered with 5 kilograms of *laddoo*s (a type of sweet) and then distributed amongst the members. Some Gujjar members volunteered to contribute wooden poles to erect the mosque. Wooden poles were valuable as they were not easily available in the village where they were relocated and the Gujjars needed them to renovate their huts. It was decided to initially construct a temporary mosque with wooden poles and a plastic-sheet roof until enough funds were collected for building a concrete one. The construction would require the labour of the men. Women were not present at the penchi, neither are they allowed to offer namaz in the mosque. The Lodhas took pride in the fact that they were constructing their own mosque. This would promote kinship solidarity among members of their clan. Members of other clans were also welcome to offer namaz in this mosque.

During the month of Ramzan, all—the young and old, men and women—intensify the reading of the Quran. It is considered as sabab. Observing a fast (*roza*) and reading the Quran is essential during Ramzan. One would hear older Gujjars asking the younger ones if they were reading the Quran in the mornings or afternoons. In the evenings namaz is offered and the Trabi is read. The holy book is wrapped in a cloth (*gulaf*); its spine is kissed and then touched to the forehead. The lines of the book are read aloud while sitting and moving back and forth like a pendulum. The younger members could not comprehend the meaning of the text; they merely read them in the hope of earning sabab.

Weakening Social Relationships

The removal of Gujjars from the forest has led to the weakening of the social relationships among the community members. In the forest, kinship played an important role for the Gujjars, as those who did not have permits from the Forest Department to access forest resources depended on their *shariq* (consanguines) or *rishtedar* (affines) to access forest lops or to migrate to the hills. Kinship in the forest context provided security of social life and livelihood for the Gujjars. Since their removal from forests, majority of the Gujjars do not require each other's help as they have been given land for cultivation. The relocated Gujjars have a substantially small number of buffaloes as they no longer have access to forests to lop trees. This has weakened their kinship bonds. The weakening of kinship ties and the uncertainty that looms ahead in the context of a new livelihood—agriculture— has led the Gujjars to salvage their social relations through the institution of religion. The ones who seek help from their kinsmen to access forest resources are the ones who have large buffalo herds but are unable to pen them due to scarcity of space in their new village. Because the kinship relations have weakened after relocation, the community feels it essential to reclaim their social relationship in another form. These relationships cannot be reclaimed through their traditional livelihood as in the context of the forest. Hence, the Gujjars strengthen their relationships through two institutions, marriage and religion.

The number of elopement weddings in the relocated village has increased compared to the forest context. Most cases of marriage referred to the political council revolved around matters related to elopement by Gujjar boys and girls married to other Gujjars. The

Gujjars stress the fact that the increase in elopement cases is due to their relocation, which has also further widened the gulf among kinsmen.

Another way through which they can reclaim their ties is in the form of religion. Many reinforce the need to pray together on Fridays and offer namaz. The community, with encouragement from the non-Gujjar religious clerics who belong to either the Barelwi seminary or the Deobandi one, through their religious messages and namaz, attempt to create a Muslim consciousness amongst the Gujjars. Gujjars stress the significance of abiding by the Islamic way of life. This leads us to the question of the reconstruction of the Gujjar identity. In the forest, they identified themselves as 'Van Gujjar' or 'jangle ke loge', suggesting the forest-dweller identity. Another indicator of changing identity is that the Gujjars have begun wearing skull-caps. In the forest, the Gujjars wore a *pag* (turban) or a traditional cap with a small woollen ball at its tip. Skull-caps have begun replacing the traditional headgear. The adoption of skull-caps suggests a tilt towards a Muslim identity. The forest is no more accessible to the Gujjars in the relocated village; trends suggest they are moving towards reshaping their identity as Muslim Gujjars. They lead an Islamic way of life amidst conflict and solidifying religious fundamentalism.

***

There is a view held by the government that agriculture is a beneficial economic pursuit and pastoralism is not ecologically and economically viable. Such a notion about livelihoods seriously impacts nomadic pastoral communities. They are made sedentary and forced to adopt agriculture as a livelihood, thereby affecting their traditional way of life, that is, pastoralism. Once communities are relocated into a new environment, they are unable to pursue their traditional livelihood as they no longer have access to the resources that facilitated it. Thus, adopting the new livelihood upsets their entire pattern of living, knowledge system, and ethos. The removal of people from their natural base and subsequent sedentarization emanates from the notion of conservation of biodiversity free of people's presence within nature. This 'scientific' approach towards conservation of nature is informed by the narratives of modernity.

This case study of Gujjar sedentarization and its consequence on religion seems to falsify Weber's idea of 'disenchantment of the world', that religion will be eroded as rationality progresses. In the Gujjar context, rationality and science are not replacing the religion of the community. On the contrary, science adopted by the state is altering the Gujjar belief and way of life. Berger's idea of pluralization is relevant in the Gujjar case, especially as different belief-systems within the Islamic religion gain significance for the community. But Berger's idea of religious revival and Oommen's idea of traditionalization may not be relevant in understanding the Gujjar case, as the community is resorting to a redefinition of their identity. The Gujjars who were once, to some extent, homogenous with regard to their identity, that is, they subscribed to a forest-dweller's identity and were Islamic, are no longer so. In the relocated context, Gujjars resort not to a single Islamic belief but to other divisions that are in conflict with one another. Moreover, the conflict is deepening within the community as each group is subscribing to a more religious-fundamentalist position. They are now becoming heterogeneous in their religious beliefs and livelihood pursuits with some holding on to pastoralism, while the others are caught between adopting agriculture and not practising either agriculture or pastoralism. They are in a state of limbo. The Gujjar case does not suggest a return to tradition but an emergence of novelty in the realm of religion laced with fundamentalism and conflict within the community. These processes play out in the context of tradition that interacts with forces of modernity.

Notes

1. There is a mutual dependence between livestock and people. People derive their livelihood by the sale of animal products such as milk, butter, clarified butter, and so forth. To sustain large herds of livestock, pastoralists move between different resource areas as these are not available around the year in the same place.

2. The high-altitude grasslands are part of the Greater Himalayas (2,400–3,600 metres); they lie between the Trans (3,600–8,000 metres) and Lesser (0–2,400 metres) Himalayas. This region is also known as the Alpine Meadows. The region is covered by vast stretches of open grasslands, ideal for grazing livestock. Gujjars migrate to this zone to graze their livestock during summer.

3. An analysis of state policy and its consequence on the Gujjars is restricted to the erstwhile United Provinces, where the Gujjars primarily lived. After independence, this geographical region became Uttar Pradesh (UP), and, in 2000, Uttarakhand was carved out of UP as a new state.

4. Sunnat is the prescribed norm based on the practices and teachings of Prophet Mohammed. It may include specific words, sentences, and practices.

5. During Ramzan, Gujjars observe a fast and offer special evening prayers during which long portions of the Quran are recited. These special prayers are called Trabi by the Gujjars. It involves many postures and can be tiring.

6. A Gujjar takes a measurement of 1 foot by closing his palms, forming a fist with each thumb sticking out and touching the other. A stick with the length of the fists is taken as a measurement of a foot. A rope measuring the length of the stick was taken as a measure of 1 foot ten times to arrive at a measurement of 10 feet. This measurement of the rope was doubled to arrive at a 20-foot measure. The mosque was temporarily constructed in the shape of a tent supported by four wooden pillars.

Bibliography

Atkinson, E.T. 1973 [1882]. *The Himalayan Gazetteer*. Delhi: Cosmo Publications.

Ben-Rafael, Eliezer, and Yitzhak Sternberg, eds. 2005. *Comparing Modernities: Pluralism versus Homogenity*. Boston: Brill.

Berger, Peter L. 2012. 'Further Thoughts on Religion and Modernity'. *Society* 49(4): 313–16. Available at http://download.springer.com/static/pdf/871/art%253A10.1007%252Fs12115-012-9551-y.pdf?auth66=1401685290_b9f b2cfc8e4891c3c3b2f3129cee70ae&ext=.pdf (last accessed 31 May 2013).

Black, Cyril E. 1966. *Dynamics of Modernization: A Study in Comparative History*. New York: Harper & Row.

Casanova, Jose. 2010. 'Religion in Modernity as Global Challenge'. In *Religion und die umstrittene Moderne*, edited by Michael Reder and Matthias Rugel, 1–16. Stuttgart: Kohlhammer. Available at http://bilder.buecher.de/zusatz/28/28042/28042081_lese_1.pdf (last accessed 28 May 2014).

Dangwal, Dhirendra Dutt. 1997. 'State, Forests and Graziers in the Hills of Uttar Pradesh: Impact of Colonial Forestry on Peasants, Gujars and Bhotiyas'. *Indian Economic Social History Review*, 34(4): 404–35.

Descola, Philippe. 1992. 'Societies of Nature and the Nature of Society'. In *Conceptualizing Society*, edited by Adam Kuper, 107–26. London: Routledge.

Eisenstadt, S.N. 2000. 'Multiple Modernities'. *Daedalus* 129(1): 1–29.

Englund, Harri, and James Leach. 2000. 'Ethnography and the Meta-Narratives of Modernity'. *Current Anthropology* 41(2): 225–48.

Gadgil, M., and Ramchandra Guha. 1992. 'State Forestry and Social Conflict in British India'. In *Peasant Resistance in India 1858–1914*, edited by David Hardiman, 259–95. New Delhi: Oxford University Press.

Hervieu-Léger, Danièle. 2005. 'Multiple Religious Modernities: A New Approach to Contemporary Religiosity'. In *Comparing Modernities: Pluralism versus Homogeneity*, edited by Eliezer Ben-Rafael and Yitzhak Sternberg, 327–38. Boston: Brill.

———. 1990. 'Religion and Modernity in the French Context: For a New Approach to Secularization'. *Sociological Analysis* 51: S15–25. Available at https://www.bc.edu/content/dam/files/centers/boisi/pdf/f09/Religion_ and_Modernity_in_the.pdf (last accessed 30 May 2014).

JPAM (Joint Protected Area Management). 1998. 'News on Action towards Joint Protected Area Management'. See http://kalpavriksh.org/images/ PAUpdate/PAUpdate1_17_Sept1994_Jul1998.pdf (last accessed 27 December 2012).

Kahn, Joel S. 2001. 'Anthropology and Modernity'. *Current Anthropology*, 42(5): 651–80.

Kumar, Anand, and Frank Welz. 2003. 'Approaching Cultural Change in the Era of Globalization: An Interview with T.K. Oommen'. *Social Identities* 9(1): 93–115.

Levi-Strauss, Claude. 1968. 'Structuralism and Ecology'. *Social Science Information* 12(1): 7–23.

Mishra, B.K., R. Badola, and A.K. Bhardwaj. 2007. 'Conservation Induced Displacement and Resettlement: A Case Study of Gujjar Rehabilitation from Rajaji National Park'. *Indian Forester* 133(10): 1341–9.

Oommen, T.K. 2005. 'Challenges of Modernity in an Age of Globalization'. In *Comparing Modernities: Pluralism versus Homogeneity*, edited by Eliezer Ben-Rafael and Yitzhak Sternberg, 149–69. Boston: Brill.

Rajvanshi, A., and J. Dasgupta. 2005. 'Assessment of Biotic Pressures and Human Dependencies on Rajaji National Park'. In *The Relationships among Large Herbivores, Habitats and Peoples in Rajaji–Corbett National Parks, Uttaranchal, Northern India*, 205–54. Dehradun: Wildlife Institute of India Publications.

Rangarajan, Mahesh. 2008. *India's Wildlife History*. New Delhi: Permanent Black.

RLEK (Rural Litigation and Entitlement Kendra). 1996. 'Community Forest Management in Protected Areas: Van Gujjar Proposals for the Rajaji Area'. Unpublished report. Dehradun: Rural Litigation and Entitlement.

Rudolph, L. Lloyd, and Susanne Hoeber Rudolph. 1987. *The Modernity of Tradition: Political Development in India*. Hyderabad: Orient Longman.

Savory, Allan. 1991. *Holistic Resource Management*. Zimbabwe: Gilmour Publishing.

Singh, C. 1986. *Common Property and Common Poverty*. New Delhi: Oxford University Press.

Thapar, Romila. 2008. 'Forests and Settlements'. In *Environmental Issues in India: A Reader*, edited by Mahesh Rangarajan, 33–41. New Delhi: Pearson Longman.

Turner, Bryan. 1990. 'Periodization and Politics in Postmodernity'. In *Theories of Modernity and Postmodernity*, edited by Bryan S. Turner, 1–14. London: Sage.

Vania, F. 1997. 'Rajaji National Park, Uttar Pradesh: Prospects for Joint Forest Management'. In *Building Bridges for Conservation*, edited by A. Kothari, F. Vania, P. Das, C. Christopher, and S. Jha, 186–221. New Delhi: IIPA.

Wade, Peter. 2007. 'Modernity and Tradition: Shifting Boundaries, Shifting Contexts'. In *When Was Latin America Modern?*, edited by Nicola Miller and Stephen Hart, 49–68. Palgrave Macmillan.

Williams, G.R.C. 1992. *Memoir of Dehra Doon*. Dehra Dun: Natraj Publishers.

6

PUSHPESH KUMAR

Religion, Erotic Sensibilities, and Marginality*

What prompts me to write this chapter is my own engagement with teaching sexuality to postgraduate students at the University of Hyderabad. The major focus of the course has been on the sexual and erotic as lived experiences and their governance and control in the specific contexts of India and South Asia. The participatory and non-hierarchic[1] approach adopted in the classroom often provided for heated debate and counter-arguments. An emphasis on historical and cultural specificity in dealing with issues related to erotic aspects of human life invariably drew the classroom discussions

* I am thankful to Vyjayanti Vasanta Mogali for facilitating this study by introducing me to several of her friends who volunteered to participate in the interviews and conversations which constitute the core of this chapter. I am also deeply obliged to Javed Pasha from Hyderabad and Hashina Khan from Awaaz-e-Niswaan, Mumbai, for specifically enlightening me on nuances of textual and lived Islam; to Krishna Naidu from Suraksha, Hyderabad, for his generous support in providing the office space for conducting interviews; and to all the interlocutors for their patience and sharing their personal stories. I am also immensely grateful to Professor Sekhar Bandyopadhyay, Professor Aloka Parasher Sen, and my colleague Professor Sasheej Hegde for encouraging me to write this chapter.

towards diverse traditions and multiple religious practices in India. Hinduism, Islam, and Buddhism, the great religious traditions, were critically evaluated in terms of their acceptance and openness to alternative erotic sensibilities.

The popular understanding that Islam is necessarily more intolerant and hostile to different erotic tastes and practices was consistently contested with the historical material made available by the prolonged, meticulous, and diligent translation and research carried out by Ruth Vanita and Saleem Kidwai (2008).[2] Kidwai, in his explorations of Islamic India, turns towards the Persian and Urdu literary traditions to see whether there was 'room' for plural erotic sensibilities and practices (Vanita and Kidwai 2008). He finds out that homoerotically inclined men are continuously visible in Muslim medieval histories and are generally described without pejorative terms.[3] He also demonstrated that *ghazals*,[4] which often gendered both the lover and the beloved as male, were subsequently heterosexualized through reformists' sanitizing of literary traditions during late nineteenth-century colonial India. These historical and literary materials do help in a way to extricate the Muslim past from alleged orthodoxies and bigotries as well as in denaturalizing the nationalist heterosexist Indian historiography. Arguing against the essentializing statements about the umbrella term 'Islam', Samar Habib (2010: xi) maintains that Islam is neither condemnatory nor forgiving, neither restrictive nor liberationist, but shaped by the cultures that adopt it, by the socioeconomic, geographic, and political states of such cultures, and by the exegetes whose interpretations are institutionalized over the centuries and by the forms of media and education that disseminate and propagate these teachings.

The Backdrop: Autonomy, Subsumption, and Interpretative Engagement

What enthralled and stimulated me to engage with this chapter, however, are the more contemporary narratives of queer Muslims' negotiation with their religious identity and erotic life within South Asia as well as in diasporic situations. Studies of religious organizations and movements, though still relevant, have failed to capture these everyday lived experiences and negotiations of religiously and culturally marginalized subjecthood. Writing about modernity and religious practices, McGuire (2008: 213) argues that scholars must study religion not as it is defined by religious organizations but as it is actually lived in people's everyday life. In globalizing situations, a particular religion's understanding of sexuality could often be incompatible with broader social and cultural developments that are moving towards greater liberalism and recognition of sexual diversity and pluralism (Yip 2009), although a simultaneous strengthening of the conservative orthodox position cannot be denied. In my attempt to explore the experiential landscape of Muslim queer erotic subjects for the purpose of initiating discussions among the participants of the course on sexuality, three broader expressions began to surface. They ranged from the distancing from formal religion through articulating 'choice' and autonomy, to living in fear and helplessness, to interpretative engagement with religious identities and erotic preferences. What follows is a concise illustration of these three delineations.

Ali Potia hails from Gujarat and works as corporate trainer and a freelance writer. He (2005) comfortably claims two identities, Muslim and gay, and critically reflects upon his religious context through his sexual self. In his illuminations, he seems to be claiming and articulating an erotic citizenship which he values over and above his own religious trappings. He writes:

> As far as I am concerned, the religion is very categorical—buggery is a sin and I will burn in hell for it. When faced with such overt hostility, why should I even bother to find legitimacy within the faith?... I may be a bad Muslim but I am perfectly upright human being ... the only reason I am stuck with the identifier of Muslim now is because of my name, and a certain missing piece of my anatomy (something I did not have a say in). (Potia 2005: 256)

This excerpt provoked me to ask certain questions. Can every Muslim person with a different erotic sensibility afford to articulate such an autonomous self and claim erotic citizenship? Do other sexually marginalized members of Potia's community split so easily and do they compartmentalize religious identity and sexual self? I came across another story, that of Saad Zahid from Pakistan, who writes about his fear and apprehension of living as a gay man in Pakistan. He ruminates:

I want to tell my family about it. I am afraid they will disown me. I love
my mom and dad so much. I can't even think to degrade them [*sic*] in
front of the whole society; I don't want them to be boycotted by society.
I will never like if they are subjected to funny jokes in the social circle
just because their son is gay. (Zahid 2013)

I encountered a third and very interesting trope of a 'progressive'
USA-based Muslim queer poet, Bushra Rehman, who once severed
her ties with Islam finding no acceptance in her religion but, in the
face of the prevalent Islamophobia in post-9/11 USA, felt an ardent
need to come back to the religious community. Bushra (2014) asserts:

After September 11, after the beatings, the mass arrests and detentions
of Muslim immigrants, after the suspension of their civil liberties, I
know that it does not matter whether or not I fast during Ramdan. I
am Muslim.... Since September 11, 2011 [I] have felt torn between my
loyalties to Muslims who do not understand my queerness and queers
who do not understand my Muslimness.

Bushra thereby feels the need to wear her Muslim identity while
retaining her queerness even if she is apprehensive of being accepted
by her own community. These three different expressions persuaded
me to explore the world of persons who follow Islam or identify
themselves as Muslims and struggle to navigate between their sexual
self and religious identity. Before I begin to unravel the narratives of
my own queer Muslim interlocutors from a few metropolitan cities
in India, it seems pertinent to philosophically reflect upon the three
different positions concerning the lived experiences of Muslim queerness outlined previously.

Potia's public acknowledgement of his queerness, his celebration
of privacy and 'exercizing of choice', and his readiness to privilege
his erotic self vis-à-vis his religious affiliations may derive from his
class position and his privileged location in the corporate world (see
his profile at http://www.sgpc.sg/wp-content/files/2015/10/Ali-Potia-
Profile.pdf [last accessed 7 June 2016]). Is Potia able to engage with his
own (gay) 'self' without having to bother too much about his religious
community—unlike Saad Zahid (trapped in family and religious
contexts)—because he associates with the politics of neoliberal times
where 'freedom' and 'right to privacy' are recoded as democratic aspirations with no concern for inequalities in commercial life and civil

society (see Duggan 2002)? In the diasporic context, Abraham (2009) perceives homonormative[5] attitudes as compatible with the neoliberal view of 'freedom' and 'privacy', which is partly responsible for the desire of some queer Muslims to closet their religion. It appears that only upwardly mobile elite gay subjects could confidently flaunt 'personal choice' and articulate 'right to privacy' while undermining whatever comes in the way. They might inhabit a world of plastic sexuality where affluence allows new ways of organizing intimate life.[6] Perhaps, here, class becomes more decisive than religion. Bushra Rehman's attempt to reconnect to Muslimness appears to be what Minawalla et al. (2005) would refer to as belonging to an interpretative community of queer Muslims located in the West who are explicitly 'progressive' albeit within the bounds of bourgeois liberalism.[7]

Considering these three registers encountered during my teaching engagements, I went about to explore the life of queer Muslims in some metropolitan cities of India. The prime concern of this chapter, then, is to understand how alternative erotic lives and religiosity are negotiated in the modernizing and globalizing context in India. Andrew Kam-Tuck Yip (2009) reiterates the need to develop a nuanced understanding of religion and the erotic as lived experiences in different geographical, political, and social contexts. Contexts throw up significant structural factors that such individuals find empowering and/or constraining (Yip 2009). At another level, the present case also intends to question the stereotype of a queer erotic subject whose life is supposed to have been extremely difficult because Islam as a religion is supposedly more vigilant, intolerant, and radically violent to those who deviate from the chartered path of religion.[8] With hindsight, I would suggest here that despite public homo-negativity and strong heterosexism among the Muslim population like their Hindu brethren, alternative erotic practices do exist and those who engage with them exhibit a sense of agency in contemporary times at least in the contexts of bigger metropolitan cities. It is pertinent to reiterate here that persons who are Muslim and espouse alternative erotic sensibilities cannot be regarded as constituting a stable cultural border (Abraham 2009). They negotiate their everyday life in a city space marked with the existence of the Internet or virtual community, civil-society connections articulating and spreading notions of sexual citizenship, and the anonymity of the city space, notwithstanding the aforementioned heterosexism and homo-negativity surrounding their lives.[9]

In a popular view, Islam is perceived as rigid in controlling all aspects of its believers' lives and intolerant of any expressions of sexuality outside the context of heterosexual marriage (Yip 2009: 2). It emphasizes the complimentary nature and unity of sexes (*zawj*), which is creative and procreative in accordance with hegemonic status of heterosexuality within marriage. Outside this framework, all sexual activities (for example, *zina* or adultery) and homosexuality are considered not only sexual deviation, but also a revolt against Allah (Abraham 2009). This popular and essentialist view fails to offer a nuanced picture of human agency, namely the capacity of individuals to construct lived experiences by resisting, contesting, and adapting religious orthodoxy and cultural hegemonic systems, as well as empowering and constraining the potentials and outcomes of such an engagement (Abraham 2009). The chapter is an effort to capture the everyday negotiations and lived experiences of queer Muslims in Indian city life.

Methodology

The study is based on the interviews with eight Muslims who identify as queer and hail from three metropolitan cities in India by using a semi-structured questionnaire. In order to gain access to participants in the interview, I took support from some local NGOs whose focus was gay men or MSM (men who have sex with men) and some queer-rights activists in these cities. My own connections with feminist collectivities enabled me to approach the only female queer Muslim included in the present sample. Four participants identify as 'transgender' (or TG), while the other three label themselves gay. Based on Abraham's (2009) study of queer Muslims in Australia, I will refer to my participants with letters of the alphabet to provide greater anonymity. A very brief introduction to my research participants is given below:

- P, male, from city H, in his mid-twenties with a BTech degree, works with an IT firm and identifies as gay. He is single and lives with his mother and sister.

- B, female, from city K, is in her mid-forties and identifies as a (trans) woman. She underwent surgery to remove her (male) sexual organ. With a diploma in Hotel Management she worked for a few years in a five-star hotel. She was earlier married to a Muslim man, whom she is now separated from as she wanted him to live free from stigma by marrying another woman and having a child. She lives by herself and works as a shadow leader with an NGO which caters to the sexually marginalized, particularly MSM and transgender people.
- R, in her early forties, considers herself as *nirvanhijra*.[10] She is a matriculate and works as a committee coordinator at an organization that provides services to and counselling for sexual minorities and victims of HIV/AIDs. She is married to a man and lives with him in a rented house.
- F, aged 24, has a BTech degree and works at a multinational company in city H. He is single and identifies as gay. He is a migrant from a small town and not out to his family.
- K is transgender woman in her mid-thirties; she has to lead a dual life of a man and a TG in order to remain within 'her' natal home. She completed her schooling and works as a community organizer at the same NGO where R works. She calls herself a modern TG. She is castrated but abstains from cross-dressing when she is with her natal family.
- T is a medico in his late twenties from city B. He was interning and expecting a good job offer at the time I interviewed him. He has plans to settle abroad to lead an open and happy life. He stays with his joint family with nine other siblings.
- S is an out lesbian from city D who identifies as a queer feminist. In her early forties, she is well-educated and associated with an organization that works towards the empowerment of Muslim women. She, along with her other queer (female) friends, initiated and established an organization for non-heterosexual women in her city. She lives with her same-sex partner.
- Q is a fresh graduate in social work from city H, speaks good English, and leads a dual life. S(he) is a hijra sex-worker during a part of the day and male when with her natal family.

All the research participants are educated. Despite differing levels of confidence they are aware of the homophobia, transphobia, and

lesbophobia. They are connected and exposed to civil-society initiatives associated with sexual-rights activism and have varying degrees
of awareness about what has gone on in the West as far as alternative-
sexuality politics are concerned. They critically engage with Section
377 of the Indian Penal Code, which criminalizes alternative sexuality,
and have been participating in Gay Pride Marches and certain cultural
activities addressing queer issues. All of them agree that bigger cities, in a way, provide anonymity enabling them to escape the family,
community, and neighbourhood at certain points in everyday life,
allowing them space for expression and fulfilment of desire in differing degrees. They have networks of friendship and community
beyond the heteronormative world; this alternative friendship and
community move beyond the single religious community. The three
gay men, particularly, are more intricately linked with cyberspaces[11]
that either initiate debates on issues related to sexual minorities or
provide cruising space for meeting and sex-dates. So, from the present
instance it appears that the self and subjectivity of queer persons in a
metropolitan space are mediated by multiple, though linked, institutions and processes. The Muslim queer community, therefore, is not a
wholly contained entity in itself, and religion, though significant, does
not yet fully delimit its existence. Abraham (2009) points out that the
contained community or neat political and cultural belonging is either
a chauvinistic logic or often questions of bureaucratic convenience.
Considering alternative friendship, kinship, community, cyberspace
engagements, and civil-society exposure of the participants, their locations appear more hybrid and diverse. It is important to emphasize this
hybridity as it enables agency and resistance in globalizing times.[12]

Questions were framed against the backdrop of the three different positions articulated by three different subjects discussed in the
beginning of this chapter. Autonomy from religion, fear of religion,
and reconciliation between the sexual self and religious self were
important points of discussion. The Islamic religious beliefs and textual prescriptions disapproving alternative erotic possibilities—zina
and *lut*—and innovative reinterpretation of the Quran *ijtihad* that
are verbalized frequently in the diasporic discourse of the (Western)
queer Muslims (see Minawalla et al. 2005) did form part of the present
dialogue and conversation.[13] The interviews were conducted in NGO
offices, face-to-face encounters in cafeterias, and also over the phone.

Navigating Desire, Negotiating Qayamat:[14] Emerging Tropes from Lived Experiences

This rather brief yet engrossed dialogic encounter unfolded several tropes which touch upon the nuances of queer Muslims' hopes and dilemmas of the everyday in some of the Indian metropolitan cities. Contesting, coping, conforming, and changing dominant worldviews about sexuality all surfaced persistently in the narratives. There may be fear of Qayamat (the Day of Judgment) but the intensity of desire is equally irresistible. If one is held accountable by Allah on the Day of Judgment, one must equally remember that Allah is also a forgiving mother who loves all her children the same. If alternative erotic desire is a deviance, there are other kinds of deviance that are taken for granted and assimilated in everyday life. The following tropes reflect the lived experiences and contestations and dilemmas of the participants.

Critiquing Duplicity, Supporting the Incongruous

Most of the participants in the interview cited a duplicitous everyday life within their immediate (Muslim) community and kin members (read male), in the sense that the 'normal heterosexual members' do not adhere to the prescribed Islamic (sexual) norms either. Spotting the slips and negligence of the powerful could be read as the resistance offered by the subalterns; this strategy is not unique to the present case but applies to any power situation (see Scott 1985). Stressing the contradictions and hiatus between the ideal and real of their own community members often remained central to the responses towards morality and sexual deviance. Participants spoke about the violations of prescribed code in mundane and everyday life by those who might despise alternative erotic sensibilities.

P, the IT professional, while reacting to the question that his sexual preference could be seen as un-Islamic by his own community, responds:

> Tell me how many people are really Islamic? Qur'an says that you should not stare at girls. We say this act [staring at girls] as—*aankhon se zinakarrahe ho* (you are *molesting* through your eyes [emphasis original]). But how many people follow this? Islam prescribes ways to have

sexual intercourse. We call it *saramga* [etiquette]. You should not be fully nude while doing sex and only penetrative sex is allowed, no foreplay or anything. But how many follow that? When I was a kid and use to play football, many boys used to deliberately fall on me—*ladke aake gidte the*. What you call them, gay or straight? Even if the community says 'we all are heterosexuals', we do exist here to question this lie and pretention.

Another gay man, F, says:

What un-Islamic? Let me tell you most of the men in my community would love to have sex with men and transgender [*sic*]. But they fear to come out because they will be shamed. Many gay men experience [their] first encounter of sex in their own families—a close relative might approach you for sex and the same person will condemn homosexuality in public. The original Qur'an was different. Men–men love was very much there.

K, the modern TG, contends: 'If same sex is un-Islamic then let me talk about the Middle-East. Same sex relation among men happens in plenty and goes un-noticed there.[15] Then who is un-Islamic?'

T, the medico, says: 'During my childhood I was abused by my own blood relative and I grew with that experience otherwise I might not have been this. Now let me ask you what is un-Islamic here? The person (the violator) leads a full "Islamic" heterosexually married life!'

S, the lesbian and women's rights' activist, argued:

Tell me a religion where homosexuals do not exist? And it depends upon where you are located and whether that location is enabling or disabling to talk about it? If you are in Turkey and Malaysia you can openly talk about your sexuality, but if you are in Pakistan or Bangladesh, the story will be different. This shows that Islam is diverse and not frozen everywhere.

Religion and Identity: We Cannot Live without Muslimness

The term 'Muslimness' from Bushra Rehman's (2014) story referred to wearing a Muslim identity while apparently being critically reflective about the enabling and delimiting possibility of such an identity from a queer perspective. While the other participants could not reflect on Muslimness with Rehman's interpretative consciousness, the majority disagreed with Ali Potia's (2005) stance of rejecting religious identity if it affected erotic life. His version of autonomy sounded little extremist to the participants. P said, 'I cannot leave my religion for the sake of my sexual desire. Rather I would like to know the real facts of Islam. Is Allah, the mother really differentiates among Her children [sic]? I am very, very happy to be a Muslim.' B, the transwoman, narrated, 'I see Allah in everyone. This is at individual level; I am in direct communication with Allah. The problem arises when everything comes to the level of *jamaat* [the community with its religious leaders]. So, in my personal communication to Allah I only see love and I love to be a Muslim, you know.' R, the nirvanhijra, dismissed Potia's position of relinquishing religion by saying: 'Islam me sabko bada martaba[16] hai [everyone is considered with distinction in Islam] yadi ek Hindu Musalmaan ban jaye to uska martaba jyada hoga [if a Hindu converts into Islam, 'he' will enjoy more eminence].' She further added: 'I regularly visit *musjid*; cannot leave this till death [*mare tak nahin chorna*]. I go in *kurta paijama* [long shirts and pants which are flexible and comfortable, worn by men in parts of South Asia] as cross-dressers are not allowed.' In F's words, 'I cannot leave my religion. Without religion, there is nothing important. I am more spiritual and less religious.' T stood firm in his argument: 'It is indecent to compare sexuality and religion and place sexuality above religion. You need to find out a way where you could be accepted by your religion and I think the time is changing and gradually it will happen.' As for K, 'Religion is bigger than individual.'

Most of the participants closet their sexual identity and prefer-ences from their respective families and communities in order to retain their religious identity externally while comfortably articulating their sexual desire during in-group situations. The latter situation is not exclusively Muslim but rather always mixed, with queer persons of other religious groups including Hindus, Christians, and others mingling and interacting with each other without necessarily being conscious of religious and ethical identities. Yip (2009), in the con-text of queer British Muslims, terms this conscious manipulation of self and identity as 'compartmentalization'; this occurs when sexual and religious identities are restricted to certain safe places. Unlike British queer subjects who might have to hide their religious identity anticipating Islamophobia, queer persons in Indian cities, at least the participants in the present study, do not have similar experiences. But homophobic and transphobic climates within private spaces such as the family and in public spaces force them to hide their sexual identity. To Seidman (quoted in Abraham 2009: 86), what characterizes the regime of the closet is deception and duplicity. Thus, if the strategy of compartmentalization is 'effective', it is merely an effective closeting; it is not an effective solution to prejudice. The effects of closeting could be psychologically devastating, as concealing one's true identity affects the 'psychological and social core of an individual's life' (Seidman, quoted in Abraham 2009: 86).

S, the lesbian participant, has been out and vocal about her sexual preference to her mother. Her professional life in a civil-society organization in a metropolitan city allows for the forging of relationships with Muslim women and demands that she downplay her sexual identity in public spaces. While encountering other Muslim women with alternative sexual desires, she felt more confident and comfortable about her own sexuality and sometimes raised the issue of Islam, women, and alternative erotic choices in certain forums when she found the audience more receptive. But she maintains, 'Even now, I cannot as strongly emphasize and vocalize or shout about my Muslim lesbian identity as strongly and confidently as I can argue and shout about the rights of Muslim women in general.'

S is not completely deterred by heteronormativity and keeps articulating her queer self wherever she finds an opportunity, sometimes even among the general Muslim audience. Many of her community members (read men) have reacted to her speech on alternative erotic desire and Muslim women not with denial but with a sort of indeterminate 'acceptance'—*accha ayese bhi log hain aur ayesa bhi ho sakta hain* (Oh! There are people of such kind and even this can happen!). So, heteronormativity and West-phobia in a way are not so sharply entrenched in her case as Abraham (2009) finds in case of Australian Muslims as a religious community. Abraham mentions that Australian queer Muslims are unable to 'come out' because of the entrenched heteronormativity of their community where being Muslim and queer is just unthinkable, unrecognizable, and unimaginable. West-phobia and association of alternative sexual identity with the Western way of life may be a reaction to the growing Islamophobia in the secular West which may not operate with the same intensity in the case of Indian metropolitan cities.

Between Fear and Desire

Many of the participants traverse the dialectical territory of desire and fear. Fear of Allah, community, and Qayamat do configure in certain narratives, while in others, the unmediated Allah is forgiving and accommodative while community-mediated norms and religious sanctions become constraining. Many feel guilty, while for a few others, the spectre of guilt does not haunt any more.

R says, 'Sab acchha hai. Sirf Allah ka dar hai [Everything is alright. I only fear Allah].' R is afraid because she got her male genitalia removed through castration. She believes that one should return to Allah with the same body that Allah had given at one's birth ('Allah ne jo diya wo leke jana. Allah ko kya jawab dungi?'). She further adds, 'Allah ke raste par chal rahin thi, saitan ke raste par bhatak gayi [I was following the path of Allah; later got deviated and began to follow Satan].' K, another transgender staying with her natal family as a man, fears community concern about the dead body during funeral rituals. She is apprehensive that her castrated body will be noticed by the members of her community, bringing shame and dishonour to her family and immediate kin. She explains this through the term *gosul* (bath). The dead body is given a bath for which the *gasal*—the ritual expert and performer—is called from outside. The body is unclothed and given a bath. At this time, the community men would see her body, which would shame her family members.'My death will be a matter of humiliation to the entire family.' But K is not much bothered about religion while talking about diminishing the family's shame and honour at the spectacle of her nude dead body sans the phallic organ. She says the hijras and transgenders are not very religious: 'Hijra is a Persian word meaning one who is independent and not in control of anyone [giggles].' P fears the Day of Judgment when people will be weighed on the *taraju* (weighing machine) with good deeds on one side and bad ones on another. Despite this, he wishes to be both gay and Muslim. Q, the social-work graduate who leads a double life of a man and a hijra sex worker, remarks, 'I feel guilty and think that I am committing the zina. To overcome the guilt I keep doing social work by offering money to poor children and doing free counseling to the needy people as I am a social worker.'

Fear is expressed mostly by transgender participants. Except for one gay person, P, others show respect for the religion but they do not fear Allah. What they worry about is their immediate family and community. Statements in defence of erotic desire were more forthcoming from gay men. Here, gender seemed to be intersecting with sexuality, with male gender being more vocal in articulating desire. T claimed that if he dare came out to his family, he might be put under house arrest or kicked out. So, he has decided never to come out to his family.

P has a lot to add about his different erotic desire which, he feels, is very natural and intrinsic. He stresses:

> You know why Allah allowed four wives? Because he knew there will be gay [people]. So, what about ladies not finding men? Gayness is very natural. I have not lifted it from somewhere and planted it in my body. I am prone to walk in certain manner. I don't do a catwalk deliberately, do I? Yadi mujhe pata hota ki ye kanton ka rasta hai to mai ise kyon chunta? [If I knew that this is the path full of thorns why would I chose it?] Par ye kanton ka rasta hi mere liye natural hain [But, the thorny path is only the natural path for me and I have no option than to go for it]. Why can't two men be in love? I wish I could marry a nice hot man! God has described angelic women. Why can't we have men of similar sort? What sin we have done after all?

But P too turns sentimental regarding his concern for his parents. He says that he can suppress his sexual feelings for their welfare. F says, 'I am just doing what my life is; what my "self" communicates to my mind.' T suggests that sometimes one just cannot hold one's desire: 'People have to resort to one-night-stand[s].

Lut and *Ijtihad*[17]

Lut is most often used to condemn male homosexuality. Lut has been reinterpreted by queer scholars who emphasize that the Quran does not state that destruction fell upon the people for a specific sin (Minawalla et al. 2005; Kugle 2003). Scholars suggest that inhospitality to strangers, for example, was among the intended transgression

(Minawalla et al. 2005; Kugle 2003). Queer Muslims in Shannahan's (2009) study expressed unease at the Sharia, which, they claim, has been corrupted by the orthodox interpretation. They emphasized on 'pure' and 'original' Islam that acknowledges ijtihad, the independent interpretation of existing law as a means of full submission to Allah which they consider to be a tool that would deepen democracy.

Research participants in the present study are not unanimous in their opinion about the progressive and independent reinterpretation of the Quran. The transgender participants remain silent about the issue. T says that a reinterpretation seems difficult as the people who are competent to do so are never going to consider sexuality as a basis for reinterpretation. He added that what was needed was to emphasize the upholding of spiritual Islam rather than jurisprudencial Islam, and says: 'Let's not believe in community justice, I believe in Love of God.' P is very clear about the story of Lut. He says that Lut's people were punished for their lust and not for love. To P, there is a difference between love and lust. He further elaborates, 'Qur'an has never mentioned anything about homosexual love. We are talking about love and not lust. How can Allah punish you for expressing love?' F surmises, 'We all need to get support from the community to revive either the original Qur'an which does not punish our love or we can press for removing the "sin" part of it.' He concludes by suggesting that every opponent of liberal Islam should see the Pakistani movie *Khuda Ke Liye* (For God's Sake) for its depiction of a liberal face of Islam and also of countering Islamophobia in the contemporary West. F and P do not deny the possibility of progressive interpretation, while S remains a bit cynical.

***

This study is one among the very few attempts to address the concerns of those who are Muslims and articulate different erotic sensibilities. The participants in the study belong to three metropolitan cities in India. These individuals remain on the margins of religion and sexuality in the sexually stratified society of India. Medieval India, which is regarded as the Islamic period, was not averse to same-sex love and alternative erotic practices did exist and flourish during the early and late medieval periods. In contemporary times when Islam is

essentially viewed as hostile and intolerant to alternative erotic practices, particularly in Western eyes, it is pertinent to understand the
life of queer Muslim subjects in modern, globalizing India. Religion
and religious life cannot be understood by focusing only on macro
aspects, but what remains equally important is to understand religion
as a lived experience. The author encountered three vantage points
while researching and teaching the life situation of queer Muslims
as part of the curriculum: (*a*) autonomy from religious context exercised by the subject; (*b*) the near subsumption of the subject within
the religion and community context; and (*c*) a rather interpretative
engagement with the sexual and religious self. Considering the experiential accounts of the participants, it appears that the autonomous
position, that is, privileging sexual autonomy and sexual identity
above religious self and identity, does not hold much relevance in the
present case. Almost every participant upholds religion and religious
identity even though they are critical about the dominant understanding of sexuality within Islamic discourse. Only one participant, S, who
identifies herself as queer and lesbian, confirms that she is an atheist.
But she disagrees that this could be a model for all queer Muslims:

I encounter many Muslim youth who feel confident both about
their sexuality and religious identity. As they say in Hindi, *mai roja
bhi rakhata hun aur apani sexuality ke bare mein bhi confident hun* [I
observe fast during Ramadan and I am equally confident about my
sexuality]. This is the spirit of the youth I admire. You cannot think
everyone to be an atheist like me.

S further reiterates, 'No matter how much I try I cannot leave
my Muslim identity so easily.' She cites the instance of the Gujarat
communal carnage of 2002, describing how Muslims were killed
indiscriminately without considering who was or was not religious,
who did or did not visit the mosque, who did or did not offer prayers.
In her opinion, people were killed because of their Muslim identity
or if they had a certain Muslimness about them. She states, 'I am
a Muslim because I carry a Muslim name and even if I am a non-
believer I might be killed in a communal riot because I carry the
name. In such situations, is it affordable to disengage with religion
and religious identity?' This articulation by S is much closer to the
third position—an interpretative engagement with Islam trying to
critically reconcile the sexual self and religious identity. In general,

the transgender persons articulate more fear of religion and community than the modern gay men but they do not wish to quit their sexual life either. Rather, the strategy of compartmentalization where one can play out either the sexual self or the religious self in context-specific situation appears to be how religion and sexuality are lived and negotiated. The queer Muslim subjects in the contemporary urban–metropolitan India inhabit a hybrid terrain including Internet and cyberspace, mobile intimacy, civil society, and NGO connections exposing them to ideas of sexual citizenship (albeit in a donor-driven vocabulary; see Kole 2007). They participate in Gay Pride Marches and traverse many counter-normative cultural landscapes such as queer film festivals and gay carnivals. This, however, does not make them completely free from the heteronormativity and homonegativity of their families, communities, and the religious world. So, the life of queer Muslim subjects in contemporary urban India traverse between the dialectics of determinate and indeterminate situations of realization and denial of self, between hopes and dilemmas in everyday life.

Notes

1. As a course teacher, I tried to democratize the classroom by provoking everyone to speak and comment on the issues and was conscious about not imposing my own views to respect the differences of opinions. Still, it is difficult to claim that the class was fully democratic as many participants chose to remain un-argumentative. There were, however, several others who created considerable space for debate and discussion in the class and many a times expressed disagreement with my position.

2. The other important writings worth considering on the subject are Indrani Chatterjee's (1999) *Gender, Slavery and Law in Colonial India* and Orsini's (2007) *Love in South Asia*. Chatterjee's book contains a section on 'Eunuchism in Nizamat Polity' which pithily demonstrates how erotic and sexual identities beyond heteronormative constructs were incorporated and assimilated in the Nizamat polity and, in certain significant contexts, eunuchs were often more valued ministers and close assistants of the emperor. Instances of passionate love between men are documented throughout the literary canon from the Abbasid period to the Andalusian and Ottoman periods. An analysis of many of these texts shows that the assertion that homosexuality did not or do not exist in the Arab or Muslim worlds is tenuous (see Habib 2010; Sharlet 2010).

3. Kidwai provides a graphic account of the homoerotic landscape from Mir's narrative poems 'Shola-i-isk', Dargah Kuli Khan's description of tombs of saints and religious shrines as sites of festivals where liquor was drunk and homoerotically inclined men congregated. There are references of boys who granted favour only for a price. Sultan Mahmud of Ghazan was in love with slave Aiyz, Mubarak Shah Khalji was in love with Khushro to the point of distraction, Jehangir's attraction to both fair and dark slave boys and sexual relations with eunuchs and their masters were frequently found. This should not lead us to connect homosexuality to medieval India. The text co-authored by Kidwai and Vanita provides enough instances of homoeroticism from ancient India as well (Vanita and Kidwai 2008). In Sufi literature, the relationship between divine and human was often expressed in homoerotic metaphors (see Merchant 2010).

4. A ghazal is a form of Persian and Urdu love poetry that invokes separation and longing and is sung by Iranian, Indian, and Pakistani musicians.

5. Homonormativity is a politics that does not contest dominant heteronormative assumptions and institutions but upholds and sustains them while promising the possibility of a 'demobilized' gay constituency and privileged depoliticized gay culture anchored in domesticity and consumption (see Duggan 2003). The simple premise of homonormativity is that the gay and lesbian bourgeoisie have a great deal in common with affluent heterosexuals and thus share a similar desire to maintain their power and privilege (Abraham 2009).

6. The term 'plastic sexuality' was introduced by Anthony Giddens (1992), describing a situation where sexuality is freed from reproduction: freed from the rule of the phallus and from the overpowering importance of male (read heterosexual) experience. In times of plastic sexuality, intimacy implies a wholesale democratizing of interpersonal domain in a manner fully compatible with democracy in the public sphere. Also see Dennis Altman (2001) on how affluence could influence sexual norms in substantial ways.

7. Queer activism, including the Islamic queer collective articulations in the West, has completely turned away from communist concerns and become complicit with the USA's imperialist policies (see Massad 2002). During the 1950s in America, at the time of the Cold War, Senator Joseph McCarthy propagated the view that both homosexuals and communists were subversive elements that together posed a threat to national security. This has led to the persecution of many gay individuals. In the 1970s, the gay movement had definite links with the Left movement, particularly reflected in the Gay Left Collective in London. However, the connection of individuals who identify as queer with communists in the USA during the Cold War (see Johnson 2004) does not remain an important trope any more in the West.

8. See Kligerman (2007) who argues against the common Western perception that Muslim societies are particularly repressive to gays. This has not always been the case. Contrary to the popular Western perspective, Kligerman argues that it is partly the rise of Western influence in the Muslim world that has created a greater social stigma against homosexuality.

9. Almost all my interlocutors in this study are associated with civil-society groups working around issues of sexuality and plural gender identities and sexual citizenship. Most of them are part of certain cyberspaces related to activism around issues of sexuality. A detailed discussion of this is brought out in the subsequent section on methodology. Across the globe, anonymity of city has been always congenial for the homosexual subculture to flourish and prosper even amidst overt hostilities (see Aldrich 2004). In globalizing times, wider access to Internet and cell phones has been impetus behind the queer revolution in India according to Ashok Rao Kavi, the leading gay-rights activist (see Trivedi 2014; for mobile intimacies, see also Nayar 2012: 43–6). Queer Muslims' negotiation of their erotic life cannot be understood in isolation from all these factors.

10. *Nirvanhijras* are those who are castrated. The hijras who do not remove their sexual organ are called *aqua* hijras. In the hijra subculture, nirvanahijras enjoy greater power and prestige vis-à-vis aqua hijras (Reddy 2005).

11. In the context of many Muslim-majority states, Krammer (2010) argues that a younger generation of Muslim men view their sexual proclivities in an 'identitary' (the term used by Kramer to describe the formation of identity-based communities as well as an individual's aspiration to identify herself with a particular ethnic, religious, national, or sexual identity) way (2010: 135–6). He perceives these shifts to be caused by young men's access to cyber world. This has its origins in the West where homosexuality has been normalized. Kramer suggests that sexual identities such as gay, lesbian, bisexual, or transgender in many Muslim-majority societies are taken voluntarily by persons who are not comfortable with their assigned sexuality and/or gender at birth. This is because of the exposure of non-Western societies to the Western model of alternative sexualities through travel, internet, television programmes, and human-rights organizations trying to reach out to LGBT communities across the globe.

12. Their awareness of sexuality issues, sense of injustice and demand from the state for removal of discriminatory laws, mingling with others like them who belong to different caste, class, and ethnic groups, their visits to pubs and clubs where social events are organized all contribute to a critical comprehension of the problem. So, the resistance does not derive from their Muslimness but from a variety of experiences in different locations and sites.

13. 'Zina' refers to sex outside marriage—both adultery and fornication. In Islam, sex within heterosexual marriage is celebrated. The word 'wedding' (*nikah*) is also the word for intercourse. All other forms of sexuality including homosexuality are illegitimate (zina). Zina is the anti-thesis of nikah and hence perceived as threat to moral and social order (see Khan 2003; Siraj 2009). The condemnation of homosexuality in the Quran is associated with the Lut story. Homosexuals are referred to as *quam lut* (Lot's people) referring to prophet Lut (known as Lot in the Christian Bible) who preached against homosexuality in the cities of Sodom and Gomorra, which were subsequently destroyed. Two angels in the guise of handsome young boys came to Lut, whose people came to snatch the boys away from him. Lut's request to his people to refrain from hurting the boys was not heard by the unrelenting crowd. Because of this sinful act, the cities were destroyed in a firestorm (see en.wikipedia.org/wiki/Lot_in_islam [last accessed 17 June 2014]). Many Muslim queer scholars and activists, however, have provided a progressive interpretation of this story. Scott Kugle (quoted in Siraj 2009; Abraham 2009), an American scholar, highlights the importance of ambiguity that exists within the story. For Kugle, the story is about infidelity through inhospitality and greed rather than about sex acts in general and on sexuality of any variation in particular. Kugle writes that it is a story of the condemnation of greed, miserliness, and sexual oppression, and a rejection of the Prophet's ethics of care. 'Ijtihad' is an Islamic legal term meaning 'independent reasoning' as opposed to *taqlid* (imitation). Islamic reformers call for a revitalization of ijtihad in modern world (see www.oxfordislamic-studies.com).

14. The followers of Islam believe that they will return to Allah when they die. On the Day of Judgment (Qayamat) every individual will be resurrected to account for their lives. God describes this event in the Quran: 'On the Day, people will come forward in separate groups to be shown their deeds.... God will weigh everyone's good and bad actions according to his mercy and justice, forgiving many sins and multiplying the rewards for many noble deeds. One who excels in goodness will be rewarded generously but one whose evils and wrongs outweigh his virtue will be punished' (www.whyislam.org).

15. Tilo Beckers (2010) argues that homosexuality due to its relegation to the private sphere can be tolerated in Muslim societies so long as prolongation of family tree is guaranteed and no possessions are lost in homosexual relations. Sharlet (2010) submits that passionate love between men is documented throughout the Arabic literary canon from the Abbasid period to the Andalusian and Ottoman periods. The assertion that homosexual identities did not or do not exist in the Arab and/or Muslim world is tenuous.

16. 'Martaba' connotes distinction or eminence; see the term on www. hamariweb.com

17. For *lut* and *ijtihad*, see note 12.

Bibliography

Abraham, Ibrahim. 2009. '"Out to Get Us": Queer Muslims and Clash of Sexual Civilisations in Australia'. *Contemporary Islam* 3(1): 79–97.

Aldrich, Robert. 2004. 'Homosexuality and City: A Historical Overview'. *Urban Studies* 41(9): 1719–37.

Altman, Dennis. 2001. *Global Sex*. Chicago: Chicago University Press.

Beckers, Tilo. 2010. 'Islam and the Acceptance of Homosexuality: The Shortage of Socioeconomic Well-Being and Responsive Democracy.' In *Islam and Homosexuality* edited by Samar Habib, 57–98. California: Praeger.

Chatterjee, Indrani. 1999. *Gender, Slavery and Law in Colonial India*. New York: Oxford University Press.

Duggan, Lisa. 2002. 'The New Homonormativity: The Sexual Politics of Neoliberalism'. In *Materializing Democracy; Towards Revitalizing Cultural Politics*, edited by Russ Castronovo and D. Nelson, 174–94. Durham: Duke University Press.

———. 2003. *The Twilight of Equality: Neoliberalism, Cultural Politics and Attack on Democracy*. Boston: Beacon Press.

Giddens, Anthony. 1992. *The Transformation of Intimacy: Sexuality, Love and Eroticism in Modern Societies*. Stanford: Stanford University Press.

Habib, Samar. 2010. 'Introduction; Islam and Homosexuality'. In *Islam and Homosexuality*, vol. 1, edited by Samar Habib, xviii–lxii. California: ABC-CLIO.

Johnson, David K. 2004. *The Lavender Scare: The Cold War Persecution of Gay and Lesbian in Federal Government*. Chicago: Chicago University Press.

Khan, Shahnaj. 2003. '"Zina" and Moral Regulation of Pakistani Women'. *Feminist Review* 75(1): 75–100.

Kligerman, Nicole. 2007. 'Homosexuality in Islam: A Difficult Paradox'. *Macalester Islam Journal* 2(3): 52–64.

Kole, Subir. 2007. 'Globalising Queer? AIDS, Homophobia and Politics of Sexual Identity in India'. *Globalisation and Health*, 3(8); DOI: 10, 1186/1744-8603-3-8.

Krammer, Max. 2010. 'Sexual Orientation: The Ideological Underpinnings of the Gay Advance in Muslim Majority Societies as Witnessed in Online Chat Rooms'. In *Islam and Homosexuality*, vol. 1, edited by Samar Habib, 133–62. California: ABC-CLIO.

Kugle, Scott Siraj al-Haqq. 2003. 'Sexuality, Diversity and Ethics'. In *Progressive Muslims: On Gender, Justice and Pluralism*, edited by Omid Saifi, 190–234. Oxford: One World Publication.

McGuire, Meredith B. 2008. *Lived Religion: Faith and Practices in Everyday Life*. Oxford: Oxford University Press.

Massad, Joseph. 2002. 'Re-orienting Desire: The Gay International and Arab World'. *Public Culture* 14(2): 361–85.

Merchant, Hoshang. 2010. *Indian Homosexuality*. New Delhi: Allied Publishers.

Minawalla, Omar, B.R. Simon Rosser, Jamie Feldman, and Christine Varga. 2005. 'Identity Experience among Progressive Gay Muslim in North America'. *Culture, Health and Sexuality* 7(2): 113–28.

Nayar, Pramod. 2012. *Digital Cool: Life in the Age of New Media*. Delhi: Orient BlackSwan.

Orsini, Francesca, ed. 2007. *Love in South Asia: A Cultural History*. Delhi: Cambridge University Press.

Potia, Ali. 2005. 'Islam and Me'. In *Because I Have a Voice: Queer Politics in India*, edited by Arvind Narrain and Gautam Bhan, 252–9. Delhi: Yoda Press.

Reddy, Gayatri. 2005. *With Respect to Sex: Negotiating Hijra Identity in South India*. Chicago: University of Chicago Press.

Rehman, Bushra. 2014. 'The Invisible Queer Muslim'. *Curve Magazine* 13(4). Available at www.queermuslim.tumblr.com/post/ curve-magazine-the invisible-queer-muslim-by-bushra (last accessed 9 June 2014).

Scott, J.C. 1985. *Weapons of the Weak: Everyday Forms of Peasant Resistance*. New Haven: Yale University Press.

Sharlet, Jocelyn. 2010. 'Public Displays of Affection: Male Homoerotic Desire and Sociability in Medieval Arabic Literature'. In *Islam and Homosexuality*, vol. 1, edited by Samar Habib, 37–56. California: ABC-CLIO.

Siraj, Asifa. 2009. 'The Construction of Homosexual Others by British Heterosexuals'. *Contemporary Islam* 3(1): 41–57.

Trivedi, Ira. 2014. *India in Love: Marriage and Sexuality in 21st Century*. New Delhi: Rupa.

Vanita, Ruth, and Saleem Kidwai. 2008. *Same Sex Love in India: A Literary History*. Delhi: Penguin.

Yip, Andrew Kam-Tuck. 2009. 'Islam and Sexuality: Orthodoxy and Contestation'. *Contemporary Islam* 3(1): 1–5.

Zahid, Saad. 2013. 'Feeling of a Gay Muslim'. *GayLaxy*, 21 January. Available at actup.org/news/Pakistan-feeling-of-a-gay-Muslim (last accessed 20 July 2016).

SECULARISM, RELIGION, AND POLITICS

7

APARNA DEVARE

Rethinking the 'Religious–Secular' Binary in Global Politics

M.A. Jinnah and Muslim Nationalism in South Asia

In dominant understandings of the role of religion in global politics today, religious ideologies and movements are often posited as repositories of tradition and an expression of atavism. They are seen as antithetical to secularism and are thereby considered dangerous trends in world politics. Islam in particular has been portrayed in Western media as a religion that has not modernized itself enough by espousing a secular culture like the West, instead letting itself be taken over by 'traditional' non-secular elements. But Hindu nationalism or extremism is no exception in this regard either. Both Hindu extremism in India and Islamic fundamentalism in Pakistan are seen to mark a disruption of the modern because of their inability to separate the religious from the political or public sphere.

The prevailing sentiment then, especially in the West, is that they have to be countered with greater secularization and modernization, since religion needs to be confined to the private sphere as it is in the 'civilized West'. This approach is echoed by intellectuals such as Samuel Huntington (1993), the practice of American foreign policy, and the attitude towards religious minorities within western Europe and even in South Asia itself—amongst its 'secular' intellectuals and scholars. However, Western notions of secularism have been highly contested in recent years in countries such as India and Turkey. The extent to which religion is confined to the private sphere in the West has also been questioned.[1] Both Hindu and Islamic extremists in the subcontinent themselves characterize their beliefs in nativist terms as an assertion of 'tradition' and 'purity' against the modern West and its 'corrupting evils'.[2] Their critics and supporters alike often portray their visions as a reaction to Westernization or globalization and as providing an alternative cultural world view and philosophy to it.[3]

It is precisely these binaries between the 'religious' and the 'secular' which persist in popular imagination that I contest in this chapter. In some respects, some of the boundaries between the West and the non-West breakdown because the secularization of Catholicism that eventually led to the rise of Protestant modernity in Europe, in which religion was increasingly relegated to the private realm in the West, has also affected other religions in similar ways. Rather, what we now see is what Ashis Nandy calls the 'imperialism of categories' (including secularism) in which both the West and the non-West participate in constituting new kinds of religio-political identities, and resistance to it, similarly, can come from spaces within both the West and the non-West.[4] Modernity has been increasingly internalized in the global South, and the very debates playing out worldwide regarding the role of religion in politics are now playing out there as well. The secularists and the extremists are locked in antagonistic relations but, in reality, both are operating in a shared language of secular values such as the demand for power, resources, territory, political identities, and so on. Physically they may clash but not ideologically, unlike what Samuel Huntington would like his readers to believe.

The religious as a separate domain outside the sphere of politics is increasingly difficult to find in the world today. Religion has been so worked over by modern secularism that one cannot say such a clear separation exists. In fact, religion has been increasingly secularized to the extent that these boundaries have become blurred and modern religion has to be increasingly understood through secular categories such as the modern nation-state and its institutions, history-writing, development, and so on. Having said that, not all religion is political. It is important to distinguish between lived religion as part of the everyday and its political forms. Mustapha Pasha makes a useful distinction between religion per say and religion as a political project, or what he refers to as religious resurgence, the latter of which is the focus of this piece. He points out that religion 'connotes no discernible political project to reshape the state or civil society but a fairly heterodox set of quotidian cultural and religious beliefs and practices. Religious resurgence is intrinsically a modern political phenomenon ... aim[ing] primarily to restructure national space, to redefine nationalisms and to redirect modernization' (Pasha 2004: 135–52). Religion as lived and practised and religion as politics are not always clearly separated and they do sometimes overlap. Various religion-based fundamentalist organizations do draw on religiosity as part of their political programmes. However, they continue to seek legitimacy in modern politics and modern secular institutions. This essay is primarily concerned with this trend or the way in which religion has often come to become the other side of the same coin of 'secular' politics.

The term 'political Islam' has been widely used to understand this phenomenon in the case of Islam by scholars such as Olivier Roy and others. Olivier Roy's work has insightfully demonstrated how deeply implicated modern ideas and processes are with Islamic extremism. According to Roy, Islamic fundamentalism is not a return to 'traditional' culture but intrinsically linked to the Westernization and globalization taking place in the Islamic world (Roy 2005: 15). He points out that Islam has been increasingly privatized and tied to an individuated form of belief much like in the West, especially amongst the large numbers of Muslim migrants living in non-Muslim societies who are more likely to search for a 'purist' and deterritorialized notion of Islam or a global *ummah*. In its encounter with the West, Islam has been politicized and secularized, including in self-proclaimed 'Islamic' countries such as Iran where, Roy argues, 'religion does not define the place of politics but the converse' (2007: 63).

In societies such as Iran, he argues, it is politics that reigns supreme over religion or traditional law and the 'effect of an Islamic regime of this kind is always its opposite: accelerated secularization with, for

Iran, a decline in religious observance' (Roy 2007: 63). Overall, for him, 'The question is thus not that of the persistence of an Islamic culture but of the sudden appearance of new ways of religion becoming ideological and of new forms of religiosity in the framework of the modern nation-state' (Roy 2007: 64). Roy suggests that it is the Islamists and extremists who are the real secularists because they 'bridge the gap between religion and a secularized society by exacerbating the religious dimension' (Roy 2005: 40) in a distinctly political fashion.

In the case of Hindu nationalism, several scholars, such as Richard Fox (2005), Vinay Lal (2003), T.N. Madan (1997), and Ashis Nandy (1997) amongst others, have pointed to its modernist underpinnings, drawing important connections between modern secular thought and Hindu nationalism. Others, such as Shamita Basu (2002), Partha Chatterjee (1999), Sudipta Kaviraj (1995), and Sanjay Seth (2006), have pointed to the secularization of Hinduism that undergirded so many attempts in imagining a Hindu nation from the nineteenth century onwards as a response to colonialism. As Shamita Basu states, 'The nationalist project of modernity could only be made possible by the political use of religion as ideology' (Basu 2002: 199).

While this is a global phenomenon, I focus on the South Asian context to demonstrate my claims. The two individuals whose political careers in many ways have mirrored the rise of religion-based political identities in South Asia are Vinayak Damodar Savarkar in the case of Hinduism and Mohammed Ali Jinnah in the case of Islam. Both can be considered the 'founding fathers' of Hindu and Islamic nationalism respectively. As I have previously written on the manner in which Hinduism gets transformed into Hindu nationalism through Savarkar's writings, both political and autobiographical (Devare 2009), in this chapter I look primarily at the life, writings, and politics of Jinnah. A close examination of Savarkar and Jinnah offers us a window to examining larger macro-processes of transformations in religion and politics in the subcontinent.

The key argument I make in this chapter is that like Savarkar's Hinduism, Jinnah's Islamism, rather than reflecting a religious world view, is secular, suggesting a separation and removal of religion as a way of life from politics.[5] Here the spiritual or transcendental hardly finds any mention. In fact these can often act as a hindrance to nation-building and the creation of political–national identities. Many steps have to be taken to convert transcendent ideas with their plural temporalities and fluid boundaries into secular ideas of the nation either rooted in 'objective' history writing as in the case of Savarkar, or exclusive identities in the political language of minority–majority as in the case of Jinnah. Both took these steps, although they were never personally religious to begin with. Ironically, both went from being secular-nationalists in the first half of their lives to 'communalists' or 'religion-based leaders', though this was much more stark in the case of Jinnah, who was known to be a staunch advocate of 'Hindu–Muslim' unity. Yet the term 'communal' or 'religion-based' does not capture the extent to which their concerns remained at base secular concentrating on political identities. In fact, the secular versus communal classifications in which much of modern Indian history is written is deeply problematic. The two well-known figures generally branded as 'communal' within Indian historiography were, ironically, irreligious and suspicious of lived religion. The tensions and contradictions of their positions and lives mirror the ironies and tragedies of how religion and politics have played out in the subcontinent in modern times.

Jinnah's Political-Muslim Vision

Jinnah had little patience for Islamic theologians, mullahs, and maulvis, whom he considered reactionary and conservative. He believed in a strict separation of the *practice* of religion and politics. There is very little in his writings that indicate that he saw religion as the basis of how the state would be imagined and governed. While many of his contemporaries talked of an Islamic nation based on the teachings and practice of Islam, Jinnah's writings, speeches, and public utterances are entirely focused on how to increase Muslim political representation so that they have a greater political voice. As he puts it, 'The question with which we started, as I understood, is of safeguarding the *rights* and the *interests* of the Mussalmans with regard to their religion, culture, language, personal laws and political rights in the national life, the government and the administration of the country' (Pirzada 1981: 254, italics mine). Nowhere does he express that religious authorities, teachings, or practices should be the basis of the state. In both his private life and his politics, he had little patience for the actual practice of religion; rather he aggressively embraced the religious marker of Islam as a political identity, wedding it to nationalism.

Part of the problem as he saw it was excessive religiosity and a lack of political awareness of a unified Muslim identity. He believed that 'Muslims in India have yet to learn the political language' (Pirzada 1981: 31), which he saw as his and the Muslim League's primary task. Much like Savarkar, he had little patience for his co-religionists,[6] and his life's mission after becoming a spokesman for the Muslims was to unify disparate Muslim sects and communities into a singular Muslim *political* identity. For Jinnah, various Islamic practices, sects, and subcommunities and their differing ways in which to follow Islamic teachings would act as a hindrance to the larger Muslim political cause. And a unified Muslim political identity, he insisted, had to coalesce under the banner of the Muslim League and no other political organization. This was an issue on which he had continued differences with Congress leaders who refused to recognize the Muslim League as the sole representative of the Muslims, but were willing to concede that it was one organization amongst others that had Muslim members.

In a response to a letter written by S.M. Zauqi, a Muslim activist who complained to Jinnah about how Muslims, especially the Khaksars,[7] were refusing to unify as Muslims under the Muslim League, Jinnah responded by writing, 'I do not approve of the different Muslim organisations. It is a sign of weakness and I entirely agree with you that Seerat and Khaksars should work as members of the Muslim League under one flag and one platform. Unity among the Musalmans ... is the urgent need of the moment' (Pirzada 1981: 393). Ali Zaheer, president of the All-India Shia Political Conference, once complained to Jinnah (himself a Shia) about the discrimination Shias faced from Sunnis and expressed concern about the fate of Shias in Pakistan. Much like Jinnah demanded safeguards for Muslims in India, Zaheer asked for similar safeguards for Shias in Pakistan once it was established. Jinnah's response to Zaheer was that his concerns of discrimination were mostly fabricated, not 'in accordance with facts', and an 'internal matter'. According to him, it was 'a great disservice to the Muslim cause to create any kind of division between the Musalmans of India' (Pirzada 1981: 337). Jinnah may not have opposed Muslims practising their own variations of Islam in their private lives; he himself was a Khoja, but none of that was acceptable to him in the public sphere where he worked hard to forge a singular political identity.

Jinnah from a Secular Nationalist to a Muslim Nationalist

Much has been written about the 'early' Jinnah being an advocate of Hindu–Muslim unity and a pro-Congress nationalist. Jinnah, along with Bal Gangadhar Tilak, was one of the main leaders of the Congress before M.K. Gandhi emerged as the primary leader of the party. He shared a very close relationship with Gopal Krishna Gokhale and was sometimes referred to as the 'Muslim Gokhale' (Gokhale, ironically, was also Gandhi's 'political guru'). However, what is less written about is that the understanding he sought to forge between Hindus and Muslims in the early years was based on a modern notion of secularism where individuals come together as nationalists (as Indians) shedding their specific religious and cultural attributes. When asked in the Parliamentary Select Committee in 1919 whether he wished 'to do away in political life with any distinction between Muhammadans and Hindus' he responded by saying, 'Yes! Nothing will please me more than when that day comes' (quoted in Jawed 1997: 91). Ironically, even in 1947 after the creation of Pakistan, he said something similar. While addressing the newly formed Constituent Assembly of Pakistan in August of that year in Karachi, he stated, 'We should begin to work in that spirit and in course of time all these angularities of the majority and minority communities, the Hindu community and the Muslim community—because even as regards Muslims you have Pathans, Punjabis, Shias, Sunnis and so on and among the Hindus you have Brahmins, Vaishnavas, Khatris, also Bengalees, Madrasis and so on— will vanish' (quoted in Wolpert 1984: 339).

These religious attributes and identities were not to be highlighted in politics but secular–nationalist causes were more important. Somehow, over time, he believed these primordial ties would be submerged under a broader identifier of a secular nationalism. Jinnah wanted to be seen as a nationalist Congress leader such as Tilak,

Gokhale, Pherozshah Mehta, and others, and not as a Muslim leader. As he told K.A. Hamied in 1927, 'Young man, you think I am a leader of the Muslims. I am not. I am a national leader of India. I cannot work for the Muslims alone' (quoted in Wolpert 1984: 436). His own self-identity was also one where he was not self-consciously Muslim but, in fact, highly Anglicized and deeply rooted in the urban cosmopolitan culture of Bombay, where these identities and their practices were often seen as 'traditionalist' or part only of the private sphere. How removed he was from orthodox Muslims will be discussed in the biography section of the chapter. Also, as a Khoja from a business community in Gujarat and a Shia Muslim, he kept his distance from the Sunni Muslim aristocracy of the United Provinces which, from the time of Syed Ahmad Khan (1817–98) onwards, had been talking about the need to assert a separate Muslim identity in order to gain greater opportunities in British India.

Contrary to the perception in Indian historiography that reformer Syed Ahmad Khan represented a singular Muslim voice, there were multiple voices even among the elite Muslims saying varied things.[8] Some Muslims remained sceptical of the British Raj and attempts to reinterpret Islam from a Western idiom as Syed Ahmad Khan was seen to be doing. Interestingly but not surprisingly, the ulema such as the Deobandis (who Jinnah stayed far away from especially in the early years) were also sceptical of Muslim appeals to a separateness tied to nationality as they emphasized Islamic universalism tied to the global ummah. Islam for them could not be contained within territorial boundaries, and this is a position many orthodox ulema held in contrast to the Muslim League's view on nationalism even in 1947 at the time of Partition.

Traditional Islamists saw Islam primarily in universal terms and were suspicious of Muslim nationalist claims made by political bodies such as the Muslim League and its leaders such as Jinnah whose Islamic credentials in any case were always suspect in their eyes. As Ayesha Jalal puts it, the orthodox Muslims, 'harbouring anti-colonial and Islamic universalist sentiments, immersed themselves in religious strictures at traditional educational institutions like *madrassahs* and *maktabs* only to end up squarely on the side of an inclusionary and "secular" Indian nationalism' (Jalal 1997: 82, italics original). These groups were therefore opponents of the 'modernizing' Muslim separatists such as Syed Ahmad Khan just as Jinnah was in his early political life but for very different reasons. For Jinnah, neither did the position of the ulema and orthodox Muslims interest him and nor did voices such as Khan's. He preferred not to highlight himself as a 'Muslim'.

Hence the indignation he felt when, in one of his early encounters with Gandhi, the latter singled out his being a Muslim. At a reception held in 1915 in Bombay hosted by the Gurjar Sabha, an association of Gujaratis, Jinnah made a speech—welcoming and praising Gandhi and Kasturba and their achievements in South Africa, especially regarding Hindu–Muslim unity. Gandhi noted in his response that he was pleased to find a 'Mohamedan member of the Gurjar Sabha as the chairman of this function', a description Jinnah, his biographers suggest, must have been displeased about as it singularly focused on his religious identity, something he preferred to downplay in those years. As Stanley Wolpert, his biographer, puts it, 'Jinnah, in fact, hoped by his Anglophile appearance and secular wit and wisdom to convince the Hindu majority of his colleagues and countrymen that he was, indeed, as qualified to lead any of their public organizations as Gokhale or Wedderburn or Dadabhai' (Wolpert 1984: 38).

On another occasion at a public gathering in Gujarat, Gandhi asked Jinnah to speak in Gujarati and not English. Jinnah agreed but quickly switched to English (it is likely he was not comfortable speaking in Gujarati and his weakness in speaking Urdu was also well known).[9] The audience laughed and Jinnah could not have been pleased.[10] Gandhi singling him out in public as a Muslim and reminding him of his inability to speak his mother tongue marked him in ways he did not want to be marked. For Gandhi, each person was embedded in their community and in their regional, linguistic, and caste identity, and interacted accordingly. When Jinnah mentioned to Gandhi that he considered himself an Indian first and then a Muslim, Gandhi responded by saying he himself was a Hindu and therefore an Indian. Gandhi's was not just a religious vision but also a non-secular/non-modern vision in which all identities (religious and otherwise) were to be worn on the individual's (as a member of a community) sleeve both in private and in public.

For instance, one of the most prominent Muslims in the Congress, and a strong supporter of Gandhi, was Maulana Azad who was steeped in Islamic scholarship and deeply religious. Secularist Jinnah could never relate to the theologically minded Azad and called him a 'Muslim show-boy' of the Congress. He saw Azad as betraying the Muslim cause by being an ally of Gandhi and a Congressman rather than a Muslim League leader. In a letter to Azad, Jinnah wrote, 'You represent neither Muslims nor Hindus. The Congress is a Hindu body. If you have self-respect resign at once. You have done your worst against the League so far' (Pirzada 1981: 33). (Interestingly, when Jinnah was a Congressman in his early years, Azad was very critical of Hindu–Muslim unity and of the Congress, but in later years the roles were reversed!)

Gandhi was more comfortable with a Muslim such as Azad and was never at ease with Jinnah's secularism since he saw it as too Anglicized (although, ironically, Jawaharlal Nehru was not altogether that different from Jinnah in this respect). Similarly, he was later uncomfortable with Jinnah's adopting the role of leader of all Muslims because he saw Jinnah as a man without piety and, therefore, not someone who could believe in a shared basis of religiosity such as the kind he comfortably shared with Azad or Khan Abdul Gaffar Khan. Jinnah's appeal towards Muslims as adopting a separatist stance did not appeal to Gandhi, who believed that religion was only one aspect of life and many other things, such as language, culture, dress, and so forth, were shared amongst communities. Even the notion of belief, or what Gandhi called *sraddha*, could be shared even if it was directed at different notions of divinity. Jinnah, too, did not know how to deal with Gandhi and often expressed frustration at his religiosity and his non-modern approach. Jinnah singularly focused on constitutional reforms and getting greater representation for Indians and Muslims and did not believe that social and religious reform as Gandhi was promulgating should be mixed with politics. Hence, he would go on to say, '... it is Mr. Gandhi who is destroying the ideal with which the Congress was started. He is the one man responsible for turning the Congress into an instrument for the revival of Hinduism' (quoted in Jawed 1997: 234).

Jinnah also strongly opposed Gandhi's embracing the Khilafat cause as part of the Congress agenda. He could not relate to those Muslims who were Khilafatists as he saw them as reactionary. He thought Gandhi was coddling religious reactionary forces on both the

Muslim and Hindu sides by making politics explicitly about religion and not sticking to constitutionalist issues such as political rights, opportunities, and representation for Indians in the British Raj. He saw the Khilafat movement as setting a dangerous precedent, stating that 'sentimental nonsense and emotions have no place in politics' (quoted in Jawed 1997: 202). Here, he was supported by Tilak who also spoke against appealing to Muslims on religious grounds. Tilak criticized Gandhi by saying that it was important to bring Muslims into the Congress by appealing to the notion of swaraj (self government) and even, if necessary, giving special privileges 'but never seek to introduce theology into our politics' (quoted in Jawed 1997: 202).

Jinnah saw himself increasingly alienated in the Congress as he could not agree with Gandhi's approach to politics, including its religious dimension, and he left the party by the time Gandhi's leadership came to the fore. In many ways, even though they had sharp personal differences, Jinnah and Nehru shared much more in common in their approach towards religion. Nehru was suspect of any religious identities entering politics, quickly dubbing them 'communal'. Nehru viewed all demands by Muslims, even those for greater representation and a political voice, as part of communal politics and believed that Muslims should be subsumed under a unified nationalist banner where religious identities were secondary. Therefore, he could never reconcile to demands made under the banner of 'Muslim separatism'. Nehru, like Jinnah, was also never entirely comfortable with Gandhi or Azad's approach of wearing one's identity on one's sleeve and approaching Indian nationalism through their religious prism and not *despite* it. For Gandhi and Azad, this separation did not exist. Neither saw their being religious as antithetical to their sense of Indian nationalism, but rather as a precondition for it.

Jinnah's greater self-identification with Muslim causes first began with the Morley–Minto Reforms (the Indian Councils Act of 1909) that introduced separate electorates.[11] Politically he would have been marginalized if he did not stand for elections in a Muslim constituency and espouse Muslim causes, which he started to do by the 1920s; but he did so by constantly attempting to bring the Muslim League and the Congress into some kind of agreement on this question of Muslim representation within the larger framework of Indian nationalism. It was only by the late 1930s that, as the primary leader of the Muslim League, he espoused the cause of 'Muslim nationalism' and the demand for a legitimate territorial space for Muslims where they were in a majority (however, it was not necessarily a demand to completely break from India at that time as Jalal (1985) has argued). But was Jinnah's breakaway from the Congress and his becoming the spokesman for Pakistan under the banner of the Muslim League a shift away from secular nationalism to communalism as is often projected (especially on the Indian side)? Or were the breaks really not all that significant?

In many ways, Jinnah went from one kind of secularism to another and did not actually reject secularism in toto. He went from a secularism that emphasized a nation that comprised both Hindus and Muslims to one that emphasized only Muslims. Like Savarkar, who called for a nation exclusively for Hindus, Jinnah too emphasized *nationalism* as the primary way for Muslim self-realization and not religiosity per se. As he put it, 'We are a nation of a hundred million, and, what is more, we are a nation with our own distinctive culture and civilization, language and literature, art and architecture, names and nomenclature, sense of value and proportion, legal laws and moral codes, customs and calendar, history and traditions, aptitudes and ambitions—in short, we have our own distinctive outlook on life and of life' (quoted in Pirzada 1981: 113). In many ways, this unity amongst Indian Muslims was for Jinnah, to paraphrase Benedict Anderson, an 'imagined community' par excellence since many internal variations were overlooked. Nation, as a political category based on a common cultural essence, remained most important for him; he did not turn to a theological way of organizing Muslims. Some of his speeches do suggest this, particularly during the build-up to Pakistan, in order to have a mass appeal amongst Muslims and project himself as a Muslim leader, but nowhere does he mention the implementation of the Sharia and other Islamic practices, laws, and customs as the basis of the state.

In fact, his speeches after the creation of Pakistan suggest he wanted it to be a secular Muslim nation along the lines of Kemal Ataturk's Turkey where religion would be secondary to the state. While speaking to Pakistan's newly formed Constituent Assembly in 1947, he remarked, 'You are free; you are free to go to your temples, you are free to go to your mosques or to any other places of worship in this State of Pakistan.... You may belong to any religion or caste or creed—that has nothing to do with the business of the State' (quoted in Wolpert 1984: 339). While this speech may appear remarkable especially given that he advocated Pakistan in the late 1940s on very different grounds, it is not really so given that Jinnah was always deep down secular. He may have become more privately religious in his later years as some commentators suggest, but he never disavowed the belief that religious precepts, leaders, and authorities were not to meddle with the affairs of the state. At the most they could play an advisory role, although he himself never encouraged it.

Jinnah as a Non-believer

Jinnah as a non-practising Muslim becomes significant in light of the fact that he became the main voice for the demand for a pure land of Islam on behalf of Muslims in South Asia. It also indicates that belief, piety, and lived religion can coexist with political mani-festations of religion but are not necessary for it. The latter can very well do without the former. In fact, the missionary zeal with which some of these leaders took up the cause of forging religio-political identities seems to have been stronger, perhaps precisely because they were nonbelievers infusing a kind of religious passion into their 'secular' approach to politics.[12] If piety was lost to them (although I concede that Jinnah may have acquired some of it along the way and may not have been purely instrumental as some claim) a kind of religious-like zeal entered the back door and influenced their deep and uncritical faith in secularism. I have made a similar argument elsewhere in the case of Savarkar, highlighting his atheism, rational-ism, and impatience for Hindu customs and religious practices and how necessary this was for his uncritical belief in modern concepts of history, nation-state, and political identities (see Devare 2013). In this section, I draw on Jinnah's biographies to suggest that his private life offers an important prism to better understand his public persona and that the two are not altogether separate.

Jinnah,[13] as the spokesman for the establishment of a purist land of Islam, would have surprised many who knew him in the early years of his political career, including perhaps his own Parsi wife. He was a staunch secularist, even in his private life, maintaining a distance from most religious beliefs and practices. He ate pork, enjoyed his alcohol socially, smoked over fifty cigarettes a day, hardly spoke Urdu, did not fast during Ramzan, did not go to mosques or was not known to pray, wore Western clothes (his biographers always mention his Savile Row suits), and regularly shaved his beard (see Jawed 1997 for details). He showed little interest in Islamic theology or learning and preferred little contact with religious leaders or authorities. In fact, he once told Tej Bahadur Sapru, 'I think I have a solution for the Hindu–Muslim problem. You destroy your orthodox priestly class and we will destroy our Mullas and there will be communal peace' (quoted in Jawed 1997: 129). Socially, he had many friends from different communities, mostly Hindus, Christians, and Parsis, 'none of whom took their respective religions as seriously as their faith in British law and Indian nationalism' (Wolpert 1984: 18). His heroes were Dadabhai Naoroji, Pherozshah Mehta, and later G.K. Gokhale.

He himself belonged to the Khoja community, many of whose members followed the Aga Khan, a sect often not considered 'Islamic enough' by orthodox Muslims. His awareness of his marginality amongst Muslims (as a Khoja and Shia) may have heightened his need to prove his Islamic credentials in later years once he was at the helm of the League. In fact, he was often reminded of this marginality. In a letter written by a Muslim named Zafarmulk (clearly Sunni) in response to Jinnah's press statement that Muslims were celebrating the twenty-first day of Ramzan and that he could not meet Gandhi on that day, the person wrote to Jinnah, stating that 'Muslims have nothing to do with the 21st Ramzan. This is a purely Shia function. Islam does not permit any mourning day. In fact the very spirit of Islam revolts against such Jewish conceptions. I know you belong to the Khoja community, a sect of the Shias, but, pardon me, you have no right to impute a Shia belief to Muslims' (Pirzada 1981: 379).

Jinnah's Anglicized manner and his Parsi wife, Rattanbai Petit, perceived as 'ultra-modern', often acted as a hindrance to his being accepted as a genuine 'Muslim'. He was once accused, in a League meeting in 1915 in Bombay, of not being a true Muslim for not sporting a beard or wearing a fez (see Jawed 1997: 138). He faced these barbs on several occasions during his political career. In the 1930s, many orthodox leaders were critical of the clothes he wore, the fact that he did not fast, could not speak Urdu properly, and married a

Parsi girl who never 'Islamized', although she converted (unlike Begum Liaqat Ali Khan, another major League leader who was not born a Muslim but converted with marriage and took her new religion very seriously). Once, during a League meeting, Jinnah's wife, Ruttie, was in attendance wearing her usual attire that, as M.C. Chagla, who was Secretary of the League, put it, was seen as 'fast' in a 'hall full of bearded Maulvis and Maulanas'. He wrote, 'They came to me in great indignation and asked me who that woman was. They demanded that she should be asked to leave, as the clothes she flaunted constituted an offence to Islamic eyes. I told them that they should shut their eyes as the lady in question was President's wife' (Jawed 1997: 20).

There were many factors that contributed to Jinnah's transformation from being regarded as very un-Islamic in the early years to later becoming the Qaid-i-Azam, the spokesman of the Muslim demand for a pure Islamic nation. Some of these include the rise of separate electorates that necessitated espousing a more overtly Muslim identity; the alienation he felt in the Congress under Gandhi as he could not relate to his non-secular approach; and the increasing need among upper-class Muslims looking for a leader[14] who could negotiate amongst groups including the British, the Congress, and so on, and Jinnah the lawyer was a master negotiator. His growing belief that Muslims needed greater political representation in a rapidly changing political scenario, the rise of right-wing elements amongst Hindus, and so on, also contributed to his shift in positions. His own political ambitions could not be ruled out once he was marginalized in the Congress, given that he once aspired to be one of its main leaders prior to Gandhi's entry. In order to be a leader of the Muslim League, he knew he had to transform himself and that is what he did.

But the notion, especially in Indian historiography, of Jinnah undergoing a conversion of sorts from being a secular nationalist to a religious ideologue, as this chapter argues, is not entirely correct. Jinnah taking on the mantle of the leader of the Muslim League was entirely a political move and did not fundamentally alter his belief that the state should be a secular one. At best, it could carry certain religious symbols and would protect the political, social, and cultural rights and interests of Muslims, but he never envisaged Pakistan as a theocratic state. Later he even went on to state that all communities should have equal rights in Pakistan and be freely allowed to practise their religions.

***

Jinnah's espousal of a political identity in the name of Islam does not indicate giving up secularism in the name of 'communalism'; rather it indicates a continuation of his overall belief in the secularization of religion, first by confining it to the private sphere for the first half of his life (if at all), and then bringing it into public life purely in political terms (that is, the call for Muslim representation and political mobilization). Nowhere does religiosity suffuse Jinnah's notion of what the realm of politics should be; in other words, he remained a secularist, whether under the banner of the Congress or that of the Muslim League. Only the kinds of political identities he chose to promote changed over time and historical circumstances.

In conclusion, an analysis of Jinnah's writings, speeches, and biographies, much like Savarkar's, suggest how the term 'communal' and its separation from 'secular' is a misrepresentation of their interventions in politics and in understanding the nature of religion and politics, broadly speaking, in modern societies. The formation of Pakistan and the ongoing attempts by the Hindu right to search for religious purity and create homogeneous nation-states and religion-based identities are fundamentally secularist projects. This insight can be extended to many religion-based movements worldwide that are often misrepresented as 'religion' versus 'modernity'. The secularization of religion requires greater attention to be paid to the nature of secularism and the manner in which it has transformed religion in the modern world.

Notes

1. See Shakman-Hurd's (2008) argument that the West is not all that secular. The United States, she points out, is heavily influenced by a Judeo-Christian value system, whereas Europe follows laicism where the separation between religion and politics is sharper.

2. As one advocate of Hindu 'cultural purity' put it, 'Democracy and capitalism join hands to give a free rein to exploitation, socialism replaced

capitalism and brought with it an end to democracy and individual freedom' (Deendayal Upadhyaya, quoted in Anderson and Damle 1987: 73).

3. Meera Nanda advocates such a view of Hindu nationalism being antagonistic to modern Enlightenment ideas. As she puts it, 'Both fascists and fundamentalists oppose the liberal, enlightenment values of individualism and secularism as decadent and alienating' (2004: 5).

4. See Ashis Nandy's *The Intimate Enemy* (1983) for a questioning of East–West binaries.

5. The claims of some Indian public figures in recent years, especially from the Bharatiya Janata Party (BJP) such as L.K. Advani and Jaswant Singh, which drew considerable opposition within their party is not entirely untrue. Many secularists and modernists in Pakistan also have pointed to Jinnah's secular credentials, and that Pakistan has strayed away from his original ideals and dreams for the new state. Islamists also claim his legacy. This tension is there within Jinnah; hence, he continues to be intepreted by different groups for different ends in South Asia. How Jinnah is interpreted across the two nations in present times is not the scope of this chapter but would make a fascinating study in itself.

6. See Devji (2013) for this view on Jinnah.

7. The Khaksars often opposed Jinnah and the Muslim League. One of them even tried to attack and harm Jinnah. They did not believe that the League adequately represented their interests.

8. Ayesha Jalal (1997) points to these differences.

9. It was Tej Bahadur Sapru who helped him translate a document that he, as a lawyer, needed to decipher in a court case. The document was written in Arabicized Persian (see Jawed 1997: 18).

10. This event is discussed in Nanda (2010: 50).

11. In the 1906 inaugural session of the Muslim League in Dacca (present Dhaka), the only prominent Muslim who came out strongly against the idea of separate electorates was Jinnah. He argued that 'our principle of separate electorates was dividing the nation against itself' (quoted in Wolpert 1984: 26).

12. Faisal Devji makes a similar point with respect to Jinnah calling his belief in Pakistan entirely faith-based and drawn from an Enlightenment conception. He writes, 'Enlightenment thought was also perversely religious, demanding the consent of its votaries in a manner so pure as to became a kind of conversion' (Devji 2013: 134).

13. He was born Muhammad Ali Jinnahbhai but later changed his name to M.A. Jinnah to Anglicize it.

14. Devji suggests that Jinnah coming from a business community also got support from the influential Bombay Muslim trading and merchant

communities. They were important enough to shape League politics, allowing it to be based in Bombay (Devji 2013: 62).

Bibliography

Andersen, Walter, and Shridhar Damle. 1987. *The Brotherhood in Saffron: The Rashtriya Swayamsevak Sangh and Hindu Revivalism.* Boulder and London: Westview Press.

Basu, Shamita. 2002. *Religious Revivalism as Nationalist Discourse: Swami Vivekananda and New Hinduism in Nineteenth-Century Bengal.* New Delhi: Oxford University Press.

Chatterjee, Partha. 1999. *The Partha Chatterjee Omnibus.* New Delhi: Oxford University Press.

Devare, Aparna. 2009. 'Secularizing Religion: Hindu Extremism as a Modernist Discourse'. *International Political Sociology* 3(2): 156–75.

———. 2013. *History and the Making of a Modern Hindu Self.* New Delhi: Routledge.

Devji, Faisal. 2013. *Muslim Zion: Pakistan as a Political Idea.* Cambridge: Harvard University Press.

Fox, Richard G. 2005. 'Communalism and Modernity'. In *Making India Hindu: Religion, Community, and the Politics of Democracy in India,* edited by David Ludden, 235–49. New Delhi: Oxford University Press.

Huntington, Samuel. 1993. 'The Clash of Civilizations'. *Foreign Affairs* 72(3): 22–49.

Jalal, Ayesha. 1997. 'Exploding Communalism: The Politics of Muslim Identity in South Asia'. In *Nationalism, Democracy and Development: State and Politics in India,* edited by Sugata Bose and Ayesha Jalal, 76–108. New Delhi: Oxford University Press.

———. 1985. *The Sole Spokesman: Jinnah, the Muslim League and the Demand for Pakistan.* Cambridge: Cambridge University Press.

Jawed, Ajeet. 1997. *Secular and Nationalist Jinnah.* New Delhi: Kitab Publishing House.

Kaviraj, Sudipta. 1995. 'Religion, Politics and Modernity'. In *Crisis and Change in Contemporary India,* edited by Upendra Baxi and Bhikhu Parekh, 295–316. New Delhi: Sage.

Lal, Vinay. 2003. *The History of History: Politics and Scholarship in Modern India.* New Delhi: Oxford University Press.

Madan, T.N. 1997. *Modern Myths, Locked Minds: Secularism and Fundamentalism in India.* New Delhi: Oxford University Press.

Nanda, B.R. 2010. *The Road to Pakistan: The Life and Times of Mohammad Ali Jinnah.* London, New York, and Delhi: Routledge.

Nanda, Meera. 2004. 'Manu's Children: Vedic Science, Hindutva and Postmodernism'. Paper presented at the 18th European Conference on Modern South Asian Studies, Lund University, Sweden, 6–9 July.

Nandy, Ashis. 1997. 'The Twilights of Certitudes: Secularism, Hindu Nationalism, and Other Masks of Enculturation'. *Alternatives* 22: 157–76.

———. 1983. *The Intimate Enemy: Loss and Recovery of Self under Colonialism*. New Delhi: Oxford University Press.

Pasha, Mustapha Kamal. 2004. 'Modernity, Civil Society and Religious Resurgence in South Asia'. In *Gods, Guns and Globalization*, edited by Mary Ann Tetreault and Robert A. Denemark, 135–52 (IPE Yearbook, vol. 13). Boulder: Lynne Rienner.

Pirzada, Syed Sharifuddin, ed. 1981. *Quaid-i-Azam Jinnah's Correspondence*. New Delhi: Metropolitan Book Co.

Roy, Olivier. 2005. *Globalised Islam: The Search for a New Ummah*. New Delhi: Rupa and Co.

———. 2007. *Secularism Confronts Islam*. New York: Columbia University Press.

Seth, Sanjay. 2006. 'The Critique of Renunciation: Bal Gangadhar Tilak's Hindu Nationalism'. *Postcolonial Studies* 9(2): 137–50.

Shakman-Hurd, Elizabeth. 2008. *The Politics of Secularism in International Relations*. Princeton: Princeton University Press.

Wolpert, Stanley. 1984. *Jinnah of Pakistan*. New Delhi: Oxford University Press.

8

SEKHAR BANDYOPADHYAY

Modernity, Citizenship, and Hindu Nationalism

Hindu Mahasabha and Its 'Reorientation' Debate, 1947–52

When India achieved independence on 15 August 1947, the All India Hindu Mahasabha (AIHM) was the political party that held the banner of Hindu nationalism. The other notable organization, the Rashtriya Swayamsevak Sangh (RSS), preferred to function more as a cultural body, avoiding any direct participation in politics. The AIHM, ever since its revival in the 1920s in the wake of the Khilafat movement, had been trying to position itself against its projected 'threatening Others', the Muslims (Jaffrelot 1993: 25–6). Yet, the majority Hindu support went towards the Congress, which, despite its secularist image, always had a Hindu 'traditionalist' strand within it (Graham 1988: 174). The AIHM tried to invent its distinctiveness after 1937 when V.D. Savarkar became president and decided to develop it as 'a political rival of the Congress' (Gondhalekar and Bhattacharya 1999: 51). He defined the ideology of Hindutva as the foundational principle of the Mahasabha, thus distinguishing it from the Congress. But its support for the Congress Nationalist Party in the 1937 election and opposition to the Quit India movement dented its popularity. When in 1942 Savarkar stepped aside for ill health and Shyama Prasad Mookherji, a Bengali moderate nationalist, took over the leadership, its distinctiveness further began to erode and doctrinal differences within the party increased, as the pragmatism and pro-Congress sympathies of Mookherji set him on a collision course with the orthodoxy of the Savarkarite group. The Mahasabha failed to initiate a mass movement and lacked a mass support base (Gondhalekar and Bhattacharya 1999: 48–74), which became crucial factors behind its electoral debacle in 1945–6, when the Mahasabha candidates lost to Congress candidates in most of the seats. It won only three seats in the provinces and none at the centre (Baxter 1969: 20–3).

At the time of Independence and Partition, there was intense group fighting within the Hindu Mahasabha between the more moderate group led by S.P. Mookherji and the conservatives led by Ashutosh Lahiry, owing allegiance to Veer Savarkar and his ideas (Bandyopadhyay 2009: 146–9). These internal rifts became sharper as the challenges it faced became deeper. Within the Congress, it could rely on support from a powerful traditionalist lobby headed by Vallabhbhai Patel and Purushottamdas Tandon. But, on the other hand, Jawaharlal Nehru wanted the Congress to be steered towards the principle of secularism, as opposed to Hindu nationalism, which was increasingly being negatively branded as 'communalism'. This internal battle was resolved in favour of the secularists after Patel's death in December 1950, and when Nehru replaced Tandon as Congress president in 1951 (Jaffrelot 1993: 80–91; Guha 2007: 127–33). At the 57th session of the Congress in New Delhi on 18 October 1951, Nehru, in his presidential address, identified two enemies of the new nation: 'communalism' and 'poverty'.[1] Nehru's vituperative attacks on communalism had however started much earlier as he considered the Hindu Mahasabha to be 'communal, anti-national and reactionary' (quoted in Prakash 1966: 2). Such attacks obviously made the Mahasabha leadership feel threatened, and they mounted a counter-attack on the Congress secularists, alleging 'hypocrisy', and branding Congress policies as 'morbidly communal, favouring one community in preference to the other'. 'The so-called Congress struggle for freedom', they argued, only resulted in the 'vivisection of this holy land' (Prakash 1947: 5, 11). Ashutosh Lahiry, the AIHM general secretary, expressed his apprehension in a press statement on 8 January 1948: 'I have the gravest apprehension that the policy pursued by our new masters is slowly and steadily driving the country towards a new autocracy,' because they have declared that 'all the political parties in Free India should be formed on economic basis alone'. And so the Mahasabha and the RSS, termed as 'communal[,] should now cease to exist'.[2] Time, therefore, had arrived for these groups to either mount an ideological assault on the Congress or be marginalized in a gradually emerging secular modern political field.

For a definition of this ideology it became imperative to identify a new 'Other', as the Muslims were no longer 'threatening' in a post-Partition India, where the Hindus were an overwhelming majority. So now, for some of the Mahasabha members, their projected Other was the Congress, with its alleged policy of 'unnecessary Moslem appeasement'. With this was also associated their attempt to define citizenship in terms of religion. India could now be claimed exclusively for the Hindus, as Pakistan had become the land of the Muslims. The 'Congress policy of nationalism based on the unity of Hindus and Muslims', Lahiry asserted, was 'obviously now an exploded myth'. The Muslims had their homeland and they 'should now take their rightful place in Pakistan and not in India'.[3] But this was not an ideological position shared by all the leaders of the AIHM; some of them accepted the modern secular definition of citizenship and preferred to open the gates of the Mahasabha to all irrespective of religion. Shyama Prasad Mookherji had joined the Nehru cabinet as the Minister for Industry and Supply. In August 1947 he warned his party that 'there can be no reason for maintaining a separate political organisation confined to Hindus as such after attainment of India's independence. We are today masters of our own destiny and we can shape State policy and administration in any way we like, acceptable to the majority of the people or their representatives.'[4] In view of these dilemmas and divisions within the Hindu nationalist camp, the AIHM felt the urgent need to redefine its ideological position within the new context of postcolonial India.

The support base of the Mahasabha at the time of independence was not that great. According to one report, in 1947 in the whole of India, the total membership of the Mahasabha was 1,080,000.[5] In the wake of Partition and its consequences, the Mahasabha leadership saw great opportunities for increasing these numbers. 'The new situation has ... opened up great opportunities for mass enrolment of members', a circular sent out to all provincial and district committees in October 1947 pointed out. 'Times are very favourable for us', it emphasized, and hence, to 'make the best use of the opportunities', '[e]nrolment of members should be taken up in right earnest and carried on vigorously and every household should be approached to get themselves enlisted as members'.[6] In some areas such as West Bengal which were more directly affected by Partition, local Mahasabha organizers could find many Hindus feeling attracted to the Hindu Mahasabha.[7] In places like Delhi too, which received thousands of battered refugees from Pakistan, the response was overwhelming (Jaffrelot 1993: 81). But in other parts of India, away from the new frontiers and less directly affected by the aftermath of Partition, the situation was different. In November 1947, Brindaban Das, the president of the Mathura Hindu Sabha, ruefully reported 'very little following behind our movement'. While the pro-Muslim policy of the Congress was resented by many and this could be exploited, '[a] gitation against their own government at a critical juncture when perhaps every ounce of energy was needed to infuse more strength in it failed to catch the imagination of the people and they rather turned hostile'.[8] In other words, so soon after decolonization, the time was not right yet to mount an attack on the Congress, which had inherited the legacy of the freedom struggle—unless there was a potent enough ideological tool to displace it.

So on 28 December 1947 the Working Committee of the AIHM decided to initiate an internal debate to reorient its ideological position. A Special Committee was to be appointed to collect and collate opinion on an internal discussion document on the 'reorientation of the Mahasabha policy and programme ... in the light of the altered circumstances of the country'.[9] In the end, the debate did not result in any major reorientation of the AIHM policies, as the old guard staunchly held the ground, and the debate was somewhat derailed by the political fallout of the assassination of Mahatma Gandhi by Nathuram Godse who had previous connections with the Mahasabha. Most of the commentators have concluded that this inability to change resulted in the eventual political demise of the AIHM. But no one has examined the debate which in itself was important as it raised some serious questions about the political modernity of the

Indian nation at the moment of its arrival. It clearly brings out the pluralism within a major Hindu nationalist group and shows how the Hindu right sought to overcome this internal crisis to establish its ideology of Hindutva that defined Indian citizenship in terms of religion. This chapter critically looks at this debate and its aftermath on Hindu nationalist politics in the wake of decolonization.

The Document

The circular (referred to earlier) that the Working Committee of the AIHM sent out to all its local branches for their members to send feedback raised several important issues about postcolonial Indian modernity. It pointed out first of all that during the British period there was a broad anti-imperialist consensus as everyone wanted to get rid of foreign rule. But there was no ideological consensus on the future trajectory of the nation once the British left the country. So, it was now the time to decide 'on what basis the edifice of Free India is to be erected' and how in that project of postcolonial nation-building the Hindu Mahasabha could position itself. It reiterated its faith in the 'Hindu rashtra', but refused to project it as a concept of a communal or theocratic state. One might argue that the basic contours of Hindu rashtra, as defined in Mahasabha's Bilaspur Resolution (1944)—for example 'joint electorate, adult franchise, no weightage to minorities, and representation on population basis'—had all been recognized and secured by the Constituent Assembly. But was it a 'complete conception of Hindu Rashtra' or did it require 'a far more precise and comprehensive definition', as the postcolonial journey of the nation was about to begin?

This question was particularly important as a powerful section within the Congress was trying to define the future trajectory of the Indian nation according to the Western model of a linear journey towards the goal of a 'democratic secular state'. Interrogating this model of modernity, where religion would be separated from politics and relegated to a private sphere of the individual, the circular raised several pertinent questions:

> Will a Secular Democratic State adequately satisfy the aspiration of the Indian masses? Will the new Free State of India solely concern itself with the material happiness and prosperity of the people or will

it endeavour to develop the spiritual urge of her people and to subordinate their purely material interests to considerations of higher culture and spiritual evolution?

Has democracy, as it has worked in Western countries, really brought about peace and prosperity of her people?... [W]ill Free India blindly imitate the West in this respect or will India forge ahead on the lines of her innate political genius?[10]

Apart from this ideological orientation, the structural realities of the new nation also had to be taken into account, and three issues were particularly important here. First of all, 'What will be the place of Moslems in Hindu Rashtra?' As many Muslims preferred to live in India, what would be the effects of communal demography on the political future of the Hindus in the new regime of joint electorate? And should the Muslims be admitted into the Hindu Mahasabha and should it now be opened to members of other religions? The second issue was about mass mobilization, as the introduction of universal adult franchise had now made the masses important as citizens. So, there was the more instrumentalist question as to whether the appeal of Hindu nationalism was effective enough to mobilize the rural poor or if the Hindu Mahasabha should adopt a more radical economic programme for this purpose. And, finally, a new party structure was emerging in free India. While Congress was positioning itself as the major ruling party, and to some extent even exhibiting an authoritarian tendency, there were other opposition parties emerging and they were contesting its claims. But none of them were strong enough to halt the massive political machine of the Congress on their own. So, should Mahasabha collaborate with the other like-minded political parties to build a strong opposition to the Congress, or should it just be concentrating on building 'a strong independent party wedded to the cult of Hindu Nationalism'?

The document evoked mixed responses informed by varied notions of history and indicating different levels of engagement with modernity. The secretary of the AIHM received nearly forty submissions, some in the form of organizational resolutions, others in the form of personal letters. It is difficult to discern any specific regional pattern influenced by recent events such as the Partition, as often opposing views were coming from the same region.[11] So, it is better to discuss them thematically. On one side of the spectrum were those who embraced a wider civilizational concept of nation, almost akin to what Mahatma Gandhi had advocated in his *Hind Swaraj* (1909). Their agendas were closer to those of the 'Hindu traditionalists' within the Congress, who believed in the Indian nation, but also in the strengthening of the culture and interests of the majority community (Jaffrelot 1993: 83–4). The general secretary of the Banaras City Hindu Mahasabha wrote to Delhi that '"Hindu" is not the name of the particular community, it also denotes the name of the Indian national [*sic*].' However, he was willing to recognize and 'honour those Muslim statesmen and saints who have made rich contributions to Hindu (Indian) culture', such as Akbar and Kabir. In other words, he was willing to incorporate Muslims into his putative 'Hindu' nation.[12] In Madras, in K.S. Ramaswamy Shastri's notion of history, India was 'never a theocratic state'; as always in the past the 'state was secular'. Hinduism, he pointed out, might 'place spiritual interest higher than material interests but that will not take away the secular character of the state'. And, for the future, he wanted India to develop into a modern democratic state where the majority would rule, but the protection of the rights of the minority would be equally important. He thought that the Constituent Assembly, by providing for universal adult franchise and joint electorate, had already ensured that.[13] In the same way, Rebati Raman Datta in Calcutta was willing to define 'Hindu' as a broad national category incorporating the Muslims as its 'integral parts', and Hindu rashtra not as a theocratic state as Western modern definition would have it but more as a spiritual concept of ethical good government—'governed by the common law of the land as decided by the common representatives of the people'. 'It was not possible to shut out western Democratic ideas', he conceded; but there should be 'no blind imitation'. 'Indian democracy has to be suitably adjusted' to the wisdom of our ancient political tradition.[14] In other words, these reformists were keen to craft a modernity which would be their own, where the state would be defined spiritually rather than in Western secular legalistic terms, but it would be inclusive at the same time. As Shyama Prasad Mookherji himself put it in one of his speeches: 'I hate the word secular—in the dictionary it is defined as "Godless, profane", we claim to be a civilised democratic State, where people will have equal rights no matter what their religion is ...'[15] And, in this moral–spiritual definition of state, the Hindu Mahasabha was expected to define its own distinctive modernity vis-à-vis the secular modernism of the Congress that was perceived to be imitative of the West.

There were of course others who would accept Mookherji's spiritual–moral definition but not share his universalism, and were more inclined to define the Hindu rashtra in an exclusive communitarian mode. 'Dharam cannot be separated from the State just as the soul cannot be separated from the body,' declared one submission to the general secretary of the AIHM. 'A mere secular democratic state in the Western sense can never satisfy the aspirations of the Hindu people.' And this state 'should not merely concern itself with the material happiness and prosperity of its people'. However, this spiritual state would also be the exclusive state of a community, as the 'Muslims [would] have no place in the Hindu Rashtra as long as they are out and out Muslims'.[16] The Raisinghnagar Praja Sevak Sangh of Bikaner also resolved that the 'Hindu rastra state must be based on Dharma', but, in this dharma rashtra, the minorities were to be defined as 'the followers of foreign born religions', who 'should not be allowed rights of citizenship until and unless they identify themselves in every way with (dress, manner of living, customs, civilisation and outlook) the Hindu people'.[17] In other words, in these thoughts 'Hindu' represented a conflation of nation and a religious community. According to Pirthi Singh of Delhi, India 'would not be a theocratic state but Hindu Democratic State of 99% Hindu Population'.[18] But even though the Hindus were a majority 'community', as the Calcutta Ward IX Hindu Mahasabha argued, they needed an exclusive political organization of their own, as 'non-communal bodies' such as the Congress could not be expected to protect the interests of the Hindus.[19]

For some others, however, Hindu majoritarianism was more selectively discriminatory towards the nation's minorities. In their perception, the memories of Partition and a wounded sense of historical injustice made the Muslims the natural 'Other' of their putative Hindu/Indian nation. Other minorities could be embraced without any malice towards them. G.V. Subba Rao of Bezwada, who served twice on the AIHM Working Committee, thought that 'the State must be a good servant of the Dharma', because 'religion is the breath of our real life', and he doubted if a proper secular state ever existed anywhere in the world except in Russia. As for the minorities, he recommended that the Hindu Mahasabha follow the dictum that '[t]he majority must constitute our confidence and minority our doubt'. But he was not equally unsympathetic to all minorities. In his reckoning, '[a]lmost all the Mussalmans in India' were 'matadrohis' (treacherous to the mother) and therefore should be 'disenfranchised statutorily' for at least twenty years. Indeed, in his view, 'the logical culmination' of the Indian freedom movement should have been 'the elimination not only of the couple of lakhs of Britishers in the country, but also of the several crores of the followers of Islam ... through assimilation or otherwise'. As for other minorities such as Christians, Parsees, and others, he was 'not in favour of any discrimination against them for obvious reasons'. On the other hand, he was all in favour of building bridges within the Hindu community through such movements as 'shuddhi, sangathan, removal of untouchability', and so forth, in order to eliminate all those 'ugly differences and inequalities which are now standing in the way of a strong and live Hindu solidarity'.[20]

Similarly, in north India, to Avadesh Narayan Singh, a *vakil* (lawyer) in Gorakhpur in the United Provinces (UP), who described himself as 'an ordinary citizen of India', a 'nation without religion is a ship without helm to guide its course through the stormy waters of materialism', and it was in this emphasis on religion that he thought 'the ideology of Congress differs from that of Mahasabha'. Hindu rashtra for him should be 'so defined as to connote an organised attempt to uplift humanity in spiritual, moral, social and lastly political spheres of life'. In this state, there should be 'perfect freedom with regard to religion'; even the Muslims should 'be given equal opportunity in all spheres of life provided they remain loyal to India'. And here lay the crux of the problem, as he thought the 'Muslim mentality' had 'not left the narrow groove of communalism and a born hatred for non-Muslims'. He was, however, willing to admit Buddhists, Jains, Sikhs, and aboriginals into the fold of the Mahasabha.[21]

If we look at all the submissions that were pouring into the AIHM head office in Delhi, it seems clear that among the Hindu Mahasabha followers throughout India, certain distinct ideological strands were taking shape. What all of them rejected was the idea of a secular state on the Western model. Its alternative, 'Hindu rashtra', had different meanings to different people. To some of the reformists it implied a spiritual concept of state, which was universalist. For them 'Hindu' was the name of a civilizational nation, not a community, and it included other religious groups. But in the minds of an increasing number of people, a communitarian definition of the Hindu rashtra was taking shape as well. For them 'Hindu' was a community—the majority community—which should legitimately dominate the nation-state in which the other minority communities were suspects. And of all the minorities, the Muslims were particularly unacceptable because of a widely shared historic sense of betrayal. And as these communitarian ideas began to take firmer roots, the reformists found their space more and more constricted. This tension reached a crisis point as the Mahasabha received its severest political blow with the assassination of Mahatma Gandhi.

The Crisis

The assassination of Mahatma Gandhi (30 January 1948) was widely believed to have been the result of a conspiracy involving the AIHM and the RSS.[22] The public outrage that followed led to a severe clampdown on both these political groups by the Government of India. Apart from state control, there was a huge popular backlash against the Hindu right-wing political organizations and their leaders. In Maharashtra, the Brahmans became targets of public attacks—their houses were burnt and properties worth about one crore rupees were destroyed.[23] In Bengal, houses of prominent Mahasabha leaders such as Shyama Prasad Mookherji were attacked by irate mobs.[24] The RSS was formally banned; the AIHM escaped the ban, but the public backlash made some of its leaders think deeply about its future. Mookherji argued that the Mahasabha now had two options: either it could wind up its political career and focus on welfare and philanthropic activities, or it could shed its communal character and throw its door open to people of all religions (Graham 1990: 13). As he argued later in a press statement, an exclusive Hindu party had lost its *raison d'etre* in post-Partition India:

> In the India of today, more than 85% of her people are Hindus and if they are unable to protect their own economic and political interests or India's inherent rights through the working of a fully Democratic constitution, no separate political party, which would confine its membership to the Hindu fold alone, could ever save Hindus or their country.

On the other hand, if the majority community itself retains its political exclusiveness it would inevitably encourage the growth of communal political organizations representing the interests of various minority groups within the country itself, leading to highly prejudicial results.[25]

On Mookherji's recommendation, the Bengal Branch of the Mahasabha on 11 February 1948 formally adopted a resolution to suspend all political activities and only exist as a social philanthropic organization.[26] Following this, the central Working Committee of the AIHM met in Delhi on 14–15 February and extended that decision to the rest of India. It decided to 'suspend its political activities and to concentrate on real Sangathan work ... for the creation of a powerful and well organized Hindu society in Independent India' (quoted in Graham 1990: 13).

This was hardly a popular decision and indeed precipitated a crisis for the organization, as the conservatives reacted sharply to what appeared to them an unnecessary knee-jerk response. Lahiry, the general secretary, found the situation 'intriguing', while B.S. Moonje, then the vice president of the AIHM, was of 'clear opinion ... against Mahasabha relinquishing politics'.[27] B.G. Khaparde, a member of the Working Committee from Poona, sent an urgent telegram to Mookherji telling him: 'You giving [sic] wrong lead in asking Sabha [to] give up politics. This is panicky advice. 87% Hindus have not Hindu minds. Sabha's aim was infusing Hindu spirit which is real nationalism and must have free expression in any democracy worth the name.' In another telegram to L.B. Bhopatkar, the president of the AIHM, he argued that Mookherji's leadership was 'misleading, in both matters': the Mahasabha 'must not abandon politics' and 'cannot admit non-Hindus'.[28] While a strong faction in Bengal under N.C. Chatterjee and Debendranath Mukherjee supported Mookherji, in public meetings he was vilified in abusive speeches.[29] A number of members of the Bengal provincial council complained to Moonje about manipulation of the meeting by the Mookherji group. This resolution, the letter stated, was the 'verdict of Dr Mukharji and Mr. [N.C.] Chatterji only and not the verdict of the Bengal Provincial Hindu Mahasabha Council'. It was passed, they complained, in 'a most undemocratic way' in a meeting that was attended by only 87 of the 350 members of the council.[30] The Hooghly District Committee

and the North Calcutta District Committees separately adopted resolutions recommending resumption of political activities and urging
the AIHM to reconsider the decision of the working committee.[31]

Frustrated radicals from villages and district towns and representatives of Hindu student bodies began to write to the general secretary
protesting against such a cowardly measure following the 'killing of a
friend of Pakistan', expressing in no uncertain words their brahmanical and masculinist anxieties.[32] The Hindu students in Bangalore
city half-heartedly accepted the suspension of political activities as a
temporary 'diplomatic move ... to meet the adverse situation created
by assassination of Gandhijee by one of our members'.[33] But their
elders were more forthright in their condemnation of the decision.
The federation of the South Indian Provincial Mahasabhas, representing Andhra, Madras City, Tamil Nadu, Kerala, Karnataka, and Mysore
states, 'after a heated discussion', adopted a resolution condemning
the Working Committee decision as

> hasty and ill-conceived and not in the best interests of the Hindudom.
> The Federation rejects altogether the theory of an 'Indian' Nation, or
> the theory that Hindus are a Community in Hindusthan. Both his-
> tory and the reason of the thing conclusively show that Hindus are the
> nation in Hindusthan. Hindu Mahasabha has the right in a democratic
> constitution to exist as a political body for undoing the great evil of
> partition of this great and sacred land.[34]

Indeed, in areas such as south India, where public backlash against
Mahasabha had been muted, the reaction of the local Mahasabha
leaders was more strident. 'Why should the leaders of the Hindu
Mahasabha become overnight obsessed with the need for reorientation?' That was the question asked by D.S. Iyer, the secretary of the
South Arcot District Hindu Mahasabha. To him, 'reorientation' meant
'an abandonment of the endeavours of our leaders like Lajpat Rai,
Malaviya & others', and it was 'motivated by fear of mob activities,
lynch law, the sensation mongering press and outbursts of Pandits and
the Socialists'. He questioned the decision of the Working Committee
in the name of democracy, both broader and internal. He agreed that
public opinion in India was shifting towards the ideal of a secular
state. 'But that would not warrant the forcible suppression of a contrary view.' Indeed, 'in a democratic country there must be a healthy
opposition', he asserted; and that was the only 'way of maintaining our

new found freedom'. And then, internally, the Working Committee was 'too small a body' to take such a momentous decision in 'such shortness of time', 'changing the nature of the institution itself'.[35]

The Working Committee of the AIHM ultimately gave in to the pressure from the grassroots and decided in a meeting on 8 August 1948 to reverse its February decision and resume political activities to fulfil the objectives of the 'free nation'.[36] However, the meeting, which included the participation of Mookherji as well, could not ignore the new political developments around them. As a conciliatory gesture towards the reformists, the 'Political Resolution' adopted at the meeting envisaged the 'development of a strong democratic State in the country', and to achieve that objective, it recommended that the All India committee should forthwith 'consider amongst other things whether the membership of the Hindu Mahasabha should not be thrown open to all citizens irrespective of caste or religion'. It also recommended immediate resumption of the initiative to institute a Reorientation Committee to suggest changes to Mahasabha policies and programmes.[37] Within the next three days a committee was formed and its membership publicly announced. It was to be chaired by Bhopatkar and convened by Lahiry. It did not include Shyama Prasad Mookherji, but his supporter from Bengal, Debendranath Mukherjee, was there. However, to counterbalance this, it also included Narendranath Das from his rival faction from Bengal. On the other hand, it had conservatives such as Mahant Digvijay Nath of Gorakhpur and moderates such as R.A. Kanitkar and S.B. Date from Maharashtra.[38]

The Debate

On resumption of political activities by the Mahasabha, both President Bhopatkar and General Secretary Lahiry made two long public statements, which set the tone for the ideological debate and the internal fissures to follow. But more importantly, these statements sought to make the distinction between the conservatives and the reformists rather blurry. Bhopatkar's speech was a persuasive response to the external critics of the Mahasabha, but through this response, he also tried to appropriate the grounds of the reformists. The 'Mahasabha may be communal in its name and style', he argued, but it was not communal in its essence because 'it made or makes no special demands for the Hindu community'. It only demanded an even playing field and tried to ensure that the minority community did not benefit at the cost of the majority. In this sense it was bad propaganda to say that Mahasabha stood for a Hindu theocratic state. On the contrary, it advocated 'a Secular Democratic State, not only in name, but also in reality, that is to say, a State where the rule of the majority shall prevail, but consistent with the fundamental rights of the minority'. In other words, it wanted a state to be fashioned after the true Western democratic model. And this justified Mahasabha's participation in politics, as '[n]o democracy worth the name is conceivable unless there is an effective parliamentary opposition to the party in power'. In modern democracy, he reiterated, opposition did not mean rebellion or any attempt to destabilize the state. On the contrary, what the Mahasabha wanted was 'Surajya i.e. fair, just and efficient government'. In other words, by appropriating the rhetoric of modernity, Bhopatkar justified a conservative position of maintaining an exclusive Hindu political party. He also referred to the 'great furore' which Dr Mookherjee's recent statements had created, both within the Mahasabha as well as in the broader Hindu community. But he avoided making any direct comment, submitting that the Working Committee in due course of time would deal with those issues.[39]

Lahiry's offensive was also overtly directed against the Congress, and was conciliatory towards the reformist position within the party. 'Excepting that the Mahasabha confined its membership to Hindu community alone', he argued, 'there is nothing in the Mahasabha programme or activities which can be called communal in the sense that it ever claimed for the Hindus anything which it sought to deny to Non-Hindus.' According to the Bilaspur resolution the minority community would be free to share in the governance of the country 'in accordance with their numerical strength', 'besides full liberty to develop their religion, culture and language'. In this sense, the Mahasabha's concept of Hindu rashtra was no different from the ideals of the Congress, and indeed it was a great triumph that all the principles that the Mahasabha stood for had now been endorsed by the Constituent Assembly. In such a context, long before the assassination of Mahatma Gandhi, the Mahasabha had initiated the discussion to throw open its gates to Muslims. The leaders of the Mahasabha had already realized that

> the political background which impelled leaders like Pandit Malaviyaji to start the Hindu Mahasabha and organise it as a citadel against Muslim aggressiveness disappeared with the quitting of the British and we now definitely feel that 28 crores [one crore = ten million] of Hindus need not have any separate exclusive organisation of their own for such purposes.

His justification for the return of the Mahasabha to politics was also carefully couched in the rhetoric of modern mass democratic politics. The masses were 'longing for other political parties' which might give new direction to the country, provide an 'effective political opposition', and rescue them from the misrule of the Congress, which was 'pursuing a policy of ruthless suppression of Civil Liberties'. Mahasabha's re-entry into politics was therefore to forestall 'the perpetuation of monopoly of power for the Congress Party'.[40]

As for the reformists within the party, Lahiry and Bhopatkar wanted to set the tone of the ensuing debate by circulating their own draft reorientation resolutions on 6 September 1948, delineating their notions of nationhood, state, and modernity, carefully presenting them in a secular, democratic language. Lahiry's document, first of all, defined 'Hindu' as the *nation*:

> A Hindu means a person who regards this land of Hindusthan from the Himalayas to the Seas as His Motherland and believed that all sections of the people of this country, irrespective of religion constitute one single Nation.

This concept of the territorial nation-state was also universalistic and recognized the rights of all individuals, but would not allow any special rights for the minorities. The Hindu Mahasabha would strive to create 'a non-communal democratic State and to that end shall abolish all special reservations for any minorities'. It would seek to create 'a new social order' in which everyone 'irrespective of caste and creed' would enjoy equal rights.[41] Bhopatkar's document also reiterated that 'the time–spirit require[d] the Dominion of India to form itself into a non-communal, democratic and socialist State'. But it should stop the 'old policy of appeasing some communal elements'. He also made it clear that if any 'non-Hindu' accepted the aims and objectives of the Hindu Mahasabha, he or she could only become its 'associate member'.

The differences between Lahiry's and Bhopatkar's statements are interesting, as the former gives a more territorial definition of Hindu, sounding more like Gandhi in *Hind Swaraj*, while the latter sticks to its religious definition. But Bhopatkar's modernity could be discerned in his recognition of the new realities of mass democracy in free India and in his prescription of a modern socialist economy—his idea of 'surajya'—where one could hardly distinguish his programme from Nehruvian socialism. In his frame of things there would be ceiling on family landholding, excess land would be redistributed among landless tillers, the tiller of the land would enjoy full fruits of his labour, modern scientific agricultural methods would be introduced to increase the yield of the land, and steps would be gradually taken towards collectivization of agriculture. However, at the same time, '[k] illing of cattle useful for agriculture shall be prohibited'. While agriculture was the main focus of his attention, he also recommended nationalization of all 'key industries', minimum wages for labourers, and steps to be taken 'to see that capital does not get concentrated in a few hands'. And finally, he recommended for India a modern welfare system where the 'state shall provide employment to all and shall undertake the maintenance of the unemployed'.[42]

As debate progressed within the Mahasabha circles, two opposing views on citizenship of the Indian nation, and consequently on the membership of the Mahasabha, emerged. One group wanted to redefine the term 'Hindu' by emptying it of its religious connotation and making it a purely geographical and civilizational concept. All those who called Hindusthan their motherland would be considered as Hindus and could become members of the Mahasabha. On the other hand, the conservatives wanted to stick to the existing religious and exclusive definition of Hindu, as was once defined by Veer Savarkar, and as a concession to the new realities of free India would perhaps accept non-Hindus as 'associate members' of the Mahasabha.[43] And, as the conservatives consolidated their position within the party, both Bhopatkar and Lahiry took their side.

The ideological rift over the nature of Indian modernity and citizenship ripped open the divisions within the Mahasabha leadership. On one side of this fault line, as Lahiry explained in a personal letter to one of his supporters, were the reformists including '[m]ost of our Maharashtrian leaders', who believed in the Western type of democracy through which they wanted to establish the dominance of the Hindus. According to them, this had already been accomplished with Independence and Partition and hence they demanded the transformation of the Mahasabha into a non-communal organization. But '[s]ome of us', wrote Lahiry, 'have not been able to see eye to eye with this fundamental approach to the problem'. They felt that a democratic tradition in India could only be developed slowly, and hence the 'spiritual and cultural heritage of India must be the sheet-anchor' of the future Indian state.[44] In the end the Reorientation Committee discussed the new draft constitution of the party, which was approved by the AIHM Working Committee on 6–7 November 1948, and it defined 'Hindu' as: 'A person who declares that he is a Hindu and regards this land of Bharatvarsha ... as his Father-land as well as his Holyland.' And within that definition, the committee decided to 'carry on its political activities without admitting any non-Hindu thereto'.[45]

However, it was possibly one of the most contested decisions that the AIHM ever took in its history. The Reorientation Committee had met on 18, 19, and 20 September 1948; in all, it had four sittings and deliberated for 13–14 hours, but in the end failed to produce a unanimous decision. The main resolution which recommended that 'the Hindu Mahasabha should carry on its political activities without admitting any non-Hindus thereto' was supported by seven members of the committee, while three members—S.R. Date, K.H. Dhamdhere, and R.A. Kanitkar—voted against it. At that point, Dhamdhere raised a point of objection that the resolution went against the specific terms of reference. The president, L.B. Bhopatkar, then ruled that the recommendation of the Reorientation Committee would be referred back to the Working Committee, where the three members could also present a Minority Report. The Working Committee and then the All India Committee would take the final decision.[46]

In a 'Minute of Dissent' the three dissident members recorded their sense of disappointment in no uncertain terms: 'Our dissent basically relates to the necessity of opening the Hindu Mahasabha to other nationals, which according to us is inevitable in the new set up, so as to enable it to function as an effective political organisation.'[47] The proceedings of the Working Committee, which sat in Delhi on

6 and 7 November 1948, do not give any indication that a separate Minority Report was ultimately placed. So the conclusion was almost foregone as the conservatives dominated the committee, and six of the seven members of the Reorientation Committee who had voted for the recommendation were among the fifteen Working Committee members who attended this meeting. But even then, it could not be passed unanimously. Debendranath Mukherjee (a known Shyama Prasad loyalist), who was a member of the Reorientation Committee but could not attend the meeting because of family reasons,[48] voted against the resolution.[49]

The decision of the Working Committee had not ended the debate; rather, it had laid bare the ideological rift within the Mahasabha very sharply, and it now began to threaten the very existence of the organization. Shortly after the Working Committee meeting, R.A. Kanitkar of Maharashtra, one of the dissenting members of the Reorientation Committee, warned the secretary: 'If Indian Union is to function as a secular state & if Hindus do not want to be dubbed hard baked conservatives, the Association must open its gates to all nationals irrespective of race & creed.' And he further warned that the 'depleted ranks of the Sabha in Berar will also melt away, leaving a few individuals, if the W.C. [Working Committee] decides to commence politics without provision for all nationals'.[50] S.R. Date, editor of the Marathi newspaper *Kal* and another dissenting member of the Reorientation Committee, wrote to Lahiry from Poona that the Hindu Mahasabha should take the name of 'Democratic Party or some other nationalist name'. If this did not happen he would resign with 'some others', because 'we do not think that with the democratic ideology in politics, we can consistently continue to be in the organisation which is mainly political and still excludes all other national elements only on account of different religion'.[51] K. Shivanandy Thevar of the Tamil Nad Hindu Mahasabha, who was a member of the Reorientation Committee but did not attend the meeting, wrote in a disappointing tone that if Dr Mookherji's views about opening up the membership were accepted, there would have been 'more chances for Hindu Mahasabha to succeed [in] its long-cherished desire with changed colours in the light of changed circumstances'.[52]

On the other hand, the conservatives mobilized their supporters as well. On 12 December 1948, the Bengal Provincial Hindu Mahasabha held a meeting which was marked by 'sharp division of camps', and the 'majority of members were found to be against the new definition [of Hindu] and in favour of Savarkarite one'.[53] Another memorandum sent by S.K. Acharya from Punjab to the AIHM argued that 'the name of the race inhabiting this country "Bharat" has always been "Hindu" from the "Day of Creation" to the day of Mahabharat and later till our times'. And they are 'distinct' from other communities such as Muslims, Parsis, or Christians, 'who may be the nationals of India by Declaration, Adoption etc'.[54] In other words, while the Hindus were the natural citizens, others were only naturalized citizens of India.

The consolidation of this communitarian position was again clearly visible in the responses to AIHM's attempt in early 1949 to develop a broad political opposition to Congress. In February, it constituted a committee for 'rallying round all really democratic and nationalistic forces in the country with a view to forming a common political platform'.[55] But the provincial responses to this endeavour were rather lukewarm. Of course, there were some positive responses: for example, the UP Provincial Hindu Mahasabha decided to hold a convention to explore possibilities to form a common platform 'to check the fascist tendencies of the Congress governments' and the 'growing menace of communism'.[56] The Bengal Provincial Hindu Mahasabha held 'fairly a big meeting' in Calcutta under the presidency of Dr Radhabinode Paul,[57] and a 'Unity Party of India' was formed.[58] But there were many others who were less enthusiastic about such a broad cross-party alliance. S.R. Date wrote back from Poona reporting that 'excluding the RSS there are scarcely any parties worth the name with whom we can make any common cause'.[59] In Madras, M.V. Ganapati, who later became a member of the Working Committee, found it 'impossible to attract any politician of the other recognised parties'. The AIHM was 'for the present unpopular', he agreed. But he was not too concerned about that because: 'The public is just a big baby with no intelligence behind it, and it is we who think and act for the best of Hinduthva.... If they are so taught there is no reason why they should not support us.' And therefore he preferred to go alone 'without changing even an iota of our ideology'.[60] Despite all the democratic rhetoric, such distrust of the masses found resonance in the utterances of the party high command as well. Ashutosh Lahiry, the general secretary of the AIHM, wrote to one of his followers: 'Democracy has to be built up slowly and steadily and cannot be over-night [*sic*] foisted on the public. The masses are ignorant, do not know how to exercise their vote ...' So until that time when the masses would be sufficiently infused with the ideology of Hindu rashtra, the AIHM had 'to see that public opinion is mobilised along these lines ... to recreate a new India in social, cultural, economic and political spheres in consonance with the ancient Indian ideals as applied to modern conditions'.[61]

It was this ascendancy of the communitarian ideas within the AIHM that further constricted the space for the reformists who wanted to forge a broad-based democratic political opposition to the Congress. Shyama Prasad Mookherji resigned from the Working Committee on 23 November and from the AIHM in December 1948; his resignation was accepted on 7 May 1949 (Baxter 1969: 27; Graham 1990: 13). In a press statement, he clarified that he was resigning 'with no ill-will to any one', and hoped that 'whatever the Mahasabha may decide in future, its activities will be directed towards the consolidation not only of Hindus but of all important interests and elements in the country, who believe in one Indian Nationhood'.[62] Other disgruntled members of the AIHM who did not resign continued to publicly criticize their central working committee's decision, breaching party discipline and incurring the wrath of the general secretary.[63] But such dissenting voices within the party, as we shall see later, could not be muffled or purged so easily.

The New Programme

The same Working Committee meeting in New Delhi that accepted Mookherji's resignation also adopted a resolution on 8 May 1949 to immediately reactivate the AIHM as a political party on the basis of its original political position and programme of actions.[64] Veer Savarkar's birthday on 28 May was to be observed as the 'Hindu Mahasabha Day', when the workers would re-launch the political programmes of the party after sixteen months of suspension.[65] It was 'gratifying', wrote Lahiry in a circular, that the day was 'enthusiastically observed all over India and evoked a very satisfactory response from the public though news agencies, for reasons not known to ourselves, blacked out all news about the Day!'[66] In June 1949, a new programme of the AIHM was issued through a document entitled *Mahasabha's New*

Stand. It pointed out categorically that there would be 'no departure, whatsoever, from our ideal of Hindu Rashtra'. '[W]e call it Hindu Rashtra', the document said, 'because the word "Indian" is foreign to us.' Any 'blind imitation' of Western democracy 'can never inspire the masses, nor can it lead our land to its desired destiny', only the ideal of Hindu rashtra can.[67] At a press conference in Calcutta on 4 November 1949, Ashutosh Lahiry, as the general secretary of the AIHM, provided a further clarification of its new anti-Congress, anti-secular ideology. '[P]olitics is inseparable from religion', he argued in a conscious attempt to dissociate Mahasabha from the Western model of secular modernity which Congress had embraced. He accepted, however, the Western model of homogenous nation-state and argued, following the Savarkarite line (Jaffrelot 1993: 31), that the 'state must aim at securing cultural homogeneity throughout the country'. And of course, this must be based on the notion of 'Hindu rashtra'. While defining the concept, his statement did take into account the new realities of post-Partition India. Hinduism today, he observed, was like 'a federal system of diverse faiths', and therefore, in the Hindu rashtra, every religion would have its right. But everyone would have to align with the cultural notion of Hindu rashtra, going back to 'ancient moorings'; it involved 'the work of *nationalising* the four crores of our Muslim brethren'.[68]

The new programme also marked a remarkable retreat from the bold socialist pronouncements of Bhopatkar a few weeks ago. *Mahasabha's New Stand* mentioned that the Hindu rashtra 'will be meaningless if it fails to alleviate the sufferings of the masses'. But unlike the Socialists or the Communists, its emphasis would be 'primarily on cultural unity and secondarily on economic read-justments' because it would like to avoid class conflicts. Therefore, their 'appeal ... [was] to subordinate the economic interests of the individual to the superior demand of a common culture and a common way of life'. The document did talk about such bold pro-grammes as land redistribution among the landless, nationalization of key industries, labourers being part-proprietors of industries, and assured minimum living wages. But ultimately, all these were to maintain social harmony—to save the country from that 'dangerous swing to communism'.[69] In a subsequent press statement, Lahiry made this stand even clearer:

We believe that the Kisan-Majdoors, the middle classes, and that section of the people which will continue to be more prosperous than the rest are all inseparable limbs in the body-politic of our Mother Country, and will all have an effective share in moulding the future of the country, each according to his merit. Those Leftists who are crying for Kishan–Majdoor Raj forget that in no country in the world today there is any such Raj.[70]

These were the same ideas that conservatives such as G.V. Subba Rao put forward in cultural terms as the 'golden rule of the Veda':

... that the landlord (Kshatriya), labourer (Shudra), capitalist (vysya) and organiser (Brahmin) are all but different limbs of the same Organism or Purusha; and it should be our unceasing endeavour to ensure that these several 'factors of Production' are all restored to their pristive [sic] and glorious position.[71]

As Christophe Jaffrelot has argued, such ideas of 'spiritual collectivism' were eventually to take the shape of a new, organicist brahmanical version of the varna system in the thinking of the Mahasabha leaders (1993: 108). The ultimate example of that was the resolution proposed by Mohant Digvijaynath at the Calcutta session of the AIHM in December 1949. It said that the Mahasabha should look with pride at the social and scientific system enjoined in the Vedas of dividing the Hindu society into the four varnas of Brahman, Kshatriya, Vaisya, and Sudra, and recommended that in tune with the modern times a new varna (*nabin varna*) should be recognized as composed of those who did not follow the rules of caste or had been brought back to the Hindu fold through *shuddhi* or reconversion.[72] This extreme casteist resolution, however, did not ultimately reach the final stages.

It was at this Calcutta session of the AIHM, held at Deshbandhu Park on 24–26 December 1949, that the new programme was confirmed. According to the official historian of the Mahasabha it was at this session that a new organization emerged into full vitality of life from the ideological debates and political confusion of the preceding years following the assassination of Gandhi (Prakash 1966: 5). It was decidedly a more conservative organization, which changed its name from All India Hindu Mahasabha to 'Akhil Bharat Hindu Mahasabha', whose objective would be to 'establish a really democratic state in Hindusthan based on the culture and traditions of the land'.[73] Veer Savarkar, while inaugurating the session, described the independence of India as a great victory for the Hindudom. For him the Hindu rashtra had already arrived, as the president, prime minister, and the deputy prime minister were all Hindus. So, now the total fulfilment of the promise of freedom for this Hindu nation would be in reversing Partition and restoring Akhand Bharat or undivided India. And, within this context, there was an even more urgent need for the Hindu Mahasabha to 'represent and protect the interests of the Hindus'. The address of the new Mahasabha president, Dr N.B. Khare, was less triumphalist in celebration of Indian independence. Freedom, Khare believed, was a hasty transfer of power, marred by the Partition. The Hindu Mahasabha, he declared, believed in a non-communal government, where every individual would be equal before law. But the Muslims had failed to become 'nationally minded', and hence the policy of 'appeasement' towards the Indian Muslims should be given up. He opposed the Hindu Code Bill and thought that the idea of a secular state only reflected 'a confused and diseased mind', as it did not exist anywhere.[74]

The question of the Indian Muslims, however, continued to cause rancour as the Mahasabha ideologues sought to establish a Hindu majoritarian position for the party. At an All India Hindu Youth's Conference, in his presidential speech, Ashutosh Lahiry sought to present the basic contours of this position. The Hindu rashtra was 'not for the Hindus alone', he argued,

> But we want Hindu Rashtra because we desire to give a predominant bias to all State activities in favour of the Culture and Heritage of the land which the overwhelming majority of its Hindu population have the inalienable right to claim.[75]

However, as the Mahasabha ideologues sought to define Hindu rashtra anchored in the nation's past, it was difficult to completely purge the Muslims out of that past. In December 1950, the Parliamentary Board of the Mahasabha in a document entitled *Mahasabha and Its Ideals* therefore sought to resolve this anomaly of history by trying to exteriorize all non-Hindus. 'Bharat' or 'Akhand Hindustan' was declared as the 'National Home for the Hindus'. 'Their "National Home" was forcibly captured, and has been retained under wrongful possession, by non-Hindu invaders, just as the Jews' Homeland was held up by non-Jews.' All non-Hindus thus became the progeny of foreign invaders, although in recognition of the present, the document also suggested that the Mahasabha would ultimately accept non-Hindus into the Hindu rashtra and they would 'enjoy the same rights and privileges as Hindus'; but the government would 'have powers to make distinction, if deemed necessary'.[76]

However, if this document sounded like the ultimate assertion of a Hindu majoritarian and communitarian position, the reformists had not given up their battle yet. When the Working Committee met in Moradabad on 2 October 1950, a campaign was again launched to throw the doors of the party open to all non-Hindus. The conservatives opposed again, fearing that this would lead to the liquidation of the party, and the Working Committee agreed only to associate non-Hindus with the parliamentary part of its activities (Prakash 1966: 99–100). Not daunted by this failure, in December 1950 the reformists again attempted to amend the official resolution on non-Hindus at the Poona session of the Working Committee, which was to endorse the principles adopted at the Calcutta session. The official resolution 'recognise[d] that the various non-Hindu minorities in India have got large stakes in the country', but allowed them entry into the Mahasabha only 'in so far as the Parliamentary part of its activities is concerned'.[77] If this was a minor concession to the reformists, the latter were still intent on making a last attempt to change the orientation of the party in order to make it into an effective democratic opposition. First of all, an amendment to the official resolution was unsuccessfully moved by Professor Om Prakash Kahol of Punjab. It pointed out that the non-Hindu minorities, 'who have completely identified their interests with the Nation', needed to be assured 'equal opportunities'. It also proposed that the Mahasabha 'may, if need be, enter into Parliamentary coalitions with other political parties, groups and individuals, as the case may be to carry out its accepted programme through legislatures'.[78] While this amendment did not go anywhere, another proposed resolution from Govindrao Desai of Poona mentioned 'the urgent need of having a strong party in opposition to the party in power'. And for that reason it suggested that 'the Hindu Mahasabha should take a bold step to convert itself into a *Hindi* Mahasabha (i.e., an assembly of all Indians) to make it possible for all irrespective of religion and community to become its members to secure the common object of having a strong and influential opposition to the Congress'.[79] Another 'Alternative Resolution', in similar vein, proposed to rally 'all nationalist and democratic elements' to form a new party as a parliamentary opposition—a new party that would be 'open to all irrespective of caste, colour and creed ... [and be] broad-based upon the principles of democracy and nationalism'.[80] These draft resolutions did not ultimately make their way to the main session.

Four months later, on 28 April 1951, a special session of the AIHM in Jaipur finally endorsed the decision of accepting non-Hindus only in its parliamentary activities. The resolution invited the 'Indian Muslims to rally under the banner of the Mahasabha to build up a Hindu rashtra in which their interests would be fully safeguarded'.[81] In other words, in the Mahasabha's ideological parlance, citizenship of India was not going to be based on the Western concept of secular individual citizenship; it was going to be defined culturally by its notions of Hindutva. The Muslims had to accept that ideology to become full citizens. In this session, Dr N.B. Khare was even more threatening in his presidential address; he proposed to 'go a step further and Hinduise all foreign faiths' (quoted in Prakash 1966: 101). The new constitution of the AIHM, as amended at Jaipur, declared:

> The Aim of the Hindu Mahasabha is to establish a really democratic Hindu State in Bharat, based on the culture and tradition of Hindu Rashtra and to re-establish Akhand Bharat by all constitutional means.[82]

We should remember, however, that at a discursive level such ascendancy of 'ethno-religious notions of citizenship' (Shani 2010: 145–73), based on a majoritarian Hindu identity, was not confined to the ranks of the Hindu Mahasabha leadership alone. In immediate post-Partition India, suspicion about Muslim loyalty and questions about their full citizenship were being raised by influencial leaders of the Congress as well as powerful members of the bureaucracy (Pandey 1999: 608–9). At an ontological level, the Muslims continued to be socially alienated and physically ghettoized in cities such as Delhi or Calcutta, where Hindu Partition refugees arrived in large numbers and Muslims became refugees in their own land. They often came to be described as 'fifth columnists' and their neighbourhoods came to be known as 'miniature Pakistans' (for moving details, see Pandey 1997; Chatterji 2005; Zamindar 2007: 79–94). Yet, it is also critical to remember that voices against such tendencies to stigmatize the Muslims and deny them full citizenship within the new nation-state of their choice were being raised not only by secular Congress leaders such as Jawaharlal Nehru or Maulana Abul Kalam Azad, but also by a number of reformists among the Hindu nationalist leaders. The marginalization of the latter and the ascendancy of the former by 1950–1 determined the future political trajectories of the two political groups, as the Indian constitution in January 1950 established the principle of individual citizenship based on complete equality, and the nation went to its first general election in January 1952 on the basis of universal adult franchise.

***

S.R. Date recalled in an oral interview in 1970 that if the reorientation debate in 1949–50 had been resolved in favour of the reformists, and the Hindu Mahasabha had evolved into something like a 'Democratic Swaraj Party which was open to all', the trajectory of Hindu nationalist politics in India might have been different.[83] That counterfactual historical possibility is worth pondering in view of the ideological debates within the Hindu right in the wake of decolonization. The Hindu right in India was by no means a political monolith—not everyone was a communalist in the same way. There was a strong dissident voice which offered a different model of modernity that recognized a legitimate space for religion in the public life of the nation, but did not accept the exclusivist communitarian ideology of Hindu rashtra that sought to exclude the Muslims from citizenship. But this reformist position found its political space gradually shrinking, as the conservatives took control of the Hindu Mahasabha and the Congress secularists represented everyone on the right as communalists and therefore not worthy of any political legitimacy in post-Independence India.

In May 1966, on the eve of the 50th anniversary of the Hindu Mahasabha, its official historian, Indra Prakash, wrote: 'Perhaps there is no other political organization in India other than the Hindu Mahasabha which has been more misunderstood or misrepresented both by friends and foes alike' (Prakash 1966: 1). This essay sought to clear some of those misperceptions and misrepresentations perpetuated by both its protagonists and detractors. David Cannadine has reminded us that 'historians need to emancipate themselves from the spurious thraldom of dichotomized modes of thinking'; they 'should be more concerned with gradations, continuums and nuances than with postulating mutually exclusive alternatives' (Cannadine 2008: 33–4). Remembering that cautionary note, this essay strives to drive home the point that binaries such as the secular–communal dichotomy, which dominate much of India's nationalist historiography and popular discourses on communalism, do not help us understand the reorientation of Hindu nationalist politics in the wake of decolonization. To understand this politics we need to take cognizance of the ideological fissures and debates within this political strand.

It is also possible to argue that this past has a presence, as these debates have not been conclusively resolved yet, and there have always been parallel strands within Hindu nationalist politics as represented by the Jana Sangh in the 1960s and 1970s and its successor, the Bharatiya Janata Party (BJP), since the 1980s, with their varying relationships with the RSS. One of these strands has been more liberal and reformist, seeking alliances with other democratic forces in the country, proposing populist economic programmes in the 1970s, and even using such rhetoric as 'Gandhian socialism' and 'positive secularism' in the 1980s. The other strand has been evidently more traditionalist and communitarian, often concerned about the dilution of the ideology of Hindutva and usually militantly exclusivist. It is difficult to pin down these two strands to specific individuals or groups striving for power, and these divisions, as Christophe Jaffrelot has argued, are often strategic rather than ideological (Jaffrelot 1996). In other words, these internal fissures and debates cannot be reduced into fixed binaries. The Hindu right has always been balancing between divergent trends, sometimes trying to forge consensus, forming alliances with other political parties, and sometimes taking extreme positions to negotiate popular pressures. As Thomas Blom Hansen and Christophe Jaffrelot have argued: 'The Jana Sangh, and later the Bharatiya Janata Party have always oscillated between a militant and a moderate approach to politics.' The Hindu right's ambition to become a national alternative to Congress materialized in the 1990s when the BJP moved towards a softer pragmatic policy of forging consensus with other opposition political parties. Yet its 'ambivalence' persisted, 'reflecting deeper tension between ideological purity and pragmatism in the Hindu nationalist movement' (Hansen and Jaffrelot 1998: 1–2). This tension, as this essay has tried to show, originated in the early days of independence.

Notes

1. *The Statesman*, 19 October 1951.

2. 'Sree Ashutosh Lahiry, General Secy, All India Hindu Mahasabha, in the course of the press conference stated', Cawnpore, 8 January 1948, Hindu Mahasabha Papers (hereafter HM), File no. C-165/1947, Nehru Memorial Museum and Library, New Delhi (hereafter NMML).

3. 'Sree Ashutosh Lahiry, General Secy, All India Hindu Mahasabha, in the course of the press conference stated', Cawnpore, 8 January 1948.

4. 'Dr. S.P. Mukerjee's statement', S.P. Mookherji Papers (hereafter SPM), I Installment, Speeches/Statements, Sl. no. 6, NMML. Also see Graham (1990: 12–13).

5. *Amrita Bazar Patrika*, 7 July 1949.

6. Ashutosh Lahiry to N.C. Chatterjee, circular letter to all Provincial Sabhas, dated nil, letter intercepted on 17 October 1947, Government of Bengal, Intelligence Branch (henceforth GB, IB), S. no.65/30, File no.103/30, West Bengal State Archives, Kolkata (hereafter WBSA).

7. Balai Chand Mukherjee to N.C. Chatterjee, 19 October 1947, intercepted letter, GB, IB, S. no. 65/30, File no.103/30, WBSA.

8. Copy of an English letter D/27.10.47 from Brindaban Das, President, Hindu Sabha, Mathura, to Ashutosh Lahiry, General Secretary, All India Hindu Mahasabha, GB, IB, S. no. 35/20, File no. 250/20, WBSA.

9. A copy of the circular can be found in HM, File no. C-175/1948-49, pp. 195–6, NMML.

10. HM, File no. C-175/1948-49, pp. 195–6, NMML.

11. See HM, File no. C-175/1948–9, NMML.

12. General Secretary, Banaras City Hindu Mahasabha to General Secretary, AIHM, 16 February 1948, HM, File no. C-175/1948–9, NMML.

13. K.S. Ramaswamy Sastri to Ashutosh Lahiry, 8 February 1948, HM, File no. C-175/1948–9, NMML.

14. Rebati Raman Datta to Ashutosh Lahiry, 10 January 1948, HM, File no. C-175/1948–9, NMML.

15. Speeches/Statements by S.P. Mookherji, SPM, I Installment, S. no. 31, NMML.

16. Submission by Satya Parkash and Purna Chandra Chakravarty, HM, File no. C-175/1948–49, NMML.

17. 'Answers to the Questionnaire issued by the General Secretary H.M.S. [Hindu Mahasabha] to know the public mind by Distt Praja Sevak Sangh Raisingh Taluka Bikaner State', 5 January 1948, HM, File no. C-175/1948–49, NMML.

18. Pirthi Singh to Ashutosh Lahiry, 3 December 1947, HM, File no. C-175/1948–49, NMML.

19. R. Biswas, G. Bhattacharjee, and B.K. Chanda, Ward IX Hindu Mahasabha, Calcutta, to General Secretary, AIHM, 10 February 1948, HM, File no. C-175/1948–49, NMML.

20. G.V. Subba Rao to Ashutosh Lahiry, 29 December 1947, HM, File no. C-175/1948–49, NMML.

21. 'A Memorandum to All India Hindu Mahasabha', submitted by Avadesh Narayan Singh, HM, File no. C-175/1948–49, NMML.

22. 'Brief History of Shri Ashutosh Lahiry', GB, IB, S. no. 45/1920, File no. 210/20, WBSA.

23. S.R. Date interview transcript, dated 17 April 1970, Cambridge South Asia Centre, no. S.32, p. 7; also see Jaffrelot (1993: 87).

24. *Anandabazar Patrika*, 15 February 1948.

25. Mookherji's press statement, 23 November 1948, Speeches/ Statements, SPM, I Installment, S. no. 6, NMML.

26. *Anandabazar Patrika*, 15 February 1948.

27. B.S. Moonje to Ashutosh Lahiry, 4 February 1948, GB, IB, S. no. 158/20, File no. 210/20, WBSA.

28. B.G. Khaparde to Indra Prakash, Provisional General Secretary, AIHM, 11 April 1948, HM, File no. C-171, NMML.

29. Ashutosh Lahiry to Narendra Nath Dass, Bengal Provincial Hindu Mahasabha, 25 February 1949, intercepted letter, GB, IB, S. no. 35/1920, File no. 210/20 (1), Part I, WBSA.

30. Enclosure to intercepted letter from B.S. Munje to N.C. Chatterji, 24 February 1948, GB, IB, S. no. 158/20, File no. 210/20, WBSA.

31. Bholanath Chakraborty, General Secretary, Hooghly District Hindu Mahasabha, to L.B. Bhopatkar, President, AIHM, 9 May 1948; from S.K. Mitra, Secretary, North Calcutta District Hindu Mahasabha, to President, AIHM, 26 April 1948, HM, File no. C-171, NMML.

32. Twenty-eight crores of Hindu Brothers and Sisters to General Secretary, AIHM, 9 February 1948, intercepted letter, GB, IB Records, S. no. 35/1923, File no. 254/23; Dewan Dwarka Khosla, Working President, All India Hindu Students Federation to Ashutosh Lahiry, 28 August 1950, intercepted letter, GB, IB, S. no. 8/1920, File no. 210/20 (1), Part II, WBSA.

33. General Secretary, Mysore State Hindu Students Federation, Bangalore City, to General Secretary, AIHM, 3 August 1948, HM, File no. C-175/1948–49, NMML.

34. Resolution of the Akhil Bharateeya Hindu Maha Sabha–Dakshina Prantheeya Sakha, 5 March 1948, HM, File no. C-171, NMML.

35. D.S. Iyer, Secretary, South Arcot D.C. Hindu Mahasabha to the General Secretary, AIHM, 10 February 1948, HM, File no. C-175/1948–49, NMML.

36. *The Statesman*, 9 August 1948.

37. Proceedings of the meeting of the Working Committee of the All India Hindu Mahasabha held on 7 and 8 August 1948, HM, File no. C-175/1948–49, NMML.

38. Press Statement, All India Hindu Mahasabha, 12 August 1948, HM, File no. C-175/1948–49, p. 135, NMML. The committee included the following people: L.B. Bhopatkar (chairman), Debendranath Mukherjee (Calcutta), Narendranath Das (Calcutta), Mahant Digvijay Nath (Gorakhpur), Tej Narain (Lucknow), Ram Singh (Delhi), Capt. Keshabchander (Amritsar), Panchanathan Aiyer (Madras), K. Shivanandy Thavar (Madura), R.A. Kanitkar (Buldhana), S.R. Date (Poona), K.B. Dhamdhare (Bombay), Indra Prakash (Delhi), and Ashutosh Lahiry (convenor).

39. Text of the speech by L.B. Bhopatkar, HM, File no. C-175/1948–49, pp. 137–41, NMML.

40. Press statement by Ashutosh Lahiry, dated 18 August 1948, Statements and Speeches, Ashutosh Lahiry Papers (hereafter AL), S. no. 9, NMML.

41. Reorientation of Mahasabha Policy (by Ashutosh Lahiry), 6 September 1948, HM, File no. C-175/1948–49, NMML.

42. L.B. Bhopatkar, 'The Political and Economic Programme of the Hindu Mahasabha', HM, File no. C-175/1948–49, NMML.

43. *The Statesman*, 11 September 1948.

44. Ashutosh Lahiry to Ramendranath Ghosh, 19 April 1949, intercepted letter, GB, IB, S. no. 158/20, File no. 210/20, WBSA.

45. All India Hindu Mahasabha, *New Political & Economic Programme* (New Delhi, 1948), Pamphlets, AL, S. no. 29, NMML.

46. Report of the Reorientation Committee, HM, File no. C-175/1948–49; also see Ashutosh Lahiry's Press Statement in Speeches/Statements, AL, S. no. 10, NMML.

47. 'Minute of Dissent', HM, File no. C-175/1948–49, NMML.

48. Telegram from Debendranath Mukherji to Ashutosh Lahiri, 18 September 1948, HM, File no. C-175/1948–49, NMML.

49. Proceedings of the Working Committee Meeting held at New Delhi on the 6 and 7 November 1948, HM, File no. C-175/1948–49, NMML.

50. R.A. Kanitkar to Ashutosh Lahiry, 28 September 1948, HM, File no. C-175/1948–49, NMML.

51. S.R. Date to Ashutosh Lahiry, 19 April 1949, HM, File no. C-175/1948–49, NMML.

52. S. Sivanandy Thevar to Ashutosh Lahiry, 17 January 1949, HM, File no. C-175/1948–49, NMML.

53. Sukumar Deb Roy to Ashutosh Lahiry, 16 December 1948, HM, File no. C-175/1948–49, NMML.

54. 'Memorandum: English Translation from Sanskrit', dated 12 September 1948, HM, File no. C-175/1948–49, NMML.

55. Memo by Ashutosh Lahiry, 20 February 1949, HM, File no. C-175/1948–49, NMML.

56. Tej Narain to Ashutosh Lahiry, 9 April 1949, HM, File no. C-175/1948–49, NMML.

57. Debendranath Mukherjee to Ashutosh Lahiry, 27 April 1949, HM, File no. C-175/1948–49, NMML.

58. 'Constitution and Rules of The Unity Party of India', HM, File no. C-175/1948–49, NMML.

59. S.R. Date to Ashutosh Lahiry, 19 April 1949, HM, File no. C-175/1948–49, NMML.

60. M.V. Ganapati to Ashutosh Lahiry, 22 April 1949, HM, File no. C-175/1948–49, NMML.

61. Ashutosh Lahiry to Ramendranath Ghose, GB, IB, S. no. 158/20, File no. 210/20, WBSA.

62. 'Dr. S.P. Mukherjee's statement', Speeches and Statements, SPM, I Installment, S. no. 6, NMML.

63. Ashutosh Lahiri to Bholanath Biswas, 1 June 1949, GB, IB, S. no. 158/20, File no. 210/20, WBSA.

64. *Anandabazar Patrika*, 9 May 1949.

65. 'Brief History of Shri Ashutosh Lahiry', GB, IB, S. no. 45/1920, File no. 210/20, WBSA.

66. Ashutosh Lahiry to Makhan Lal Biswas, Circular No.2, GB, IB, S. no. 158/20, File no. 210/20, WBSA.

67. *Mahasabha's New Stand* (New Delhi, June 1949), pp. 5–6, Pamphlets, AL, S. no. 31, NMML.

68. See the transcript of the press conference in GB, IB, S. no. 35/1920, File no. 210/20 (1), WBSA; italics added.

69. *Mahasabha's New Stand*, pp. 6–8, 17–15.

70. Speeches/Statements by Ashutosh Lahiry, AL, S. no. 13, NMML.

71. G.V. Subba Rao to Ashutosh Lahiry, 29 December 1947, HM, File no. C-175/1948–49, NMML.

72. Mohant Digvijaynath to the President, AIHM, 15 December 1949, HM, File no. C-180/ 1949–50, NMML.
73. Twenty-eighth Session of the Akhil Bharat Hindu Mahasabha, Calcutta, 24–26 December 1949, Full Proceedings, pp. 30–5.
74. *Amrita Bazaar Patrika*, 25 and 26 December 1949.
75. Pamphlets, AL, S. no. 37, NMML.
76. *Mahasabha and Its Ideals* (Calcutta, December 1950), pp. 3–7, Pamphlets, AL, S. no. 38, NMML.
77. 'Non-Hindu Minorities', HM, File no. C-184(II), NMML.
78. 'Amendment to the official resolution no. 8 regarding non-Hindu Minorities', HM, File no. C-184(I), NMML.
79. Govind Gopal Desai to Dr N.B. Khare, 18 December 1950, HM, File no. C-184(II), NMML. Emphasis original.
80. 'Alternative Resolution No. 8: Formation of a New Party', HM, File no. C-186, NMML.
81. *The Statesman*, 29 and 30 April 1951.
82. 'The Hindu Mahasabha: Constitution. Aims, Objects and Rules. As amended at the Special Session of the All India Hindu Mahasabha held at Jaipur on 28 and 29 April 1951', Pamphlets, AL, S. no. 42, NMML.
83. S.R. Date interview transcript, dated 17 April 1970, pp. 8–9.

Bibliography

Bandyopadhyay, Sekhar. 2009. *Decolonization in South Asia: Meanings of Freedom in Post-Independence West Bengal, 1947–52.* London, New York: Routledge.
Baxter, Craig. 1969. *The Jana Sangh: A Biography of an Indian Political Party.* Philadelphia: University of Pennsylvania Press.
Cannadine, David. 2008. *Making History, Now and Then: Discoveries, Controversies and Explorations.* Basingstoke: Palgrave.
Chatterji, Joya. 2005. 'Of Graveyard and Ghettos: Muslims in Partitioned West Bengal, 1947–67'. In *Living Together Separately: Cultural India in History and Politics,* edited by Mushirul Hasan and Asim Roy, 222–49. New Delhi: Oxford University Press.
Gondhalekar, Nandini, and Sanjoy Bhattachrya. 1999. 'The All India Hindu Mahasabha and the End of British Rule in India, 1939–1947'. *Social Scientist* 27(314–15): 48–74.
Graham, B. 1988. 'The Congress and Hindu Nationalism'. In *The Indian National Congress,* edited by D.A. Low, 170–87. New Delhi: Oxford University Press.
———. 1990. *Hindu Nationalism and Indian Politics: The Origins and Development of the Bharatiya Jana Sangh.* Cambridge: Cambridge University Press.

Guha, Ramchandra. 2007. *India After Gandhi: The History of the World's Largest Democracy*. London: Macmillan.

Hansen, T.B. and Christophe Jaffrelot. 1998. 'Introduction: The BJP after 1996 Election'. In *The BJP and the Compulsions of Politics in India*, edited by T.B. Hansen and Cristophe Jaffrelot, 1–21. New Delhi: Oxford University Press.

Jaffrelot, Christophe. 1993. *The Hindu Nationalist Movement and Indian Politics: 1925 to the 1990s*. London: Hurst & Co.

————. 1996. *The Hindu Nationalist Movement in India*. New York: Columbia University Press.

Pandey, Gyanendra. 1997. 'Partition and Independence in Delhi: 1947–48'. *Economic and Political Weekly* 32(36): 2261–72.

————. 1999. 'Can a Muslim Be an Indian?' *Comparative Studies in Society and History*, 41(4): 608–29.

Prakash, Indra. 1947. *A Tale of Blunders*. New Delhi: The Hindu Mission Pustak Bhandar.

————. 1966. *Hindu Mahasabha: Its Contribution to India's Politics*. New Delhi: Akhil Bharat Hindu Mahasabha.

Shani, Ornit. 2010. 'Conceptions of Citizenship in India and the "Muslim Question"'. *Modern Asian Studies*, 44(Special Issue 01): 145–73.

Zamindar, Vazira Fazila-Yacoobali. 2007. *The Long Partition and the Making of Modern South Asia*. New York: Columbia University Press.

9

B.L. BIJU

Bipolar Coalition System in Kerala

Carriers and Gatekeepers of Communal Forces in Politics

Community organizations based on castes and religions have an enduring presence in Kerala's democratic politics. The political parties of the left and right are vulnerable to the pressure tactics of communities in varying degrees and for varying reasons. The left component of the party system in Kerala, including the Communist Party of India (Marxist) (CPI[M]) and the Communist Party of India (CPI), are believed to be less susceptible to direct pressure than the right of the party system, which includes the Indian National Congress, Muslim League, and Kerala Congress parties.[1]

The influence of communal pressure groups in politics began from the period of competitive community-based social mobilization for internal reforms, recognition, and status. They had been mobilizing people for community-wise representation in state power since the last quarter of the nineteenth century. Before state reorganization in 1956, Kerala was comprised of three political units—the princely states of Travancore, Cochin (present Kochi), and the British Malabar. The principal agents of political mobilization of people in the three regions were caste–community organizations, class organizations, and the national movement. By the 1940s, in the British Malabar, the strength of class organizations under the communists was gaining ascendency. In the princely states, the Congress held a clear advantage in constructing community coalitions within its party organization. This strategy was also extended to mobilize people during the national struggle. The relative influence and strength of the three currents in mobilizing people in Travancore-Cochin, and Malabar were largely determined by the nature of state structure, relative strength of popular reception for community- and class-based mobilization in the three regions, and the ideology of the principal political-party actor. In south Kerala (old Travancore-Cochin), the strength of Hindu caste organizations and Christian churches in influencing political parties is higher than that in the north. In north Kerala it is only a single community, the Muslims, that has a clear voice in politics through political mobilization on communal lines. When the three regions were combined to form united Kerala, the political processes also got fused. The Hindu right wing has not been a remarkable force in representative democracy across the state until very recently,[2] and the caste organizations have not enjoyed power over the electorate in north Kerala in comparison to their success in the southern parts.

After a long period of ministerial instability due to a high level of organized social polarities and related fragmentations in the party system, the principal political players, by realizing their inability to form a durable single-party government, forged a stable bipolar coalition. In 1964–5, CPI split into two parties (CPI and CPI[M]) based on ideological divisions and the Congress split on communal lines giving birth to the Kerala Congress.[3] Since then, coalition politics became the norm in elections and attained stability by the 1980s. CPI(M) formed the Left Democratic Front (LDF), and the Congress constructed the United Democratic Front (UDF) in the early 1980s.

Coalition politics in Kerala is highly representative of the four major communities (Ezhavas, Muslims, Christians, and Nairs) and guards itself against any precarious takeover of state politics by any single communal party. At present, except for Muslims (mainly in north Kerala), no other community has been successful in forming a community-based political party that has won such a large number of seats in assembly elections. The Kerala Congress parties have the support of Christian churches. But due to the diverse composition of communities in the constituencies where they contest elections in south Kerala, they also have to seek support from the Hindu caste organizations of the Ezhavas and Nairs. Contrary to this, the Indian Union Muslim League (IUML) barely needs the votes of Hindu caste organizations to win elections in their strongholds in north Kerala because of the high concentration of the Muslim population there. Demographically, Hindus form 56 per cent of the population in Kerala, followed by Muslims (25 per cent) and Christians (19 per cent). Christians are believed to be strongly affiliated with the Congress and Kerala Congress parties. Hindus are deeply divided into caste groupings in which Ezhavas outnumber the Nairs. Ezhavas are supporters of left parties in general, while the Nairs give support to the Congress.[4] Nadars, another powerful caste/community which is divided along religious lines into Christians and Hindus, are limited to certain constituencies in Trivandrum district. Scheduled Castes (SCs) comprise 9.1 per cent of the population in Kerala. The Scheduled Tribes (STs), which account for 1.45 per cent of the total population, are concentrated in some areas but do not have big enough numbers to influence the election results. Even though in party politics community-based mobilization seeks opportunities through the Congress-led coalition, it is unable to always assure electoral victory.

Interestingly, the community organizations and their political outfits are also cautious to hide their community-centred agenda from public platforms by pretending to be secular and universal in outlook in public political communication.[5] There are also very few audible voices in Kerala's civil society circles that oppose secularism.[6] All this shows the possibility and strength of an inclusive secular public space in Kerala.

The two coalitions are divided by a narrow vote share in elections. Only in a couple of elections since the 1980s has the difference in their vote share reached 5 per cent, the maximum. The inability of the CPI(M)-led coalition to attract more votes than its opponent shows that the voters in Kerala are more or less equally divided between communal and secular politics. The failure of the left to gain a clear supremacy in electoral politics shall be read as being due to the weakness of its class-secular strategy to pull a clear majority to its side. This chapter qualitatively looks at the nature of interaction between community organizations and political-party system by focusing on public-policy making, electoral competition, and political campaigning.

Communities in Politics: Recognition and Distribution through Bourgeois Competition and Populism

The left-leaning politics under the leadership of CPI(M) in Kerala cannot be treated as solely anchoring on class issues. The class politics of the left, which was truly a secular initiative, appeared on the scene in the 1930s when the society was facing strong communal polarization and its competitive bargaining for non-class but progressive reformative demands vis-à-vis the state. Under colonial modernity the population was mobilized on communal lines and demanded equal recognition and internal reforms. In this course, community identities were reformulated and their demands readjusted with changes in the general system. The social-reform movements organized by caste and religious groupings under the leadership of Western-educated middle-class men were using ascriptive identities for mobilization against the evils generated by the ideas and values of the premodern social structure. The common ground between them was their commitment to a more progressive Kerala society through modernization. Secularism, as they envisaged, was based on creating a democratic state structure and progressive society devoid of community-based discrimination. At the most radical level, the most enlightened sections strived hard for eliminating community-based identities by creating a truly secular citizenship. These efforts helped the formation of public forums representing different groups as part of a greater humanity devoid of manifest discriminations based on caste and religion. The spiritual reformers had set the objective of the social-reform movements as making the Malayalees (a term commonly used in the vernacular to refer to the people of Kerala) more humane in character. The maxim of Sree Narayana Guru, a spiritual reformer from the Ezhava community, exhorted, 'One caste, one religion and one god for all.' There was an urge for the transcendence of communal identity in favour of secular citizenship. Political parties leading national and class movements were an outcome of this process.

Broadly, political parties were the first ensemble of secular public organizations in modernizing Kerala. Social-reform movements supplied leaders to political parties even for the communist party. Even though community organizations had risen to visibility as communal, they had temporal demands for democracy through equal representation and state support to start educational institutions for the uplift of members of the community. They also garnered state support for their well-off sections, especially by lobbying for their respective members in intra-class economic competitions. It substantiates the argument that the road to secularization in Kerala was basically communal in character. The social-reform movements galvanized support by engaging with both the spiritual and temporal lives of the community's population (Mathew 1987). While spiritual reforms were confined to internal reforms, in the emerging democratic politics, they rallied their people for temporal gains. To put it differently, the organizations were fighting for secular objectives by mobilizing people on the basis of community. Their significance in connecting people with politics in temporal matters faced competition with the political parties that were anchored to nationalism and class struggles. Since the formation of party politics in pre-independent Kerala, the party system has exhibited sectarian, integrationist, accommodative, and oppositional currents regarding the political parties' relationship with the community-based organizations.

The left parties were, from the beginning, cautious to appraise the progressive virtues of the community-based social-reform movements. They successfully organized anti-caste class struggles and replaced the Congress from the leadership of national movement in Malabar even more successfully. The communists were fighting class injustice within the communities of caste and religion. They were also opposed the efforts of community organizations to act as pressure groups in politics. The class-wise political mobilization at the initiative of political left was able to split each community along class lines. It also brought a cross-community representation in its class support base. Although left politics in Kerala upheld the modern point of view to treat communalism as a transient phase in the trajectory of transformation, its visionary leadership was aiming at a victory through a critical engagement with questions of caste. The communist party was making its presence in national and social-reform movements in addition to class struggles (Desai 2007). However, since all the major community organizations had a leadership subservient to the upper-class elites, the left political party formations always came into conflict with them.

The attempts of the left for class-wise mobilization had produced enormous trouble in the prevalent community-based mobilization and their trailblazers. For instance, the land-reform movement by and large went against Hindu upper-caste landlords, but it could also attract a large number of tenants and pauperized peasants of the same castes to the side of the left. Likewise, the mobilization by the left of school teachers in quite a large number of private schools run by the religious and caste organizations, in matters of their service and wages, divided employees and employers belonging to the same social identity. The old material base of the caste system in Kerala was debilitating at the beginning of the twentieth century. All the organizationally powerful communities—the Nairs, Ezhavas, Christians, and Muslims—had landlords, traders, and aspiring entrepreneurs. So the peasant movements and trade unions of the left had to confront their enemies in all the major communities. The community organizations also vied for buying plantations and establishing educational and health institutions. The transformation of the basic thrust of community organizations from philanthropy to surplus generation gave additional support to the dominant classes within them. In politics, quite naturally, the relationship between the economically powerful groups and their respective community organizations was based on mutual benefits. The dominant classes needed support of the community to pressurize the political parties and the premodern but gradually democratizing governments. The richer sections were necessary for the community organizations for fundraising and to buy political leaders. It was more prevalent in the princely states than in Malabar. The party formations responded to this situation differently. The Congress and its national movement were found to be more congenial to community pressure groups and their economic classes, while the left politics, which was activating the demands for surplus distribution, went against the dominant classes and thereby got alienated from the community organizations.

Even though the left intellectuals, to a great extent, were able to educate the people about the evils of community politics, the intellectual opposition was not sufficient to ward off the influence of the community organizations in people's daily lives. Community organizations had established strong influence in the lives of the people through engaging with temporal matters such as education and employment, as well as in the rituals of marriage and death. The constitutional democracy of independent India later legitimized spaces for the expression of community identities. The civil–political and economic life of the Malayalees, like other regional groups in India, has a secular and communal component to pull their intellectual and emotional make-up in contrasting directions. Although the left-aligned party tried to replace community organizations from engagement in marriages and funerals, the strategy was not equally successful in all regions and across all communities. The intellectuals and activists who had shifted their loyalties from caste groups and religious sects to the political organizations of the left had to face scathing treatment from their respective communities.[7] Decades ago, it was unthinkable to see a party man in a prayer home or in a community meeting.

The legislative reforms of the left-led governments in education and agriculture received the angst of the dominant classes, and it was rooted through their respective community organizations. Class politics of the left faced, in the late 1950s, the biggest ever consolidated form of political opposition combining landlord–bourgeois–communal forces that toppled the first communist government from power. The left faced strong opposition to its policies of secular control of education because the communities owning a large majority of educational institutions viewed it as a political challenge. Ownership and control of educational institutions was a status symbol for each community and also a means to inform their members of their significance in their lives.

The community groupings had carved out a space in politics as constituents of political parties, for instance, the Congress. While transcendence of communal identity was mandatory for those recruited to the communist party, the Congress, as a grand coalition of social groups, did not make it necessary for party membership. Similarly, while the class movement gained independent strength mainly by seizing advantage of the economic polarization within each community, the Congress took care to forge a unity across classes and a coalition of communities. In fact, communist politics, as else-where, was pitted against both the Congress and the community organizations in Kerala. Their independent strength in organizing class struggles, an anti-imperialist national movement, and, later, the efforts to organize movements for a unified Kerala added strength and legitimacy to their secular class politics. The Congress could not take a lead in the movement for a linguistic state due to opposition from its national leadership and due to the differential stakes that its constituent communities in the princely states (in south Kerala) anticipated in the politics of a united Kerala. The communists played a crucial role in constructing a 'national popular' and gained political benefits from it. Although there have been a number of criticisms about the caste, gender, and religious basis of the 'national popular' and the cultural politics of the left in Kerala in recent times, its efficacy in garnering a huge level of political support for the left parties and acceptance for its political view point was spectacular in the beginning (Mannathukkaren 2013).

The accommodative strategy of the national movement by making a consensus between and concessions for the elites of different communities and the promise of the Congress about greater and equal representation for all in the party organization and government was successful in south Kerala. The Congress strategy of building up a communal coalition in politics worked better in the south, where the community organizations had an earlier and decisive presence, than in the north of Kerala (British Malabar). The accommodative strategy of the Congress, the class polarization brought about by communist politics vis-à-vis community groups, and the new enthusiasm of people to forge a secular, national, and sub-national identity moderated the singular strength of community organizations over time. It had also mitigated the chances of large-scale violent and open communal conflicts in the state. While the left was carving out political support without directly appealing to community identity, the community organizations realized their actual strength and mostly preferred to continue as pressure groups rather than as political parties. This was more so in the south, where the caste organizations of Ezhavas, Christians, and Nairs exerted pressure on state independently, through the Congress, or by forming alliances between each other. By the time of Independence, this had become an intriguing relationship between state power, community organizations, and the rich.

There is also regional variation in people's general perceptions about communalism in Kerala. In south Kerala, which used to tolerate the intervention of caste-based pressure groups and Christian churches in the party system, there was a general wariness about 'the Muslim communalism' coming from the north. Therefore, the previous attempts by the CPI(M) to come to electoral understandings with political parties and organizations linked to Muslim communities in certain constituencies in northern Kerala cost them votes in south Kerala. Even though both Christians and Muslims are numerically powerful minorities in Kerala and are represented by political parties, the Christian community, which is strongly present in south-central Kerala, is also exonerated from being called 'communal' because their demands, compared with Muslims, seem to be related to secular objectives such as education. The Christian community across different denominations was more or less influenced by Protestant ethics under colonialism, and later found convenience in logic of entrepreneurship and hegemony of developmentalism (Mathew 1987; Devika and Varghese 2010). In fact, the term 'communal' in Kerala common sense applies to those sections and movements which are relatively less susceptible to the concerns of Kerala's local version of modernity.

The highly contentious term 'communalism' has been translated for use in Malayalam in two ways—'saamudaayikatha' and 'vargeeyatha'. In the vernacular, when communalism is translated as 'saamudaayikatha', it denotes a softer and acceptable form of consolidation of communal identities of caste and religion for political bargaining. But when communalism is translated into 'vargeeyatha', it gives a related but different meaning by referring to extremely unacceptable and violent behaviour and mentality based on a religious identity for political purposes. In the horizon of the common sense of Kerala politics under discussion, 'saamudaayikatha' implies a modern, civilized, and democratic expression of interests of the social identities of religion and caste, while 'vargeeyatha' confines its implication to a premodern, violent, and undemocratic expression of community identity. Both the vernacular versions of communalism, if explained from the modern vantage point of secularism, are the same in substance, but are operationally different. In due course of time, 'saamudaayikatha' has been used to generally describe the politics of caste associations and non-violent interest-group and pressure-group politics of religions.

In fact a transformation from 'vargeeyatha' to 'saamudaayikatha' is becoming a requisite for religious organizations to legitimately intervene in politics. This denotes a process of secularization that Kerala politics had achieved in the past. Both LDF and UDF used to claim that they have no allies bearing 'vargeeyatha' in the coalitions. But the left can appear more secular because they are insulated to a higher degree from striking compromises even with the accept-able forms of 'saamudaayikatha' in comparison with UDF. There is resistance from various caste and religious outfits across the board against cataloguing them as forces of 'vargeeyatha' by the left intellec-tuals and political parties. Mostly the political religious organizations, especially those of Muslims and Hindus, are considered as potential sources of 'vargeeyatha' in common parlance and in the language of the press. To encounter this, they struggle hard to present themselves as spokespersons of 'saamudaayikatha' instead of 'vargeeyatha'. The Hindu right tries to assume a cultural-nationalist and spiritualist out-look to evade the negative labelling for its organizational appearances. But by and large the Muslim organizations are finding it difficult to escape the criticism of representing 'vargeeyatha' even though there have been only sporadic instances to show that the Muslim organi-zations adopted openly violent political options in state politics. The secular common sense and its slightly Hinduized versions bear heav-ily upon the Muslim organizations to point out 'vargeeyatha' behind every form of political expression of their identity. The Christian organizations can usually evade such criticisms compared with their Muslim counterparts. In the coalition politics, LDF and UDF are very careful in perpetuating the distinction between 'vargeeyatha' and 'saamudaayikatha' to define their commitment to secularism while seeking political alliance with community groups, even though LDF has been showing a greater drive to distance itself from both the versions of communalism. While the Congress is more powerful as an alliance-maker between communities of castes and religions, the CPI(M) is more interventionist, critical, and a potential architect capable of aggravating secular fissions within each community group.

The religious minorities are relatively insulated from the left move-ment. The lack of the kind of religious reforms in these communities that were experienced by Hindu caste groups and the more inward-looking institutionalization strategies of Muslims and Christians are cited as the reasons for this (Thomas Isaac and Tharakan 1995). Therefore, in spite of a large number of beneficiaries of the class-based agitations of the left and the welfare policies of left governments, the two minority religions hold an anti-left orientation in their political affiliation.

Muslims in Kerala are mainly concentrated in Malabar (north Kerala). In the past, they were mainly mobilized by the clergy and a political party of their own known as Indian Union Muslim League (IUML). The nature of religiosity of the community, the economic backwardness of a large majority of them, and the clout of orthodox religious leadership rendered it impervious to modernity's pressure for a long time. Their reform movements were distinctive in their reluctance to share the dominant premises and frameworks in common use since the nineteenth century by other social groups for community mobilization and internal reforms. The community was also alienated from mainstream politics in Malabar after a movement known as the Mappila Rebellion (1921), inspired by the ecclesiastical leadership against Hindu landlords and the British government, ended in communal violence and state repression. The rebellion corresponded to the religious reformism gaining currency among the Muslims in the northern region, but both the state and the movement resorted to violence as the final option. It was an exception to the emerging pattern of interaction between community organizations and the state in the formative stages of movement politics in Kerala. The poorer members of the community in the north remained to a great extent unreachable to the political left's class strategy. While other communities were organized for both material and symbolic benefits, Muslims in Malabar were predominantly mobilized for symbolic and religious gains for a long period of time under the political leadership of IUML. The community was also suffering from the lack of a visible middle class to confidently represent the community in the modernizing public until they gained the material and cultural benefits of migration to the Gulf countries in the 1970s. It is also a consequence of the slow process of internal reforms. In fact, the circulation of intellectuals and leaders between Muslims and left-wing political parties to act as mediators for dialogic relations has been far less frequent in comparison with other communities.

In the pre-Independence period, British Malabar was witnessing land struggles and agrarian agitations against the state and the landlords more actively than in the south, whereas in the princely states the rulers conceded to the demands of middle-class peasants through some piecemeal land and agrarian reforms under pressure from some caste organizations and their peasant groups. The different state structures before Independence in the north and south have some implications for assessing the interaction between community groups and political parties in Kerala's democratic politics after Independence. The three strong social groups—Ezhavas, Nairs, and Christians—and their organizations were very decisive for political parties in electoral competitions in south Kerala. The units of Congress in the two princely states of Travancore and Cochin were mainly the political organs representing these three communities. The Congress faced a community-wise split in 1964, and the breakaway fraction carried the name Kerala Congress. Unlike in Malabar where the class politics of the left had never faced a crucial challenge from community-centred mobilization except from the Muslims, in the south it could only hope for a political victory when the experiment of communal combination conducted by the Congress was facing internal frictions. It has been pointed out that the failure of the Congress to maintain a balance between the three major communities of the time contributed to the victory of the undivided CPI in the 1957 elections (Nair 1965).

Class divisions were present in all communities, but the left did not have equal success in mobilizing the lower classes from all of them. The class politics of the left attracted the Dalits and Ezhavas in which a sizeable majority was from the lower classes. The identical class and caste identity of Dalits in the social hierarchy came in handy for the communists to gain their support. Ezhavas were a mobility-seeking caste in both class and caste terms. The Congress faced limits in making concessions to the Ezhava elites due to the combined pressure from Nairs and Christians. The political affiliation of the Ezhavas and Dalits to class parties was moved faster than any other community in Kerala because they also were largely represented as the lower class. There was an instance of the transformation of the Ezhava coir-worker community-based organization into a secular trade union in Alappey in south Kerala

(Jeffrey 1984; Thomas Isaac 1985). Comparable events were rare in the case of Nairs, Muslims, and Christians even though many people from these two communities became political leaders and intellectuals of left politics.[8] Steven Wilkinson (2004: 181) describes the CPI(M) in Kerala as an Ezhava-dominated party. The left have been looked as a political formation cutting across communities, but this cross-community mobilization of people does not show equal share from all communities. Even though a majority of Muslims by all socioeconomic indices were backward, they remained aloof to class movements.

The Congress was also mobilizing people from all communities, but confined itself to giving representatives of different communities a share in organizational positions, ministerial portfolios, and concessions from public policies. Traditionally, class-wise cross-community mobilization was followed by the left. The Congress preferred elite-oriented cross-community mobilization. The communists have to compromise more than the Congress on their basic approach when they form coalition. One commentator argued:

> The Left could remain insulated from such pressures as long as it focused on class interests alone. However, with the polity becoming increasingly wary of ideological identities, and the increasing need for expanding the vote base, the Left appears to have chosen the easy way out. The rising number of Independents on their list of candidates [in 2014 parliament election] and their social identities point to the disturbing trend. (Jacob 2014)

The electoral outcome after the formation of a bipolar coalition shows that the intermittent victories of the UDF and LDF in assembly elections have been over a narrow vote margin. But the seat share may vary depending on the efficacy of community coalitions forged by the UDF and the possibility of the LDF winning UDF seats when an internal friction, among other things, occurs within the latter. Both fronts keep an eye on the constituency-wise strength of different communities before fielding candidates in elections.

Dalits and tribals are dispersed geographically. However, the two minorities, Christians and Muslims, possess the advantage of being influential in electoral politics because of their concentration in some regions. Close to one-third of the total Muslim population of Kerala resides in a single district, Malappuram. Hindus comprise less than 30 per cent of the population in that district. Kannur, Kozhikode, and

Kasaragod (all in north Kerala) are the other districts with a sizeable Muslim population. Christians are more concentrated in the south-central districts of Kottayam, Idukki, Ernakulam, and Pathanamthitta. In sum, while Hindus are spread across the states, the population of other religions are actually concentrated in particular districts (Kailash 2010). It greatly gives advantage to minority religions to float political parties in state politics. A group of the Kerala Congress represents Christians. The Muslim League represents a big majority of Muslims from north Kerala.

Kerala politics provides scope for community-centred demands regarding both recognition and distribution. The politics of recognition initiated by the community movements in the social-reform period have become as deeply entrenched as the politics of distribution organized on the initiative of the communists. The Congress and CPI(M) concentrate heavily on recognition and distribution respectively. Therefore, the community organizations that are overwhelmed with demands for recognition and interested in bourgeois competition are galvanized to Congress-led coalition. The distributive political strategy of the left, however, compelled the Congress and also other community-linked political parties to pay attention to distribution. The lack of a big difference in the social spending of the governments is a case in point (Singh 2011).[9] Besides, community organizations from the Muslim League and Christian Church to Hindu upper-caste organizations hardly miss any opportunity to swear in the name of their poorer members in order to substantiate their demands for recognition. It seems that distribution has a little headway over recognition in Kerala's politics of communalism. The political demands for recognition by community organizations had to always be distributive, at least in rhetoric. Their discontentment about distribution would be visible only when the left-led agitations and the governments make attempts to rob Peter to pay Paul.

Public Policies and the Communities

Public policies are generally the blueprints of political parties exemplifying their political agenda based on the major demands of people mobilized under their leadership. Depending on the concerns of the support base and the principles adopted for mobilizing people, the

public policies may be both proactive and reactive. On class questions, the policies of the left governments are proactive and that of the
Congress is reactive. But as far as the demands of communities go,
the Congress seems to be more proactive than the left. Most often the
policies of the left towards community-centred demands have been
election-oriented, administrative responses without much organizational clarity on the position. In coalition politics, the left governments practise a fewer number of confrontationist policies vis-à-vis
the interest of the community organizations, and most of its policies
are adaptive and transformative in nature. Their strength and efficacy
in promoting a dialogical relationship with community organizations
and the community sentiments of the population largely depend on
the publicity of such policies in the media. A cursory glance at the
left's public policies in a select number of cases brings to attention
their efforts to engage with communities in the past and the reasons
for the failure of them to catch community votes. A crucial distinction between the left and the Congress in public-policy making is
also worth mentioning here. The focus on class while mobilizing
people gave the left clarity on public-policy making on class questions.
Explicit policy prescriptions are made on a large number of issues
by the left on class questions. But the Congress adopts a strategy of
coming to a consensus between community organizations through
in-camera negotiations including on matters concerning class.

The left parties have been more active than others in waging
scathing criticisms of internal affairs of the communities, while the
Congress gave greater weight to autonomy of community leadership.
The left urged for the necessity of transcendence of 'false' community
identity to form a concrete class identity. The traditional strategy was
to divide each community on class lines. Since the 1960s, mainly
under the leadership of E.M.S. Namboodiripad (henceforth EMS),
the CPI(M) adopted a different strategy by identifying progressive factions inside the communities and seeking alliance with them.

There were some policy initiatives carried out by the 1957 left
government in favour of the Muslim community. The provision of
10 per cent special reservations for Muslims, school-fee incentives
for Muslim children, the lifting of restrictions on the construction of
mosques, madrasas, and congregational marches in front of mosques,
the upgrading of Arabic teachers to full-time teachers, and so forth,

are some examples. The government also withdrew the draconian and anti-Muslim Mappila Outrages Act (Thomas Isaac 2009). The 1967 left coalition government gave a green signal to form Malappuram district by grouping together the Muslim-populated areas. But whether this resulted in favourable returns in terms of votes from the community to the political left during elections is not certain. Even though the CPI(M)'s vote share increased in Malappuram, only on a few occasions did it defeat the Muslim League candidates. This is mainly due to the over-consciousness of the CPI(M) to project the community-specific policies within the secularizing scheme. It wanted to portray each of these measures as justifiable on secular principles such as civil rights, anti-imperialism, workers' rights, and economic development. On the other side, the League, which had maintained a sway over the educationally backward Muslims' communication channels with the outside world through religious institutions, interpreted it as a victory for political recognition of their community-based mobilization and bargaining. This might have taught the left a lesson regarding the necessity of engaging with religious institutions.

There were many efforts from the political left to engage with the Hindu community by nominating members to the temple administration committees, known as 'dewaswam boards', while in power in the state government. The left government of 2006 proposed caste-based reservations for membership to these committees. Democratic control over them was justified to mitigate corruption. Caste-based reservation in temple administration committees was intended to bring equal opportunity to all sections. It was also aimed at fighting the growing influence of the social and political outfits of the Hindu right wing through temples. The left-led trade unions also made efforts to mobilize the employees and priests in these temples for matters related to their service and wages (Nirmala 2009: 87). While there was better scope for such mobilization in Hindu temples, the strategy has lesser scope vis-à-vis the workforce of the religious and administrative bodies of the minority religions. Besides the constitutional protection to prevent the state's intervention in religious affairs, the Christian churches in Kerala are politically powerful and possess sufficient economic resources to take care of their clergy's material needs. The employees' unions organized by the political left are confined to the secular institutions managed by the churches in education and business instead of the Church as such. Though the Congress-led governments tried to introduce pensions for priests of religious institutions, they did not attempt to mobilize them from below. In addition, the Congress-led coalitions hardly worried about giving any secular justifications behind their interventions in religion. They exhibit a political behaviour of appeasement towards all religions. The effort to equally appease all religions is convenient for the Congress, as it is able to call itself a secular party.

The class-wise engagement of the party with the institutions run by communities in education, plantations, and hospitals was by and large interpreted as a direct threat to the community as a whole or as attempts to infringe on minority rights. The image of the party being dissatisfied with the Indian Constitution and the strong weight of atheism in the open communiqué of the party leaders gave momentum to the propaganda of the community organizations against it.

In order to engage with minority religions, the party followed a strategy of facilitating debates on the dialectical materialist understanding of the party about religion. There were a series of debates between the spiritual leaders of all the communities and party leaders, mainly EMS, in the 1980s–90s. The liberal intelligentsia of the Muslim community and some adherents of liberation theology from the Christian church were active in this debate. In fact, the party's intellectual position on religious issues was clarified during this period by mitigating bourgeois rational atheism (Nirmala 2009). It is, however, doubtful whether the party was capable of communicating its transformation intelligibly to the minority communities and among its rank and file. The critical position of the CPI(M) on Islamic Sharia in the 1980s was the immediate reason for the 'progressive' fraction of the League to break its relationship with LDF and migrate back to the Muslim League. On the positive side, this dialogue helped to reduce the distance of the party from the Church and the Muslim community. Many religious leaders were invited to the party-sponsored International Congress on Kerala Studies, held four times since 1994, for talks and interaction (Thomas Isaac and Tharakan 2004). On the negative side, in some instances it brought about the brokering of a political deal during elections with the ortho-dox segments of Muslim community. The decision of the CPI(M) to field a candidate supported by the People's Democratic Party in the 2009 Lok Sabha elections created a factional criticism inside the organization.[10]

The CPI(M)'s strategy to make inroads into the Muslim community by actively supporting them in some national and international issues, such as the demolition of Babri Masjid, the Gujarat riots, the Israel–Palestine conflict, and the US invasion of Iraq, only ended in mixed results. There are several reasons for this. For example, the Muslim community in Kerala does not face any strong political threat of Hindu communalism inside the state, and, if there is any, they can effectively deal with it through the League and the alliance struck with the Congress. Therefore, the efforts of CPI(M) in forming a relationship with this community on the principles of minority rights and anti-imperialism seem to be offering them very little in material and cultural terms. The economic gains that the elites of the community struggle for and the recognition-related aspirations of the masses face no challenge from the coalition with the Congress in state politics. In addition, the CPI(M) leadership has had to openly admit after facing criticism for its electoral alliances with community-backed independents that the approach of the party was merely a strategy. As mentioned earlier, the 'Hindu-secular' opinion of south Kerala against Muslim extremism is a disadvantage for the party to forge an alliance with Muslim organizations (Biju 2010). However, there has been a moderate increase in the percentage of minorities in CPI(M)'s total membership since late 1990s. This is generally viewed as a result of the conscious efforts of the party to bridge the gaps between itself and people from minority religions. Since the 1990s, the left parties have also attempted to promote symbolic representation for persons from minority religions in leadership positions, especially in its youth and student-wing organizations. CPI(M) and CPI also fielded some of them as candidates in general elections. The flexible recruitment to leadership has generated disciplinary issues, and some of the leaders defected after a brief stay with the left parties by citing the incompatibility between their religious views and the ideology of the parties as a reason. If media reports are believable, the floor-crossing of the young members between CPI(M) and the Muslim League and CPI(M) and the Bharatiya Janata Party (BJP) has also been more frequent since 2010.

Certain new policy initiatives of the left coalition governments since the late 1980s enhanced the gravity of the mass-mobilization strategy over trade-union-based class mobilization of the CPI(M) (Heller 1995). The administrative decision of the left government of 1987 to mobilize a state-wide popular campaign for total literacy was appealing to the Muslim sections in north Kerala. The government's public relations department used to appraise people about the necessity of literacy by citing the plight of the wives of Gulf migrants who sought the help of their neighbours to read the letters from their husbands. The focus of the campaign was the Muslim community, which faced large-scale illiteracy and had a strong contingent of Gulf migrants. A large number of teachers and unemployed youth linked to the left parties were deployed state-wide to the success of the mass-literacy campaign. It became an inspiration for the party to undertake non-class mobilization techniques to engage with the community.

In 1997, the implementation of decentralized governance through local self-government institutions also gave preference to community-centred development activities at the grassroots. The elections to local bodies to an extent helped the party to make alliances with rival parties of the UDF and necessitated a shared sense of governance at the local level. The Christian Church, the Ezhavas, and Muslim organizations actively floated developmental NGOs (non-governmental organizations) and collaborated with party representatives in local bodies in many panchayats. Here too, CPI(M) had to justify its policy based on inclusive secularism rather than hard secularism and primarily for the benefit of local economic development. Parallel to this, the promotion of the women's self-help group called Kudumbashree and the leadership role of the All India Democratic Women's Association (AIDWA) opened new avenues of collaboration with the non-party public and women from different communities (Biju and Kumar 2013).[11] However, the increasing focus on social groups in local development and the resultant polarization in voting is not well-researched. The failure of the LDF in the 2010 panchayat elections is a case in point.

The left had also implemented several public policies that invited negative community-based reactions. Reform in education is more prominent among them. The left had to encounter all the community organizations in carrying out these reforms since the community management boards owned a large number of the educational institutions in the state. The instructions of the left governments for reforms in the education sector, which included regulation of teacher appointments and student admissions, were resisted tooth and nail by all the community organizations. Its efforts to implement educational reforms were necessary to safeguard the interests of poor students and the teaching staff to show the leading party's class-based commitment. But, to achieve this, the left parties and their governments always had to confront the issue of profit to the management boards and the managerial rights of the minorities in educational institutions. In fact, in the period after economic liberalization, the capitalists have been reacting more vociferously against the left governments under the disguise of community interest.

Control over educational institutions is crucial for the community leadership to exercise an influence upon the lives of its members. In addition to the improvement in the number of educated members, each community organization considered the ownership of educational institutions as a status symbol. Therefore, they were in conflict with the left governments which wanted to implement public control of these institutions. The first communist government which came to power in 1957 discouraged allotment of new educational institutions to caste and religious organizations even though it did not raise much objection to institutions run by private individuals. Decommunalization of ownership of educational institutions was a consistent demand from the left-wing students' organizations and teachers' unions in the state since the very beginning. The education reform act introduced by the government of 1957 is still a nightmare for the private management boards whenever the left front is elected to power.

Since the 1990s, when the state witnessed a phenomenal growth in self-financing professional colleges under two UDF dispensations during 1991–6 and 2001–6, the community organizations and the political left formed warring camps. The major communities became powerful educational management bodies, and the self-financing institutions attracted a good investment from rich individuals and corporates linked to all major communities. The regulations brought about by the left governments in 1997 and 2006 followed a legal battle in the courts and big negative propaganda from the community organizations. Even though the friction between community managements and the left in educational reforms was almost the same as earlier, this time the community organizations could not gain strength for their call for a 'second liberation struggle' against the 2006 government. The left front government's decision to introduce social and economic reservations in admissions of students to all self-financed private colleges generated internal divisions within the communities. This time, some factions representing the economically backward groups from different communities staged demonstrations in favour of the regulations brought by the left government. In the assembly elections of 2011, the LDF was able to narrow down the victory margin of the UDF to four seats. The success of the UDF was largely due to the improved performance of the League by capturing Muslim votes (Biju 2011).

Now, the land question in Kerala is not an issue that invites any interest from the major community organizations. The demands and agitations for land are confined to sections of Dalits and Adivasis. The left governments failed to find any substantive solutions to this, and it faces a community-wise challenge from the Dalits. To absorb the community-wise consolidation of tribals and Dalits, the CPI(M) recently launched the Adivasi Kshema Sabha and Scheduled Caste Welfare Organization. Although the SCs had a propensity to initiate caste-based movements along with other caste groups since the beginning of the twentieth century, by and large they were absorbed into the class movements organized by the left. But, the quest for a new community identity by the Dalits and tribals since the 1990s poses a political challenge to the left. They want to confront the political parties for treating them mainly as the welfare subjects of the state. The new organizations enlighten the members about their relatively weak political assertion through community organizations, citing this as a reason for their deprivation and abjection in comparison with other major communities (Devika 2012). Similar patterns of mobilization by citing abjection take place among the Muslims and the marine-fishing community as well. The social character of the poor is also marching ahead of its class character.

After economic liberalization, the public policies of the two coalitions in Kerala show that while popular mobilization under the leadership of progressive political forces induced the state to maintain doses of welfarism (Prabhash 2004), there is a consensus out of willingness from the UDF and out of compulsions for the LDF that the demands should not disturb the interests of the propertied classes or communities. Liberalization in education and health gave new impetus to the consolidation of communal capitalism. The new private investors, mainly non-resident Keralites searching for opportunities in the post-liberalization economy, have plenty of cronies within the community organizations. In many of the ventures in education and health, the already existing community-based management boards also try to expand their reach in collaboration with the private entrepreneurs by influencing the political leadership. Thus, new capital can take a communal route to enter Kerala's economy. Even though labour agitations are gaining currency in the health and education sectors, they have been rendered weak in challenging the clout of capital couched in community ownership more than ever before (Biju 2013).

Community Votes in Elections

As stated previously, the demands for political representation in Kerala were on community lines. Each community organization looks for preferential treatment in the selection of candidates by political parties. The political parties of the left and Congress are cautious about being responsive to community equations during elections. Minority communities largely practice community-voting in elections, especially in those constituencies where they are concentrated. The left coalition faces a dilemma in dealing with this. It has no party in the coalition to claim the support of Muslims and Christians in a big way. Therefore, the LDF fields party candidates from specific communities and even experiments with independent candidates. At the level of symbolism, both fronts are adaptive to community-based representation. Rare instances of winning elections without paying attention to the communal composition of each constituency are largely to the credit of LDF rather than UDF. Barring one election (the 1987 assembly election), the CPI(M) did not reject community votes openly in coalition politics. The party may not discourage its candidates from paying courtesy visits to offices of different caste and religious organizations in constituencies during elections. Over time, the left parties were able to find leaders from localities that favoured them to help split community votes. Even then, based on substantive representation for the community organizations, the left coalition does not seem attractive. This is exemplified by the fact that community organizations fail to bargain for community-based representation in portfolio allotments in left ministries. The UDF, on the other hand, leaves better scope for communal representation in the ministry, in addition to its concessions to communities and their economic elites in public policies.

The Congress in Kerala has a comparative advantage over CPI(M) in wooing community voters. The party has a culture of internal representation of different communities by different party leaders. In addition, the coalition consists of the Muslim League and Kerala Congress parties claiming support of two big minority communities. The CPI(M) lacks both, and its strategy to make a tactical alliance with community voters is confined to fielding some independent candidates and through outsourcing the task of communal vote-capturing to allied parties in the front. But after a faction of the Kerala Congress decided to leave the left coalition in 2010 and the Muslim League consolidated its support base against the rival political factions willing to lend support to LDF, for instance, the People's Democratic Party and Indian National League, LDF has no gain to claim from community voters. Even though in the 2014 Lok Sabha elections LDF fielded five independent candidates and half of its total candidates were from minority religions, the election results were not at all impressive, except in two constituencies. The minority voters preferred substantive representation rather than a symbolic one.

In 2013, the efforts of the rival caste organizations of the Nairs and Ezhavas to unite against the minorities, the third attempt in history, was soon foiled through an accommodative strategy of UDF. The Nair Service Society (NSS) and the Sree Narayana Dharma Paripalanayogam (SNDP) thrice tried to forge an alliance in Kerala. But the efforts did not last because of the conflicting position on the question of economic reservation for upper castes. The UDF leaders were tactful in dealing with the two by conceding to their demands in the private education sector. The Muslim League, which holds the education portfolio, claimed equal consideration for all private managements in education. The UDF and the Congress did not find the community-based reactions of the NSS and SNDP difficult to handle due to the willingness of the government to privatize education on communal lines. Therefore, it is difficult to assume that the opposition of NSS and SNDP to growing representation of Muslims and Christians within the UDF ministry would become detrimental to the UDF to fetch benefits for LDF. As a gesture of appeasement to Hindu upper castes and Syrian Christians, who are outside the purview of the affirmative-action policies of the state and ineligible for reservations in education and government jobs, the UDF government (2011–16) set up the Kerala State Welfare Corporation for Forward Communities Limited to look into the concerns of economically backward sections of these groups.[12] In fact, the two caste organizations are inferior to minority religions due to the relative strength of the latter to garner support for the UDF through the League and Kerala Congress.[13] The recent delimitation added two more assembly constituencies in Malappuram district, giving an advantage to the League.

***

Democratic politics in Kerala upholds two meanings of secularism—equal accommodation of all communities in politics or non-discrimination, and the separation of community organizations from politics. The Congress subscribes to the first, and the left parties under the CPI(M) take efforts to preserve secularism as per the second principle. In the second meaning of secularism, that is to save politics from direct or mediated takeover by communal forces, Kerala is a partial success. The political common sense about secularism in Kerala allows communities to exert pressure on political parties for recognition and resources. The left is also careful to avoid charges of community-based discrimination. Hard secularism in Kerala, as perceived in the second meaning of the concept, is a half-won battle under the leadership of the left, even though the tensions between the primordial loyalties and emerging civic loyalties contributed to the secularism of accommodation gaining ground in state politics and public space. The necessity of coalition politics for the CPI(M) to succeed in elections in Kerala shows that its class politics and the wider support for secularism in civil society are in no way sufficient to effectively challenge the communal character of the coalition politics of the Congress. Politics in Kerala largely gives support to the accommodative, non-discriminatory, and inclusive version of secularism, one of the main currents of old social-reform movements that shaped modernity in Kerala at large. Ironically, communalism also creeps into politics on the back of this heritage. The demand for hard secularism remains to be sidelined in coalition politics, though the CPI(M) is still the biggest single-party organization, and the vote share of its coalition in competition with the UDF, the main rival, did not fall beyond a 5 per cent maximum in any of the previous elections. The left-led coalition performs the gatekeeping function vis-à-vis the entry of communal forces which most often take the UDF as the carrier.

The state-assembly elections of 2016 boosted the prospects of BJP-led National Democratic Alliance (NDA) in Kerala politics. The major ally was the Bharatiya Dharma Jana Sena (BDJS), a political party comprising thirty Hindu caste-organizations led by the SNDP. The NDA–BDJS alliance garnered 15.01 per cent of the total votes, which is the highest ever for any BJP-led coalition in Kerala politics. It was triple the number of votes gained by NDA in 2011. However, the LDF's 43.37 per cent votes is 4.57 per cent higher than the UDF, which secured only 38.8 per cent of the total votes. There is a nearly 2 per cent decrease in the LDF's vote share in the total votes polled in 2016 as compared with the 2011 elections. But significant still is the fact that in comparison with the UDF, the LDF was able to increase its total number of votes between 2011 and 2016. Between 2011 and 2016, the UDF's vote share decreased by 7 per cent. This decline in the UDF's votes, the highest ever decrease, also shows that the growth of the BJP-led coalition is a result of Hindu votes shifting from the Congress. The experiment of the 'inclusively secular' but caste-conscious and communal UDF coalition is facing an unexpected hit from the BJP's rise in the state, which has caused high polarization of communal votes. It also indirectly raises the left's hopes by leaving Hindu communal votes divided between the UDF and the BJP. It keeps an eye on minority voters who perhaps prefer a more powerful secular government to deal with the growing Hindutva in Kerala, before which the Congress has always been pliant. In the emerging tri-polar coalition politics too, hard secularism would still be more a minor political option, even for the left.

Notes

1. Just before the 2014 Lok Sabha elections, one faction of RSP (Revolutionary Socialist Party) moved to the United Democratic Front (UDF)

due to a conflict over denial of seats. The United Democratic Front has a total of nine parties including (figures in parenthesis show the number of Members of Legislative Assembly [MLAs] in the 2011–16 Legislative Assembly): Indian National Congress (39); Indian Union Muslim League (20); Kerala Congress (Mani) (9); RSP (2); RSP (Bolshevik) (1); Socialist Janatha (2); Kerala Congress (Pillai) (1); Kerala Congress (Jacob) (1); and Communist Marxist Party (CMP) (0). The Left Democratic Front (LDF) includes: Communist Party of India (Marxist) (44); Communist Party of India (13); Janatha (Secular) (4); National Congress Party (2); Indian Congress (Socialist) (0); and Kerala Congress (Thomas) (0).

2. The Bharatiya Janata Party (BJP) gained 10.3 per cent votes in Lok Sabha election 2014 and came second in Trivandrum constituency. The data of vote share in previous elections from 1980s onwards showed high variation, between 3 and 10 per cent, for the party in Kerala. The performance of BJP after forging an alliance with around thirty Hindu caste organizations, in the civic elections of 2015 and the assembly elections 2016, was most striking. The BJP secured 13.28 per cent of votes in the civic polls and 15.01 per cent in the assembly elections. For the first time in history, it won an assembly constituency and came second in seven other constituencies. It is also keen to capitalize on the dissatisfaction of the Hindu caste organizations which believe that Christians and Muslims receive greater preference in the UDF coalition.

3. Later on, the Kerala Congress experienced a series of splits to give birth to smaller parties. The splinter parties retain the same title usually suffixed by some additions in parentheses, for example, Kerala Congress (Mani), Kerala Congress (Jacob), Kerala Congress (Secular), Kerala Congress (Joseph), Kerala Congress (Balakrishna Pillai), and so on.

4. There is a mismatch between the support of Ezhavas to left parties and the official stand of their caste organization, Sree Narayana Dharma Paripalanayogam (SNDP). However, S.I. Wilkinson (2004: 117–19) notes that CPI(M) in Kerala is (predominantly) an Ezhava party.

5. The names of political parties formed by two caste organizations in Kerala can reflect this point. The Nairs formed a party in 1974 named the National Democratic Party (NDP). 'N'can signify either 'National' or 'Nair' as the reader sees fit. The Ezhavas also formed a party in 1976 called the Socialist Republican Party (SRP). The letter 'S' can be expanded as 'Socialist' or 'Sree Narayana' (the name of their spiritual leader) as one wishes to imply. This double ambition of communal parties to represent both secular and non-secular values is an interesting aspect in analysing their claims over politics in Kerala. Some Muslim outfits formed since the 1990s also carry secular titles.

6. The various criticisms against Nehruvian secularism and the anti-secular intellectual trends within Indian academia since the 1980s have attracted little attention in Kerala so far. Likewise, Kerala's political commentators and academics in social science disciplines have been greatly critical of caste influence in politics in other states even though caste parties have a progressive connotation for democratic politics elsewhere. However, the protagonists of the new postmodern identity politics are a rising current in intellectual debates in the state, but the reverberation of their ideas in the structure of party politics is marginal.

7. The party members from minority communities faced strong objection from their community organizations. The acceptance of a communist party member within the circles of the community depends greatly on the degree of internal reforms and amount of radicalism within the community.

8. Unofficial accounts estimate that 4 per cent of the CPI(M) membership is Christian and 10 per cent is Muslim.

9. However, the findings on parity between the two coalitions in social spending hardly bring out the differential efforts behind it. While the UDF's expenditure is equal to that of the left, the role of the left in realizing its aims through mobilizing people for distributional demands is far greater than the UDF. As Patrick Heller points out, the active role played by the left in organizing trade unions was responded by the non-left political parties to bring up strong trade unions in the state under their banner (Heller 1999).

10. For a detailed analysis of CPI(M) dilemma with Muslim community during elections, see Prabhash (2000).

11. However, the political dividend of this for the party is not quite convincing. In the 2010 local-body elections, the LDF faced a clear setback in spite of implementing a 50 per cent reservation for women.

12. Reservation for those who are economically very poor in the forward communities (mainly Brahmans, Nairs, and Syrian Christians) in government jobs was a suggestion made by the Administrative Reforms Commission appointed by the first communist government of 1957. But it was extremely difficult for political parties to counter the pressure from Ezhavas and Muslims, who are significant beneficiaries of the current reservation policy based on social backwardness and under-representation, to take this suggestion forward.

13. The Muslim League categorically states that the very existence of the UDF, more than any other, is necessary for the League. However, the Kerala Congress (Mani), after three months of the UDF's failure in the 2016 election, quite unexpectedly quit the alliance and decided to sit as a separate bloc in the assembly.

Bibliography

Biju, B.L. 2010. 'CPI(M) at Risk in Kerala Politics: Role of Mediated Social Scrutiny of Politics, and Civil Society'. *Journal of Polity and Society* 3(1): 32–51.

———. 2011. 'Kerala Assembly Election 2011: A Not-Quite-There Victory for Welfare Policies, Consolidation of Minority Votes, and V.S. Factor'. *Socialist Perspectives* 39(1–2): 23–56.

———. 2013. 'Angels are Turning Red: Nurses' Strikes in Kerala'. *Economic and Political Weekly* 48(52): 25–8.

Biju, B.L., and K.G. Abhilash Kumar. 2013. 'Class Feminism: Kudumbashree Agitation in Kerala'. *Economic and Political Weekly* 48(9): 22–6.

Desai, Manali. 2007. *State Formation and Radical Democracy in India*. New York: Routledge.

Devika, J. 2012. 'Contemporary Dalit Assertions in Kerala: Governmental Categories versus Identity Politics'. *History and Sociology of South Asia* 7(1): 1–17.

Devika, J., and V.J. Varghese. 2010. 'To Survive or to Flourish? Minority Rights and Syrian Christian Community in 20th Century Travancore/Kerala'. Working Paper no. 427, Centre for Development Studies, Trivandrum.

Heller, Patrick. 1995. 'From Class Struggle to Class Compromise: Redistribution and Growth in a South Indian State'. *Journal of Development Studies* 31(50): 645–75.

———. 1999. *Labor of Development: Workers and Transformation of Capitalism in Kerala*. Ithaca and London: Cornell University Press.

Jacob, George. 2014. 'Communal Politics and Realpolitik'. *The Hindu*, March 27.

Jeffrey, Robin. 1984. 'Destroy Capitalism! Growing Solidarity of Allepey's Coir Workers, 1930– 40', *Economic and Political Weekly* 19(29): 1159–64.

Kailash, K.K. 2010. 'Political Outsourcing as a Coalition Strategy in Kerala'. In *Accommodating Diversity: Ideas and Institutional Practices*, edited by G. Mahajan, 182–205. New Delhi: Oxford University Press.

Mannathukkaren, Nissim. 2013. 'The Rise of the National-Popular and Its Limits: Communism and the Cultural in Kerala'. *Inter-Asia Cultural Studies* 14(4): 494–518.

Mathew, George. 1987. *Communal Road to Secularism in Kerala*. New Delhi: Concept Publishing Company.

Nair, Ramakrishnan. 1965. *How Communists Came to Power in Kerala*. Trivandrum: Kerala Academy of Social Sciences.

Nirmala, V.U. 2009. 'Civil Society and Left Politics: A Study on Their Inter-relationship in Kerala'. Unpublished MPhil dissertation, University of Hyderabad.

Prabhash, J. 2000. 'Kerala: CPI(M)'s Muslim League Dilemma'. *Economic and Political Weekly* 35(34): 3009–11.

———. 2004. 'State and Public Policy in Kerala'. *Indian Journal of Political Science* 65(3): 403–18.

Singh, Prerna. 2011. 'We-ness and Welfare: A Longitudinal Analysis of Social Development in Kerala, India'. *World Development* 39(2): 282–93.

Thomas Isaac, T.M. 1985. 'From Caste Consciousness to Class Consciousness: Alleppey Coir Workers during Inter-War Period'. *Economic and Political Weekly* 20(4): 5–18.

———. 2009. 'The Left Position on Ponnani'. Available at http://www.pragoti.in/node/3293 (last accessed 21 October 2013).

Thomas Isaac, T.M., and Michael Tharakan. 1995. 'Kerala: Towards a New Agenda'. *Economic and Political Weekly* 30(31–32): 1993–2004.

Wilkinson, S.I. 2004. *Votes and Violence: Electoral Competition and Ethnic Riots in India*. Cambridge: Cambridge University Press.

10

N. SUDHAKAR RAO

M. RAVIKUMAR

The Ritual of Power and Power of the Ritual

An Interface between Religion and Politics

S ome traditional Hindu religious practices continue to be popular in modern Indian society—in fact, they enjoy high esteem. Their significance becomes quite meaningful in certain geographical locations given the historical experience of Muslim domination in the past and the continuation of its legacy in the present. The contemporary democratic political environment and interests of various groups—castes, communities, political parties, and so forth—encourage and support such religious practices against the spirit of modernity where science, technology, objectivity, and rationality act as guiding principles. In this context, the present chapter discusses the development of a Hindu temple and performance of a ritual (*jathara/bonalu*) in the old city of Hyderabad. Villagers near the old city used to organize the low-key ritual at a small shrine in honour of a village deity called Maisammma before 1950. Over a period of time, the deity became Mahankali and the shrine transformed into an important temple in Hyderabad city that now attracts several politicians, bureaucrats, and cinema actors, along with the media. Once patronized by the Nizam, the temple turned out to be a source of communal tension between Hindu and Muslim populations surrounding it due to the importance attached to the processions taken out in celebration of the jathara which did not have such importance earlier. The temple organizing committees, which did not exist earlier, are now taking an active mediatory role between the people and the politicians or bureaucrats, and for some, membership to these committees became a point of entry to the formal local political field. With the experience and popularity gained while working for the temple committees, they contested municipal elections as councillors, division members, and so on. The media plays a significant role covering various aspects of the ritual, the visitors, and various activities at the temple and during the processions. The media thus became instrumental in popularizing the temple.

Anthropology and Ritual

The huge body of anthropological literature available on south Indian village rituals[1] shows that the village rituals reproduce the social order[2] wherein members of all the castes take up roles related to their traditional occupations. The most important discussion among anthropologists centres on the association between the system of religious values—purity and impurity contained in the ritual practices and social behaviour—and hierarchy among the castes giving coherence to the social system.[3] In this debate there is apparently very little discussion on the political dimensions reflected in the village rituals with reference to the village and outside society.

Villagers seek the benevolence of the goddess who is believed to be one of the forms of Durga/Kali, the consort of Lord Shiva, through the ritual. She is also known as Shakti, which means power, and this power, it is believed, manifests itself not only by fulfilling the desires of people but also, if she is not honoured, by inflicting diseases and death on people along with animals. The ritual itself is power-filled, for people come together to honour the goddess wherein members of each caste play the specific role traditionally assigned to them.[4] In this process there is a re-creation of the social order that reproduces the social hierarchy maintained through ritual as well as political and economic power relations. Social anthropologists have lately recognized the significance of non-ritual power. Here, power needs to be conceptualized in terms of its coercive and visible form expressed through outbursts and protests in addition to its non-coercive and invisible form that manifests in various ways in everyday actions. Although the village is an isolated whole, it is connected to the outside world through political, economic, and cultural networks and administrative systems. The external affairs of the villagers do affect the ritual, which is an internal affair.

While summarizing the theoretical developments in anthropology since the 1960s, Sherry Ortner (1984) calls for a shift from structure to practice and everyday life. Nicholas Dirks (1988) writes that there is a move, among anthropologists, from symbolic analysis of the ritual to its practice, increasing focus on both everyday social behaviour and the non-ritual. He further argues that in social-science thinking, 'order' is presented as universal need subsequently getting naturalized, with disorder becoming marginal and unnatural. In this thinking, 'power' is virtually synonymous with order. Order is seen as an effect of power rather than its condition, but it is neither a cause nor a first principle— power is a relation, or rather an endless series of relations. Order needs to be denaturalized in this conceptualization of power, and resistance, while relieved of the obligation of establishing a new order, is significant as it indicates the presence of power. Reflecting on current anthropological writing on ritual, Dirks says that there is an 'underplay, both at the level of kingdoms or large political units and at the level of village rituals and festivals, [of] the social fact that ritual constitutes a tremendously important arena for the cultural construction of authority and the dramatic display of the social lineaments of power' (1988: 13). From this perspective, everyday forms of resistance shall find a place in ritual as well, and the disorder or disruption of order that exists with conflicts of interests and power struggles constitutes the natural order of the ritual. The present study takes into consideration the power—struggles for power with political dimension—and 'everyday' of the ritual.

Worship of Maisamma

Maisamma, who is now called Mahankali, was at one time a crude stone located on the outskirts of a village that abutted the walled city of Hyderabad, on the western side at a distance of 100 metres from Lal Darwaza gate[5] (Luther 2012: xxvii). Initially Madigas[6] alone used to worship the deity, but later the Goudas of the village joined them when they found that their business of selling *kallu*, the sap of the palmyra tree, had increased since they started worshipping the deity, which was considered the effect of her benevolent power. Later, Yadavas[7] also joined in worshipping the deity. Together they then erected a small shrine over the stone deity. They started organizing an annual celebration in which the Goudas used to offer *saaka* (the liquid offered to the deity, generally kallu), while others also participated. However, tradition says that the deity gained popularity in 1908 when the city experienced dangerous floods due to the overflowing of River Musi. It is believed that the deity appeared in a dream to the prime minister of the Nizam of Hyderabad, Raja Kishan Parishad, and told him that the flood could be controlled if the Nizam and the raja worshipped her. Persuaded by the prime minister, the Nizam worshipped the deity and the floods receded. Again, in 1921, when there was outbreak of plague, cholera, smallpox, and malaria, the epidemics were brought under control when the prime minister and the Nizam worshipped the deity. Thereafter, the Nizam sent a silk sari, jewellery, turmeric, and saffron powder on the day of worship every year as a mark of his homage or obeisance to the deity (Luther 2012: 48; 2012: 174).

The Ritual before 1953

Before 1953, the village elders belonging to the Gouda and Yadava castes began the ritual with the purchase of a male buffalo and handing it over to the Erpula families, a sub-caste of the Madigas. Taking the buffalo and beating a drum, they paid door-to-door visits to members of all castes in the locality. Women in the households worshipped the buffalo and gave some cash or grains to the Madigas as gift.

On day one, the first activity was *ghatasthapana*, which meant installation of the goddess Maisamma.[8] This was the symbolic movement of the mother goddess from her conjugal family to her natal house upon being invited to participate in the re-enactment of her marriage with Lord Shiva. Following this, the elders accompanied by others would go to the house of the Madigas while beating drums to bring the buffalo in a procession and tie it to a pole at the temple. They would then divide into small groups, each one responsible for fetching different items. One group would bring *putta mannu*,[9] *puste*,[10] and *mettelu*[11] from the goldsmith; another group would get a new sari from the weaver, a pot of toddy from a Gouda household, and wooden idols of Maisamma and Shiva from the carpenter of the village. Plastering the precincts of the shrine with putta mannu, the Madiga would place the wooden idols of Maisamma and Shiva on the ground and perform the marriage rituals of the goddess.[12] Meanwhile, a huge amount of rice would be cooked and kept ready for the ritual. Then, a Madiga would behead the buffalo and sprinkle its blood on the rice which was called *rati*. This entire process was known as *baliharana*. A foreleg of the animal would be cut and inserted horizontally in the mouth of the buffalo, and the head of the animal would be placed in front of the shrine. A Madiga would take three fistfuls of cooked rice, rati, and place it before the goddess. The remaining rice was filled into baskets (called *baligampas*) and into a pot. After this a small goat would be killed by an Erpula who dipped a cloth in its blood and removed its liver. A Chakali caste person wore this blood-soaked cloth around his waist and held the liver of the goat between his teeth. He also held another foreleg of the buffalo in one hand and was garlanded with the goat's intestines. Most of his body would be covered with blood and look very terrifying. He then followed the running group of men around the boundaries of the community who shouted 'kobali' or 'bali', while the Erpula Madiga man held the baligampa on one hand and sprinkled rati on the way with the other hand. No individual was supposed to move or come across the baligampa. The head of the buffalo would be kept at the shrine till the evening of that day. Then, women of all caste backgrounds carried *bonam*[13] and men carried camphor from their homes as offerings to the goddess, and the convention was that the potter's household would offer the first bonam followed by the others. This was followed by the worship of Potharaju, a man identified earlier for this purpose. He came out of the temple and ran around in a frenzy when he was possessed by the goddess and, when a ram was offered to him, bit at its neck and sucked its blood. This was followed by *bahishyavani* (foretelling). In this activity, a woman from the Erpula caste, identified earlier, would be possessed by the goddess and, standing on an earthen pot, would foretell events about the socioeconomic life, drought, rainfall, and so forth, in the ensuing year. In the evening, as part of the last activity of the festival, a procession would take place with the wooden statues of the god and goddess, with the head of the sacrificed buffalo kept in a winnowing-fan and carried as a head-load by a Byagari belonging to the Mala sub-caste,[14] and a *ghatam*[15] carried by an Erpula man from the Madiga sub-caste, and a potter. The procession would go up to Nallavaagu, a stream, where the wooden idols were immersed in water, their feet and faces washed, and then returned to the temple. The head of the buffalo was dropped on the banks. The following Sunday, the potter would offer a bonam to the goddess, which was called *maru bonam*. Those who had not offered bonam on the day of the festival could offer bonams on this day. With this, the bonalu festival would come to an end.

The Ritual in Other Villages

The celebrations of jatharas at Chinna Komerla in Kadapa and Kanupuru in Nellore districts observed during February–March 1991 were very similar, although the deities worshipped were different.[16] The central theme in both the cases is the worship of the male buffalo and its sacrifice to the deity. The dominant castes, that is, the Reddys and Berisettys, were the principal organizers in their respective villages while all other castes were participants. The major difference with the Maisamma jathara was that there were no marriage rituals performed between the goddess and Shiva in the other villages. What is important to note for the present is the 'everyday' of the ritual, that is, the emergence of non-ritual aspects which arise from political and economic power relations inherent in the caste society. In the first case, the father of one Ramakrishnaiah Mudaliar, a Berisetty, used to conduct the Kanupuru jathara until his death about seven years ago. Then, Ramakrishnaiah Mudaliar, who became the *sarpanch*[17] of the village, succeeded him in spite of pressure from his cousins, headed by Abbai Mudaliar, who desired to appropriate the leadership role in the ritual. The reason for this was that a Reddy who maintained illicit relations with Ramakrishnaiah's father's sister had been assisting Ramakrishnaiah and even his father in the ritual performance. Abbai Mudaliar and others felt that the prominence of Reddys in the ritual would increase or that they might even usurp the leadership if Ramakrishnaiah continued to officiate the ritual. They were also upset about the illicit affair with the Reddy.

These two groups supported two rival political parties: the Telugu Desam Party (TDP) and the Congress. Ramakrishnaiah Mudaliar, the sarpanch of the village, supported the Telugu Desam, whereas Abbai Mudaliar supported the Congress. Ramakrishnaiah sued Abbai in the local court for his alleged attempts to grab the leadership for the ritual in 1985, for which the court gave an injunction to maintain status quo for the next five years. With this, he continued directing the ritual for the next four years. During this period, since the Telugu Desam Party was in power in the state, Abbai Mudaliar's group did not meddle with Ramakrishnaiah's leadership. But when the state government changed from the Telugu Desam Party to the Congress in 1990, Abbai Mudaliar and his group went ahead with the performance of the ritual and threatened to beat up the other group if they arrived to stop them. When they started preparations by worshipping the deity to determine a date for the celebrations, Ramakrishnaiah Mudaliar and his supporters went to stop them because they were still legally entitled to perform the ritual that year. But they were assaulted and driven away and later the ritual was conducted by Abbai Mudaliar. Expecting troubles again, the district administration sent police troops to avert fighting between these rival groups during the ritual that was observed in 1991.

In the Chinnakomerla jathara too, there was struggle for domination and recognition of status. There were two Reddy groups involved in fights and murders, and even received punishments and jail sentences. Even after the resumption of peace between them, one Reddy group attempted to seize the privilege that was not due to them. The order of buffalo worship used to come from the chief of the Karnataka Reddys. These people were supposed to have been very prominent in the past, but their importance has gradually declined. But the ritual followed the old practice giving the privilege of first worship to the Karnataka Reddys. Since this group was no longer influential in the village, another Reddy, a non-Karnataka Reddy, attempted to appropriate the privilege by superseding some Karnataka Reddys.

The aforementioned facts confirm the observation made by Dirks (1987: 303–5) that the ritual performance is the locus of conflicts and contestations because of the play of honour and the emergence of political, economic, and other forms of power. The ritual unambiguously reflects the domination of high castes whose power is neither despotic nor coercive but seeks cooperation, willingness to share, and the submission of the lower castes.

In the Maisamma jathara, such conflicts and struggles for power, as noted in the other jatharas, may have existed before 1953, but they were not considered significant for the reason of Muslim domination. Further, with urbanization the village gradually disappeared as the physical and social gaps between the village and the walled city of Hyderabad eventually faded away. Along with urbanization, some other changes that occurred in temple maintenance, which are discussed later, have affected the leadership. There is a change in the entire scenario of worship besides the physical structure of the temple with the introduction of new deities and the priests therein.

The Ritual between 1953 and 1968

Around 1953, changes started occurring in the worship of the goddess with the discontinuation of animal sacrifices under the influence of one B. Venkataswamy, a leader of the Arya Samaj who was also a municipal councillor. He was able to organize the village elders who elected members to form an active temple committee for a fixed period and also an advisory committee to advise the temple committee that took care of the day-to-day affairs of the temple. He successfully convinced the elders to stop killing animals and substitute them with vegetables. The buffalo was replaced with a pumpkin, the goat or ram with a bottle gourd, and the blood with saffron powder. In the beginning, the elders used to go to the houses of Madigas with a pumpkin, but later the practice was given up altogether. The pumpkin was now brought directly from the house of the Madigas to the temple in a procession. Potharaju's activities changed; he bit the bottle gourd, not the neck of ram. Besides this, Venkataswamy also advised the elders to change the route of the procession on the last day towards Purana Pul (a bridge) of the Musi River instead of the Nallavagu stream. Further, he was able to convince elders of the temples at Lal Darwaza, Haribowli, Gowlipura, and Chandulal Bela to come together and organize a joint procession. Accordingly, the procession of the goddess did not go to Nallavagu, but to the Musi River along with other deities of the locality.

The actions of Venkataswamy have to be understood against the background of the political situation before and after Independence. The Nizam eagerly looked forward to regaining his independent state within India, but the Indian government wanted a merger of the Nizam's state with the Indian Union. The political situation was such that the Hindus wanted Hindu India and the Muslims wanted to resist the merger with India and restore the Nizam's power or Muslim hegemony. At this juncture, an armed group of Muslims called *razakar*s rose in support of the Nizam to enable him to re-establish his rule. The razakar movement totally destroyed the friendly Hindu–Muslim relations. At the same time, the Hindus dreamt of an independent India that would enable them to obtain their original power and authority. After driving away the British, Hindus wanted the Muslims to remain as non-dominant neighbours. But the situation was different as the Muslims continued their domination by numbers that enabled them to capture constitutional positions, which shall be explained later. For this they needed the consolidation of Hindu forces in the area. In this context, the changes that have taken place in the worship of Maisamma and organization of the bonalu festival at Lal Darwaza need to be understood.

Encouraged by the achievements made in changing the course of the collective procession of the deities in the Muslim-dominated areas and the response of the Hindu masses, the people of Lal Darwaza wanted to bring about some more changes. In 1964, the Maisamma Temple Committee sought help from Sri Marri Chenna Reddy, the minister of Andhra Pradesh, for getting an idol made of the goddess. He advised them to meet Ganapati Sthapati, a great architect, builder, and sculptor. Sthapati said it was not difficult to make a statue, but its installation in the old city might not be possible due to communal tensions in the area, as the Muslims might resist such a move. But he promised help in making an idol and suggested that they should meet Sri Sri Sri Jagadguru Chandrashekharendra Swamy, the popular Hindu religious guru of Kanchi Kamakoti Peetam, whenever he visited Hyderabad. When the Swamy was visiting Hyderabad in 1968, the committee met him and requested permission for the installation of the idol made by Sthapati at Lal Darwaza temple. He readily agreed.

The government gave police security and permission to take a procession from Charminar on 27 May 1968 to the Maisamma Temple of

Lal Darwaza. Sri Chandrashekharendra Swamy walked in front of the elephant that carried him till Charminar from Shankar Mutt. Several devotees and members of the general public followed him. With police escort, the procession moved from Charminar to Shah-Ali-Banda to Lal Darwaza Mode and to Lal Darwaza. It moved so slowly through huge crowds that it took more than three hours just to cover a distance of 1.5 kilometres or so. The Swami installed the new idol, the goddess sitting on a lion. Since then the name Maisamma has been changed to Shimha Vahini Mahankali because the goddess is seated on a lion as her vehicle. The Swami also suggested that the committee continued the regular worship of the goddess, let the temple remain open for 365 days, and also bring about a change in the pattern of worship. The three-day ritual became the eleven-day festival. This event energized the Hindus into taking the collective procession of the deities through the streets of the old city, demonstrating their physical strength and symbolic domination where the Muslim population was concentrated. A Brahman priest was also appointed to conduct day-to-day and special rituals.

The Ritual after 1968

The Temple Committee followed the suggestions of Swami Sri Sri Sri Chandrashekharendra Swamy and implemented the new practices in the temple functions since 1968. Every year the bonalu festival starts on a Friday. For nine days, the priest adorns the goddess and performs the *poojas* as shown in Table 10.1.

A new method of worship called Shanti Kalyanam was added in 1979. Shanti Kalyanam is performed by newly married couples on the evening of the last Sunday of the festival. This is the special worship offered in connection with the vow made by the parents who prayed for the marriage of their son or daughter. It is a gesture of gratitude expressed for the answered prayer.

In 2008 when the temple completed 100 years, reckoning 1908 as the beginning when the Musi flood occurred and Raja Kishen Parishad and Nizam realized the power of the goddess, the Temple Committee invited Sri Sri Jayendra Saraswati who had succeeded Sri Sri Sri Chandrashekharendra Swamy, and Vijayendra Saraswati, the disciple of Sri Jayendra Saraswati, as special invitees. A noticeable

Table 10.1 *Poojas* during bonalu festival at Mahankali Temple of Lal Darwaza

Day	Name of the *pooja*	Activity
Friday	Abhishekam	Pooja is performed by pouring turmeric water, *kumkuma* (saffron) water, and so forth, on the goddess, and *paarani*, the utterance of 800 names of the goddess.
Saturday	Akshitarchana	One lakh raw rice grains mixed with turmeric and kumkuma are counted and pooja is performed.
Sunday	Ghatasthapana/ Ghatotsavam	Ghatam is installed.
Monday	Bilwarchana	Pooja is performed by counting one lakh leaves.
Tuesday	Deepotsavam	Lighting of traditional decoration lamps.
Wednesday	Shakambari pooja	The goddess is adorned with vegetables and worshipped.
Thursday	Pushparchana	The goddess is adorned with flowers.
Friday	Kumkumarchana	Pooja is performed by transferring one lakh pinches of kumkuma from one plate to another.
Saturday	Chandihomam and Tottela Uregimpu	Ghatam procession is taken out.
Sunday	Baliharana, Bonalu	The sacrifice of a buffalo and goat takes place symbolically by the breaking of a pumpkin and bottle gourd respectively; food is offered to the goddess.
Monday	Potharaju, Rangam	Breaking of a bottle gourd by Potharaju (since 1986); *Rangam*— the foretelling or prophetic utterances about socio-economic conditions of the people in the year—is performed; and a procession is taken to the Musi River.

Source: Compiled by authors.

element about the centenary celebrations was the installation of the statue of Lord Ganesh, which was not there earlier. Usually, in the temples of mother goddesses, one can find only the goddess and Potharaju, without Ganesh, but this temple is different in this regard.

Ghatasthapana

As stated previously, the festival begins on a Friday with Abhishekam, and the pooja of Akshitarchana is performed on Saturday. On Sunday the ritual of Ghatasthapana is performed. Earlier, the Ghatasthapana used to take place individually and separately in a simple manner by the elders of each temple on the very first day of the festival but now it takes place on the third day. On this day, the elders of the temples at Haribowli, Gowlipura, and Chandulal Bela[18] used to separately collect the ghatams from the Shiva Temple of Shah-Ali Banda, carry them individually, and place them in the respective temples. However, with the formation of the Ummadi Devalaya Committee (Joint Temple Committee) in 1968 under the leadership of B. Venkataswamy, the pattern of Ghatasthapana has changed. According to the new pattern, all the temples at Lal Darwaza, Haribowli, Gowlipura, and Bela take the ghatam from the Shiva Temple at Shah-Ali Banda. These ghatams are made anew every year but the idols of the goddesses in the temples remain the same. The objective is to bring together all Hindus on a single platform in the Muslim-dominated area. Then, all of them go in a procession to Lal Darwaza Mode. During this procession, the ghatam of Mahankali of Lal Darwaza is in the forefront leading the rest, since Mahankali is the eldest among the goddesses. The last but not least that stands in this procession is the deity of Haribowli.

At the Lal Darwaza Mode, the Ummadi Devalaya Committee welcomes the ghatams along with political leaders or officials who are invited to participate in the ritual. Two stages are set up: one at Lal Darwaza temple and the other at the Lal Darwaza Mode. As soon as the ghatams arrive, the chairman of the committee invites some important leaders and officials onto the stage who deliver speeches about the goddesses and the significance of the bonalu festival. After this, the ghatams depart for their respective temples. At Lal Darwaza temple, the chief advisor of the advisory board and chairman of the temple committee welcome the ghatam of Mahankali upon its arrival.

The stage set up at the Lal Darwaza temple is used for two purposes: first, for the delivery of speeches by dignitaries who visit the temple throughout the nine days of the festival; and second, for performance of cultural programmes sponsored by the Endowment Department of the state government. These programmes are organized particularly in the evening.

After the Ghatasthapana on Sunday, the great traditional rituals of Bilwarchana would take place on Monday, Deepalankarana on Tuesday, Shakambari pooja on Wednesday, Pushparchana on Thursday, Kumkumarchan on Friday, and Navachandiyagam on Saturday. On Sunday, the traditional practices come into play, that is, baliharana and bonalu, with the changes introduced after 1953 under the influence of B. Venkatswamy. On Monday, the activities of Potharaju and rangam are undertaken, followed by the final procession.

Tottela Uregimpu

The Tottela Uregimpu presets the final, that is, the ninth day of the procession. It was introduced as a new activity for Monday in 1968. It is the procession of *tottelu*,[19] which did not exist before 1968. The *totte*,[20] which was made by an expert, was taken to the temple on the first day itself by the elders of the temple. Two days before the final procession, that is, on Saturday, the Temple Committee of each temple gathers at Lal Darwaza Mode with the totte of the temple, and, when all gather, each committee with its totte returns to its temple in procession and places it there.

Appaginthalu

The final procession in which all the ghatams are carried for immersion in Musi River is called Appaginthalu.[21] On Monday evening when the *bhavishyavani* (foretelling the future) or *rangam karyakramam* (the programme of the rangam performance) is over, the procession of the deities along with ghatam takes place. This ghatam is held by a potter who sits on a chariot, which is actually a truck or tractor, and the totte is also placed on the chariot. When all the chariots of different temples gather at Lal Darwaza Mode, the procession begins with the chariot of Haribowli temple. During this procession, the Lal

Darwaza temple's chariot is placed at the end of the procession. All the temple chariots have their own music system; people dance in front of each of the chariots, a practice that has replaced the earlier custom of Madigas beating drums. People also consume alcohol during the procession and dance to the tunes. They decorate the chariots in a unique way with good lighting. At last they reach the Purana Pul, clean the ghatam, leave the tottelu and other items over there, and return silently without any fanfare.

By the time the procession begins at Lal Darwaza Mode, a stage is set up at Charminar. There the Ummadi Devalaya Committee makes arrangements for the speeches of the political leaders and other dignitaries while the procession of the deities starts at Lal Darwaza Mode.

A week after the bonalu, the temple committees arrange *anna daana karyakramam* (free distribution of food) at their respective temples. Some hundreds of people attend irrespective of caste or class to receive food. On the festival days, the committee arranges free food in the afternoon for the poor. The worship of the goddess was confined to the local community even fifty years ago, but now it draws thousands of people from the new city, the old city, and also from neighbouring towns and villages. The final procession is a great attraction; it is a delightful sight of each uniquely decorated chariot proceeding in a line while people dance to the tunes of music with passion. Those who watch the show stand on either side of the road and on the roofs of their houses.

An attempt has been made to understand the local Hindu religion in the background of power, caste, politics, and the role of media through the description (see Table 10.2) of the jathara or bonalu festival for Maisamma in the beginning and Mahankali later. The everyday life becomes significant in the analysis. There is an inherent interrelationship between the power of the goddess and sociopolitical power of the dominant caste within the locality which has connections and networks outside of the locality. The temple, as a religious institution, stands out as an informal learning centre to develop leadership in the community. The participation in rituals provides an opportunity to make decisions, help and work in cooperation with others, and also enable leadership development. The media mediates between politicians and people in general but in particular with the temple functionaries and local leaders, and indirectly provides a galvanizing effect on the people about the power of the goddess.

Table 10.2 Changes in the temple of Lal Darwaza

	Before 1953	Between 1953 and 1964	From 1964 till date
Physical structure	• Small shrine in an open site • Mother goddess—a black stone two feet high • Worshipped by Madigas	• New temple constructed • Gopuram covered with bronze plate	• New statue installed • Idol of Lord Ganesh installed • Silver sanctorum made • Bronze Gopuram replaced by golden Gopuram
People	• Participation of all castes • Participation by Nizam and other officials of his court	• Domination of Goudas extended • Temple committee created • Informal Advisory Committee created	• Brahman priests appointed • Participation of political leaders, religious gurus, and other officials • Formal Advisory Committee formed
Rituals	• One-day ritual • Maisamma installed • Deity decorated • Buffalo taken by Madigas into the community for worship • Wedding of the deity with Shiva performed by a Madiga • Buffalo and goat sacrificed • *Poli* thrown • Bonalu offered • Potharaju possessed by deity • Events foretold	• Animal sacrifice stopped • Animals replaced by pumpkin and bottle gourd • Three-day festival • Worship conducted with Sanskritic pooja on first two days; worship of village deity on final day	• Eleven-day festival; stage set up for various cultural activities • New worship of Shanti Kalyanam introduced • Madigas' entry into the community stopped • Anna daana karyakramam introduced

(Cont'd)

Table 10.2 (Cont'd)

	Before 1953	Between 1953 and 1964	From 1964 till date
Processions	• Procession taken to Nallavaagu • Procession not joined by other temples • Maru bonam offered	• Procession taken to Purana Pul • Procession joined by temples of surrounding areas	• Temple Committee meetings held by government • Separate processions of ghatam and totte taken • Chariots included in final day of procession to Purana Pul • Political leaders felicitated and speeches given

Source: Compiled by authors.

Sovereignty, Construction of Authority, and Dominant Castes

The sacrifice of buffaloes and goats during bonalu closely resembles the rites of the great horse-sacrifice that was performed by kings with the aid of Brahman priests during the Vedic period (see Ramanujam 1986). The performance of this ritual in medieval times, as Stein (1984) shows, took a different form and meaning. The kings of south India, especially the maharaja of Mysore, made this sacrificial ritual public and associated it with Puranic gods or heroes such as Lord Rama and Goddess Durga. According to Stein, every year the ritual assumes a political significance when the king is reconsecrated and made divine. Dumont has rightly observed that the Indian village is a 'reduced version' of the kingdom and 'there is a homology between the function of dominance at village level and the royal function at the level of a larger territory' (1970: 160, 162). The village head-man, as the counterpart of the king, protects the 'dharma' and caste order. In the rituals described earlier, the dominant role of the village headman and his caste is obvious. Therefore, the ritual legitimizes the authority of the village headman and authorizes its organization by the dominant caste or castes, thus strengthening their existing political and economic power. The ritual also determines different roles to be undertaken by different caste members that reinforce the extant social order. The conflicts in this regard play the role of legitimizing the village leadership besides recognizing the status of various castes and individuals. This is evident in case of Kanupuru and Chinkomerla jatharas. Dirks (1987: 303–5) makes a similar observation about another Tamil Nadu ritual regarding the play of political and economic power.

The scenario of the bonalu festival of Lal Darwaza Mahankali is of a different kind where traditional inheritance of leadership has transformed into a democratic electoral system. Yet what is clear is the gradual downplaying of the importance of Madigas and Malas and the entry of local politics. The Temple Committee is constituted as per the norms developed by the elders of Lal Darwaza representing the Gouda, Yadava, Mudiraj, Sanga, and other castes. However, the jathara begins with the worship of the elder of the Yadava caste, the first bonam is offered by the Kummari (potter) elder's family, and, finally, the eleven-day festival ends with the worship conducted by a member of the Gouda caste; in the recent past, this is done by Devender Gouda, an MLA (Member of Legislative Assembly) and former minister of the state. For the last four years, the committees are experiencing some conflicts because of their affiliations to various political parties. If majority of the members who attend the meetings are associated with the Congress party, they propose the name of someone who is a Congress-party member to be the chairman, which creates dissent among the Telugu Desam Party followers. The next problem relates to caste: Goudas, Yadavs, Mudirajs, and others attend the meetings. Sometimes, if the chairman belongs to the Gouda caste, he likes to have more of his caste members in the committee, which is not acceptable to others. This caste favouritism creates discomfort for those who want to work as members of the temple committee. But the significant fact is that they never include people from the (SCs) even though they have a vital role to play in the temple functions.

Location, Religion, and Politics

In this Lal Darwaza area where the temple of Mahankali is located, there is a good proportion of Muslims though the Hindu population is predominant. However, the Muslims have dominated the political arena due to their representation in the formal political institutions such as the municipal corporations, legislative assembly, and Parliament. Muslims try to hold on to their legacy of domination and continue to organize huge rallies during Muharram. Hindus argue that the political domination of Muslims continues in the Lal Darwaza area because the Hindus are politically divided even though they outnumber the Muslims. While Hindus support different political parties, which are mentioned later, and thus divided, the Muslims are politically united and support Muslims' parties only. But the Hindus no longer like to be political subordinates. They feel they have remained powerless for a long time in this area unlike their brethren who dominate in other localities of Hyderabad where the Muslim populations are smaller. They opine that Independence has not really granted them freedom from the domination of local Muslims in this area.

In Hyderabad, relations between Hindus and Muslims were said to have been cordial until the 1930s. The Hindus participated in Muharram activities and shared their joy on Ramadan along with their friends. But, in the following years, these relations became very fragile. Communal hatred and conflicts increased, particularly due to the razakar movement that emerged during this period (see Luther (2012: 224). These incidents had completely destroyed the brotherly relations between the Hindus and the Muslims. Consequently, Hindus in the old city stopped participating in the Muharram festivities. Muslims did not allow the bonalu festival to take place. The development of communal feelings between Hindus and Muslims led the two religious communities to show their strength and unity on occasions, such as during conflicts, elections, and the organization of festivals. Hindus found in the jathara/bonalu festival a means of keeping themselves united. The community came forward to celebrate the bonalu festival together in a manner that would excel the celebration of Muharram, which is observed with great religious fervour in the old city. In this context, Venkataswamy took the initiative and played a leading role in the construction of the temple and reorganization of the temple activities with the help of the elders of Lal Darwaza, as described earlier. In 1954, it was Venkataswamy's motivation that led to the formation of the Temple Committee and, in 1964, of the Ummadi Devalaya Committee. The first procession was held under the chairmanship of Venkataswamy. He believed that for the Hindus to gain power and resist Muslim domination, the procession had to change its route and pass through the Muslim-dominated areas in order to show their physical and numerical strength, will power, and their unity.[22] Because of his efforts, the procession of the goddess has shifted from the old city to the new city, and was made successful by all the Hindus coming together.

Interests of the Political Leaders

The city of Hyderabad is divided into different constituencies. The old city has four constituencies: Chandrayangutta, Bahadurpura, Yakutpura, and Charminar. Before the changes made by the Delimitation Commission in 2008, the entire Lal Darwaza area was part of the Chandrayangutta constituency. Until then, the positions of MLAs and Members of Parliament (MPs) were always held by Muslims due to their numerical strength. After implementation of the Delimitation Act, the area was divided into four parts and each part merged with different constituencies. Lal Darwaza, with three wards, was carved up between Yakutpura, Bahadurpura, and Charminar constituencies, with one ward in each constituency. Even then, the situation has not changed in any way. The Hindus continue to be unrepresented from this area.

Various political parties in the old city, such as the All India Majlis-e-Ittehadul Muslimeen (AIMIM), the Indian National Congress, the Telugu Desam Party (TDP), the Telangana Rashtra Samiti (TRS), the Bharatiya Janata Party (BJP), the Majlis Bachau Tehreek party (MBT), the Praja Rajyam Party (PRP), and so forth, participate in municipal, assembly, and Parliamentary elections. Of these political parties, some are secular while others are non-secular. The AIMIM supports Muslims, the BJP supports Hindus, notwithstanding its claim of being a secular party, and other parties stand on secular ground. The winning of elections in these areas mostly depends on the candidate's religion, caste, and political-party affiliation. By and large, Muslims vote for a Muslim candidate and Hindus vote for a Hindu. The candidates contesting elections meet the informal local leaders such as members of the temple committees, advisory committees, or procession committees and seek their support. For a member of any of the religious committees, religion and political party are two sides of the same coin. As far as religion is concerned, no party affiliation should interfere with it, but as a Hindu one would oppose any of the Muslim parties, and as a Muslim one would oppose a non-Muslim party.

Leaders of almost all the political parties such as AIMIM, MBT, TDP, INC, BJP, MBT, and PRP participate in the bonalu festival. The temple has been visited by the following leaders who belonged to different political parties at different times, including Prime Ministers Indira Gandhi, Rajiv Gandhi, and P.V. Narsimha Rao, President Sarvepalli Radhakrishnan, and several MPs, MLAs, corporators (members of municipal corporations), governors, chief ministers, and police commissioners of Andhra Pradesh. Here, religion and politics have become inseparable and interdependent. Political leaders show interest in participating in the temple functions in order to come closer to the voters and become familiar with the public. They also like to know the local leaders in order to take help from them during the elections, as they are influential at the grassroots.

A good network between the informal and formal leaders has been built. The common people in the locality seek help from these informal leaders to get their problems relating to ration cards, old-age pension, and so forth, solved. This builds a good rapport between the informal leaders and the public. If the informal leader cannot solve someone's problem at his level, he approaches the formal leader who may be an MLA for a solution. Thus, the informal leaders bridge the gap between the common man and the formal leader. So, in course of time these informal leaders become more popular and find opportunities to enter the political field.

The networks help them to fulfil their vested interests and try to clear their way for entry into local politics at the community or division level. Politicians also look for candidates who can work for the development of their party from that locality and mobilize the public for rallies and other similar events. Such candidates are usually temple functionaries who could easily mediate between the people and the politicians, and who have developed their oratory skills, expertise in mobilizing people, and an understanding of the problems of the common people. In such a situation, two temple functionaries joined the newly established PRP. One of them got a PRP ticket to contest the state assembly elections of 2009, but lost. The other person tried very hard to get a ticket for the same election but, ultimately, in vain. He then contested the elections as an independent candidate, but without success.

The members of the temple committee, as stated earlier, are not detached from political inclinations and squabbles. It is obvious that they use their role in the temple activities to get political mileage. For instance, there is a need to acquire more space for the temple as the number of pilgrims and devotees is increasing every day, making the temple area very congested. But because of internal political conflicts, the committee has been unable to buy the surrounding piece of land. This is due to the fact that if one group of the committee members proposes to acquire land, the other group opposes it as the former might take credit for expanding the space of the temple. Therefore, political intentions and religious affairs are interlinked in subtle ways, though not openly.

Political Leaders and Communal Riots

Communal riots can take place on any day a religious group organizes a procession. Communal feelings may arise due to provocation from either side—Hindus or Muslims. Any incident of conflict between a Muslim and a Hindu can spark violence. Instances of what might lead to riots could be shouting slogans that provoke others or making loud noises when passing through areas inhabited by people of the other religion. In 1966, Hindus were attacked by Muslims in two places, at Shah-Ali Banda and Patharghati, when they were returning to their homes from the Musi River. Around ten to fifteen Hindus were injured. On 23 November 1979, Muslims desecrated the Bhagyalaxmi temple of Charminar by setting it on fire. On 22 July 1984, Muslims attacked Hindus who were participating in the procession of the Mahankali goddess at Moghulpura. Such incidents increased communal feelings and tensions between the two communities. This was the time for intervention by officials and political leaders. Political leaders reacted or interfered in the issues related to riots.[23] Both Muslim and Hindu leaders have tried to settle the disputes because they are nurtured by these parties.[24] On the day of Maha Shivratri in 2011, Hindus had to stop playing music at a particular place on the demand of the Muslims but then started playing the music at some other temple. This shows the competition and religious feeling between the two communities: one group does not want to listen to another religious group. When problems arise, they need leaders to settle the issues. Therefore, the political leaders are welcomed in the bonalu festival.

Role of the Press/Media

During the eleven days of bonalu, the media plays a significant role by covering all the activities of the temple each day and the visits of the various dignitaries. This coverage has an impact in two ways: first, it facilitates the visit of a large number of devotees, and second, it helps in strengthening relations between the politicians, bureaucrats, and temple functionaries. The first impact is the media effect, but it has cultural implications for the people. When people watch television and read newspapers about the visits by officials, cinema actors, and other luminaries, besides large numbers of common people, they feel encouraged to visit the goddess and their faith in the goddess also increases. This increased faith is related to the belief that the goddess is very powerful and answers all prayers, and this is why many people, including the dignitaries, visit the goddess. Therefore, visits from a large number of devotees is a reflection of the power of the goddess, and the media plays a significant role in that.

Second, when politicians visit the temple and deliver speeches, they strongly desire media coverage of their visits. They want publicity about them among the masses. They want the people to know about them so that they are recognized as important and powerful personalities who will be able to solve their problems and thus secure votes for themselves during elections. Further, they want to show their faith in the goddess—an assertion of their common religious identity is likely to impress the Hindu voters. The temple functionaries and other local leaders like the media to cover their meetings with politicians and bureaucrats who visit the temple. They use these meetings for continued association so as to obtain official favours for them or for the local people in future. The media coverage also helps in building their image in public for their association with the dignitaries. Since people come to know about the association of the temple functionaries with the officials through media, they approach the temple functionaries to take their issues up with the officials for finding solutions. The temple functionaries thus become mediators between the local people and officials or politicians.

***

The foregoing analysis and description reveal the fact that traditional village rituals continue to enjoy high esteem in both urban and rural contemporary Indian society. Religion, in particular the observance of village rituals, has not been free from the influence of politics, power struggles, or efforts to establish the hegemony of a particular caste. However, in the present case, the presence of Muslims and their rule in the past and the strained relations over the years have given a communal dimension to the village rituals. It is not uncommon for several non-Sanskritic deities to become Sanskritic deities. Maisamma has been transformed into Mahankali, who represents the ferocious form of Durga/Kali, who also symbolizes Hindu power vis-à-vis the local Muslim domination. Given the emergence of a communal element and a source for drawing political clout, political parties are attracted to the festival. The temple organization, ritual performance, and procession-taking have also become means for entry into politics for some individuals. Thus, the temple is the place where religion and politics come together, and this has magnified the effect on the general public due to both historical reasons and strained relations in contemporary times between the two dominant religious communities in Hyderabad city.

Notes

1. See Beals (1964); Dirks (1987); Dube (1955); Dumont (1986); Elmore (1915); Fuller (1987, 1992); Harper (1959, 1964); Heibert (1971); Pandian (1983); Moffatt (1979); Nuckolls (1997); Pfaffenberger (1980); Rao (1998); Reddy (1952); Srinivas (1965); Tapper (1979); Whitehead (1921); and, more recently, Mines (2002) and several others.

2. Leach writes, '... ritual action and belief are alike to be understood as forms of symbolic statements about the social order' (1964: 14). 'The structure which is symbolised in ritual is the system of socially approved "proper" relations between individuals and groups' (Leach 1964: 15).

3. Cf. Dumont (1957); Harper (1959, 1964); Marriot (1955); Srinivas (1965); and Sharma (1970).

4. It is in the sense of collective consciousness. There is also a blend of mechanical and organic solidarity.

5. Until the early twentieth century, Hyderabad remained a walled city with fourteen gates and an equal number of *khidkis* (postern gates).

6. The lowest caste in the social hierarchy.

7. A low caste in the middle level of the social hierarchy.

8. A bust-size idol made of silver, which is housed in the temple of Śiva at Shah-Ali-Banda, decorated with flowers, and carried by a potter.

9. *Putta mannu* is mud collected from an ant hill, which is used for plastering floor of a house.

10. *Puste* is a small golden badge tied to a cotton thread which is tied around the woman's neck by the husband at the time of marriage. It is the symbol of marriage for the woman, which is supposed to be worn all her life.

11. *Mettelu* are rings put on the second toes of a married woman's feet to symbolize her marital status.

12. Such a marriage between Lord Shiva and Selliyamman, the village deity, has been noted in Tamil Nadu (Moffatt 1979).

13. It consisted of cooked rice in a pot decorated with lime, vermillion, turmeric spots, and neem leaves.

14. One of the lowest castes in the social hierarchy.

15. Originally the term 'ghatam' was used to refer to the decorated bust-size image of the goddess made of mud or the decorated earthenware image of the goddess, also of bust-size. Since this is carried by people from place to place, it is mobile in this sense. Nowadays, the image is made of silver which is mobile and called 'ghatam'. The opposite of 'ghatam' is the immobile and fixed image of the deity made of wood or stone, which remains permanently in the sanctorum of the temple for worship.

16. For details, see Rao (1998: 107–48).

17. Elected head of the village council.

18. Different deities were enshrined in these temples, and bonalu was organized on different dates.

19. 'Totte' is the singular, while 'tottelu' is the plural.

20. 'Totte' is a mound or pyramidal or conical but elongated structure, approximately 5 or 6 feet high, made of split bamboo reeds. The structure is conical at the top and rectangular at the bottom, with each side (width)

measuring a foot. All its sides from top to bottom are covered with coloured transparent papers, and it is often decorated with flower garlands.

21. 'Appaginthalu' means handing over. This is a ritual in marriages in which the bride is handed over to the groom. It symbolizes the goddess being handed over to her husband, Lord Shiva.

22. Kaur (2003) notes the role of the public procession in connection with the Ganesh festival organized by Lokmanya Bala Gangadhara Tilak, which brought about the unity of Hindus and gave a political message. The procession is cultural, religious, and symbolic of the city's politics.

23. Naidu (1990) has also observed that communal conflicts occurred in connection with the bonalu processions and commented on the involvement of political leaders in resolving these conflicts.

24. Both Muslim and Hindu local leaders meet the police officials when they come to know about the riots and the arrest of their supporters by the police. They try to influence the police in not registering cases against these individuals and prosecuting them. The mutual dependence between the leaders and their followers is such that it is an obligation on the part of the leaders, whether Hindu or Muslim, to help their respective supporters at the time of crisis, in this case, point police custody. As leaders who are not directly involved in the riots, they attempt to diffuse tensions between the two communal groups so that the situation does not go out of control. The riots that happen during the festival often have had their roots in earlier unresolved disputes that surface at this time on some pretext or the other. At this juncture, therefore, the leaders attempt to settle these old and new disputes when their followers are in trouble. By doing so, the leaders obtain the goodwill of their supporters. In a way, with the support of the leaders, the individuals get encouraged to be involved in riots in the future because they have the backing of their leaders. As a cyclical chain of events, the leaders in this sense seem to encourage the riots, because they help them to gain the supporters' goodwill.

Bibliography

Appadurai, Arjun. 1981. *Worship and Conflict under Colonial Rule*. Cambridge: Cambridge University Press.

Babb, Lawrence. 1975. *The Divine Hierarchy: Popular Hinduism in Central India*. New York: Columbia Press.

Beals, A.R. 1964. 'Conflict and Inter-local Festivals in a South Indian Region'. *Journal of Asian Studies* 23(special issue): 95–113.

Bourdieu, Pierre. 1977. *Outline of a Theory of Practice*. Cambridge: Cambridge University Press.

Carol, Lucy. 1977. '"Sanskritization", "Westernisation", and "Social Mobility"'. *Journal of Anthropological Research* 33(4): 355–71.

Dirks, Nicholas. 1987. *The Hollow Crown: Ethnohistory of an Indian Kingdom.* Cambridge: Cambridge University Press.

———. 1988. 'Ritual of Resistance: Subversion as a Social Fact'. CSST Working Papers. Ann Arbor: The University of Michigan.

Dube, S.C. 1955. *Indian Village.* Ithaca: Cornell University Press.

Dumont, Louis. 1957. *Une Sous Caste de L'inde du sud.* Paris: Mouton.

———. 1970. *Homo Hierarchicus.* Chicago: Chicago University Press.

———. 1986. *A South Indian Sub-Caste: Social Organization and Religion of the Pramalai Kallar.* New York: Oxford University Press.

Elmore, W.T. 1915. *Dravidian Gods in Modern Hinduism: A Study of the Local and Village Deities of Southern India.* University Studies, vol. 15. Lincoln: University of Nebraska.

Fuller, C.J. 1987. 'Sacrifice (Bali) in the South Indian Temple'. In *Religion and Society in South India*, edited by V. Sudarsen, P. Reddy, and M. Suryanarayana, 21–35. Delhi: B.R Publications.

———. 1992. *The Camphor Flame: Popular Hinduism and Society in India.* Princeton: Princeton University Press.

Harper, E.B. 1959. 'Two Systems of Economic Exchange in Village India'. *American Anthropologist* 61(5): 760–78.

———. 1964. 'A Hindu Village Pantheon'. *South Western Journal of Anthropology* 15(3): 227–34.

Heibert, Paul. 1971. *Konduru: Structure and Integration in a South India Village.* Minneapolis, MN: University of Minnesota Press.

Kaur, Raminder. 2003. *Performative Politics and Culture of Hinduism.* Delhi: Permanent Black.

Kelly, John D., and Martha Kaplan. 1990. 'History, Structure, and Ritual'. *Annual Review of Anthropology* 19: 119–50.

Leach, E.R. 1964. *Political Systems of Highland Burma.* Boston: Beacon Press.

Luther, Narendra. 2012 [2006]. *Hyderabad: A Biography.* New Delhi: Oxford University Press, revised and updated edition.

Marriot, McKim. 1955. *Village India: Studies in the Little Community.* Chicago: The University of Chicago Press.

Mines, Diane P. 2002. 'Hindu Nationalism, Untouchable Reform, and the Ritual Production of a South Indian Village'. *American Ethnologist* 29(1): 58–85.

Moffatt, Michael. 1979. *An Untouchable Community in South India: Structure and Consensus.* Princeton: Princeton University Press.

Naidu, Ratna. 1990. *Old Cities, New Predicaments.* New Delhi: Sage Publications.

Nuckolls , Charles W. 1997. 'Fathers and Daughters in a South Indian Goddess Myth: Cultural Ambivalence and the Dynamics of Desire'. *Contributions to Indian Sociology*, 3(1): 51–7.

Ortner, Sherry B. 1979. *Sherpas through Their Rituals*. Cambridge: Cambridge University Press.

————. 1984. 'Theory in Anthropology Since the Sixties'. *Comparative Studies in Society and History* 26(1): 126–66.

Pandian, Jacob. 1983. 'The Sacred Symbol of the Mother Goddess in a Tamil Village: A Parochial Model of Hinduism'. In *Religion in Moderm India*, edited by Giri Raj Gupta, 198–214. Delhi: Vikas.

Pfaffenberger, B. 1980. 'Social Communication in Dravidian Ritual'. *Journal of Anthropological Research* 36(2): 196–219.

Ramanujam, A.K. 1986. 'Two Realms of Kannada Folklore'. In *Another Harmony*, edited by Stuart H. Blackburn and A.K. Ramanujam, 41–75. Berkeley: University of California Press.

Rao, N.S. 1998. *Organized Power and Unorganized Resistance*. New Delhi: Aravali Books International.

Reddy, N.S. 1952. 'Transition in Caste Structure in Andhra Desh with Particular Reference to Depressed Castes'. Ph.D. dissertation, Lucknow University.

Sharma, Ursula. 1970. 'The Problem of Village Hinduism: "Fragmentation" and Integration'. *Contributions to Indian Sociology*, n.s. 4:1–21.

Srinivas, M.N. 1965. *Religion and Society among the Coorgs of South India*. Bombay: Asia Publishing House.

Stein, Burton. 1984. *All the King's Mana: Papers on Medieval South Indian History*. Madras: New Era Publishers.

Tapper, B.E. 1979. 'Widows and Goddess: Female Roles in Deity Symbolism in a South Indian Village'. *Contributions to Indian Sociology*, n.s. 13(1): 1–31.

Whitehead, Henry. 1921. *The Village Gods of South India*. Calcutta: Association Press.

RELIGIOUS PRACTICES OF THE DIASPORA

Cultural Reproduction and Religious Practices of the Diaspora

11

APARNA RAYAPROL

Cultural Reproduction and the Reconstruction of Identities in the Indian Diaspora

In the twenty-first century, one can see the ways in which religion has taken interesting turns to reinvent itself in the diasporas. Diasporas have seen the resurrection of religious practices in new avatars and, with modernity, the influence of the host communities on the practice of religion and rituals in a new social and cultural location. Elements of tradition find their way into reclaiming pasts in diasporic contexts after major terrorist attacks such as 9/11. Modernity does not necessarily mean more openness, but it implies a further discrimination of minorities in the face of religion. For instance, the expression of religion in the form of a veil or a turban or in the renewed imparting of religious education in a temple is a reactive endeavour. Many Muslim women in the contemporary world feel compelled to be in a veil, something that was dispensed with by their mothers in the face of modernity, particularly in post-Independence India. There is a pressure to engage in the reproduction of culture when they become the other, or minorities, in migrant or diasporic contexts. The expression of religious sentiments in modern nation-states takes many diverse forms, but the establishment of religious institutions in the diaspora is a simple but emphatic concrete assertion of one's identity.

Construction of Hindu temples, ethnic churches, synagogues, and Islamic centres are examples of such assertions.

Hindu temples around the world have functioned as places of worship, meeting places for political purposes, and also for simply reproducing and recreating culture. In the contemporary world, it is hard to ascertain the exact number of Hindu temples outside India, but the temples are surely of different kinds based on their class, caste, and regional and cultural lineages. These temples reflect the diversity of Hindus in India as well as of the diasporas around the world. In the contemporary world, it is hard to ascertain the number of Hindu temples outside India, but there are several. An analysis of the temples shows that the diversity of religion, caste, class, and region that is present in India is slowly but surely seen in the diasporas as well. There are temples built by the old diaspora in the subaltern world, and there are temples built in the new diasporas in the twentieth-century postcolonial world. Rituals are often reproduced or transformed to suit the needs of the host communities (Clothey 2007). The South Asian immigrant bourgeoisie, particularly in the West, have a vested interest in the preservation of 'traditional' culture, and have now joined forces with the nation-state to preserve not only culture but also a particular aspect of it, patriarchal authority. For the first generation of the diaspora, it was crucial to have their children reproduce Indian culture in other parts of the world. Mapping the number of Hindu temples and Indian-classical-dance schools around the world indicates that the success rate of the first generation is quite high, and that Indian culture has become an important part of global culture. My earlier work on the first generation was based on an ethnography of a south Indian Hindu temple in the United States where women were the pillars of building a strong religious community (Rayaprol 1997). This chapter will draw from some of that work while also attempting to understand the way that religion has been changing meanings in different social and political contexts in diasporas around the world. Subsequently, the second and third generations have to contend with constructions of traditional and 'authentic' Indian values that are being propagated by right-wing Hindu-fundamentalist groups. Many children go to summer camps organized by the Hindu Student Council, which is a branch of the Vishwa Hindu Parishad. Recently, in California, Shubha Mudgal, a

Hindustani classical musician from India, was interrupted before her performance by a temple-committee member, as she was known to have made some anti-Narendra Modi remarks in the past (*The Hindu* 2014). Finally, the other organizers apologized on his behalf and persuaded her to sing. Therefore, while some temples are surely involved in merging politics with religion, most temples in the diasporas function as religious and ritual spaces involved in reproducing culture for the second generation in the form of religion. Arjun Appadurai characterizes the immigrant predicament as one where they face 'the seductiveness of plural belonging, of becoming American while staying somehow diasporic, of an expansive attachment to an unbounded fantasy' (Appadurai 1993: 422).

Immigrants carry with them, from their countries of origin, culturally imagined roles and values which complicate the process of acculturation (Fong and Peskin 1973).[1] Many immigrants prefer to retain their ethnic distinctiveness in a plural society rather than assimilate into a non-existing melting pot (Hirschman 1983). One of the ways immigrant groups cope with the alien environment is by remaining allied to the values and ideologies of their cultures of origin. Another coping strategy is to try to integrate aspects of both the parent and host cultures that are felt to be most amenable to the development of self-esteem and identity (Sue 1973). Whatever strategy they might adopt, immigrants are primarily concerned with 'cultural reproduction' or the process by which they seek to transmit their knowledge, values, belief systems, and behavioural norms to the next generation (Mallea 1988). This idea of reproduction cannot be conceptualized merely as a mechanistic replication, but as a generative process involving innovation and creativity (Jenks 1993: 5). Possibilities of change and new combinations in cultural reproduction become particularly significant in the immigrant context.

Raymond Williams has written that emigration involves a 'crisis of epistemology' that focuses people's attention on their traditions or narrative in order to establish a 'known world' (Williams 1988: 31). One way in which Hindu immigrant groups try to resolve this crisis is by building temples and establishing indigenous social and cultural activities in the new society. The salience of religion for early immigrants to the United States was noted in several studies including Herberg's classic work, *Protestant–Catholic–Jew* (1955), and Miller and

Marzik's *Immigrants and Religion in Urban America* (1977). Herberg describes the transformation of America from the land of immigrants to the 'triple melting pot' comprising three major religious faiths, Protestantism, Catholicism, and Judaism. While the second-generation immigrants tried to assimilate into American culture, the third generation sought to discover their origins. He says that it was the 'dialectic of the third-generation interest' in their heritage that made religion an important form of identity in the United States:

> ... what he [the grandson] can 'remember' is obviously not his grandfather's foreign language, or even his culture; it is rather his grandfather's *religion*—America does not demand of him the abandonment of the ancestral religion as it does of the ancestral language and culture. (Herberg 1955: 257; emphasis added)

Religion is an accepted part of the 'American way of life', and by the middle of the twentieth century, religion was firmly institutionalized. Herberg goes further to explain that America has emerged as a three-religion nation and anyone who was anything but a Protestant, Catholic, or Jew was a 'foreigner'. Half a century after Herberg's classic work, the three religions continue to be the dominant ones in the United States, but the arrival of people of many other religions and the consequent move towards cultural pluralism have made the slow acceptance of other religions possible. In the case of Indian immigrants, it was the first generation that made a visible attempt to institutionalize religion. A number of studies have shown that Indian immigrants have retained their religious values and other forms of cultural expression regardless of the country to which they have emigrated (Clothey 1983; Burghart 1987; Williams 1988).

Immigrant religious institutions are not only places of worship but centres for various cultural and social activities that bind the participants into a close-knit community. My own work found that the Sri Venkateswara Temple in Pittsburgh, Pennsylvania, USA, was conceived by its members to be

> more than a religious institution! It is a cultural center—a place of dialogue—for Indian adults to reaffirm their heritage—for their children to discover who they are—for all Americans as a reminder of the diversity that has shaped this country. (Saptagiri 1975: 3)

south Indian immigrant women who frequent the temple play a cru-cial role in this process of reaffirming their cultural heritage and in shaping the identities of their children (Rayaprol 1997). As part of an elite group of people who emigrated from India in the pursuit of professional success, the south Indian immigrants have the resources to engage in representations of the past and reconstruct identities for themselves and their children. The identities that are built and the memories that are invoked in the process are not fixed in space and time, but are constructions of reality that change over time (Gillis 1994). The south Indian immigrant women played a central role in creating a familiar world for themselves as well as for their families.

Nostalgia and the Celebration of Community

An important feature of deterritorialized groups such as immigrants is that they dwell in 'imagined worlds' (Appadurai 1990). Nostalgia is the critical building material for the construction of such an imagined world, a new cultural space, inhabited by the diasporic inhabitants. The word 'diaspora' implies the dispersal of people and their eventual return to the homeland, and this idea is often sustained by nostal-gia. An *archetypal diaspora* is comprised of a group whose members seek to hold on to an 'imaginal memory' that includes the idea of return (Armstrong 1982). In the case of the Indian diaspora, the idea of return is not necessarily a physical, but a cultural phenomenon (Nadarajah 1994). The building of the temple in Pittsburgh can be seen as an expression of nostalgia, symbolizing an act of cultural return. By reproducing the 'authentic' architectural style (that of its parent temple in Tirupati), the community demonstrated its resolve to recreate and reproduce a familiar cultural institution in an alien world. Clothey sees the temple as affirming 'a world—a psychic space—in which the community lives and acts out its identity' (Clothey 1983: 196). Temples have been a central part of south Indian culture in India, and this centrality is also visible in the building of temples by south Indian Hindus in the various countries to which they have moved. The temple in Pittsburgh became an example of the ways in which the upper-caste south Indian diaspora perceived an ideal temple to be.

Many respondents in my Pittsburgh study reported that their first visit to the temple made them feel like they were in India. This is a sentiment that has driven a lot of work on building such institutions in different parts of the world. Some compared it to the temple in Tirupati, while others said they were 'thrilled' to see a temple such as this one in a foreign land. One woman noted that the temple was 'really authentic', and on each visit, she made a special effort to dress traditionally as she felt she was 'going to India'. Perceptions of the temple's 'authenticity' are clearly based on nostalgic images of the temple in Tirupati which they had visited several years ago. Another expression of nostalgia can be seen in the yearning among many women to celebrate festivals as their mothers would have done back home. They try their best to replicate the ceremonies as closely as possible.

Although it was obvious from my research that men share this nostalgia, it is the women, in their traditional roles as transmitters of culture, who take a more active part in giving these memories a concrete shape in the form of festivals, ethnic food, dress, and religious and language classes. 'Memory work', like any other kind of labour, is carried out within a complex set of gender, class, and power relations which determine who 'remembers' what and to what purpose (Gillis 1994). Gillis argues that women, more often than men, tend to serve as unpaid keepers and embodiments of memory. While the men are on the 'fast track' of individualism in American society, it is the women who are expected to stay in touch with the past and remind the men of their cultural background. All these expressions of nostalgia among the Indian immigrants reinforce a deeply held belief that the entire group or subgroups within it have a common ancestry, a common history, a common present, and a common immigrant situation.[2] It is this belief that the many ethnic group events in the temple ritualize. Often the longing to maintain symbolic and emotional links with the past is the driving force for being a regular visitor to the temple. Thus, the Indian immigrant group is not merely a moral community in the sense of a religious group, but, in Robert Bellah's phrase, 'a community of memory'.

> In order not to forget that past, a community is involved in retelling its story, its constitutive narrative, and in so doing, it offers examples of the men and women who have embodied and exemplified the meaning

of the community. These stories of collective history and exemplary individuals are an important part of the tradition that is so central to a community of memory. (Bellah et al 1985: 153)

The immigrants who frequent the temple see themselves as part of a *Gemeinschaft* (community), participating collectively not only in worship but also in a celebration of their nostalgia and community spirit. For instance, a festival gathering certainly serves more than a religious function.

The Social Functions of Religion

During some festivals, scenes from famous Hindu myths and epics are often performed in temple auditoriums. The atmosphere is that of a wedding or any other big social event in India. Temples in the diasporas serve as locales for the performance of traditional weddings as well. The Pittsburgh temple was a favourite location before many such temples were built all over North America. Today it is quite common to have weddings celebrated in a temple close to their homes and ensure the blessings of the community as well. The idea of religion performing a social function is quite Durkheimian. For Durkheim, religion was a mode of representing social realities. He saw religion as performing social functions, both as a system of communication of ideas and sentiments and as a means of specifying and regulating social relationships. For him, 'social life, in all its aspects and in every period of its history, is made possible only by a vast symbolism' (Durkheim 1915: 264).

The need for the temple is felt very strongly, particularly at a time when the second generation is in the process of 'becoming American'. Many immigrant parents expressed the sentiment that going to the temple establishes for their children some roots within the traditional culture. Some people go to the temple for the ritual observance of the festival on the day it actually appears in the traditional calendar. Work schedules do not permit celebration of the festival, but today, in large Indian communities, like the Bridgewater Temple in New Jersey and the Rama Temple in Chicago, there are people who come on the actual festival day as well. As the diasporic community ages, there are senior citizens who have more time for religion along with those parents who are visiting from India for long periods of time. But usually families come with their children on the weekends, when the social event is conveniently celebrated by all members of the ethnic group. This is the 'expressive' role of religion that Durkheim refers to when he asserts that symbolic representations are indispensable to the group. He observes that the functions performed by religion are common to all societies as there is, according to him,

> no society which does not feel the need of upholding and reaffirming at regular intervals the collective sentiments and the collective ideas which make its unity and its personality. Now this moral remaking cannot be achieved except by the means of reunions, assemblies and meetings where the individuals, being closely united to one another, reaffirm in common their common sentiments. (Durkheim 1915: 474–5)

A festival is a time when people belonging to a common ethnic group (for example, Telugus for Ugadi, Tamils for Pongal) unite and celebrate their common religious myths and beliefs. In the different programmes of music, dance, and drama performed on these festive occasions, religious myths and fables are explained and enacted. Today, the second generation has had a good exposure to those aspects of religion and culture that their parents have carefully crafted for them. Language identity is less important for them, but religion continues to persist. Meeting as families in the temple helps parents concretize abstractions about Hinduism and Indian culture that they find difficult to explain to their children at home.

The Symbolism of Ethnic Food

For many Hindu immigrants, the temple has become the central site (in place of the home) for the celebration of festivals, with many of their constitutive features such as rituals and traditional food. Hindu festivals in India are major events in the lives of women, who take great care to authentically perform 'devotional' rituals (Wadley 1989; Robinson 1985).[3] The different kinds of items needed for the rituals and an elaborate menu for the festival meal all require a great deal of planning and preparation. The south Indian women in Pittsburgh have told me that since they cannot celebrate festivals and share the customary meal with their extended families in India, they do so with members of their surrogate extended family at the temple.

Organizing potluck lunches and dinners is one way of strengthening the surrogate extended family. Food becomes a symbol of the immigrants' shared roots (Firth 1973; Macchiwalla 1990). Ethnic food, as Kraut (1979) showed in his study of early Jewish immigrants, has historically been a distinctive feature of immigrant lives, helping forge communal solidarity. Food plays a significant role in the lives of the immigrant Indians in my study as well. A great deal of organization is involved in providing food to hundreds of people who attend the major festivals at the temple. For instance, in New Jersey, the temples are sometimes not big enough and the festivals are thus celebrated in hired open grounds during Dussehra and Diwali. As far as the second generation is concerned, one can say that food is one of the main features of their Indian identity. Leonard, in her work on the Hyderabadi diaspora (2007), says that the one thing that all Hyderabadis—Muslim, Hindu, or Christian—around the world consider as tradition is the biryani. Similarly, in contemporary Hyderabad, the Arabian culture can be seen in the mushrooming of restaurants and international cuisine, while reiterating traditional food such as *haleem* during religious festivals.

Cultural Reproduction and the Second Generation

The anxiety over the possible assimilation of their children into American culture leads parents, especially the mothers, to make conscious efforts to socialize their children into becoming 'good Indians' or 'good Hindus'. Of course, this dilemma is shared by all ethnic groups in a pluralistic culture such as that of the United States and many of them use religion as a means of maintaining ethnic identity (Hammond 1988). Stephen Wieting (1975), in an examination of intergenerational patterns of religious belief, speaks of

> the threat to society posed by the possibility that the young might not adopt the essential wisdom and values of that society.... If a society is to continue its existence beyond one generation, the members must transmit what they consider to be necessary knowledge and values. The continuity of a social system by definition requires transmission between generations.

Immigrants have often pointed out the importance of transmitting their own religious beliefs to their children's generation. Fenton (1988), in his study of Asian Indians in Atlanta, found that as first-generation immigrants began to realize that their return to India was unlikely, many became concerned that their children might lose contact with their heritage.

Religiosity and Children

Diasporic people consciously seek to do things as they were done by their mothers and hope that their children will do the same when they grow up. As such, they seek to establish a kind of ritual continuity with the past. Some people are confident of their ability to extend the tradition to their children's generation, but are worried about the succeeding generations. About half of my respondents in the Pittsburgh study admit that they themselves have become more religious after the birth of their children. Other studies on religiosity have also reported increasing levels of religious activity during childbearing years and later (see, for example, Albrecht and Cornwall 1989). Shalini's[4] words on this subject sum up the views of many of my first-generation respondents:

> I became more devoted to the temple after my children were born. Sometimes when they want to stay at home and watch a television program, I discourage that and push them to come to the temple.... My parents are very religious at home [in India]. Now for Sankranthi I try to do everything like my mother did. I hope you understand, I do all this for my children. I find myself becoming an India-fanatic because I want my children to get exposed as much as possible to our culture. Once they are out of our culture it is very frightening to imagine what will happen.... I think if we take them to the temple one hundred times, at least once something might go into the child's head.

This view of the continuity of tradition and heightened religiosity after the birth of children is mirrored in studies of other Hindu immigrant groups (Williams 1988; Clothey 1983). It was a similar concern for children's religious education that made Pakistani immigrants in Great Britain participate in Islamic centres on a regular basis (Anwar 1979).

This attempt to inculcate religious values among children extends beyond mere visits to the temple and permeates many of the children's activities organized at the temple. In cultural performances such as dances and dramas, ideas are incorporated from Hindu myths and legends. For one Sankranthi[5] celebration, for instance, little children dressed up as different Hindu gods and goddesses explained the religious and ritual significance of the festival. Williams sees cultural performances and instruction in ethnic dance, music, and arts as 'variations of the rituals that preserve in powerful forms elements of the religious traditions' (Williams 1988: 287).

Dance and Music as Cultural Reproduction

Indian classical dance in a patriarchal society is considered a girls' activity and it is also one of the ways in which the diasporic population constructs its identity as Hindu and Indian. Bharata Natyam, outside India, is synonymous with traditional Indian culture and highly valued by expatriate Indian communities. In its modern late-twentieth-century manifestation, Bharata Natyam occupies almost the same niche that ballet occupied in the West in the nineteenth century (Leslie 1991). This Indian classical dance form has become quite popular among not only Indian immigrants but people from other cultures as well. Just as ballet has been appropriated as part of American middle-class culture, it is possible that in a few decades Bharata Natyam will infiltrate into the cultural milieu of the West.

In the Sri Venkateswara Temple, a south Indian woman has been teaching Bharata Natyam ever since the temple's foundation was laid. In 1991, Kuchipudi (another south Indian classical dance form) classes were also started in the temple. A number of young girls have been learning Bharata Natyam and have had their *arangetrams* (formal graduation and first public performance). Some of these girls learn Kuchipudi on Saturdays and Bharata Natyam on Sundays. Similarly, other locations in the United States and other diasporas have examples of the second generations learning classical music. However, Skype lessons from India for music and languages are the new realities in the global digital spaces (Hegde 2011). Musicians in Chennai are transmitting their skills to clients in New Zealand and New York City. For those who want to pursue the arts more seriously, the digital media allows for shrinking spaces and new forms of the reproduction of this culture.

Temples as Locales for Organized Religious Education

Children are encouraged to read about Hinduism in the temple library and watch videos of Hindu mythological dramas shown on Indian television. Temples hold Sanskrit and other language classes on a weekly basis.[6] The members of the diasporic population who are concerned about religious identity feel that they themselves have to be able to understand the meaning of rituals before they transmit them to their children. For some, the performance of rituals was part of their own socialization in India, but they said their participation had been merely ritualistic and the motivation to learn the meaning of many of those rituals was not very high. A few young boys and girls are also taking Sanskrit classes, although they are outnumbered by women. Hindu immigrant women have taken an active part in understanding the culture that they want to hand down to the next generation. The temples become spaces for reproducing rituals that were otherwise expensive in temples in India.

Finally, I must emphasize the special role of the temple as an institution in perpetuating a religious tradition in a new location. As Kim Knott in her study of Hindu temple rituals in Britain put it, religious practice in temples, whether in the form of regular rituals or annual festivals, provides 'an opportunity for the intensification of social relationships and the reinforcement of religious traditions' (Knott 1987: 177). If institutionalization of tradition is not achieved, then the perpetuation of tradition would depend on the efforts of individual families. This might result in the private retention of religious values and culture, but 'it is difficult to see how Hinduism as a religious and social system would be perpetuated in an alien environment without undergoing some kind of institutionalization' (Knott 1987: 178). The establishment and institutionalization of the Sri Venkateswara Temple is a major part of the process of identity formation for the Hindu immigrants in Pittsburgh. This is quite similar of other temples in the world which subsequently saw the Pittsburgh temple as a model to imitate.

Managing Difference: Multiple Identities at the Temple

One of the concerns of immigrants in general and the Hindu immigrants I have studied in particular is the issue of their identity in terms of nation, region, religion, and language. Maxine Fisher's (1980) analogy of a multi-layered cake to describe multiple identities among Indian immigrants illustrates the complicated task of placing oneself in a particular group.[7] First, there is the national identity of being an Indian. Second, the fact that these Indians are frequenting the Sri Venkateswara Temple shows the salience of Hindu religious identity. Third, within the nation, frequent visitors to the temple identify themselves as south Indian, which typically includes people who are originally from the four states of Andhra Pradesh (including present Telangana), Tamil Nadu, Karnataka, and Kerala. Fourth, people from each of the four states speak four different languages—Telugu, Tamil, Kannada, and Malayalam respectively—constituting a linguistic identity. Fifth, there is the gender identity that cuts across all of the other levels of identity. Finally, like all Hindus, the Indian immigrants in my study have caste identities which are ascribed to them at birth. These different identities come into play in complex ways as the Indian immigrants interact with the outside world as well as with each other.[8] Today, there are new temples in the diaspora where subtle caste-based distinctions exist (Kumar 2015).

National and Religious Identities

In spite of the seemingly confusing collage of multiple identities, different levels of identity surface in different circumstances (Barth 1969). Most of the people in my study make a conscious and deliberate attempt, in Goffman's words, to 'mark the boundaries' of ethnicity. In interacting with the wider American environment, for instance, the Indian and Hindu identities are emphasized. The idea of the nation for the immigrant does not merely denote a geographically bounded space, but is an 'ideological force' (Bhattacharjee 1992). Just like Indians have many ideas of what the nation means to them, the diaspora too has several of these differences. Although nations are often imagined by immigrants as being internally homogeneous in cultural content, internal diversity of region, ethnicity, class, gender, and religion is celebrated (Handler 1994). Hindu immigrants regard the diasporic temple as a manifestation of their religious aspirations and the rituals performed therein as symbolic assertions of their communal identity. The religious institutions sometimes come in the way of identities that are cemented on secular Indianness like the Hyderabadi identities. In the current world of internet and social media, transnational identities cut across region, religion, culture, and nation. Communities are virtual and based on common interests and affiliations.

Regional and Linguistic Identities

Within the larger national and religious identities, various subgroups construct more distinctive identities for themselves on the basis of region and language. Feelings of being south Indian as against north Indian are strong among many who frequent the Sri Venkateswara temple. The boundary between the two signifies the line between the inside and outside as well as feelings of 'us' and 'them'. The south Indian temple 'serves to dramatize and define key South Indian ideas concerning authority, exchange and worship' that its visitors identify with (Appadurai 1981: 18). Symbolic of the difference between the two groups is the existence of two different Hindu temples in Pittsburgh serving two different clientele. Speaking of the Hindu–Jain temple in Murraysville (a suburb of Pittsburgh), barely two miles away, Revathi, a south Indian woman respondent, said:

> It is a North Indian temple and we are not used to it. We cannot merge with them, as their culture is very different.

Even within the south Indians, other identities manifest themselves in the form of language. Each subgroup, like the Tamils and the Telugus, marks members off from non-members both in their interactions with other temple-goers and in the organization of their cultural activities. As a Telugu-speaking person, I myself experienced this when I went to the Tamils' celebration of the Pongal festival. Tamil subculture was asserted through language, type of food, and dress. The auditorium resonated with people speaking Tamil, men wore lungis (the traditional Tamil dress), performers on stage delivered Tamil jokes, and everyone later feasted on Tamil food.

These particularistic affiliations in the temple as 'primordial attachments' are, according to Geertz, regional and kinship ties that include communities based on shared religion, language, and social practices. In his attempt to conceptualize the dynamics of ethnicity, Geertz (1973: 259) argued that one is bound to a community as the result not merely of personal affection, practical necessity, common interest, or incurred obligation, but at least in great part by virtue of some unaccountable absolute import attributed to the very tie itself.

In the organization of many of the temple's religious and cultural activities, these differences are taken into primary consideration. The religious committee as well as the priests plan the religious events for the year according to the religious calendars of the four south Indian states. If a particular puja has to be performed on different days for two different ethnic groups, then the temple observes the rituals on both days according to each group's particular traditions. As women who have worked on the religious committee said, 'We try to please everyone'. That same accommodative principle applies as well to the organization of the activities by the temple's cultural committee. Special festivals of particular ethnic groups, like the Tamils' Pongal described earlier, are celebrated with their own cultural performances.

Acculturation: Accommodation and Resistance

The influences of the dominant culture on the immigrant community's adaptation process are quite substantial. Among the cultural changes that could occur through acculturation is the alteration of original linguistic, religious, educational, and other institutions (Berry 1988). As pointed out by Pye (1979: 17) in a comparative study of Christianity and Buddhism,

the transmission of religion from one culture to another whether geographically or chronologically means that new cultural elements are introduced to the tradition and new demands are made upon it.

Although immigrant churches and other institutions have attempted to reproduce the traditions of the parent institutions in the home country, many

were not transplants of traditional institutions but communities of commitment and, therefore, arenas of change. Often founded by lay persons and always dependent on voluntary support, their structures, leadership, and liturgy had to be shaped to meet pressing human needs. (Smith 1978: 1178)

The temple in Pittsburgh was constructed by so-called lay people who had no training in either religious scriptures or temple rituals. Also, the physical setting itself has undergone innovations and adaptations to suit the needs of the country in which it is situated. Clothey (1983) described some of these innovations such as the use of brick and mortar instead of stone in the temple construction, the inclusion of rest rooms below the sanctuary in the same building, the opening of the inner worship area to non-Hindus, use of milk in cartons, and the serving and preparation of food by non-Brahmans on the temple premises. There are coke machines as well as pay phones in the temple area, adding to the non-traditional components of the traditional setting. Nevertheless, resistance to change can be seen in the fact that the sculptors were flown in from India and the installation (*pratisthapana*) of the idols (that were shipped all the way from Tirupati, India) was done strictly according to the Vaishnava tradition. Lynn Davidman (1991) points out in her comparative study of two Jewish Orthodox communities that many Orthodox communities can be placed along a continuum of accommodation and resistance to forces of modernity. The Hindu immigrants in Pittsburgh both accommodate forces of modernity as well as consciously resist assimilation into the dominant culture.

The processes of accommodation can be seen in the ritual sphere. The *abhishekam* (a ritual bath of the idol) of the principal deity, Lord Venkateswara, is traditionally performed in Tirupati on Saturday (the deity's auspicious day of the week). However, at the Sri Venkateswara temple in Pittsburgh and many other temples in the diaspora, this abhishekam is performed at 11 a.m. on Sundays to suit the schedules of the devotees. Christians go to church on Sunday, and Hindus come to the temple perhaps in an attempt to create an institution that is parallel to the Sunday church.[9]

Some rituals which are usually performed in the main worship area are moved to the auditorium on special festivals to accommodate more people and to avoid excessive smoke from the sacred fire near the shrine. On these occasions, many devotees sit in chairs instead of on the floor or on the carpet as is done traditionally, giving it the aura of a church or synagogue service. During one such ritual, I observed that people did not care to remove their shoes as they would have done if a puja was going on in the main worship area or even at the home shrine. Fenton predicts that the temples might eventually lose their distinctive character:

In America, Hindu temples tend to become like other American voluntary associations, and in time they will begin to resemble American synagogues and churches. (Fenton 1988: 179)

The multilingual character of the temple's visitors presents interesting dynamics in the process of accommodation. For example, English is used on some religious occasions, suggesting a transformation of traditions among the immigrants. The temple priests often use English to address an audience during collective worship sessions. Although the priests (who are conversant in most of the four south Indian languages) speak an Indian language with people they know can understand it, they make it a point to address a larger group of devotees in English. A common Hindu ritual performed by a married couple or a family is the Satyanarayana puja during which a priest usually narrates a mythological legend in an Indian language. At the temple, the priest performs the ritual but asks the devotees to read an English translation of the legend. Immigrants' lament about the apparent weakening of tradition can, however, be offset by ample evidence of resistance to change in the temple. One example of such resistance is the recitation of hymns and prayers by the priests in Sanskrit in spite of the fact that it is an archaic language understood by few. On these occasions only a handful of devotees, who are familiar with the particular prayers, recite along with the priests. Another instance of a steadfast adherence to convention is the priests' wearing of a dhoti and a thin shawl flung over their bare chests even in winter.

In an immigrant context, adaptations and compromises in religious practices are often greater than in the country of origin.[10] In another accommodative gesture, candy is used instead of tropical fruits for blessing children on festivals such as Sankranthi or Pongal. Often on these occasions, food is served on separate tables for adults and children, keeping in view the latter's lack of enthusiasm for the traditional spicy fare. The children almost always feast on an American menu consisting of cup cakes, brownies, potato chips, french fries, macaroni and cheese, and fruit salad.

Conversations between parents and children are another indication of the acculturation process. Most parents try to talk to their children in their native language, but few children respond in that language. Parents feel that children should be able to speak in native languages at least when they go back to India and meet their grandparents. However, most children speak in English, and even if they occasionally use their native language, they are self-conscious of their American accents. One of my respondents, Rajni, who has been in Pittsburgh for over twenty-five years, told me that in her early years in this country she used to speak to her children in English out of a fear that they might not grow up speaking good English. But with the coming of age of the second generation, English becomes the mode of communication and the mother tongue is the one that is consumed through the media, satellite television with Telugu and Tamil serials, and Bollywood and Tollywood films. These instances of accommodation and resistance, or continuity and change, demonstrate, in Wuthnow's words, that

> [m]odern religion is resilient and yet subject to cultural influences; it does not merely survive or decline, but adapts to its environment in complex ways. (Wuthnow 1988: 475)

I have examined the various ways in which south Indian immigrants in Pittsburgh attempt to cling on to the values of their country of origin while at the same time adapting and accommodating some of the cultural features of the host country. They are engaged in the process of cultural *reproduction* which involves *creating* a new diasporic culture that they seek to transmit to successive generations. The Hindu immigrants grapple with different identities, and the temple becomes a site on which these identities interact within the larger diasporic identity. As the second generation comes of age, the ways in which the temples are being used transforms. They are able to use the temple as a space for celebrating life-cycle rituals such as birth, puberty, and sometimes even weddings. Festivals were now celebrated with a surrogate extended family in the temple (Rayaprol 2005). The marriages of second- and third-generation diasporic youth with new migrants from India creates a symbiosis of culture, and temples continue to thrive but also take on new meanings with new generations. As the temples become a part of the landscape of the new nations, the diasporic populations begin to influence the way religion is practised in the homeland as well. The proliferation of Swaminarayan Temples is a major contribution of the Gujarati diaspora in different parts of the world, and, with the new Modi government taking over, one needs to see the ways in which the ties between the diasporic population conflate with the political goals of nation-state. Additionally, religious institutions in the diaspora cater to larger ethnic-group affiliations and are sometimes open even to mother religious groups. Religious travel becomes harder across continents, and the diasporic population has become used to having a temple close to their homes. They seem to be coming back to India as returnees and building temples that have several different influences, for example, in the performance space planned within the temple premises. Robin Cohen's (1997: 189) perspective is that while religions do not constitute diasporas themselves, they 'provide additional cement to bind a diasporic consciousness'. The meaning of religious consciousness undergoes a complete change as the generations change. A very complex set of patriarchal traditions influences the lives of South Asian women in the diaspora. Western notions of sexism related to body politics are combined with Eastern sensibilities about the woman being the bearer of tradition and create dissonance in the high-achieving career-oriented feminist ideology. Contemporary feminist work challenges the representation of women as passive victims and offers a perspective of women as architects of change. Temples may be vehicles of change, and sometimes even secular values are ironically promoted in the temples with women playing leadership roles in inculcating those values. In the larger context of understanding the relationship between religion and modernity, one must use a feminist lens to offer a meaningful analysis. The role of gender in the articulation of religious practice is central particularly in migrant and diasporic contexts.

Notes

1. Acculturation has usually been defined as cultural change that results from continuous first-hand contact between two distinct cultural groups (Redfield et al. 1936).

2. At the least, they aspire to make their history seem uniform and, on festive occasions, attempt to underplay the differences that are present.

3. Although these anthropological studies are based on field-work in rural north India, the situation in the urban areas is not very different.

Today the food blogs from different areas have successfully made the ethnic food global.

4. Shalini was one of the first-generation immigrants to Pittsburgh. She became the symbol of the celebration of community life there and the icon of cultural reproduction for her children.

5. Sankranthi is the Telugu harvest festival in January which is celebrated as Pongal in other south Indian states. Many have elaborate celebrations which can be compared with Christmas and Hannukah.

6. Sanskrit is the language of the sacred Hindu texts and scriptures, and is no longer in common use in India. Many contemporary Indian languages, however, are derived from Sanskrit.

7. Contemporary society requires that we play different roles to suit particular situations and some of us are affected by 'multiphrenia', a term Kenneth Gergen (1991) used to explain a psychological condition where an individual has many conflicting identities or selves.

8. Although caste might well be a significant form of identity among the Indian immigrants, it does not manifest itself in the functioning of the temple. The rituals are Vaishnavaite and based on the parent temple in Tirupati. But in other areas, temples have been built according to particular caste identities, for instance, the Mariamman temples in Malaysia.

9. This is perhaps similar to some Reform Jewish temples in the late nineteenth and early twentieth centuries holding their services on Sundays as opposed to Saturdays.

10. Hindu temples are traditionally not carpeted and require worshippers to enter barefoot after having washed their feet at the entrance. Although devotees in the Pittsburgh temple take their shoes off before entering, many still keep their socks on and it is not the same as walking barefoot on a floor that is cleaned and washed daily.

Bibliography

Albrecht, Stan L., and Marie Cornwall. 1989. "Life Events and Religious Change'. *Review of Religious Research* 31(1): 23–38.

Anwar, Muhammad. 1979. *The Myth of Return: Pakistanis in Britain*. London: Heinemann.

Appadurai, Arjun. 1981. *Worship and Conflict under Colonial Rule: A South Indian Case Study*. Cambridge: Cambridge University Press.

———. 1988. "Putting Hierarchy in Its Place'. *Cultural Anthropology* 3(1): 36–49.

———. 1990. 'Disjuncture and Difference in the Global Cultural Economy'. *Public Culture* 2(2): 1–24.

————.1993. 'Patriotism and Its Futures'. *Public Culture* 5(3): 411–29.

Armstrong, John A. 1982. *Nation and Nationalism*. Chapel Hill: The University of North Carolina Press.

Barth, Fredrik, ed. 1969. *Ethnic Groups and Boundaries*. Boston: Little, Brown and Company.

Bellah, Robert N., Richard Madsen, William M. Sullivan, Ann Swidler, and Steven M. Tipton. 1985. *Habits of the Heart: Individualism and Commitment in American Life*. New York: Harper and Row.

Berry, J.W. 1988. 'Acculturation and Psychological Adaptation: A Conceptual Overview'. In *Ethnic Psychology: Research and Practice with Immigrants, Refugees, Native Peoples, Ethnic Groups, and Sojourners*, edited by J.W. Berry and R.C. Annis, 41–52. Amsterdam: Swets & Zeitlinger.

Bhattacharjee, Anannya. 1992. 'The Habit of Ex-Nomination: Nation, Woman, and the Indian Immigrant Bourgeoisie'. *Public Culture*, 5(1): 19–44.

Burghart, Richard. 1987. *Hinduism in Great Britain: The Perpetuation of Religion in an Alien Social Milieu*. London Tavistock.

Clothey, Fred W. 1983. *Rhythm and Intent: Ritual Studies from South India*. Madras: Blackie & Son.

————. 2007. *Ritualizing on the Boundaries: Continuity and Innovation in the Tamil Diaspora*. Columbia: University of South Carolina Press.

Cohen, Robin. 1997. *Global Diasporas: An Introduction*. London: UCL Press.

Davidman, Lynn. 1991. *Religion in a Rootless World: Women Turn to Orthodox Judaism*. Berkeley: University of California Press.

Durkheim, Emile. 1915. *The Elementary Forms of Religious Life*. London: G. Allen & Unwin.

Fenton, John Y. 1988. *Transplanting Religious Traditions: Asian Indians in America*. New York: Praeger.

Fong, S.L.M., and H. Peskin. 1973. 'Sex Role Strain and Personality Adjustment of China-born Students in America: A Pilot Study'. In *Asian-Americans: Psychological Perspectives*, edited by S. Sue and N. Wagner, 79–85. Ben Lommand, CA: Science and Behavior Books.

Firth, R. 1973. *Symbols: Public and Private*. Ithaca: Cornell University Press.

Fisher, Maxine P. 1980. *The Indians of New York City: A Study of Immigrants from India and Pakistan*. Columbia, MO: South Asia Books.

Geertz, Clifford. 1973. *The Interpretation of Cultures*. New York: Basic Books.

Gergen, Kenneth J. 1991. *The Saturated Self: Dilemmas of Identity in Contemporary Life*. New York: Basic Books (Perseus).

Gillis, John R. 1994. *Commemorations: The Politics of National Identity*. New Jersey: Princeton University Press.

Hammond, Philip. 1988. 'Religion and the Persistence of Identity'. *Journal for the Scientific Study of Religion* 27(1): 1–11.

Handler, Richard. 1994. 'Is "Identity" a Useful Cross-cultural Concept?' In *Commemorations: The Politics of National Identity*, edited by John R. Gillis, 27–40. Princeton, NJ: Princeton University Press.

Hegde, Radha S. 2011. 'Digital Gurus, Online Classicism: Diasporic Pursuits of Authenticity'. Paper presented at the International Association for Media and Communication Research (IAMCR), Istanbul.

Herberg, Will. 1955. *Protestant–Catholic–Jew*. Garden City, NY: Doubleday.

Hirschman, Charles. 1983. 'America's Melting Pot Reconsidered'. *Annual Review of Sociology* 9: 397–423.

Jenks, Chris, ed. 1993. *Cultural Reproduction*. London and New York: Routledge.

Knott, Kim. 1987. 'Hindu Temple Rituals in Britain: The Reinterpretation of Tradition'. In *Hinduism in Great Britain: The Perpetuation of Religion in an Alien Cultural Milieu*, edited by Richard Burghart. London: Tavistock Publications.

Kraut, Alan M. 1979. 'Ethnic Foodways: The Significance of Food in the Designation of Cultural Boundaries between Immigrant Groups'. *Journal of American Culture* 2(3): 409–20.

Kumar, Pratap. 2015. *Indian Diaspora: Socio-Cultural and Religious Worlds*. Leiden: Brill Academic Publishing.

Leonard, Karen. 2007. *Locating Home: India's Hyderabadis Abroad*. California: Stanford University Press.

Leslie, Julia. 1991. *Roles and Rituals for Hindu Women*. Rutherford: Fairleigh Dickinson University Press.

Macchiwalla, Tasqeen. 1990. 'A Sense of Belonging: Identity and Ritual at the Muslim Community Center of Greater Pittsburgh'. Master's Thesis, University of Pittsburgh, Pittsburgh, USA.

Malkki, Liisa. 1992. 'National Geographic: The Rooting of Peoples and the Territorialization of National Identity among Scholars and Refugees'. *Cultural Anthropology* 7(1): 24–44.

Mallea, J. 1988. 'Canadian Dualism and Pluralism: Tensions, Contradictions and Emerging Resolutions'. In *Ethnic Psychology: Research and Practice with Immigrants, Refugees, Native Peoples, Ethnic Groups and Sojourners*, edited by J.W. Berry and R.C. Annis, 13–37. Berwyn, PA: Swets North America.

Miller, Randall M., and Thomas D. Marzik. 1977. *Immigrants and Religion in Urban America*. Philadelphia: Temple University Press.

Nadarajah, M. 1994. 'Diaspora and Nostalgia: Towards a Semiotic Theory of the Indian Diaspora'. Paper presented at the International Conference on the Indian Diaspora, Hyderabad.

Pye, E.M. 1979. 'On Comparing Buddhism and Christianity'. *Studies* 5: 1–20.

Rayaprol, Aparna. 1997. *Negotiating Identities: Women in the Indian Diaspora*. New Delhi: Oxford University Press.

————. 2005. 'Being American, Learning to Be Indian: Gender and Generation in the Context of Transnational Migration'. In *Transnational Migration and the Politics of Identity*, edited by Meenkashi Thapan, 130–49. New Delhi: Sage.

Redfield, R., R. Linton, and M.J. Herskovitz. 1936. 'Memorandum for the Study of Acculturation'. *American Anthropologist* 38: 149–52.

Robinson, Sandra. 1985. 'Hindu Paradigms of Women: Images and Values'. In *Women in Culture and Society*, edited by Yvonne Yazbeck Haddad and Ellison Banks Findly, 389–417. Albany: State University of New York Press.

Saptagiri, Vani. 1975. *A Newsletter of the Sri Venkateswara Temple*. Pittsburgh, PA: The Sri Venkateshwara Temple.

Smith, Timothy L. 1978. 'Religion and Ethnicity in America'. *American Historical Review*, 83(5): 1155–85.

Sue, D.W. 1973. 'Ethnic Identity: The Impact of Two Cultures on the Psychological Development of Asians in America'. In *Asian Americans: Psychological Perspectives*, edited by S. Sue and N. Wagner, 140–9. Ben Lomond, CA: Science and Behavior Books.

The Hindu. 2014. 'Mudgal "Threatened" at California Concert for Anti-Modi Stance'. 9 June. Available at http://www.thehindu.com/news/national/mudgal-threatened-at-california-concert-for-antimodi-stance/article6097929.ece (last accessed 21 July 2016).

Wadley, Susan S. 1989. 'Hindu Women's Family and Household Rites in a North Indian Village'. In *Unspoken Worlds: Women's Religious Lives in Non-Western Cultures*, edited by Nancy A. Falk and Rita M. Gross, 94–109. San Francisco: Harper and Row.

Weiting, Stephen G. 1975. 'An Examination of Intergenerational Patterns of Religious Belief and Practice'. *Sociological Analysis* 36(2): 137–49.

Williams, Raymond. 1988. *Religions of Immigrants from India and Pakistan: New Threads in the American Tapestry*. Cambridge: Cambridge University Press.

Wuthnow, Robert. 1988. 'Sociology of Religion'. In *Handbook of Sociology*, edited by Neil J. Smelser, 473–510. Newbury Park, CA: SAGE.

12

BRENT HOWITT OTTO

ROBYN ANDREWS

Durability and Change

Anglo-Indian Religious Practice in India and the Diaspora

The encounter between India and Europe that began in the late fifteenth century gave rise to a small community of mixed origin, known today as Anglo-Indians. While always a very small hybrid group, Anglo-Indians nevertheless developed into a distinct community that has long struggled to find a settled place for itself within the broader milieu both in India and in the places to which many of them have migrated in large numbers, mostly since Indian Independence in 1947. One distinguishing feature of Anglo-Indians is that they are almost universally Christian, yet this aspect of their identity and way of life has been largely ignored by scholars. We have attempted to focus upon it in a collaborative project, which we describe later. In this chapter we explore the interplay between Anglo-Indian religiosity and migration. In comparing the religiosity of Anglo-Indians in India with those who have migrated we have found a trend of durability more than of change in religiosity, which we develop using Swidler's (2001) concept of 'settling'. Our findings suggest that Anglo-Indians are in a uniquely ambiguous position because they draw on both

Western and Indian conceptions of modernity in their relationship with religion.

The Anglo-Indian Story and the Importance of Their Religious Practice

Who Are the Anglo-Indians?

Anglo-Indians are a colonial mixed-descent minority community resident in India and a diaspora stretching principally throughout the British Commonwealth. They have always been a 'micro-minority', whose numbers have probably never exceeded half a million. The Anglo-Indian community traces its roots to the first Europeans who arrived in India from the end of the fifteenth century as petty traders and missionaries, in time expanding their influence, acquiring rights to territorial control to support growing trade, and eventually going to war with some indigenous rulers and, in some cases, supplanting them. From the sixteenth through the eighteenth centuries, therefore, Europeans in India established relationships with Indian women, sometimes of concubinage but more commonly of marriage (Andrews 2005; Blunt 2005; Caplan 2001; Otto 2010). As European women were virtually prevented from going to India until the early nineteenth century, and Europeans often would never return to Europe, these mixed-race unions were seen as natural, normative, and were officially encouraged by the policies of the East India Company, the chartered company which represented British interests in India. The following is from a policy document of the Company in 1687:

> The marriage of our soldiers to the native women of Fort St. George ... is a matter of such consequence to posterity that we shall be content to encourage it with some expense ... to appoint a Pagoda to be paid to the mother of any child that shall hereafter be born of any such future marriage. (Abel 1988)

Over time, in light of the growth of the mixed community and anti-colonial rebellions led by mixed communities elsewhere (for example, the *mullatoes* in Haiti), policy turned against Anglo-Indians. This is reflected in an influential report that was commissioned by the British authorities a hundred years later:

The most rapidly accumulating evil in Bengal is the increase of half-caste children.... In every country where this intermediate caste has been permitted to rise, it has ultimately tended to its ruin. Spanish-America and San Domingo are examples of this fact. (Valentia 1809: 241, cited in Gist and Wright 1973: 13)

Moreover, Eurasians, as Anglo-Indians were then called, threatened the job prospects for the sons of shareholders within the East India Company, because being bilingual and born in India they had a skills advantage over Europeans. In a series of proscriptions in the last two decades of the eighteenth century, Eurasians were thus banned from going to England for education, serving in the responsible posts of the East India Company, and bearing arms in the military units of the Company (Abel 1988: 15–17). Effectively, Anglo-Indians could no longer follow in their European fathers' footsteps. Cultural prejudice aside, following in the Indian traditions of their mothers was almost never an option, usually because marrying a European was a violation of caste that resulted in the woman's estrangement from her family. Anglo-Indians thus found themselves living unsettled lives, not easily permitted to fit in the categories and cultures of their European and Indian reference groups due to political, social, racial, and religious exclusion or prejudice.

Anglo-Indians tried, with marginal results, to navigate these waters through a combination of political protestations and self-help initiatives intended to widen the social and economic space they could occupy (Stark 1934). If anything good came from these British and Indian prejudices and proscriptions, it was that they helped Anglo-Indians forge a sense of solidarity and self-consciousness as a distinct community, even though it came about through being branded as 'other' by both Europeans and other Indians. The community became virtually endogamous by the mid-nineteenth century, a sign of both their solidarity and their pronounced 'otherness' (Hawes 1996).

Unfortunately, the undergirding of most of these early nineteenth-century efforts was directed towards 'passing' as European in various ways. This meant proving that they were just as European in habit and attitude as the Europeans and often implied taking on deeper prejudices towards Indians in order to situate themselves above them and nearer to Europeans. This pattern of trying to pass as European, or nearly so, carried on right into the twentieth century, only diminishing appreciably as Independence approached (1947) and thereafter.

Yet forms of racism, colour consciousness, and their limited numbers have been inescapable sources of prejudice, reminding Anglo-Indians of their in-betweenness: that they are 'not quite' in relation to both Europeans and Indians. Many of these pressures have continued in the postcolonial context in India, causing Anglo-Indians always to lead somewhat 'unsettled lives'. This resulted in the large-scale migration of Anglo-Indians to foreign countries (usually English-speaking, Commonwealth countries), which took place in two great waves—the first one between Independence (1947) and the middle of the 1950s, and the second between the mid-1960s and 1980—but this trend continues today. This testifies that their lives became no more easily 'settled' in postcolonial than colonial India; on the contrary, the rather European cultural attributes of Anglo-Indians highlighted their difference from other Indians in the absence of British rule and with new power dynamics. But migration also presented challenges for Anglo-Indians who sought to settle in Western countries, where their differences also stood out.

Anglo-Indian Religiosity

Despite the historically tenuous nature of Anglo-Indian identity, we contend that religion has long provided a special place where Anglo-Indians could most nearly 'settle' their mixed identity. From the earliest days, Anglo-Indians adopted Christianity since between the loss of caste or social estrangement suffered by their Indian mothers, and the power dynamics that privileged the culture of their European fathers, Anglo-Indians have almost uniformly been Christian. This involved more than just church attendance, because most Anglo-Indians received their entire education in Christian schools. This trend began in the eighteenth century when Anglo-Indian children were often left orphaned because their European fathers would die in war or due to illness and their Indian mothers often could neither support them on their own nor return to their families after having consorted with a foreigner. The orphanages and boarding schools were usually set up with some church support. Further, when Anglo-Indians were legally prevented from going to England for their education, there was huge pressure to provide high-quality European-styled education in India. The arrival of missionaries into East India Company territories after restrictions were relaxed by the Charter Act of 1813 saw the multiplication of church-run schools, first by Protestants and later by Catholics, in which European and Anglo-Indian children, in many cases, made up the majority of the student body.

According to our recent survey, 80.1 per cent of Anglo-Indians report having attended Christian schools, and a full 75 per cent attend church at least once weekly, and this holds true fairly consistently for both genders, across age groups, and regardless of whether one remains in India or has migrated (as an adult) to a foreign country (Andrews and Otto 2013). In essence, to be Anglo-Indian means virtually to be raised in a practising Christian household, church, and school, frequently where there are appreciable numbers of Anglo-Indians among the parishioners or students.

This is magnified by the many social functions, such as dances, fêtes, *housie* (bingo), and picnics that are organized through both churches and schools. These are all ostensibly Western forms of socializing, although they are enacted with distinctly Anglo-Indian flairs that are recognized as such both in India and abroad.

In the devotional and domestic spheres, Anglo-Indians are often daily communicants, frequently pray the rosary, and commonly have a devotion to the Sacred Heart, an image of which is prominently displayed in many homes. What we, the authors, would term 'faith talk' is a feature of many Anglo-Indian households. Anglo-Indians often speak of the 'hand of God' when referring to the events of their lives, especially when good has come following a time of struggle. This carries special meaning in light of the unsettled and vulnerable political, economic, and social space their mixed origin has always entailed for them, in India as well as in the migrant diaspora. Blessings are often given upon the comings and goings of family or guests, in both verbal and tactile ways. For example, one might be sent off with a blessing by having the Cross traced on one's forehead or signed in the air, or being hugged and kissed on the cheeks accompanied by words of blessing. Pilgrimages to sites of miracles and Marian apparitions are popular with Anglo-Indians. Today, many Anglo-Indians in India and from the diaspora make pilgrimages to a Marian apparition site in south India called Vailankanni. In these ways Anglo-Indians demonstrate that religious expression provides an arena of belonging, where their uniqueness as Anglo-Indians is largely appreciated and celebrated.

In this sense, Anglo-Indians have an ambiguous position with respect to modernity. On the one hand with their Western social habits, Christian background, and alliance on many levels with colonial institutions and industry—perhaps mostly as functionaries but nevertheless as regular exponents of its ideology—they are children of modernity and purveyors of it. Their religiosity, on the other hand, is contrary to the increasingly secular predilections of Western modernity, and similarly inconsistent with the relegation of faith to a primarily private sphere. Religion for Anglo-Indians is socially meaningful and enacted publicly, even if accompanied by privately performed pieties.

The Need for Further Research

The Anglo-Indian religious profile has shifted over time by denomination, yet virtually all Anglo-Indians have been and continue to be practising Christians. The importance of religion to Anglo-Indian life even today is quite obvious to anyone acquainted with the community. Nevertheless, no scholarship on Anglo-Indians has attempted to study their religiosity. Most of the literature on Anglo-Indians has conceived of the group as constituted in political or racial terms (Hawes 1996), or by their importance to parts of the colonial administration or economy, for example, in the railways (Bear 2007) or the military. This failure to thoroughly explore religion in the lives of Anglo-Indians is likely the result of a number of factors. It reflects a presupposition that Anglo-Indians are a community of Westernizing, colonial/postcolonial moderns, for whom Christianity, though normative, is nonetheless a private, incidental, and in no way determinative compartment of the group's identity. In any case, both Western and Indian scholarship of the twentieth century was so affected by Marxist analysis that religion had fallen out of favour as a category of enquiry.

If religion is mentioned at all, scholars of Anglo-Indians frequently depend on 'received knowledge' about Anglo-Indian religiosity, containing many untested assumptions or assertions. For example, it has generally been said that just over half of Anglo-Indians are Catholic and the remainder are mostly Anglican. Many also imply the presumption that Christianity affirms only the European cultural bent of the community, not its hybridity, or that diasporic Anglo-Indians largely give up their faith in light of Western secularism. These assumptions begged for testing and nuance, which was part of our motivation to undertake the Anglo-Indian Religion Research Project.

Our research attempts to understand the role of religion in the life of Anglo-Indians both in India and throughout the diaspora. The project was divided into two phases: (*a*) a survey and (*b*) in-depth interviews. The first phase was to design and administer a survey to a broad representation of Anglo-Indians. We launched the survey online so that we could easily reach Anglo-Indians throughout the diaspora by promoting it through social media and Anglo-Indian organizations with a web presence. We also actively promoted the survey (with paper forms as well) during the triennial Anglo-Indian World Reunion in Kolkata in January 2013, attended by approximately 1,500 Anglo-Indians. The survey remained open for four months, closing on 30 April 2013, having been taken by a total of 515 Anglo-Indians. Roughly two-thirds of respondents (63.5 per cent) lived in India and one-third (36.7 per cent) lived outside India. Respondents ranged in age from 16 through 98 years old, with the largest age groups being those between 46 and 75. Respondents were almost equally men and women. The second phase was to conduct in-depth interviews of survey respondents who expressed an interest in being interviewed. Our argument draws principally upon the data produced by the survey— both quantitative and qualitative—from the first phase of the study.

Salient Categories and Considerations for Research on Anglo-Indian Religion: Settled versus Unsettled Lives

In trying to understand Anglo-Indian life, it is helpful to appropriate a concept that Ann Swidler has used in her book, *Talk of Love* (2001), to speak of the social condition experienced by persons or groups whose attributes diverge from that of the mainstream. Swidler speaks of 'unsettled' versus 'settled' lives to name this divergence or convergence respectively. People can 'settle' their lives not only by conforming to the mainstream (if that is possible), but also by finding a community that affirms their divergent attributes. While Swidler studied lives that were settled or unsettled in relation to norms concerning love, marriage, partnership, single life, and so forth, the concepts of settled and unsettled can be applied to Anglo-Indians, whose identity is almost always tenuous. Anglo-Indians, both in India and in the diaspora, experience a degree of 'unsettledness' because wherever they are, they are a minority which is ethnically and culturally hybrid and their numbers have never been sufficient for them to claim a majority or significant power. The task of 'settling' has variously been pursued by Anglo-Indians through adaptation to the mainstream as well as by finding places of 'settledness' within their day-to-day social reality. As this chapter demonstrates, the practice of Christian faith is, for many Anglo-Indians, one of those spaces where they can 'settle' their lives. Religion serves as both a site of *some* adaptation to the mainstream, and a site where uniquely Anglo-Indian ways are valourized. Yet both produce a sense of 'settledness'.

The Broader Discourse on Immigrant Religiosity

It is worth asking whether Anglo-Indians fall into patterns that are considered typical of other migrant groups with respect to religion. A migrant community may intensify its religiosity when it arrives in a new country, establishing ethnic churches that play an enormous social role in providing security, social life, cultural preservation, and a means of adaptation to the mainstream culture. In *Getting Saved in America* (2008), Carolyn Chen explores this phenomenon within the Taiwanese American immigrant community, which gravitates both to evangelical Christianity and Buddhism, and creates in these religious communities the kind of support they found in other places in their homeland. A similar pattern can be identified in many European Christian ethnicities that immigrated to the United States or throughout the British world—to Canada, Australia, or New Zealand.

Closer to the experience of Anglo-Indians, though, are the many other, non-Anglo-Indian, Christians who migrate from South Asia to various parts of the world. As the authors of *South Asian Christian Diaspora: Invisible Diaspora in Europe and North America* (Jacobsen and Raj 2008) note, when Christians migrate they do not generally build churches as their own places of worship (as Hindus build temples, Muslims mosques, and Sikhs gurdwaras); rather they use some 'space' provided by an existing Christian church which is of the same denomination. The space may be physical and/or temporal; for example, Knut Jacobsen (2008: 117–32) describes the creation of separate Sri Lankan spaces for this diasporic community in Catholic churches in Norway where there are significant numbers of Catholic Tamils. Language and ritual elements from Sri Lanka are incorporated into weekly Masses in Tamil, and ritual spaces are being made 'for the celebration of St Anthony,... and for our Lady of Madhu, the most important Catholic pilgrimage shrine in Sri Lanka' (2008: 117).

While this chapter will demonstrate that religion has played a role in helping Anglo-Indians to adjust to a new life and even to preserve their ethnic identity, it does not fit the same pattern as other immigrant groups. Most importantly, as a small community, Anglo-Indians have almost never arrived in any foreign destination in large enough numbers to found ethnic churches as some immigrant groups do. Even if they had, Anglo-Indians would, we think, generally shun such an idea, believing that they are culturally similar enough to the host religious community, particularly in terms of shared language, to fit in easily. Fitting in, somehow, within a largely different mainstream is just as likely to be the Anglo-Indian mode of life in India. Structurally, at least, little is new for Anglo-Indians migrants as religion for Anglo-Indians is already an important marker of identity, a settled space amidst the unsettledness of Anglo-Indian life as a minority in India. Anglo-Indian migrants, in an act of continuity with their past, claim their religiosity as a familiar place of belonging which helps to situate them as 'settled' despite the ways they are different—and thus potentially unsettled—amidst the mainstream.

Understanding the Religiosity of Anglo-Indian Migrants

In this section, we look at the various ways in which Anglo-Indians manifest their religiosity, and look at whether, and, if so, how these practices wax or wane in the process of settling their lives in India and abroad. We begin with Sunday church attendance followed by other expressions of Christian faith practice, and then move into what Anglo-Indians say of their own practices and how they have stayed the same or changed when they have migrated to other countries.

Church Attendance

Church attendance on Sundays is a cornerstone of Anglo-Indian religiosity, as it is of institutionalized Christian practice in general. Seventy-five per cent of Anglo-Indians surveyed attend church services at least once a week. Nearly 12 per cent attend more than once a week, and another 7 per cent go daily. This reflects the predominance of Catholics (82.2 per cent), who have a tradition of the daily celebration of Mass as an optional but encouraged devotional practice. When analysed along the lines of domicile, 84 per cent of the Anglo-Indians surveyed in India go to church at least once a week, while for Anglo-Indians living in the diaspora it is 57 per cent. While this could appear to be a steep decline, Anglo-Indian church attendance presents a stark contrast to the general practice of Catholics in the principal countries to which Anglo-Indians have migrated. For instance, a 2011 survey of Australian Catholics shows that only 12.5 per cent (one-eighth) attend Mass on Sunday (Australian Catholic Bishops' Conference Office of Pastoral Research 2011). From this perspective, Anglo-Indian migrants are four times more likely to be weekly churchgoers than Australian Catholics. Moreover, most Anglo-Indian migrants surveyed left India during the 1980s, meaning that twenty-five or more years have passed during which the cultural disposition towards churchgoing abroad (in the West) could have worked to erode their own devotion or adherence to this practice. So, Anglo-Indian religious practice in the diaspora appears to be quite durable over time, not diminished very much by a broader culture that does not encourage church attendance.

When survey respondents were asked about the church attendance of their children, a very different picture emerged. Of respondents in India, 84 per cent reported that all of their children attended church services regularly, and an additional 10 per cent said that some of their children did. The vast majority of their children were regular churchgoers. In contrast, only 25 per cent of respondents in the diaspora claimed that all of their children were regular churchgoers, but an additional one-third (33 per cent) reported that *some* of their children were. Virtually no respondent resident in India reported that none of their children attended religious services regularly, but a full 33 per cent of Anglo-Indians in other countries did.

An important factor in understanding the religiosity of the children of Anglo-Indian migrants is to note that 70 per cent of survey respondents did not yet have children at the time they migrated. The vast majority were born abroad or at least spent most of their formative years in a culture different from their parents'. That the children of Anglo-Indian migrants are far more likely to be churchgoers than their non-Anglo-Indian peers (that is, at least twice as likely as the average Australian) testifies to the strong influence of their parents' religiosity. The particularly high number of Anglo-Indian migrants who report that none of their children attend church regularly (33 per cent), as compared with only 1.3 per cent of Anglo-Indians in India, implies that to choose not to practise communal and institutionalized religion is a valid choice abroad which possibly does not exist or is at least inhibited in India.

Leadership and Responsibility

About 35 per cent of Anglo-Indians express their religiosity in part by taking on roles of leadership or responsibility within religious organizations. Whether they live in India or have migrated abroad seems to have no effect on their likelihood of taking on such roles. Many are highly involved as volunteers in various liturgical roles, that is, to do with communal worship. Others volunteer in administrative and organizational roles within parish churches or other organizations. Still others engage in local charitable works, or prayer or study groups. A number of them are involved in regional and national associations of Catholics dedicated to spiritual enrichment, and ethical and charitable concerns. For example, Anglo-Indian women in both India and Canada report taking on leadership roles in the Catholic Women's League of each country respectively. Those resident in India appear particularly likely to be involved in prayer and faith-sharing groups, such as the Small Christian Communities (the equivalent of the Comunidades Eclesiales de Base in Latin America), charismatic prayer groups (for example, centred on the Sacred Heart Devotion), sodalities, confraternities, Bible studies, and the Legion of Mary. This suggests that Anglo-Indian religiosity in India is expressed in more social rather than private forms of prayer and devotion. Anglo-Indians in India more often reported involvement in 'Associations of the faithful', such as the Ambassadors for Jesus (founded by Calcutta-based Anglo-Indian Melvyn Brown), or the Lay Missionaries of Charity. Involvement with Christian associations at the local, regional, and national levels (for example, the Catholic Association of Bengal) also seems to be especially popular with Anglo-Indians in India, possibly reflecting the impulse of religious minorities towards solidarity. This may be especially true in recent years, as Christians in India have suffered violent attacks in certain places at the hands of Hindu fundamentalists fuelled by communal politics.

What Anglo-Indian Migrants Say of Religion and Change

Without denying the durability of religiosity among Anglo-Indian migrants, marked by churchgoing and responsibilities within religious organizations, we now focus upon the minority who have not kept up these forms of religious practice, because it will highlight the inevitable challenges and changes that Anglo-Indian migrants have had to confront and assimilate by moving into a different culture. Anglo-Indian migrants gave numerous reasons for lessening or stopping their former religious practices, which fall roughly into four principal categories: (*a*) a culture of busy-ness; (*b*) a secular milieu; (*c*) the privatization of faith; and (*d*) the dissonance between religious experience in India and in the West. These are all attributes of Western modernity which entail a secular public sphere, the diminishment of religion's social value in structuring life, in favour of relegating it to the private sphere.

First, one of the most commonly cited reasons for going to church less often is that life in the West is busier than in India. Whereas most Anglo-Indians would have had domestic help in India, they have to do everything for themselves in their new homes. Jobs seem to demand more, and the usually more suburban dwelling places in Australia, Canada, and elsewhere entail more time spent travelling great distances between home, church, school, and work than is required in India. Many of these respondents were regretful over this reality and wished they went to church more often.

Second, others cited the more secular milieu, reducing social pressure to practise one's faith and permitting non-practice. For example, one respondent stated, 'America is a very secular culture, so it was easy not to practice my religion without incurring negative feedback.' For a handful of respondents, this empowered them to leave Christianity altogether, to embrace atheism, agnosticism, or even paganism.

Third, an increased emphasis on the personal and private practice of faith over the communal and public forms more familiar in India constitute another recurring theme. Some Anglo-Indians claim a new religious balance that involves less churchgoing and more private prayer or meditation at home. 'I see myself as a secular Christian with a private and personal relationship to God ... though I do occasionally attend Anglican services.' Another stated, 'I am not a traditional practicing Catholic but have become a more spiritual person having exposed my mind to all the major religions.' Thus, what it means to be religious seems to shift for some Anglo-Indians, to reflect general trends in the West. They de-emphasize communal worship in favour of what the individual decides she or he wants or needs, and some are even willing to draw from the wisdom of other faiths besides their native Christianity.

Fourth, the contrast between the religious experience they had in India and those they encountered in the West has sometimes been a source of disillusionment. Some complain that the people and priests in their new countries lack fervour or dedication they experienced in India. Others have been turned off by the revelations of sex abuse among the clergy in recent years, or the perceived inflexibility they experience in (particularly Catholic) Church teachings, which they may have not experienced, been aware of, or questioned in India. Some miss the communal social and ritual traditions that marked their religious life in India, as indicated by this survey respondent: 'The Christian culture here is very much different. There is no Christmas carol groups going house to house. No cribs for Christmas. Not many Anglo-Indian families to have get-togethers or parties with.' Another has disdain towards the politicized Christianity perceived in America: 'I don't even really like to tell people I'm Christian because in the U.S. this comes with a set of assumptions that I resist. I do not care for most white American conservative Christians. (For starters, many of them hate immigrants and people of mixed racial heritage.)'

While these four aspects of challenge have, for some Anglo-Indians, contributed to a reduction in churchgoing and institutionalized practices of Christianity, the majority have responded to these factors differently. The continuity of churchgoing and involvement with religious activities and organizations among Anglo-Indian migrants suggests that most have surmounted the challenges or reconciled them with their traditional forms of Christian religiosity. One respondent explicitly claimed, 'I am more keen to live an outwardly Christian life as this country becomes less Christian by the day.' The challenge of secularism for this person provides the impetus for a more evangelical approach to religion. Yet most Anglo-Indian migrant respondents (71.6 per cent) claim they have not changed their faith practices after leaving India, making continuity the principal trend we observe.

Anglo-Indian Identity and Religious Practice in the Diaspora

As stated earlier, Anglo-Indian migrants have usually found themselves in places where there are few Anglo-Indians; therefore, in no social institutions, including churches, could they find the kind of ethnic support they may have experienced in India. Yet it is interesting to note the high degree to which Anglo-Indian migrants surveyed explained how their Christianity has supported the expression of their Anglo-Indian identity. Although fewer than half of Anglo-Indian respondents (43 per cent) stated in the survey that one had to be Christian to be Anglo-Indian (this is likely to be reflecting the legal definition that has prevailed for the better part of a century which is exclusively racialized and gendered, and not marked by religion), still, 99.3 per cent of Anglo-Indians surveyed were Christian. Moreover, many Anglo-Indian migrants wrote that being Christian is part and parcel with being Anglo-Indian. 'To me Anglo-Indians and strong Christian beliefs go hand-in-hand,' reported one respondent. For another, 'Identifying with Catholic faith [is] partly as a result of being Anglo-Indian.' Others said they have never known an Anglo-Indian who is not Christian, and the numbers certainly support this claim. While this testifies to the importance of Christianity to Anglo-Indian self-identity, it does not explain how Christianity has helped them to live 'settled' Anglo-Indian lives in countries where there are few Anglo-Indians and little knowledge of the community's background or even of its existence.

From the responses of Anglo-Indian migrants it would appear that Christian practice is a way of finding a sense of belonging in their host country, despite their racial and cultural hybridity. Christianity is a place where Anglo-Indian migrants can 'settle' their lives. Unlike other South Asians who migrate to Western countries, Anglo-Indians already adhere to largely Western customs in part stemming from their Christianity, as this response indicates:

> An Anglo-Indian Christian seems to have had many European values and components and as such we tended to live like Europeans in many ways that made us different from our fellow Indians. In our host countries this Western, Christian mindset along with a fluent command of the English language enabled us to settle into our adopted country very easily.

The kind of reception Anglo-Indian immigrants have received appears to have pivoted partly on their Christian practice distinguishing them as more Western than other South Asian immigrants.

Being Christian has also helped some to explain what it is to be a hybrid Anglo-Indian, against the tendency to generalize all Indians into a singular (false) category: 'It helps explain my ethnic background and separates me from the understanding most people have of what is traditionally Indian.' Rochelle Almeida also writes, based on her research in London, about the desire on the part of Anglo-Indian migrants to be seen as being distinct from 'other Indians' (Almeida 2013). Another respondent in Britain writes, '[It] has helped me to explain to indigenous British who have no understanding of the Anglo-Indian community, the influence that Britain and my Christian faith had on my upbringing in India.'

If a racial or socio-ethnic hierarchy remains in Western countries, Anglo-Indians sometimes have deployed their Christianity to claim a higher place in this hierarchy: '[Christian faith] identifies the difference between being an Anglo-Indian as compared to a *pure* Indian Immigrant [emphasis added].' Another writes, 'It is easier to explain to *other Australians* that we are *not native Indians* or else we would have belonged to a Hindu or Muslim faith [emphasis added].' Although this is just one person's opinion, it is striking that the Anglo-Indian who wrote it considers herself an Australian while rejecting that Anglo-Indians collectively are natives of India. The latter assertion is literally false, but it provides an extreme example of the need some

Anglo-Indians feel to justify their presence as immigrants in reference to the culture and race of the 'white' population that dominates
their new home. Likewise, some had felt a similar need to justify their
presence among the wider population in India. Christian faith allows
them to establish a claim to kinship and belonging amongst the populations in the West, who might otherwise have marginalized them on
the basis of their country of origin or complexion.

Other Anglo-Indian migrants emphasized that going to church
provided them with a social environment that welcomed them and
helped them to adjust, even if they were the only Anglo-Indians
around:

> ... the first thing I did when I arrived in England was to find myself
> a Christian community into which I could integrate and via which I
> could thence integrate into wider British society. Being Christian and
> mixed-race from India naturally provoked the curiosity of all those I
> met in England, but much rather than attitudes being hostile, they
> were, perhaps precisely on account of those factors, highly welcoming.

This Anglo-Indian migrant found his Christianity was an entry ticket
to a welcoming community that valued his South Asian mixed-race
background and could help him to adjust to the possibly less-welcom-
ing broader society.

For some Anglo-Indians, it was at church that they first met other
Anglo-Indians in their adopted country. Church became more than
a worshiping community, but also a place to meet and socialize with
other Anglo-Indians. In a few diasporic settings there is a relatively
large and concentrated Anglo-Indian community, where churches
have sometimes been able to play this role. Moreover, Anglo-Indian
Associations have been established worldwide in cities where there
is an appreciable population, providing regular social events and
facilitating both a local and an international network of ethnic cohe-
sion. Anglo-Indian association events and meetings are nuanced
by their Christianity; for example, 'business' meetings, such as the
Annual General Meetings (AGMs) of the World Federation of Anglo-
Indian Associations, begin with the Lord's Prayer, and offices of the
associations often have holy pictures, such as *The Last Supper*, on
their walls. The activities of these associations are regularly intertwined with church communities by celebrating religious feasts in
distinctly Anglo-Indian ways, often meeting in church facilities, and

sharing overlapping membership with mainly Catholic and Anglican churches. Christian practice in the diaspora in this way helps Anglo-Indians to settle their lives within communities based on religious kinship, which provide them access to other Anglo-Indians or at least acceptance of their Anglo-Indianness, but ultimately Christian practice helps them to settle their lives within the larger non-Anglo-Indian world.

***

In conclusion, contrary to what one might expect from a hybrid community long stereotyped for its eager reproduction of Western cultural habits, based on responses to our survey, Anglo-Indian migrants to the West appear not to have rapidly gone the way of the general population and fallen away from the institutionalized practice of Christianity. Nor have they seemed to reduce their involvement and leadership within religious organizations. Religiosity measured on the basis of churchgoing and leadership in religious organizations remains more similar than different between Anglo-Indians in India and Anglo-Indians in the diaspora. Yet such quantitative indications of stability can belie the qualitative change in how Anglo-Indians appropriate their faith in a different cultural context. Meanwhile, not only do Anglo-Indian migrants face assimilating cultural change, but so do Anglo-Indians in a rapidly changing India.

Like other stories about the Anglo-Indian community, the story of their religiosity in the diaspora is far from monolithic and defies some of the presumed categories and patterns one might find with other immigrant groups. This should be no surprise for a community whose hybrid identity, although quite distinct, discernable, and integral, even to the uninitiated outsider, has always been the site of contestation of their belonging—in India and abroad—amidst inevitably larger and more empowered populations. The stability of the religious practices of Anglo-Indians moving into the diaspora demonstrates how essential the Christian faith is to Anglo-Indian identity, and that through religion Anglo-Indians find (or actively claim) a place of belonging where their lives can become 'settled' in a new country. The ways in which some Anglo-Indian migrants have adapted their religious practice to Western secularism, individualism, and other differences—in essence, adapting to a different, Western kind of secular modernity from the sort which they experienced and of which they were, in some ways, the historical standard bearers in India—are consistent with the acute need of this minority to adapt to changing circumstances outside of its control. Yet the stability and relatively little *attested* change in religious practice among diasporic Anglo-Indians is a parallel reality, which underlines the high priority Anglo-Indians give to religion. Religion anchors all Anglo-Indian identities to a believing community of belonging because it affirms parts of their racial and cultural heritage, while simultaneously transcending all such marks of race and culture.

Bibliography

Abel, Evelyn. 1988. *The Anglo-Indian Community: Survival in India*. Delhi: Chanakya.

Almeida, Rochelle. 2013. 'Paradoxes of Belonging: Individuality and Community Identity'. *International Journal of Anglo-Indian Studies*, available at http://home.alphalink.com.au/~agilbert/al13.html (last accessed 15 July 2016).

Andrews, Robyn. 2005. 'Being Anglo-Indian: Practices and Stories from Calcutta'. PhD thesis, Massey University, Palmerston North, New Zealand.

Andrews, Robyn, and Brent Howitt Otto. 2013. 'Anglo-Indian Religion Research: A Project to Understand the Role of Religion in Anglo-Indian Identity, Today and Yesterday: Report of Survey Results'. Available at http://anglo-indianreligionresearch.net/ (last accessed 23 October 2015).

Australian Catholic Bishops' Conference Office of Pastoral Research. 2011. 'A Profile of the Catholic Community of Australia'. Available at http://pro.catholic.org.au/pdf/ACBC%20PRO%20Catholic%20profile%202013.pdf (last accessed 23 October 2015).

Bear, Laura. 2007. *Lines of the Nation: Indian Railway Workers, Bureaucracy, and the Intimate Historical Self*. New York: Columbia University Press.

Blunt, Alison. 2005. *Domicile and Diaspora: Anglo-Indian Women and the Spatial Politics of Home*. Oxford: Blackwell.

Caplan, Lionel. 2001. *Children of Colonialism: Anglo-Indians in a Post-Colonial World*. Oxford: Berg.

Chen, Carolyn. 2008. *Getting Saved in America*. Princeton: Princeton University Press.

Gist, Noel P., and Roy Dean Wright. 1973. *Marginality and Identity: Anglo-Indians as a Racially-Mixed Minority in India*. Leiden: E.J. Brill.

Hawes, Christopher. 1996. *Poor Relations: The Making of a Eurasian Community in British India 1773–1833*. Surrey: Curzon Press.

Jacobsen, Knut A. 2008. 'Creating Sri Lankan Catholic Space in the South Asian Diaspora in Norway'. In *South Asian Christian Diaspora: Invisible Diaspora in Europe and North America*, edited by K.A. Jacobsen and S.J. Raj, 117–32. Surrey: Ashgate.

Jacobsen, Knut A., and Selva J. Raj, eds. 2008. *South Asian Christian Diaspora: Invisible Diaspora in Europe and North America*. Surrey: Ashgate.

Otto, Brent Howitt. 2010. 'Anglo-Indians in the Tumultuous Years: Community, Nationality, Identity and Migration, 1939–1955'. Unpublished Master's thesis, Columbia University, New York, and the London School of Economics and Political Science, London.

Stark, Herbert Alick. 1934. *John Ricketts and His Times: Being a Narrative Account of Anglo-Indian Affairs during the Eventful Years from 1791–1835*. Calcutta: Wilsone & Son, Printers.

Swidler, Ann 2001. *Talk of Love*. Chicago: University of Chicago.

Valentia, Viscount George. 1809. *Voyages and Travels in Ceylon, The Red Sea, Abyssinia and Egypt in the Years 1802, 1804, and 1806*, vol. 1. London: William Hiller.

Notes on Editors and Contributors

Editors

Sekhar Bandyopadhyay is Director of the New Zealand India Research Institute and Professor of Asian History at Victoria University of Wellington, New Zealand. His primary research interest is in the history of nationalism and the caste system in colonial and postcolonial India. He is also interested in the history of Indian migration and the Indian diaspora. He has written seven books, edited or co-edited nine books, and published more than forty book chapters and journal articles. His most recent books are *From Plassey to Partition and After: A History of Modern India* (second edition, 2015) and (ed.) *Decolonisation and the Politics of Transition in South Asia* (2016). He is a Fellow of the Royal Society of New Zealand and a recipient of the Rabindra-smriti Puraskar (2014).

Aloka Parasher Sen has been teaching at the University of Hyderabad, India, since 1979 where she is currently Professor of History and Director, International Affairs. She has travelled widely on academic assignments and, most recently, was the first occupant of the Saroj and Prem Singhmar Chair in Classical Indian Polity and Society (2008–11), Department of History and Classics, University of Alberta, Canada. She is the author and editor of seven books and numerous articles in journals and edited volumes on various aspects on the economy, society, religion, and culture of early India with special reference to the Deccan. She is the author of *Mlecchas in Early India* (1991) and has prepared a *Reader on Subordinate and Marginal Groups in Early India up to 1500 AD* (2004; second edition, 2007). She has edited *Social and Economic History of Early Deccan—Some Interpretations* (1993) and *Kevala-Bodhi: The Buddhist and Jaina History of the Deccan* (2003).

Contributors

Robyn Andrews is Senior Lecturer of Social Anthropology at Massey University, New Zealand. Her research focuses primarily on the Anglo-Indian community, beginning with her PhD thesis, 'Being Anglo-Indian: Practices and Stories from Calcutta' (2005), and continuing with projects in India and the diaspora. Her interests include their Christianity, pilgrimage, ageing, education, migration, and diaspora. She writes both academic and community publications, which includes her book *Christmas in Calcutta: Anglo-Indian Stories and Essays* (2014). She co-edits the *International Journal of Anglo-Indian Studies* with Brent Howitt Otto.

B.L. Biju is Assistant Professor in Department of Political Science at the University of Hyderabad, India, since 2007. His research interest is in Indian politics, theories of class, and the politics of globalization. He is currently pursuing research on the politics of protests in Kerala. He has published ten research articles in journals and as chapters in edited books.

Aparna Devare is Assistant Professor in the Department of Political Science, University of Hyderabad, India. Her research areas include International Relations theory, postcolonialism, the politics of history-writing, Indian political thought, religion, and secularism. Her major publications include *History and the Making of a Modern Hindu Self* (2011).

Ranjeeta Dutta teaches at the Centre for Historical Studies, Jawaharlal Nehru University. Previously, she taught at the Department of History and Culture in Jamia Millia Islamia, New Delhi. Her research interests are religion and religious identities with special emphasis on the peninsular region. Her publications include a monograph titled *From Hagiographies to Biographies: Ramanuja in Tradition and History* (2014) and an edited volume (co-edited with Rameshwar Prasad Bahuguna and Farhat Nasreen) titled *Negotiating Religion: Perspectives from Indian History* (2012).

Pushpesh Kumar teaches at the Department of Sociology, University of Hyderabad, India. He has published on gender, sexuality, and pedagogical issues in reputed journals and edited volumes. He received the M.N. Srinivas Memorial Prize for Young Sociologist in 2007. He was also a British Academy Visiting Fellow in 2009 at Department of Anthropology, London School of Economics, UK. He is working on a book project on 'subordinate masculinity in western India'. His recent research engages with the issues of 'cities and sexual geographies' and 'emerging queer consumerism in contemporary India'. He is also interested in understanding academic cultures in regional contexts and their impact on pedagogical practices in social sciences and sociology.

Aditya Malik is Professor and Dean of the School of Historical Studies at Nalanda University. His main research interests are in South Asian pilgrimage, folk religion, oral narratives and ritual performance, the interface between religion, law, and justice, as well as historiography in medieval western India. He has written three books, edited or co-edited six books, and published more than thirty book chapters and journal articles. His most recent publications are *Tales of Justice and Rituals of Divine Embodiment: Oral Narratives from the Central Himalayas* (2016) and *Hinduism in India: Modern and Contemporary Movements* (co-edited with Will Sweetman, 2016).

T.K. Oommen is presently Professor Emeritus at Jawaharlal Nehru University, New Delhi, from where he retired after being a professor for twenty-six years. He was president of the International Sociological Association as well as the Indian Sociological Society. He was also a Visiting Professor/Research Fellow at several universities including University of California, Berkeley, USA; Australian National University, Canberra; Institute of Advanced Studies, Budapest, Hungary; and Uppsala University, Sweden. He has authored twenty and edited ten books. He is a recipient the V.K.R.V. Rao Prize in Sociology (1981), the G.S. Ghurye Prize in Sociology and Social Anthropology (1985), and the Swami Pranavanda Award in Sociology (1997). He was a National Fellow of the Indian Council of Social Science Research. Professor Oommen was conferred the Padma Bhushan in 2008 in recognition of his contribution to higher education.

Brent Howitt Otto is a doctoral student in South Asian History at the University of California, Berkeley, USA. In the course of post-graduate degrees in global history from Columbia University, New York, USA, and the London School of Economics, UK, and a theological degree in Indian Church history, Brent has researched Indian Catholic education, Anglo-Indian migration and diaspora, and Christian religious identity and performance. Collaborative research with Robyn Andrews formed the basis of the chapter in this volume. Brent is also a Catholic priest of the Jesuit order. Since 2013 Brent has served as co-editor of the *International Journal of Anglo-Indian Studies* and has published in two Anglo-Indian collected volumes and presented at several academic conferences and researchers' workshops.

Alok Kumar Pandey has been teaching Anthropology at the University of Hyderabad, India. His research interests include ecology, biodiversity conservation, natural resource management, development, nomadism, and pastoralism. He has carried out fieldwork with the nomadic pastoral Van Gujjars in the Himalayas and the pastoral Todas of the Nilgiri hills of south India. He has also worked as a consultant to the National Commission for Denotified, Nomadic and Semi-nomadic Tribes (NCDNT&SNT), Ministry of Social Justice and Empowerment, Government of India.

R. Siva Prasad is Professor, Department of Anthropology, University of Hyderabad, India. He has held several positions including the Reserve Bank of India (RBI) Chair Professor and a consultant for the National Commission for Denotified, Nomadic and Semi-Nomadic Tribes (NCDNT&SNT), Ministry of Social Justice and Empowerment, Government of India. He briefly served as the Regional Director at the Council for Social Development, Hyderabad, India, and was also a member of two Danish Missions (1989 and 2003). His areas of research include ecology and environment, natural resources management and livelihood systems, social stratification and mobility, anthropological theory and methodology, public health, self-help groups and microcredit, development, displacement and resettlement, entrepreneurship, and customary modes of dispute resolution.

N. Sudhakar Rao has specialized in social/cultural anthropology. Before joining the University of Hyderabad, India, he was Professor of Sociology at the Assam University, Silchar. He started his career as a social researcher undertaking urban studies and later as action anthropologist for the Indian Space Research Organization. He gradually developed an interest in South Asian social systems, caste ideology, religion, and state in India. As co-author and author he has published four books and contributed several papers to edited volumes and articles for academic journals of social sciences.

M. Ravikumar obtained his MA and MPhil degrees in social/cultural anthropology from the University of Hyderabad, India. He studied the Mahankali Temple of Lal Darwaza in the old city of Hyderabad and role of its functionaries in local politics of Hyderabad for his MPhil research. Currently, he is a doctoral candidate at the Centre for Economic and Social Studies, Hyderabad, focusing on religion and politics in urban public spaces.

Aparna Rayaprol is Professor of Sociology at the University of Hyderabad, India. She has worked on the Indian diaspora in the USA and is the author of *Negotiating Identities: Women in the Indian Diaspora* (1997).

Will Sweetman is Associate Professor of Asian Religions and Head of Department, Department of Theology and Religion, University of Otago, New Zealand. His research interests centre on interactions between the religions of Asia and the West in the modern period. He has published three books and several articles on historical and theoretical aspects of the study of Hinduism, and has edited three collections. His most recent books are *Bibliotheca Malabarica: Bartholomäus Ziegenbalg's Tamil Library* (2012) and *Hinduism in India: Modern and Contemporary Movements* (co-edited with Aditya Malik, 2016).

Index

National Democratic Party (NDP),
243n5
national identities, 5, 161, 216,
279–80
nation-state, 11, 13, 16, 22, 32, 54,
108, 159–60, 169, 172, 185, 190,
196, 201, 267–8, 285
nature–people relationship,
conception of state, 108–9
Nehru, Jawaharlal, 167, 177, 201
neutrality, 6
nirguna brahmana, 88
nomadic pastoralism, 113–14
non-duality, 47–8
no preference doctrine, 6
Nāthamuni, 102n2

Orientalist discourse, 98–9
Orthodox communities, 282
Ortner, Sherry, 240

Pakistan, 168–9, 172
Parishad, Raja Kishan, 241
Pasha, Mustapha, 159
pastoral forest-dwelling community,
impacts of modernization
projects, 12
physical and spiritual
displacement, 12
Patel, Vallabhbhai, 177
Paul, Dr Radhabinode, 194
Petit, Rattanbai, 170
pluralization, 11, 30–2
political Islam, 159
political-party system in Kerala. *See*
Kerala's politics of communalism
politics and religion, relationship,
13, 158
Hindu nationalist politics. *See*
All India Hindu Mahasabha
(AIHM)

in Kerala, 14
in Telangana, 14
polytheism, 31
Pope, George, 68
pre-colonial Christianity, 23, 32n3
Protestant ethics, 2
Protestantism, 270
Protestant missions in the north of
India, 69
Protestant modernity, 158

queer activism, 137, 150n7
queer Muslims. *See* Muslim gay
community, study of negotiation
with religious identity and erotic
life

radical alterity, 45, 52–5
radical doubt, 41
Rai, Lajpat, 187
Rajaji National Park (RNP), 114,
119–20, 122
Rāmānuja, 87, 90–1, 101
concept of the 'guru', 89
as a 'social reformer', 99–100
on Śrīvaiṣṇava community
identity, 90–2
Viśiṣṭādvaita philosophy, 88
Ramaswamy, E.V., 101
Rama Temple, Chicago, 273
Rao, G.V. Subba, 183, 197
Rao, T.A. Gopinath, 97
Rashtriya Swayamsevak Sangh
(RSS), 176, 185, 202
Ravi Pathasalas (Sunday schools), 30
reflexive traditions, 9
religion, conceptualization of, 2
early Indian religious traditions,
5
modernity and, 3, 6
in terms of secularism, 5